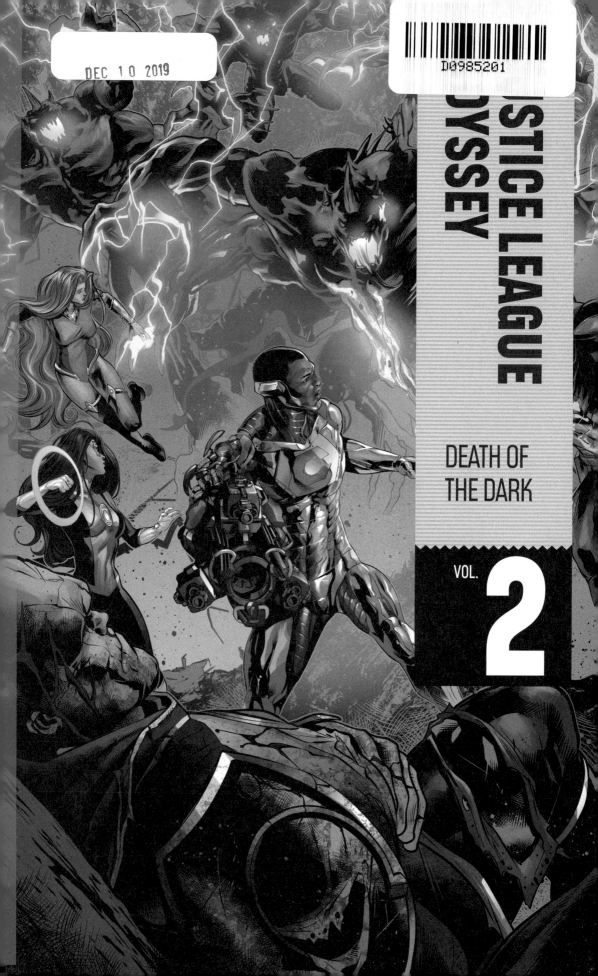

JUSTICE LEAGUE ODYSSEY

DEATH OF
THE DARK

VOL. **2**

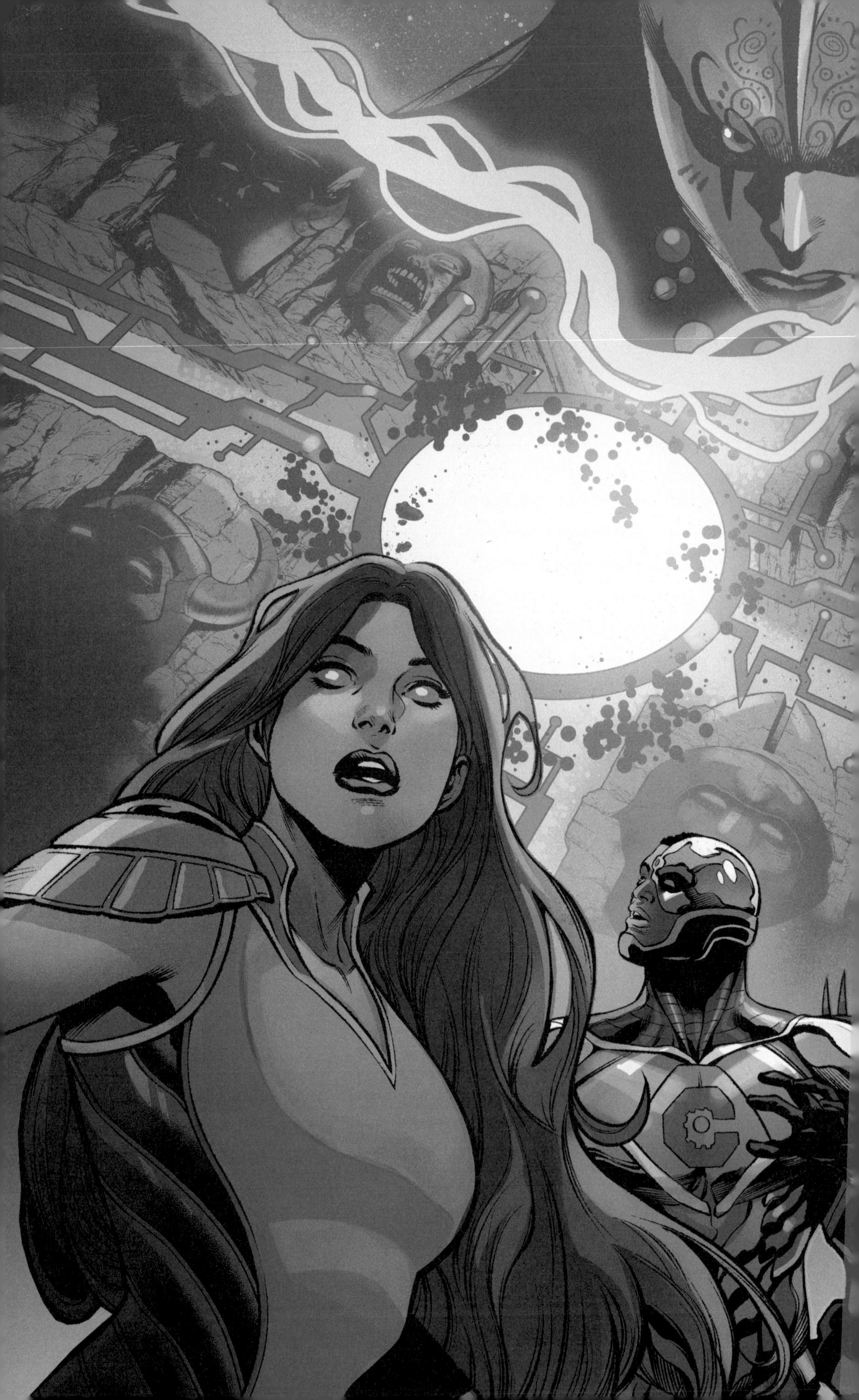

JUSTICE LEAGUE ODYSSEY

DEATH OF THE DARK

writer

DAN ABNETT

artists

WILL CONRAD
DANIEL SAMPERE
JUAN ALBARRAN
CARMINE DI GIANDOMENICO

colorists

IVAN PLASCENCIA
RAIN BEREDO
PETE PANTAZIS

letterer

ANDWORLD DESIGN

collection cover art

CARMINE DI GIANDOMENICO
and IVAN PLASCENCIA

original series cover art

CARMINE DI GIANDOMENICO and
IVAN PLASCENCIA
DANIEL SAMPERE, JUAN ALBARRAN,
and IVAN PLASCENCIA
CARLOS D'ANDA
WILL CONRAD and IVAN NUNES

VOL. **2**

ROB LEVIN
HARVEY RICHARDS Editors – Original Series
JEB WOODARD Group Editor – Collected Editions
SCOTT NYBAKKEN Editor – Collected Edition
STEVE COOK Design Director – Books
LOUIS PRANDI Publication Design
ERIN VANOVER Publication Production

BOB HARRAS Senior VP – Editor-in-Chief, DC Comics
PAT McCALLUM Executive Editor, DC Comics

DAN DiDIO Publisher
JIM LEE Publisher & Chief Creative Officer
BOBBIE CHASE VP – New Publishing Initiatives & Talent Development
DON FALLETTI VP – Manufacturing Operations & Workflow Management
LAWRENCE GANEM VP – Talent Services
ALISON GILL Senior VP – Manufacturing & Operations
HANK KANALZ Senior VP – Publishing Strategy & Support Services
DAN MIRON VP – Publishing Operations
NICK J. NAPOLITANO VP – Manufacturing Administration & Design
NANCY SPEARS VP – Sales
MICHELE R. WELLS VP & Executive Editor, Young Reader

JUSTICE LEAGUE ODYSSEY VOL. 2: DEATH OF THE DARK

DC Comics, 2900 West Alameda Ave., Burbank, CA 91505
Printed by LSC Communications, Owensville, MO, USA. 10/18/19. First Printing.
ISBN: 978-1-4012-9506-6

Library of Congress Cataloging-in-Publication Data is available.

PEFC Certified
This product is from
sustainably managed
forests and controlled
sources

PEFC/29-31-337 www.pefc.org

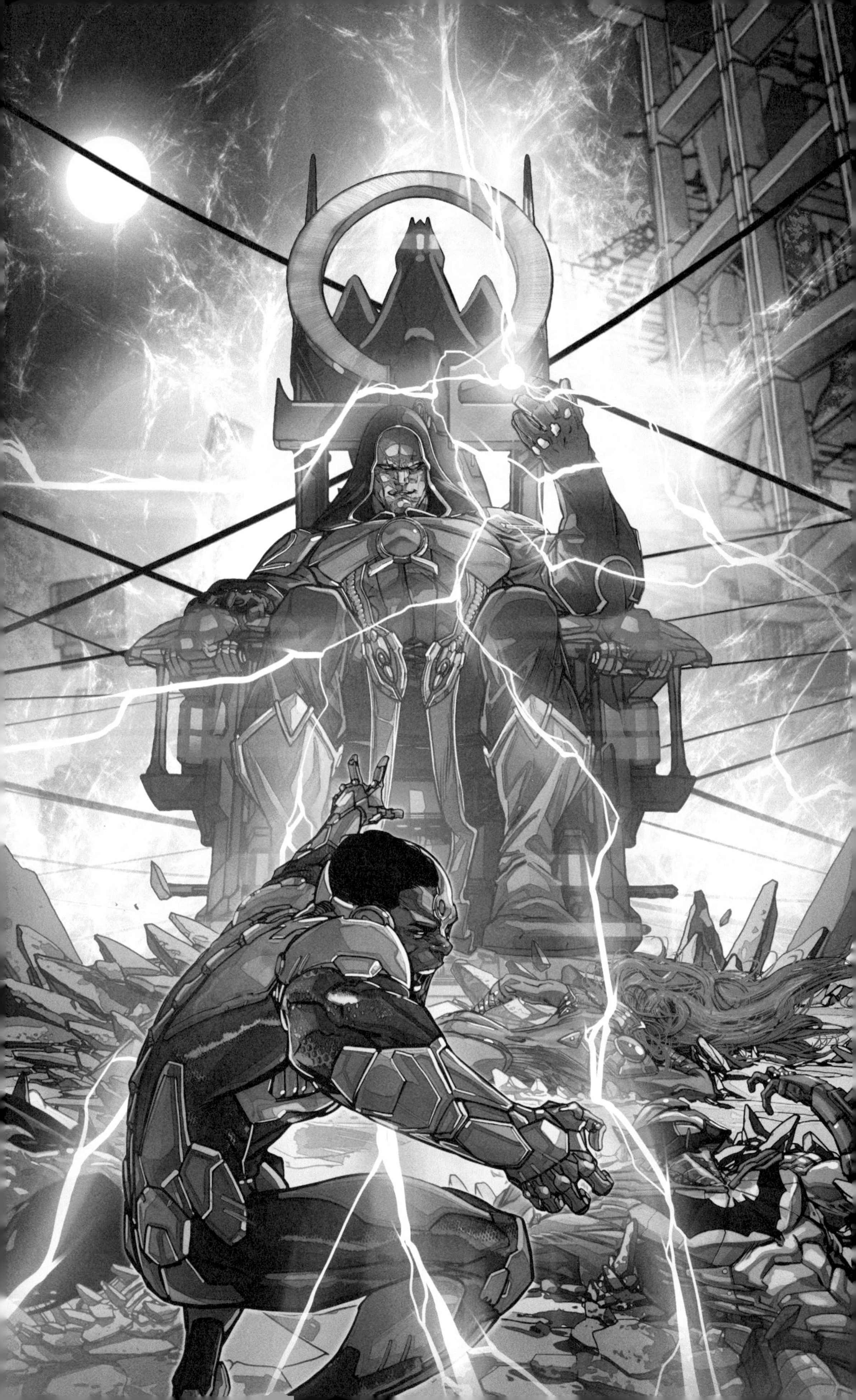

Variant cover art for issue #6 by TONI INFANTE

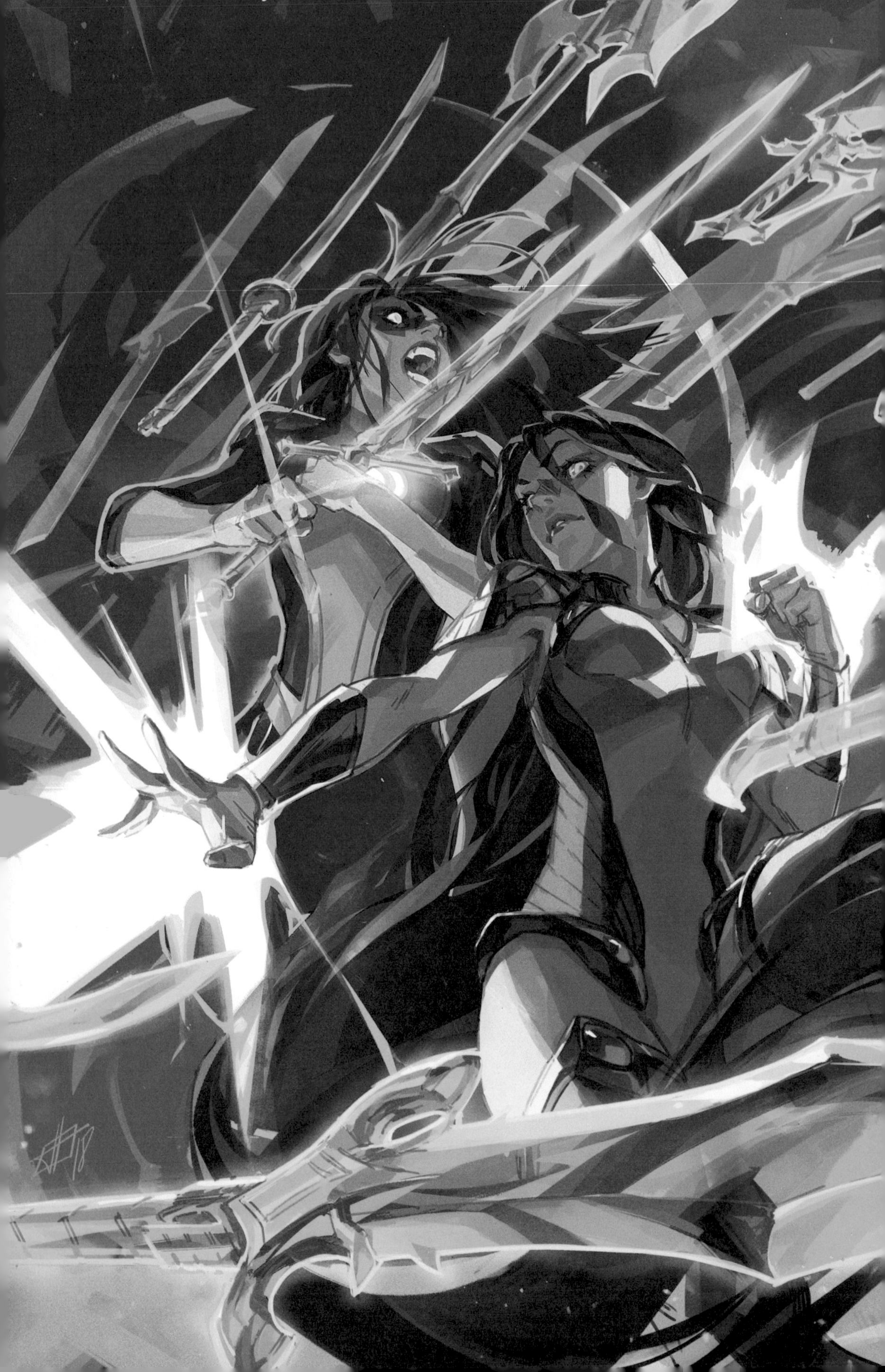

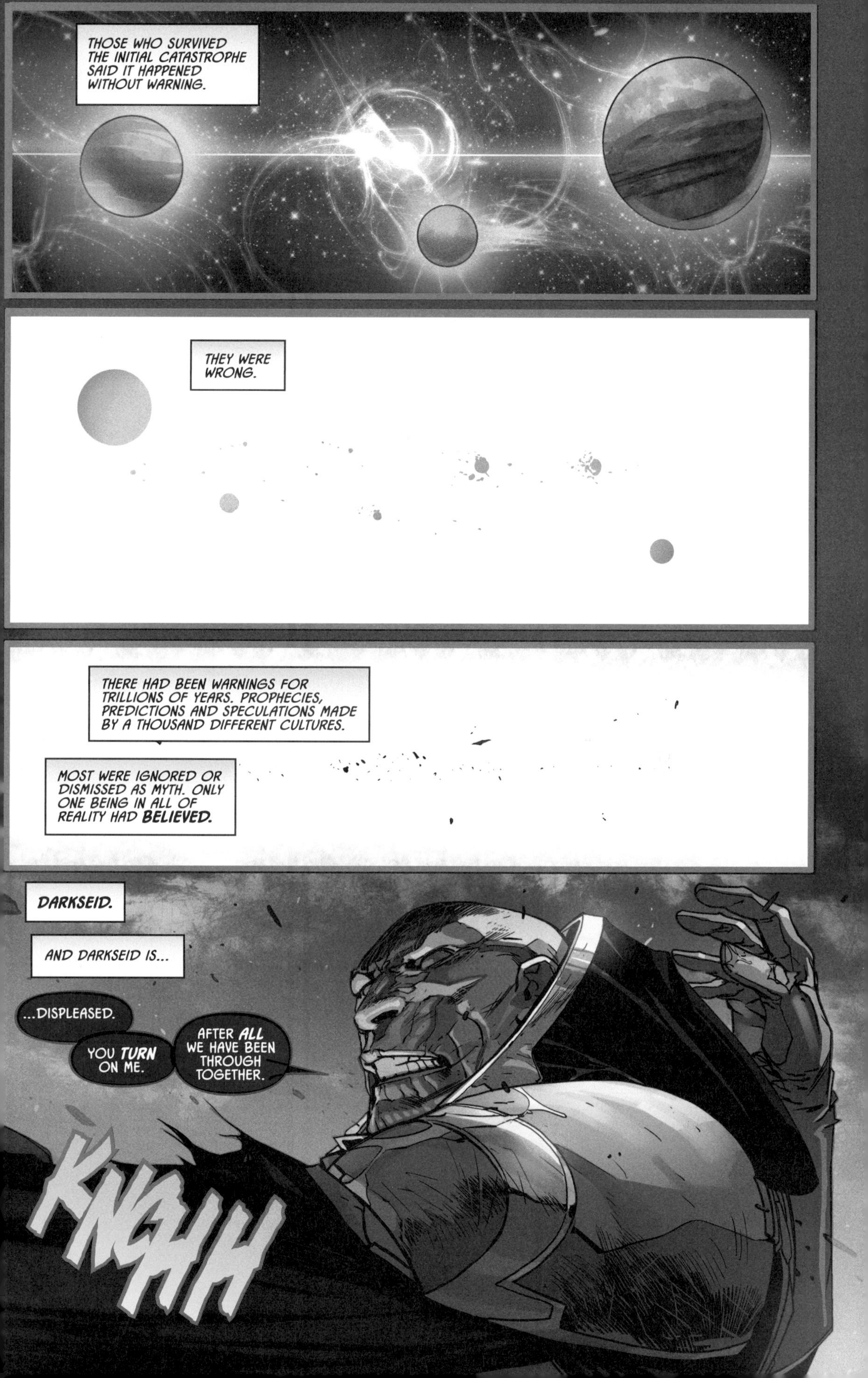
THOSE WHO SURVIVED THE INITIAL CATASTROPHE SAID IT HAPPENED WITHOUT WARNING.
THEY WERE WRONG.
THERE HAD BEEN WARNINGS FOR TRILLIONS OF YEARS. PROPHECIES, PREDICTIONS AND SPECULATIONS MADE BY A THOUSAND DIFFERENT CULTURES.
MOST WERE IGNORED OR DISMISSED AS MYTH. ONLY ONE BEING IN ALL OF REALITY HAD BELIEVED.
DARKSEID.
AND DARKSEID IS...
...DISPLEASED.
YOU TURN ON ME.
AFTER ALL WE HAVE BEEN THROUGH TOGETHER.
KNGHH

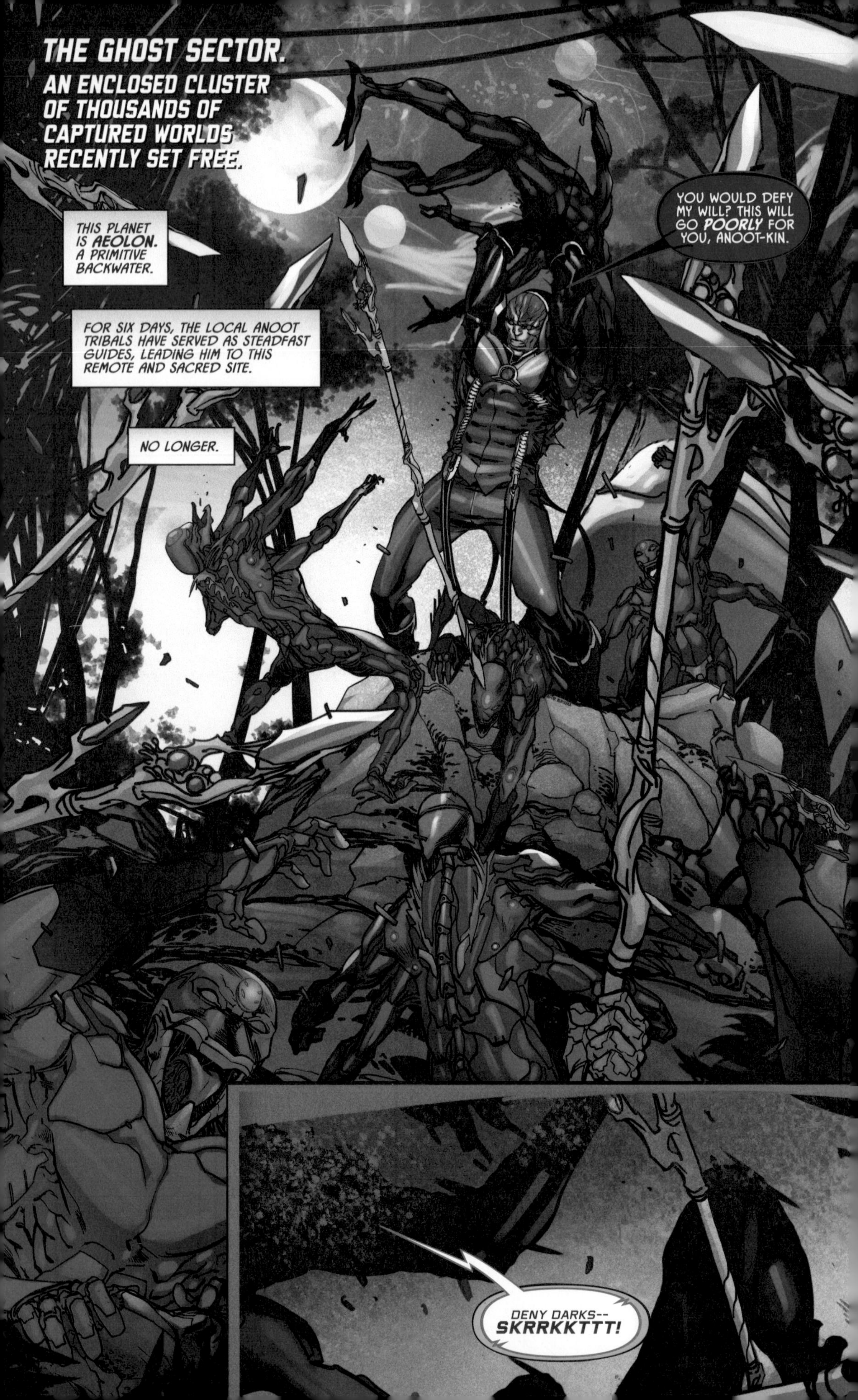
THE GHOST SECTOR.
AN ENCLOSED CLUSTER OF THOUSANDS OF CAPTURED WORLDS RECENTLY SET FREE.
THIS PLANET IS AEOLON. A PRIMITIVE BACKWATER.
FOR SIX DAYS, THE LOCAL ANOOT TRIBALS HAVE SERVED AS STEADFAST GUIDES, LEADING HIM TO THIS REMOTE AND SACRED SITE.
NO LONGER.
YOU WOULD DEFY MY WILL? THIS WILL GO POORLY FOR YOU, ANOOT-KIN.
DENY DARKS-- SKRRKKTTT!

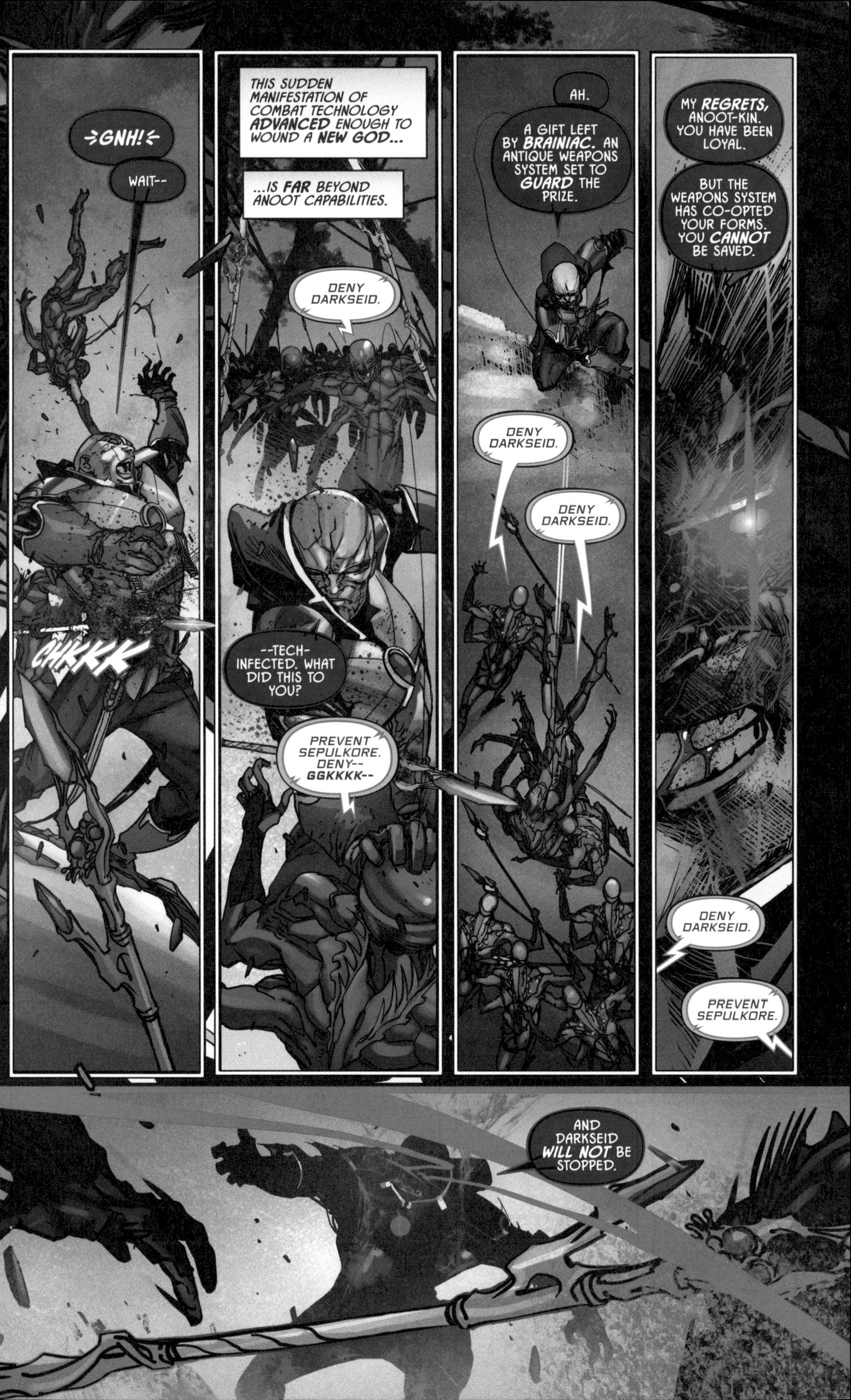

⇝GNH!⇜
WAIT--
CHKKK
THIS SUDDEN MANIFESTATION OF COMBAT TECHNOLOGY ADVANCED ENOUGH TO WOUND A NEW GOD...
...IS FAR BEYOND ANOOT CAPABILITIES.
DENY DARKSEID.
--TECH-INFECTED. WHAT DID THIS TO YOU?
PREVENT SEPULKORE. DENY-- GGKKKK--
AH.
A GIFT LEFT BY BRAINIAC. AN ANTIQUE WEAPONS SYSTEM SET TO GUARD THE PRIZE.
DENY DARKSEID.
DENY DARKSEID.
MY REGRETS, ANOOT-KIN. YOU HAVE BEEN LOYAL.
BUT THE WEAPONS SYSTEM HAS CO-OPTED YOUR FORMS. YOU CANNOT BE SAVED.
DENY DARKSEID.
PREVENT SEPULKORE.
AND DARKSEID WILL NOT BE STOPPED.

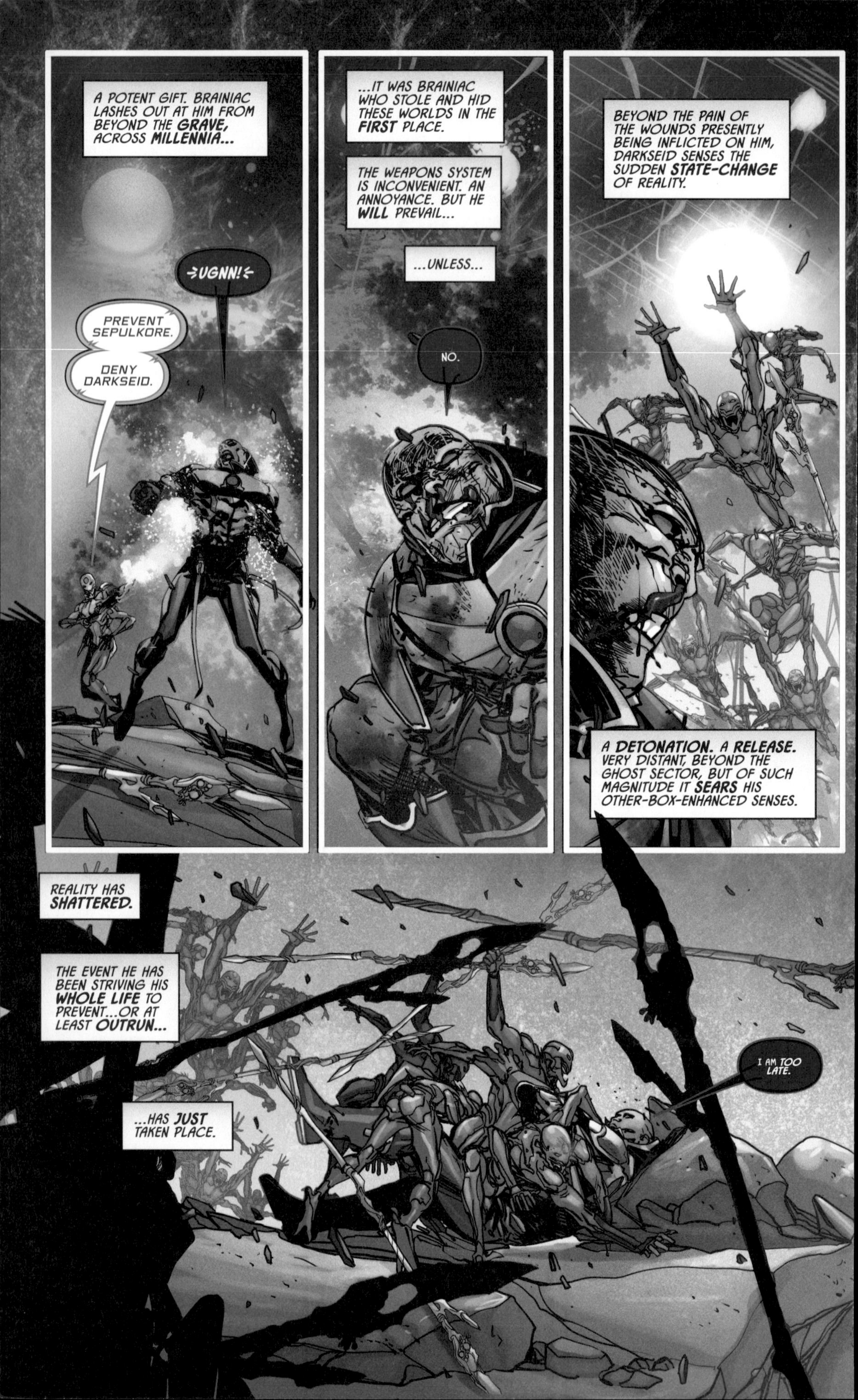

A POTENT GIFT. BRAINIAC LASHES OUT AT HIM FROM BEYOND THE GRAVE, ACROSS MILLENNIA...
UGNN!
PREVENT SEPULKORE.
DENY DARKSEID.
...IT WAS BRAINIAC WHO STOLE AND HID THESE WORLDS IN THE FIRST PLACE.
THE WEAPONS SYSTEM IS INCONVENIENT. AN ANNOYANCE. BUT HE WILL PREVAIL...
...UNLESS...
NO.
BEYOND THE PAIN OF THE WOUNDS PRESENTLY BEING INFLICTED ON HIM, DARKSEID SENSES THE SUDDEN STATE-CHANGE OF REALITY.
A DETONATION. A RELEASE. VERY DISTANT, BEYOND THE GHOST SECTOR, BUT OF SUCH MAGNITUDE IT SEARS HIS OTHER-BOX-ENHANCED SENSES.
REALITY HAS SHATTERED.
THE EVENT HE HAS BEEN STRIVING HIS WHOLE LIFE TO PREVENT...OR AT LEAST OUTRUN...
...HAS JUST TAKEN PLACE.
I AM TOO LATE.

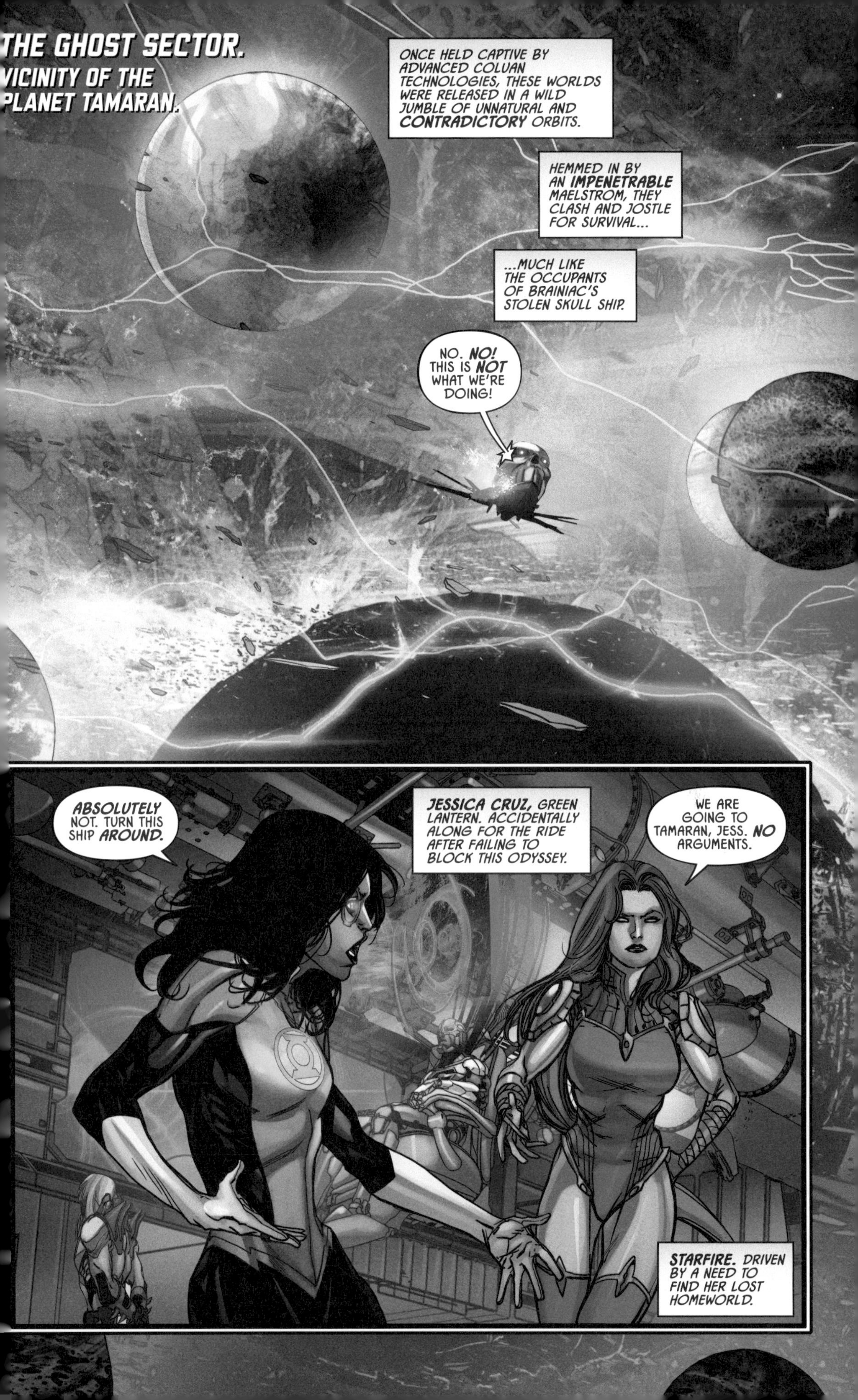
THE GHOST SECTOR.
VICINITY OF THE PLANET TAMARAN.
ONCE HELD CAPTIVE BY ADVANCED COLUAN TECHNOLOGIES, THESE WORLDS WERE RELEASED IN A WILD JUMBLE OF UNNATURAL AND CONTRADICTORY ORBITS.
HEMMED IN BY AN IMPENETRABLE MAELSTROM, THEY CLASH AND JOSTLE FOR SURVIVAL...
...MUCH LIKE THE OCCUPANTS OF BRAINIAC'S STOLEN SKULL SHIP.
NO. NO! THIS IS NOT WHAT WE'RE DOING!
ABSOLUTELY NOT. TURN THIS SHIP AROUND.
JESSICA CRUZ, GREEN LANTERN. ACCIDENTALLY ALONG FOR THE RIDE AFTER FAILING TO BLOCK THIS ODYSSEY.
WE ARE GOING TO TAMARAN, JESS. NO ARGUMENTS.
STARFIRE. DRIVEN BY A NEED TO FIND HER LOST HOMEWORLD.

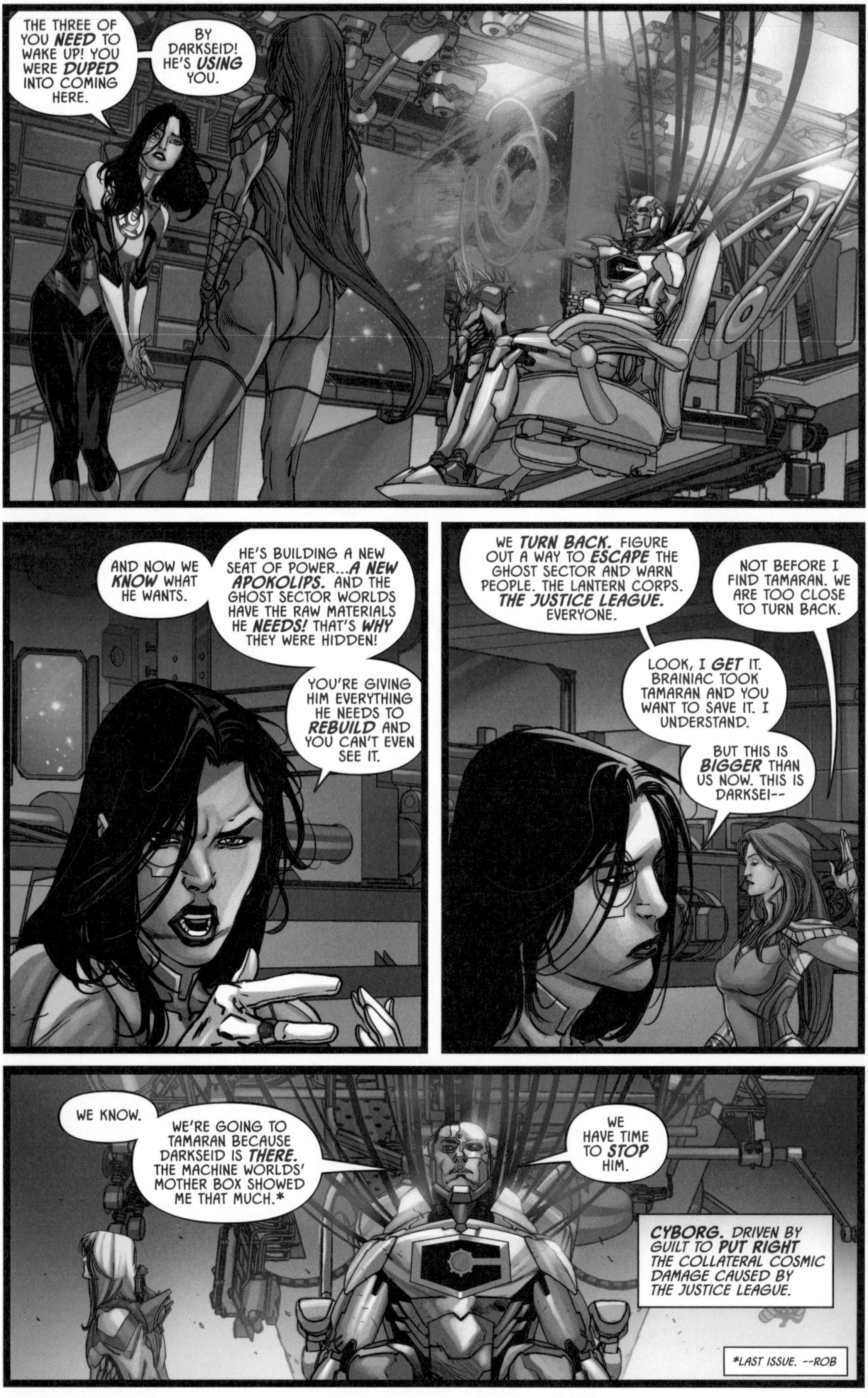
THE THREE OF YOU NEED TO WAKE UP! YOU WERE DUPED INTO COMING HERE.
BY DARKSEID! HE'S USING YOU.
AND NOW WE KNOW WHAT HE WANTS.
HE'S BUILDING A NEW SEAT OF POWER...A NEW APOKOLIPS. AND THE GHOST SECTOR WORLDS HAVE THE RAW MATERIALS HE NEEDS! THAT'S WHY THEY WERE HIDDEN!
YOU'RE GIVING HIM EVERYTHING HE NEEDS TO REBUILD AND YOU CAN'T EVEN SEE IT.
WE TURN BACK. FIGURE OUT A WAY TO ESCAPE THE GHOST SECTOR AND WARN PEOPLE. THE LANTERN CORPS. THE JUSTICE LEAGUE. EVERYONE.
NOT BEFORE I FIND TAMARAN. WE ARE TOO CLOSE TO TURN BACK.
LOOK, I GET IT. BRAINIAC TOOK TAMARAN AND YOU WANT TO SAVE IT. I UNDERSTAND.
BUT THIS IS BIGGER THAN US NOW. THIS IS DARKSEI--
WE KNOW.
WE'RE GOING TO TAMARAN BECAUSE DARKSEID IS THERE. THE MACHINE WORLDS' MOTHER BOX SHOWED ME THAT MUCH.*
WE HAVE TIME TO STOP HIM.
CYBORG. DRIVEN BY GUILT TO PUT RIGHT THE COLLATERAL COSMIC DAMAGE CAUSED BY THE JUSTICE LEAGUE.
*LAST ISSUE. --ROB

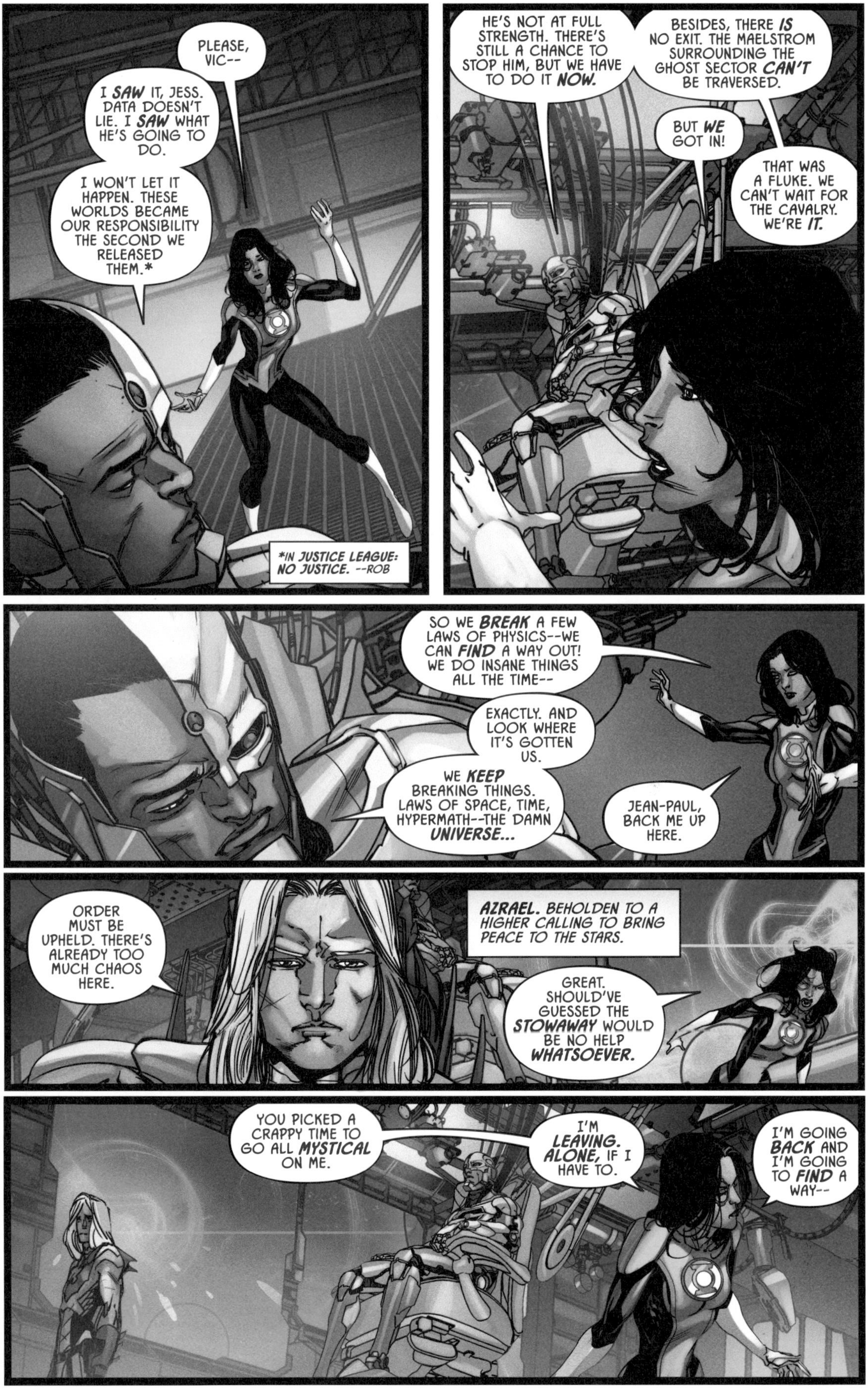
PLEASE, VIC--
I SAW IT, JESS. DATA DOESN'T LIE. I SAW WHAT HE'S GOING TO DO.
I WON'T LET IT HAPPEN. THESE WORLDS BECAME OUR RESPONSIBILITY THE SECOND WE RELEASED THEM.*
*IN JUSTICE LEAGUE: NO JUSTICE. --ROB
HE'S NOT AT FULL STRENGTH. THERE'S STILL A CHANCE TO STOP HIM, BUT WE HAVE TO DO IT NOW.
BESIDES, THERE IS NO EXIT. THE MAELSTROM SURROUNDING THE GHOST SECTOR CAN'T BE TRAVERSED.
BUT WE GOT IN!
THAT WAS A FLUKE. WE CAN'T WAIT FOR THE CAVALRY. WE'RE IT.
SO WE BREAK A FEW LAWS OF PHYSICS--WE CAN FIND A WAY OUT! WE DO INSANE THINGS ALL THE TIME--
EXACTLY. AND LOOK WHERE IT'S GOTTEN US.
WE KEEP BREAKING THINGS. LAWS OF SPACE, TIME, HYPERMATH--THE DAMN UNIVERSE...
JEAN-PAUL, BACK ME UP HERE.
ORDER MUST BE UPHELD. THERE'S ALREADY TOO MUCH CHAOS HERE.
AZRAEL. BEHOLDEN TO A HIGHER CALLING TO BRING PEACE TO THE STARS.
GREAT. SHOULD'VE GUESSED THE STOWAWAY WOULD BE NO HELP WHATSOEVER.
YOU PICKED A CRAPPY TIME TO GO ALL MYSTICAL ON ME.
I'M LEAVING. ALONE, IF I HAVE TO.
I'M GOING BACK AND I'M GOING TO FIND A WAY--

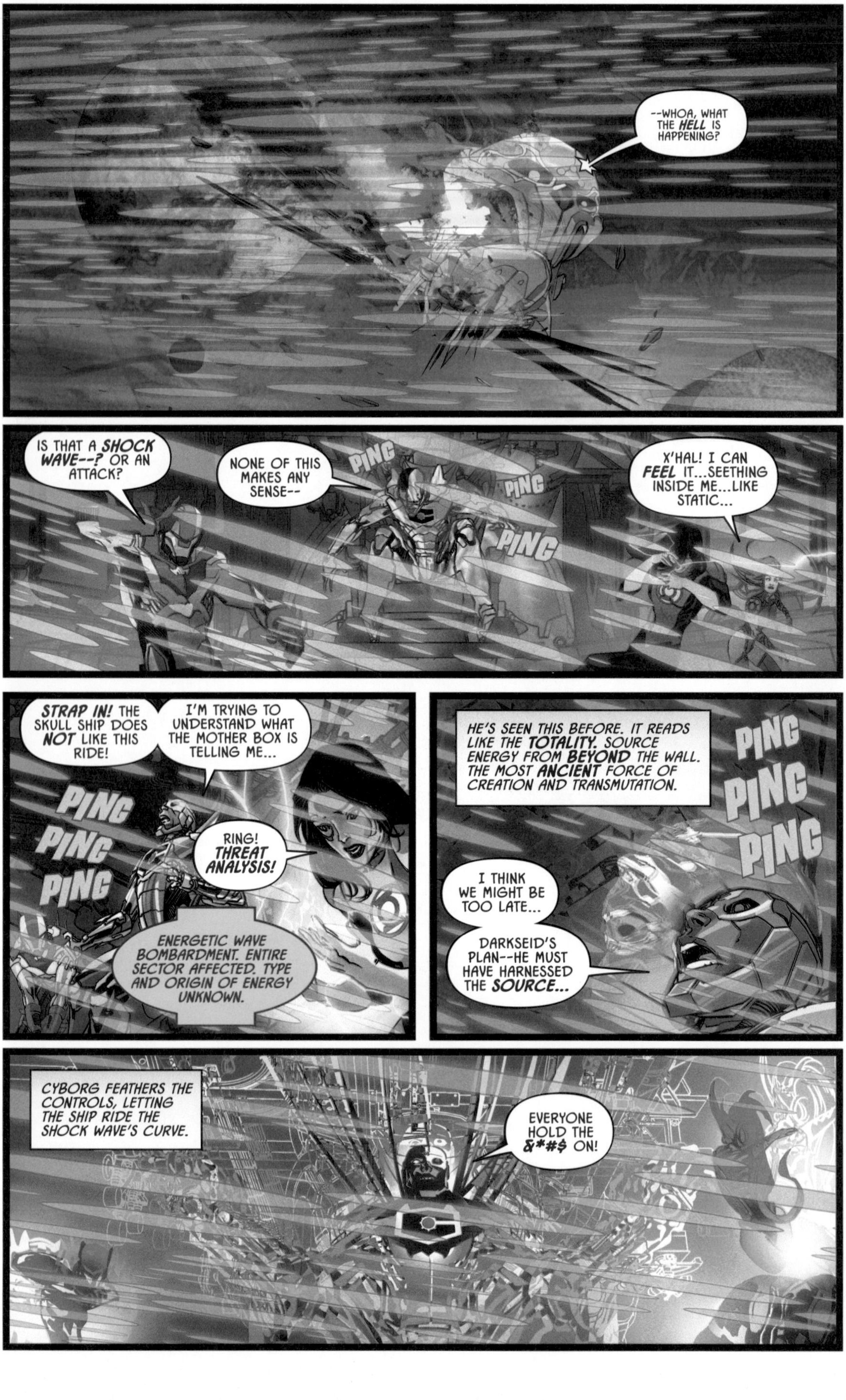
--WHOA, WHAT THE HELL IS HAPPENING?
IS THAT A SHOCK WAVE--? OR AN ATTACK?
NONE OF THIS MAKES ANY SENSE--
PING
PING
PING
X'HAL! I CAN FEEL IT...SEETHING INSIDE ME...LIKE STATIC...
STRAP IN! THE SKULL SHIP DOES NOT LIKE THIS RIDE!
I'M TRYING TO UNDERSTAND WHAT THE MOTHER BOX IS TELLING ME...
PING
PING
PING
RING! THREAT ANALYSIS!
ENERGETIC WAVE BOMBARDMENT. ENTIRE SECTOR AFFECTED. TYPE AND ORIGIN OF ENERGY UNKNOWN.
HE'S SEEN THIS BEFORE. IT READS LIKE THE TOTALITY. SOURCE ENERGY FROM BEYOND THE WALL. THE MOST ANCIENT FORCE OF CREATION AND TRANSMUTATION.
PING
PING
PING
I THINK WE MIGHT BE TOO LATE...
DARKSEID'S PLAN--HE MUST HAVE HARNESSED THE SOURCE...
CYBORG FEATHERS THE CONTROLS, LETTING THE SHIP RIDE THE SHOCK WAVE'S CURVE.
EVERYONE HOLD THE &*#$ ON!

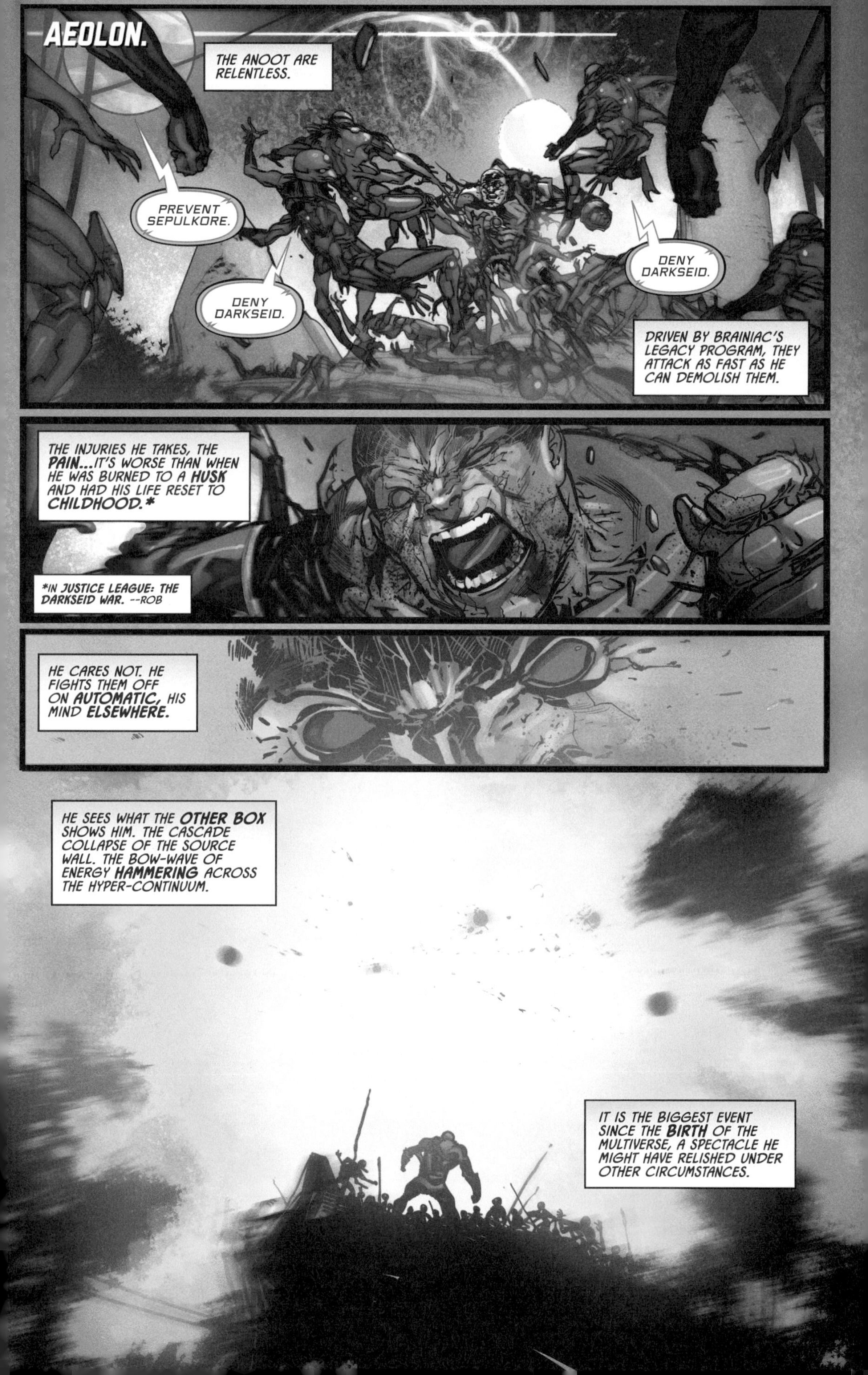
AEOLON.
THE ANOOT ARE RELENTLESS.
PREVENT SEPULKORE.
DENY DARKSEID.
DENY DARKSEID.
DRIVEN BY BRAINIAC'S LEGACY PROGRAM, THEY ATTACK AS FAST AS HE CAN DEMOLISH THEM.
THE INJURIES HE TAKES, THE PAIN...IT'S WORSE THAN WHEN HE WAS BURNED TO A HUSK AND HAD HIS LIFE RESET TO CHILDHOOD.*
*IN JUSTICE LEAGUE: THE DARKSEID WAR. --ROB
HE CARES NOT. HE FIGHTS THEM OFF ON AUTOMATIC, HIS MIND ELSEWHERE.
HE SEES WHAT THE OTHER BOX SHOWS HIM. THE CASCADE COLLAPSE OF THE SOURCE WALL. THE BOW-WAVE OF ENERGY HAMMERING ACROSS THE HYPER-CONTINUUM.
IT IS THE BIGGEST EVENT SINCE THE BIRTH OF THE MULTIVERSE, A SPECTACLE HE MIGHT HAVE RELISHED UNDER OTHER CIRCUMSTANCES.

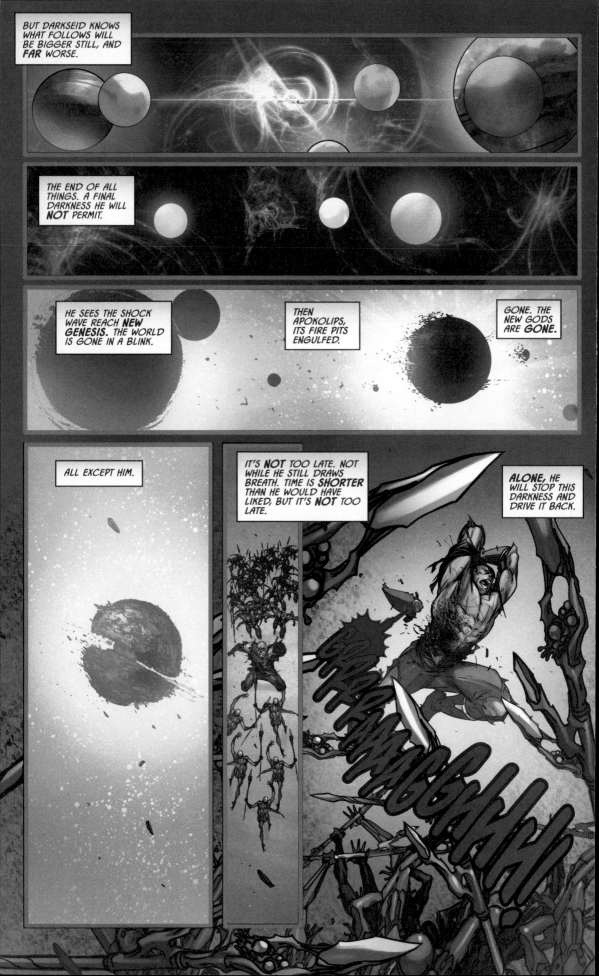

BUT DARKSEID KNOWS WHAT FOLLOWS WILL BE BIGGER STILL, AND *FAR* WORSE.

THE END OF ALL THINGS. A FINAL DARKNESS HE WILL *NOT* PERMIT.

HE SEES THE SHOCK WAVE REACH *NEW GENESIS.* THE WORLD IS GONE IN A BLINK.

THEN APOKOLIPS, ITS FIRE PITS ENGULFED.

GONE. THE NEW GODS ARE *GONE.*

ALL EXCEPT HIM.

IT'S *NOT* TOO LATE. NOT WHILE HE STILL DRAWS BREATH. TIME IS *SHORTER* THAN HE WOULD HAVE LIKED, BUT IT'S *NOT* TOO LATE.

ALONE, HE WILL STOP THIS DARKNESS AND DRIVE IT BACK.

BRRRAAAAAAAGHH!

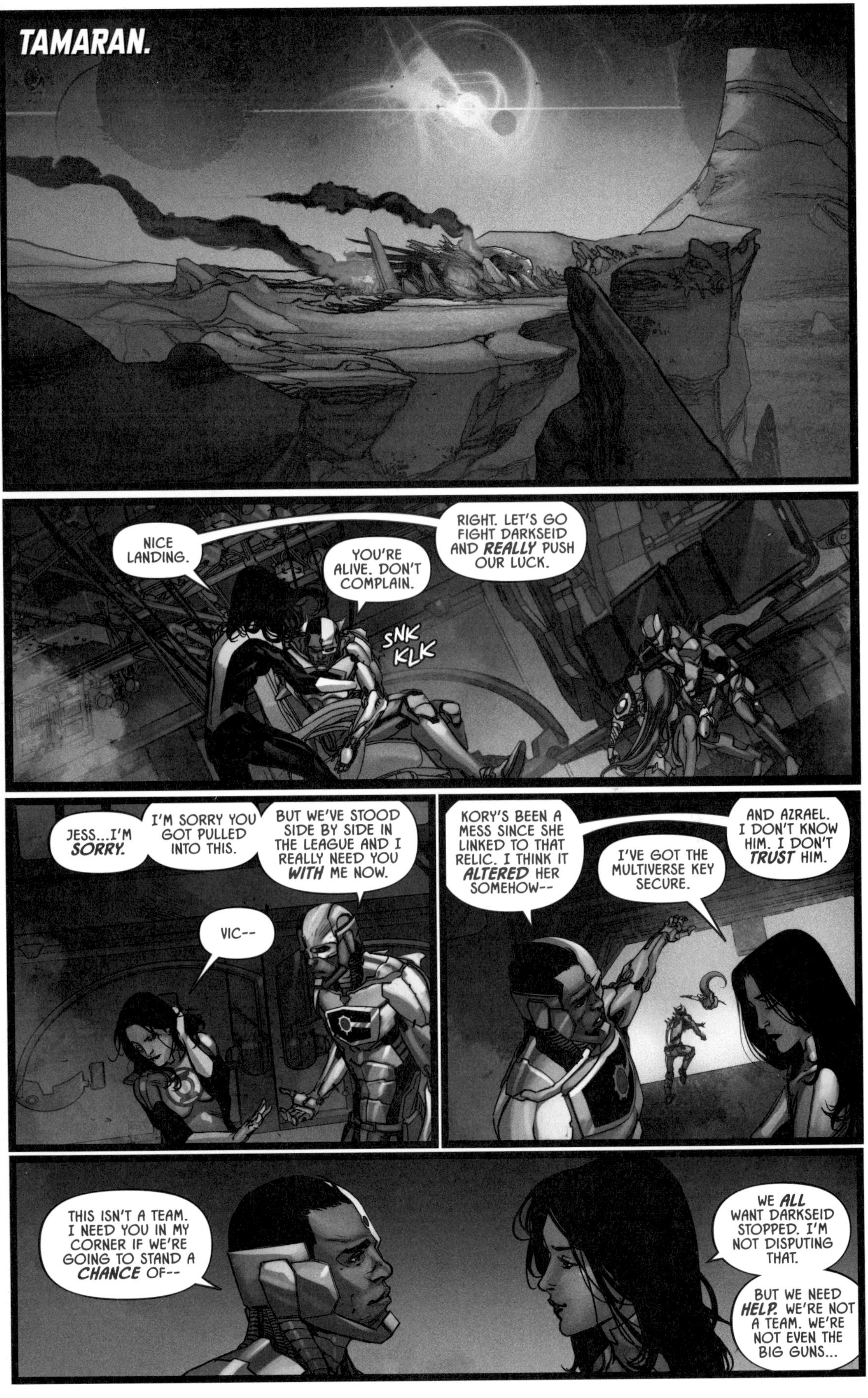
TAMARAN.
NICE LANDING.
YOU'RE ALIVE. DON'T COMPLAIN.
RIGHT. LET'S GO FIGHT DARKSEID AND REALLY PUSH OUR LUCK.
SNK KLK
JESS...I'M SORRY.
I'M SORRY YOU GOT PULLED INTO THIS.
BUT WE'VE STOOD SIDE BY SIDE IN THE LEAGUE AND I REALLY NEED YOU WITH ME NOW.
VIC--
KORY'S BEEN A MESS SINCE SHE LINKED TO THAT RELIC. I THINK IT ALTERED HER SOMEHOW--
I'VE GOT THE MULTIVERSE KEY SECURE.
AND AZRAEL. I DON'T KNOW HIM. I DON'T TRUST HIM.
THIS ISN'T A TEAM. I NEED YOU IN MY CORNER IF WE'RE GOING TO STAND A CHANCE OF--
WE ALL WANT DARKSEID STOPPED. I'M NOT DISPUTING THAT.
BUT WE NEED HELP. WE'RE NOT A TEAM. WE'RE NOT EVEN THE BIG GUNS...

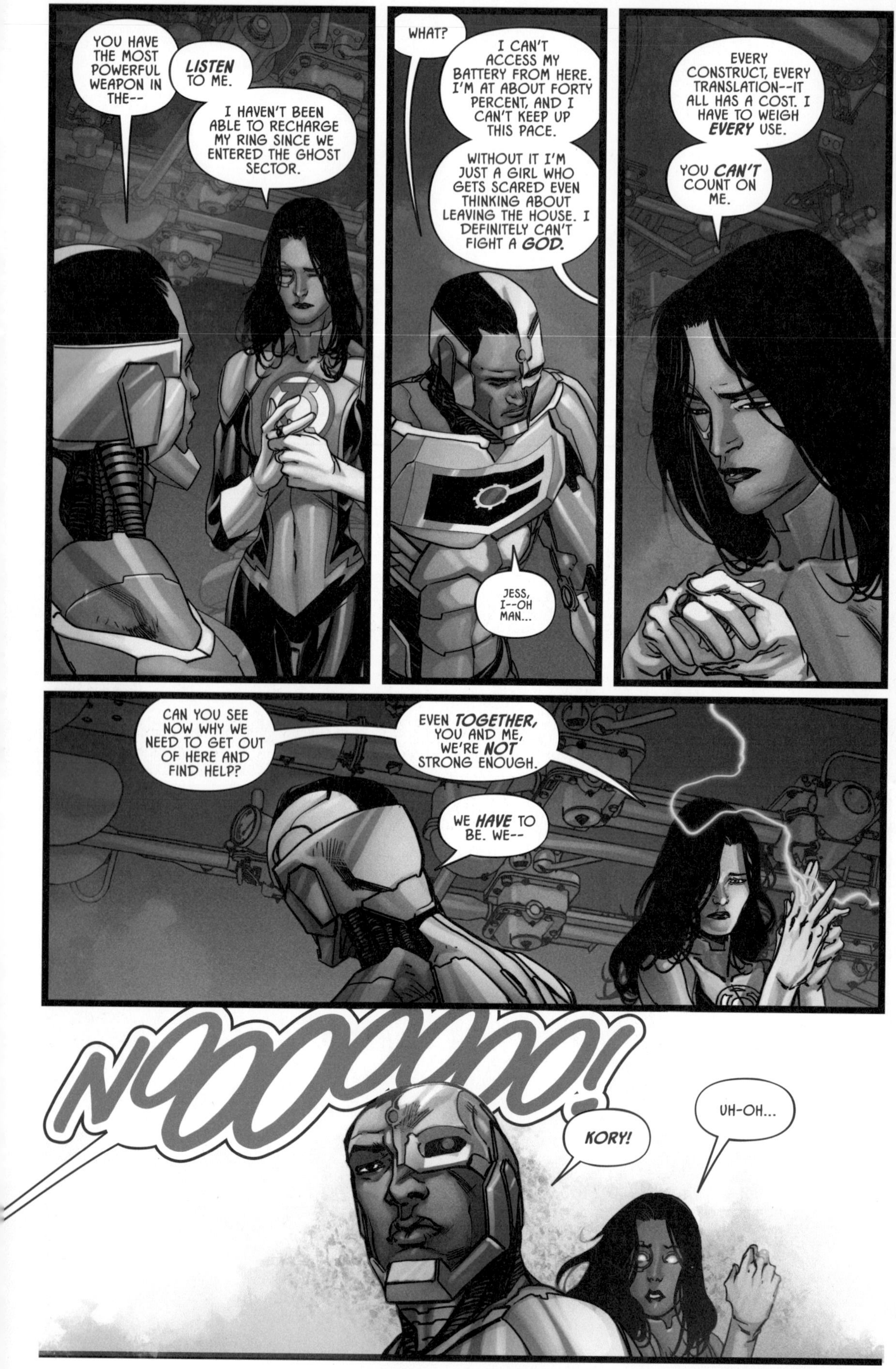
YOU HAVE THE MOST POWERFUL WEAPON IN THE--
LISTEN TO ME.
I HAVEN'T BEEN ABLE TO RECHARGE MY RING SINCE WE ENTERED THE GHOST SECTOR.
WHAT?
I CAN'T ACCESS MY BATTERY FROM HERE. I'M AT ABOUT FORTY PERCENT, AND I CAN'T KEEP UP THIS PACE.
WITHOUT IT I'M JUST A GIRL WHO GETS SCARED EVEN THINKING ABOUT LEAVING THE HOUSE. I DEFINITELY CAN'T FIGHT A GOD.
JESS, I--OH MAN...
EVERY CONSTRUCT, EVERY TRANSLATION--IT ALL HAS A COST. I HAVE TO WEIGH EVERY USE.
YOU CAN'T COUNT ON ME.
CAN YOU SEE NOW WHY WE NEED TO GET OUT OF HERE AND FIND HELP?
EVEN TOGETHER, YOU AND ME, WE'RE NOT STRONG ENOUGH.
WE HAVE TO BE. WE--
NOOOOOO!
KORY!
UH-OH...

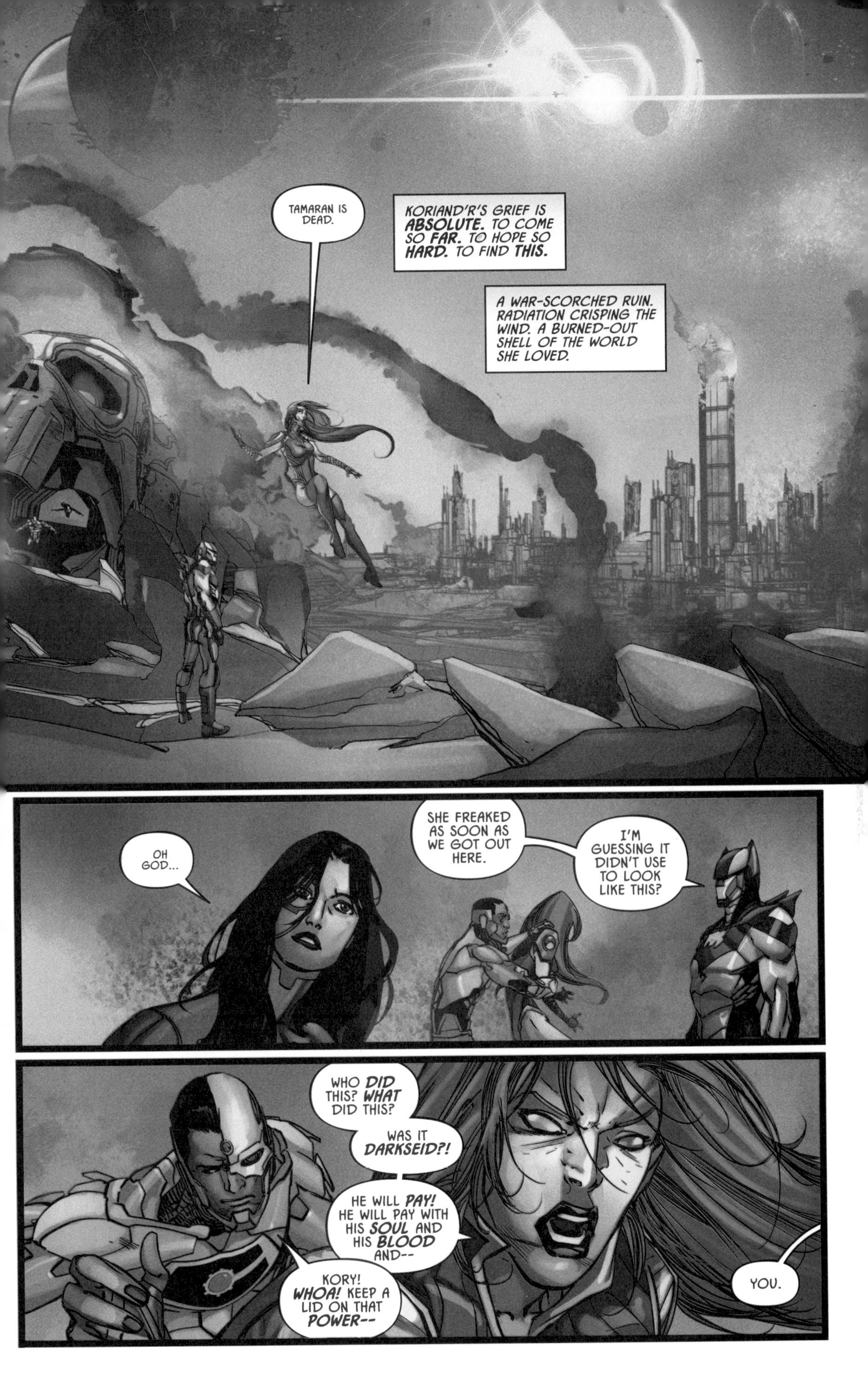

TAMARAN IS DEAD.
KORIAND'R'S GRIEF IS ABSOLUTE. TO COME SO FAR. TO HOPE SO HARD. TO FIND THIS.
A WAR-SCORCHED RUIN. RADIATION CRISPING THE WIND. A BURNED-OUT SHELL OF THE WORLD SHE LOVED.
OH GOD...
SHE FREAKED AS SOON AS WE GOT OUT HERE.
I'M GUESSING IT DIDN'T USE TO LOOK LIKE THIS?
WHO DID THIS? WHAT DID THIS?
WAS IT DARKSEID?!
HE WILL PAY! HE WILL PAY WITH HIS SOUL AND HIS BLOOD AND--
KORY! WHOA! KEEP A LID ON THAT POWER--
YOU.

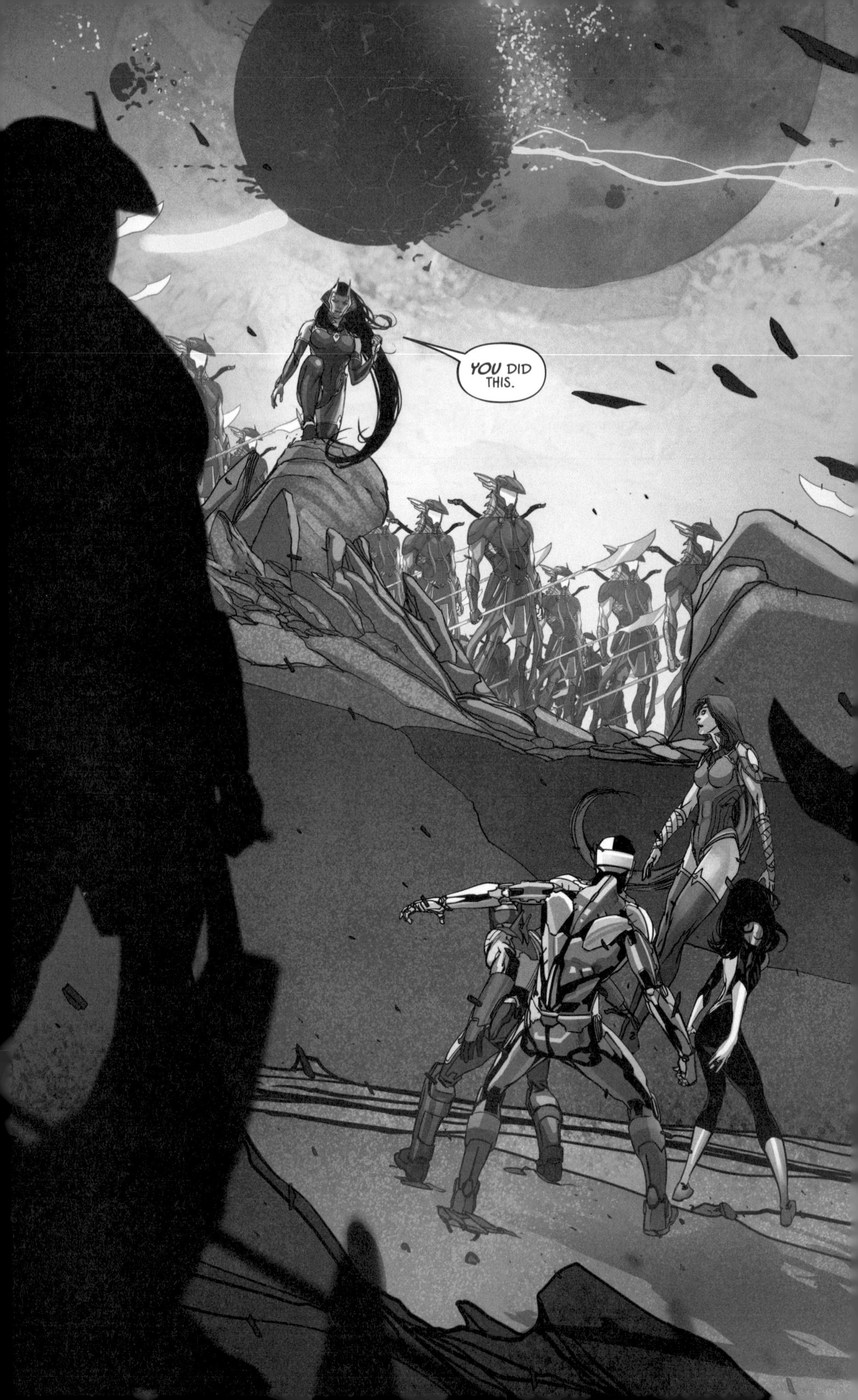
YOU DID THIS.

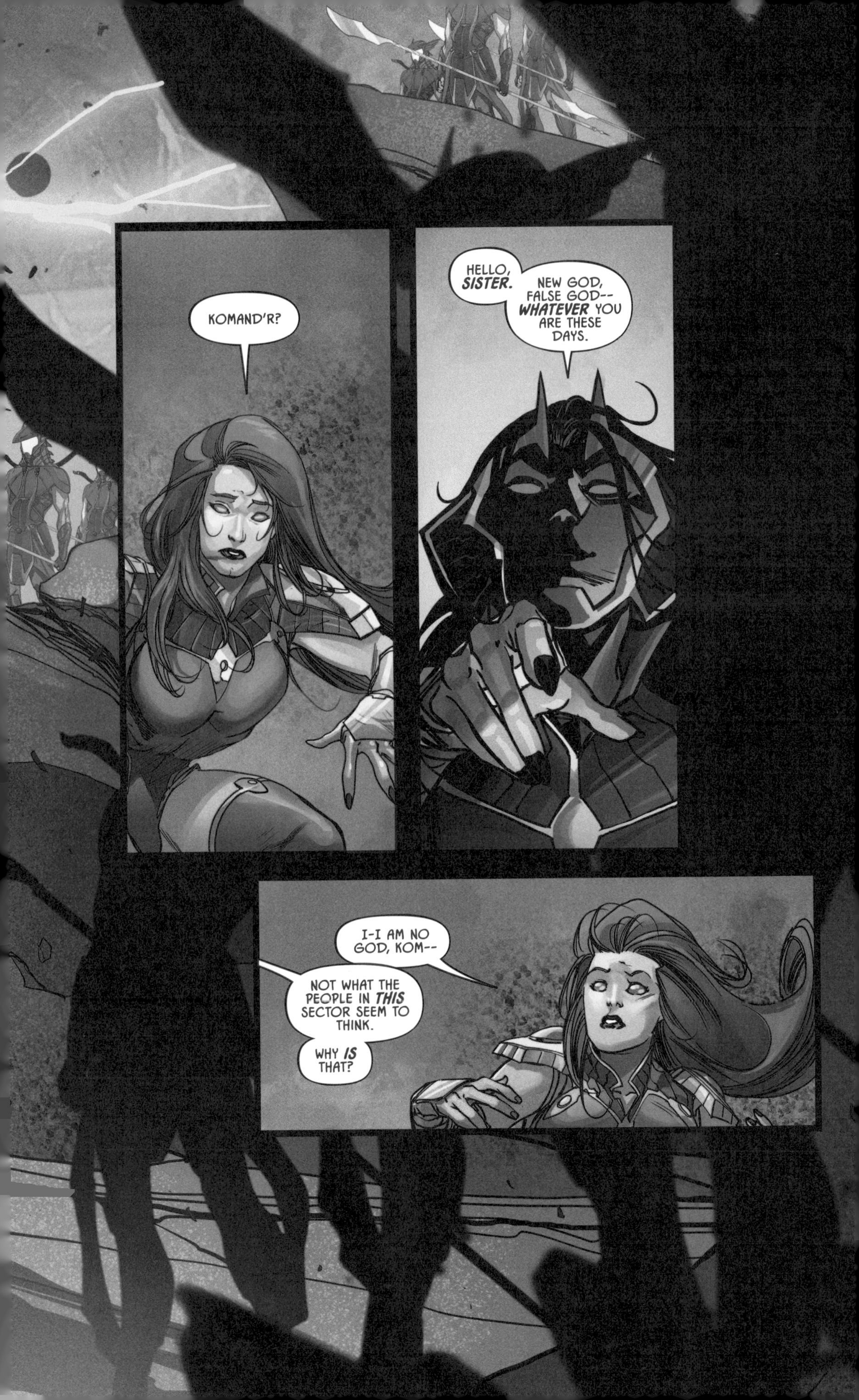
KOMAND'R?
HELLO, SISTER.
NEW GOD, FALSE GOD-- WHATEVER YOU ARE THESE DAYS.
I-I AM NO GOD, KOM--
NOT WHAT THE PEOPLE IN THIS SECTOR SEEM TO THINK.
WHY IS THAT?

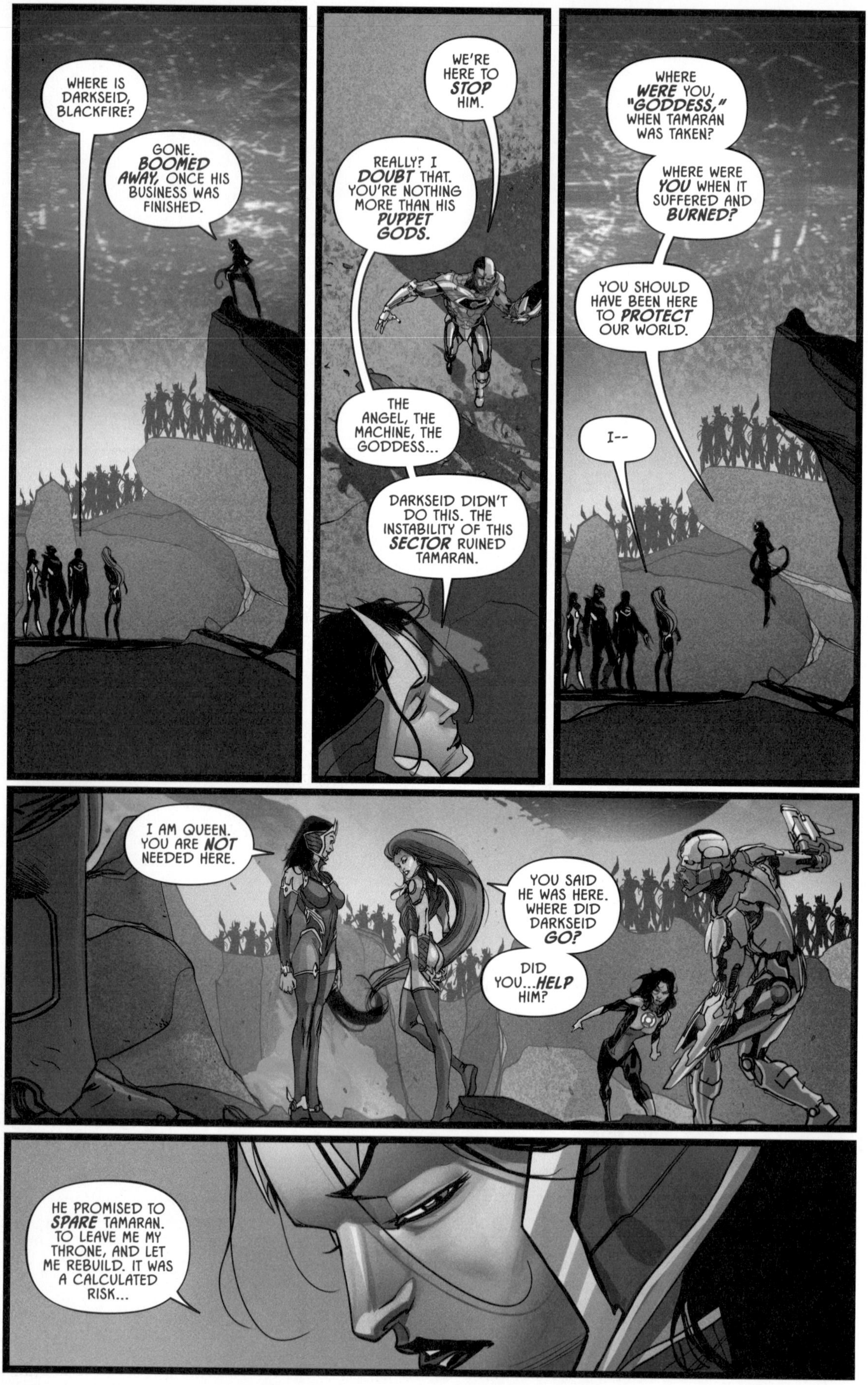

WHERE IS DARKSEID, BLACKFIRE?
GONE. BOOMED AWAY, ONCE HIS BUSINESS WAS FINISHED.
WE'RE HERE TO STOP HIM.
REALLY? I DOUBT THAT. YOU'RE NOTHING MORE THAN HIS PUPPET GODS.
THE ANGEL, THE MACHINE, THE GODDESS...
DARKSEID DIDN'T DO THIS. THE INSTABILITY OF THIS SECTOR RUINED TAMARAN.
WHERE WERE YOU, "GODDESS," WHEN TAMARAN WAS TAKEN?
WHERE WERE YOU WHEN IT SUFFERED AND BURNED?
YOU SHOULD HAVE BEEN HERE TO PROTECT OUR WORLD.
I--
I AM QUEEN. YOU ARE NOT NEEDED HERE.
YOU SAID HE WAS HERE. WHERE DID DARKSEID GO?
DID YOU...HELP HIM?
HE PROMISED TO SPARE TAMARAN. TO LEAVE ME MY THRONE, AND LET ME REBUILD. IT WAS A CALCULATED RISK...

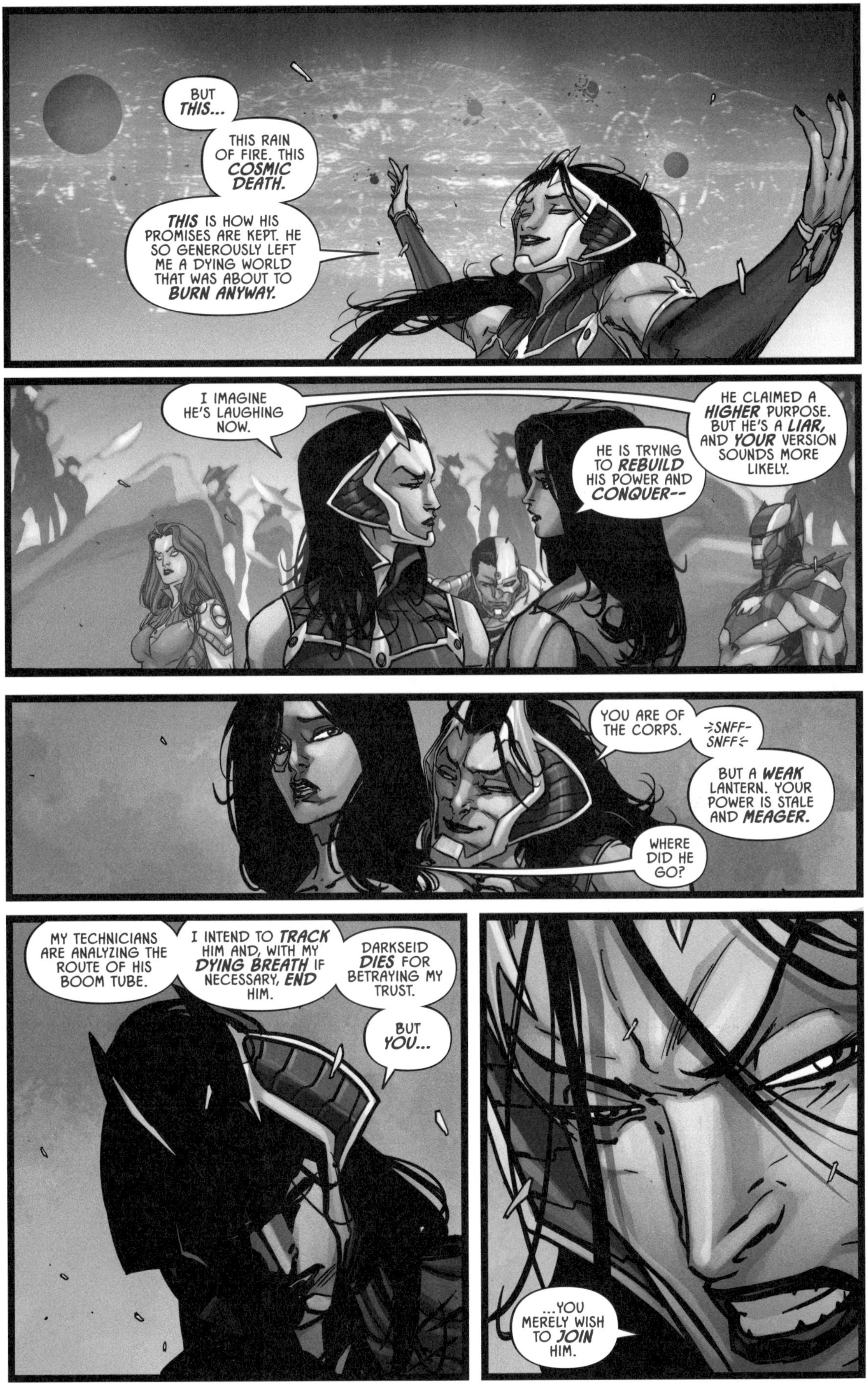
BUT THIS...
THIS RAIN OF FIRE. THIS COSMIC DEATH.
THIS IS HOW HIS PROMISES ARE KEPT. HE SO GENEROUSLY LEFT ME A DYING WORLD THAT WAS ABOUT TO BURN ANYWAY.
I IMAGINE HE'S LAUGHING NOW.
HE CLAIMED A HIGHER PURPOSE. BUT HE'S A LIAR, AND YOUR VERSION SOUNDS MORE LIKELY.
HE IS TRYING TO REBUILD HIS POWER AND CONQUER--
YOU ARE OF THE CORPS.
SNFF- SNFF
BUT A WEAK LANTERN. YOUR POWER IS STALE AND MEAGER.
WHERE DID HE GO?
MY TECHNICIANS ARE ANALYZING THE ROUTE OF HIS BOOM TUBE.
I INTEND TO TRACK HIM AND, WITH MY DYING BREATH IF NECESSARY, END HIM.
DARKSEID DIES FOR BETRAYING MY TRUST.
BUT YOU...
...YOU MERELY WISH TO JOIN HIM.

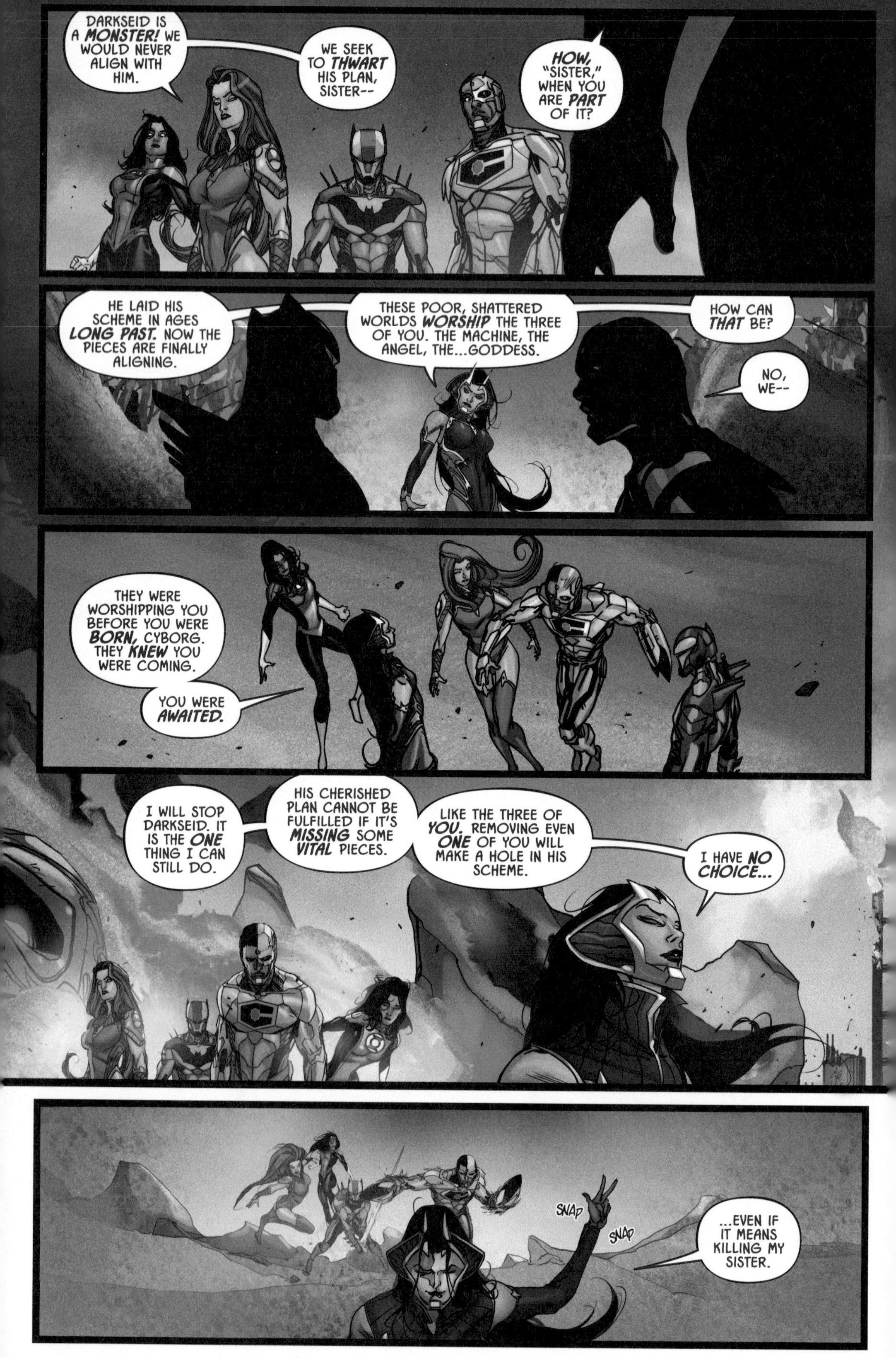

DARKSEID IS A MONSTER! WE WOULD NEVER ALIGN WITH HIM.
WE SEEK TO THWART HIS PLAN, SISTER--
HOW, "SISTER," WHEN YOU ARE PART OF IT?
HE LAID HIS SCHEME IN AGES LONG PAST. NOW THE PIECES ARE FINALLY ALIGNING.
THESE POOR, SHATTERED WORLDS WORSHIP THE THREE OF YOU. THE MACHINE, THE ANGEL, THE...GODDESS.
HOW CAN THAT BE?
NO, WE--
THEY WERE WORSHIPPING YOU BEFORE YOU WERE BORN, CYBORG. THEY KNEW YOU WERE COMING.
YOU WERE AWAITED.
I WILL STOP DARKSEID. IT IS THE ONE THING I CAN STILL DO.
HIS CHERISHED PLAN CANNOT BE FULFILLED IF IT'S MISSING SOME VITAL PIECES.
LIKE THE THREE OF YOU. REMOVING EVEN ONE OF YOU WILL MAKE A HOLE IN HIS SCHEME.
I HAVE NO CHOICE...
SNAP
SNAP
...EVEN IF IT MEANS KILLING MY SISTER.

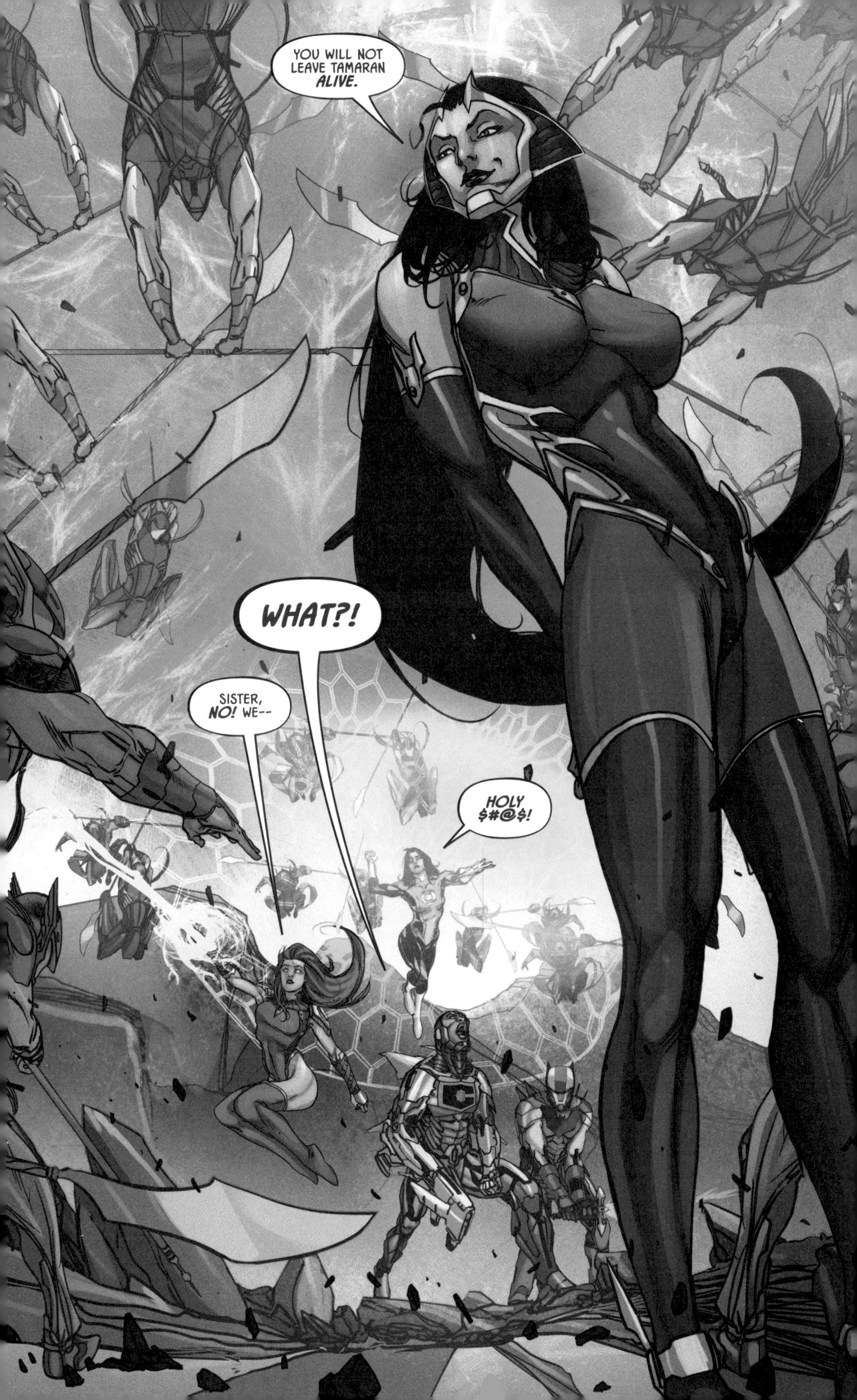
YOU WILL NOT LEAVE TAMARAN ALIVE.
WHAT?!
SISTER, NO! WE--
HOLY $#@$!

AEOLON.

THE LAST OF BRAINIAC'S WEAPONS IS SLAIN.

UHN...UHN... UHN...

DARKSEID HAS PREVAILED. THE **NEXT** RELIC IS HIS.

ANOTHER SEGMENT OF THE ANCIENT PLAN.

HE MUST **IGNORE** THE PAIN.

UNITE THE RELIC WITH THE **OTHER BOX.** COMMENCE **CONSTRUCTION.**

WITH EACH ADDED PIECE, HIS STRENGTH WILL RETURN.

IT IS **NOT** TOO LATE. THE SOURCE WALL HAS FALLEN, BUT THERE IS **STILL** TIME.

TIME TO IMPLEMENT THE ANCIENT CONTINGENCY PLAN. TO BUILD **SEPULKORE.**

TO **ARREST** THE SWIFT DECAY OF REALITY AND--

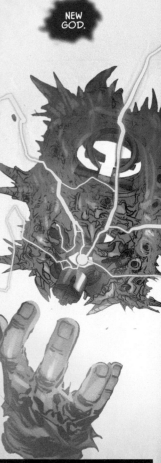

NEW GOD.

WHO SPEAKS?

ANOTHER OF BRAINIAC'S TRICKS?

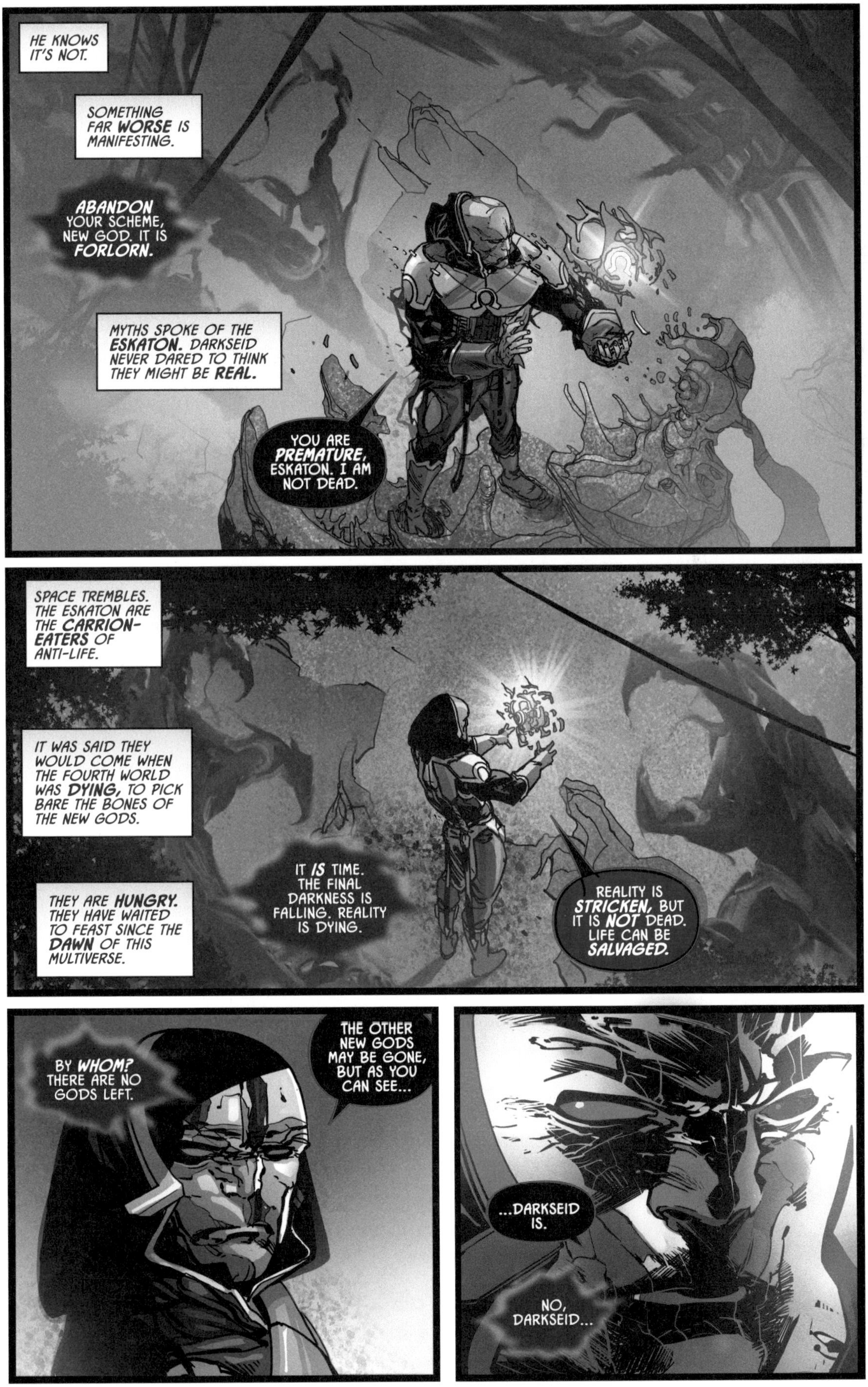
HE KNOWS IT'S NOT.
SOMETHING FAR WORSE IS MANIFESTING.
ABANDON YOUR SCHEME, NEW GOD. IT IS FORLORN.
MYTHS SPOKE OF THE ESKATON. DARKSEID NEVER DARED TO THINK THEY MIGHT BE REAL.
YOU ARE PREMATURE, ESKATON. I AM NOT DEAD.
SPACE TREMBLES. THE ESKATON ARE THE CARRION-EATERS OF ANTI-LIFE.
IT WAS SAID THEY WOULD COME WHEN THE FOURTH WORLD WAS DYING, TO PICK BARE THE BONES OF THE NEW GODS.
THEY ARE HUNGRY. THEY HAVE WAITED TO FEAST SINCE THE DAWN OF THIS MULTIVERSE.
IT IS TIME. THE FINAL DARKNESS IS FALLING. REALITY IS DYING.
REALITY IS STRICKEN, BUT IT IS NOT DEAD. LIFE CAN BE SALVAGED.
BY WHOM? THERE ARE NO GODS LEFT.
THE OTHER NEW GODS MAY BE GONE, BUT AS YOU CAN SEE...
...DARKSEID IS.
NO, DARKSEID...

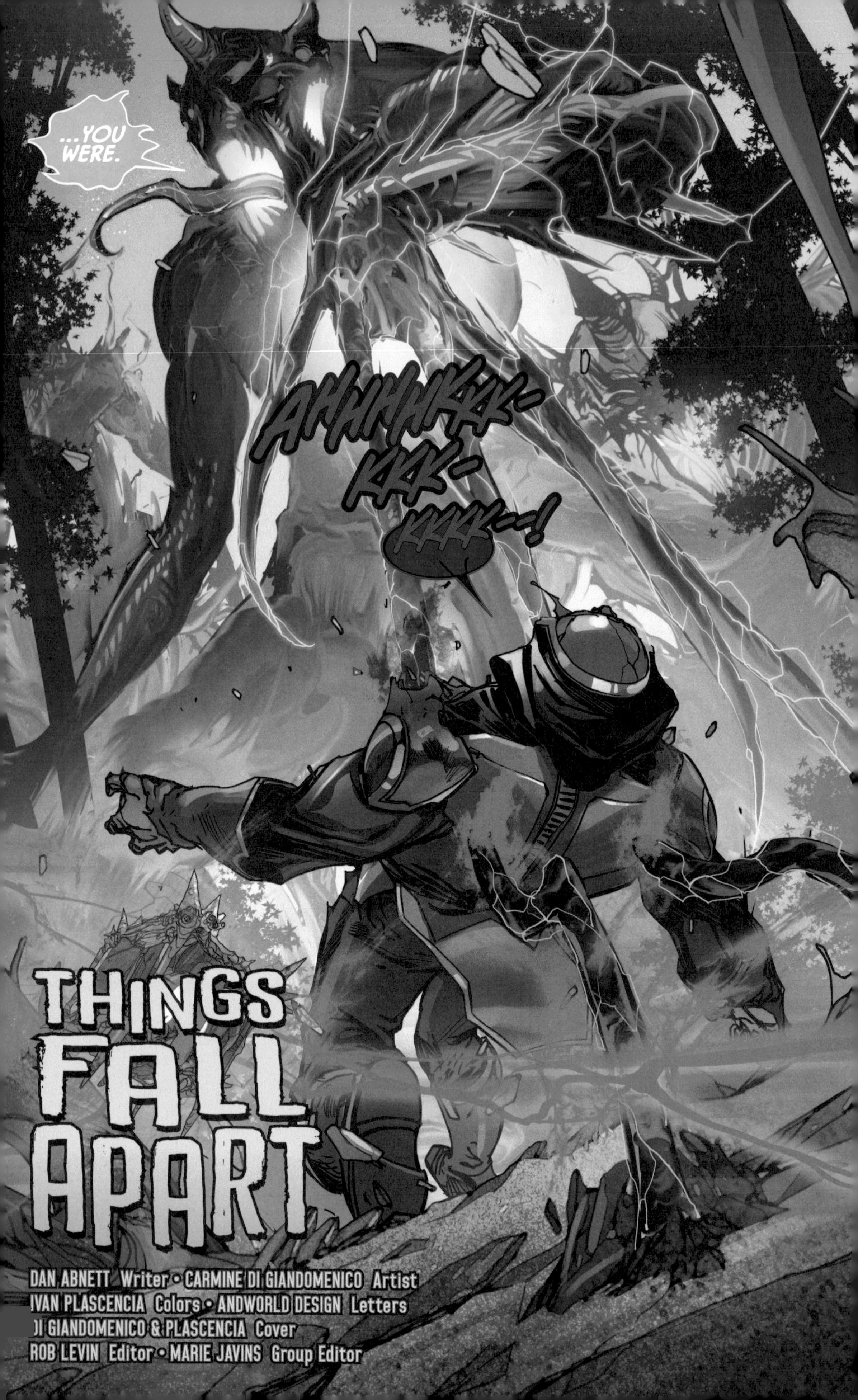
...YOU WERE.
AHHHHKKK- KKK- KKKK--!
THINGS FALL APART
DAN ABNETT Writer • CARMINE DI GIANDOMENICO Artist
IVAN PLASCENCIA Colors • ANDWORLD DESIGN Letters
DI GIANDOMENICO & PLASCENCIA Cover
ROB LEVIN Editor • MARIE JAVINS Group Editor

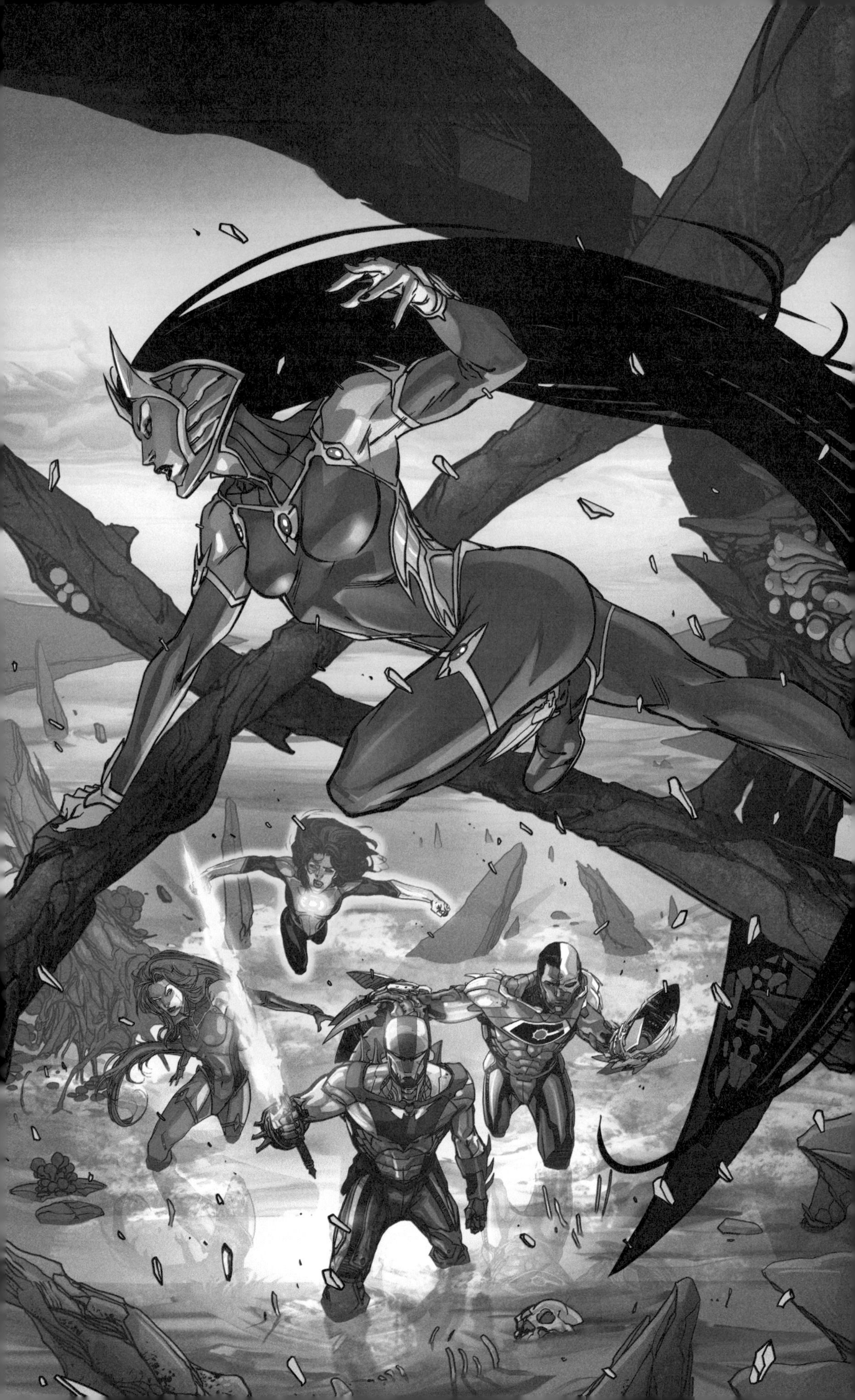

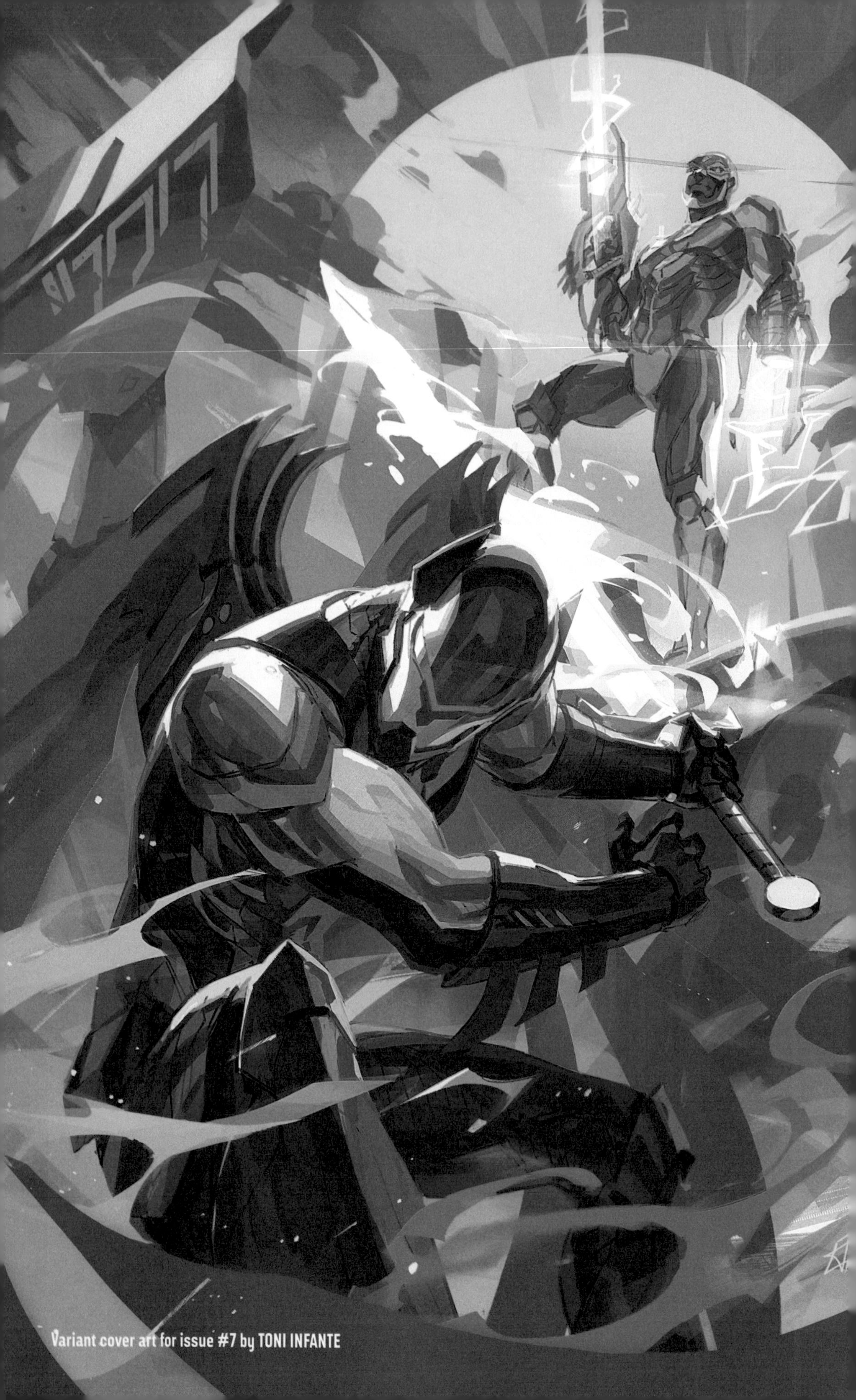

Variant cover art for issue #7 by TONI INFANTE

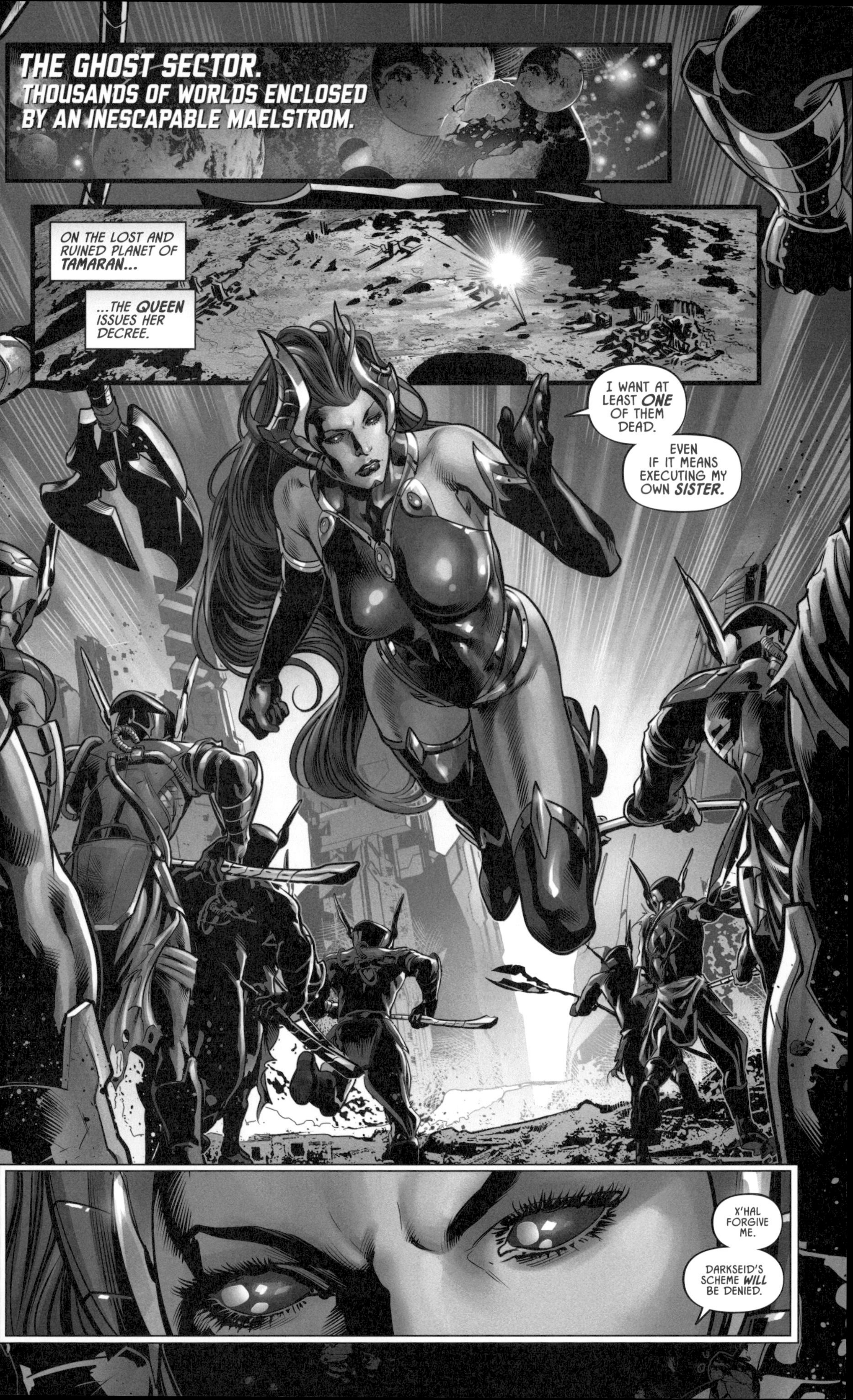
THE GHOST SECTOR.
THOUSANDS OF WORLDS ENCLOSED BY AN INESCAPABLE MAELSTROM.
ON THE LOST AND RUINED PLANET OF TAMARAN...
...THE QUEEN ISSUES HER DECREE.
I WANT AT LEAST ONE OF THEM DEAD.
EVEN IF IT MEANS EXECUTING MY OWN SISTER.
X'HAL FORGIVE ME.
DARKSEID'S SCHEME WILL BE DENIED.

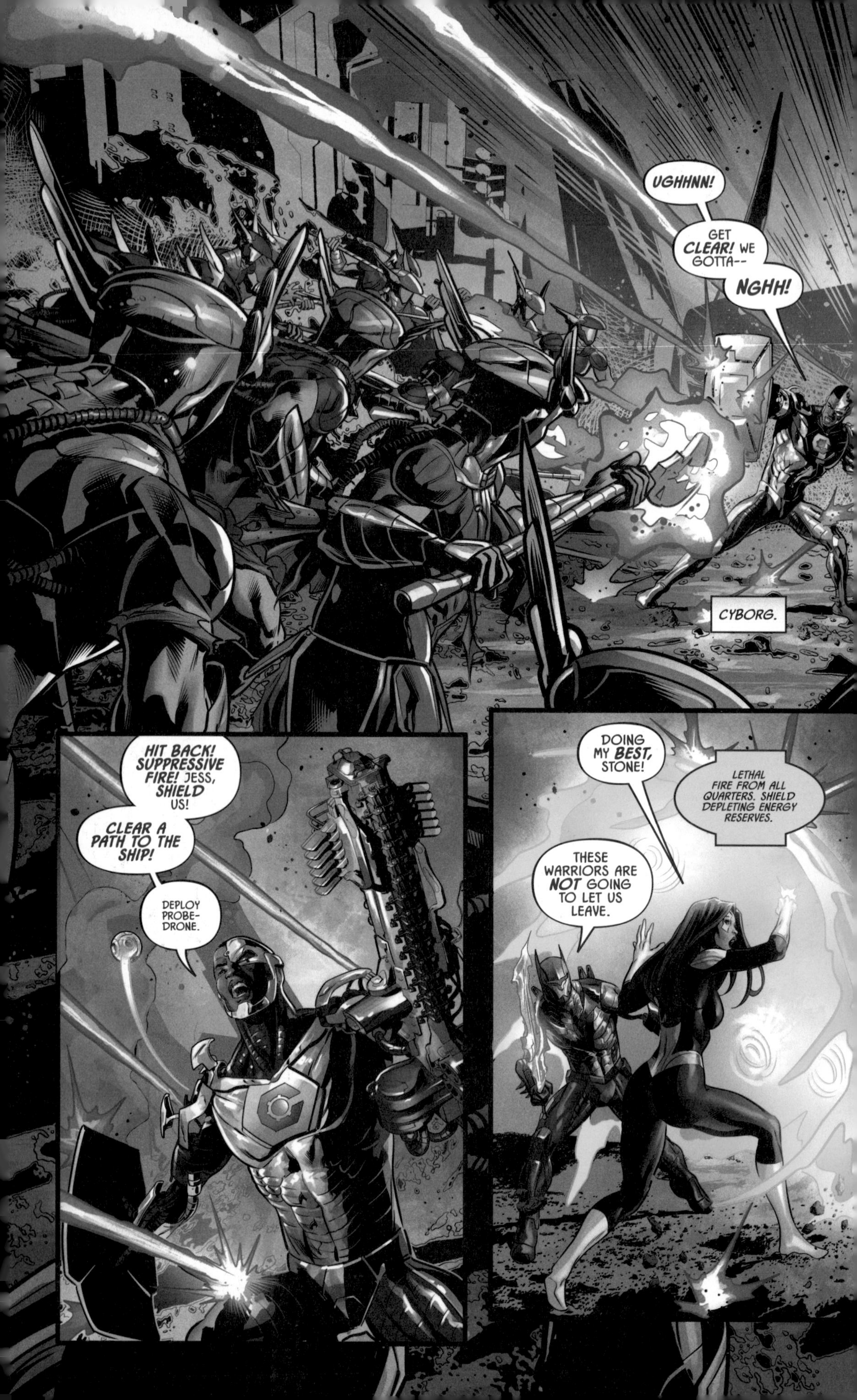

UGHHNN!
GET CLEAR! WE GOTTA--
NGHH!
CYBORG.
HIT BACK! SUPPRESSIVE FIRE! JESS, SHIELD US!
CLEAR A PATH TO THE SHIP!
DEPLOY PROBE-DRONE.
DOING MY BEST, STONE!
LETHAL FIRE FROM ALL QUARTERS. SHIELD DEPLETING ENERGY RESERVES.
THESE WARRIORS ARE NOT GOING TO LET US LEAVE.

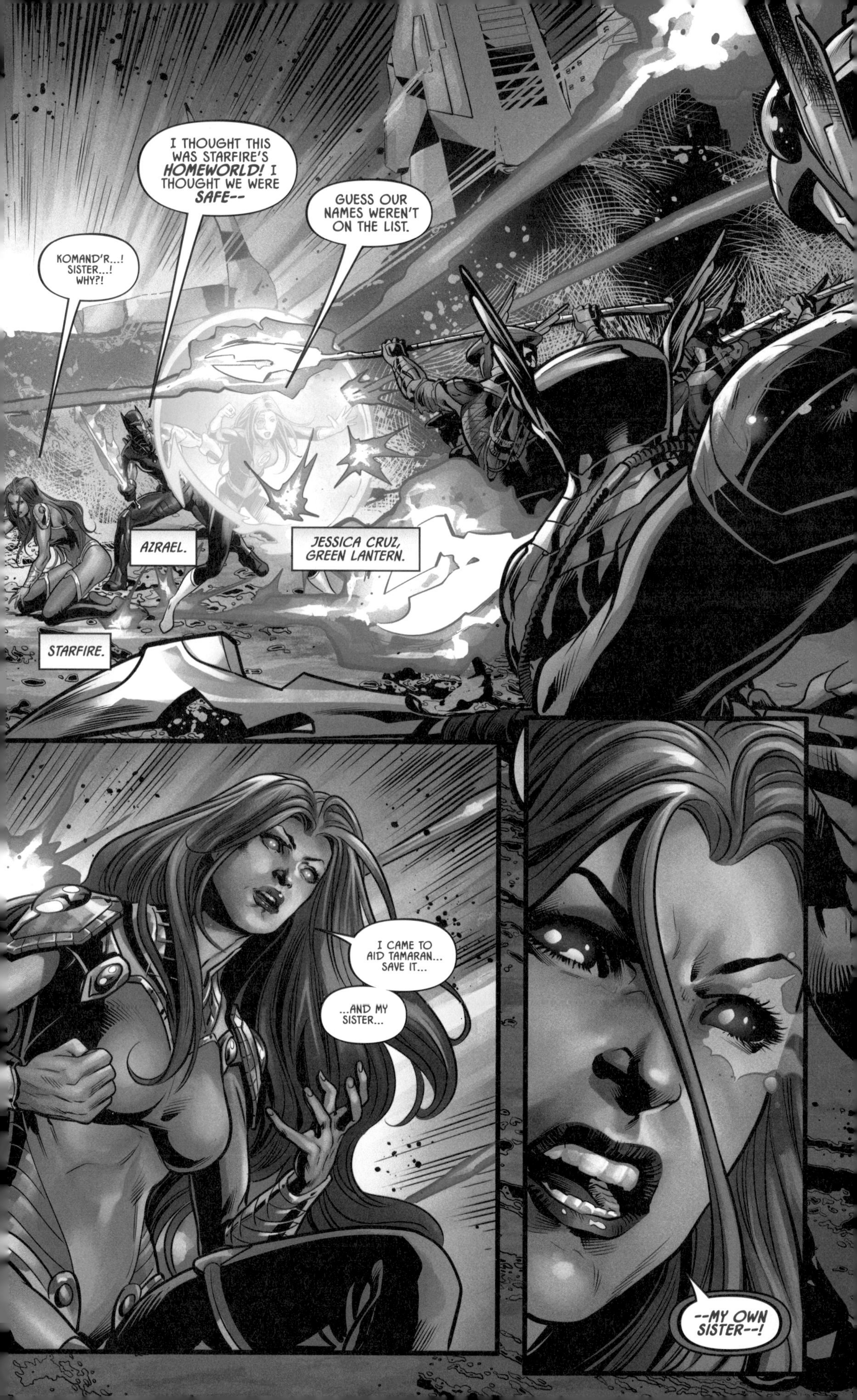
I THOUGHT THIS WAS STARFIRE'S **HOMEWORLD!** I THOUGHT WE WERE **SAFE--**
KOMAND'R...! SISTER...! WHY?!
GUESS OUR NAMES WEREN'T ON THE LIST.
AZRAEL.
JESSICA CRUZ, GREEN LANTERN.
STARFIRE.
I CAME TO AID TAMARAN... SAVE IT...
...AND MY SISTER...
--MY OWN SISTER--!

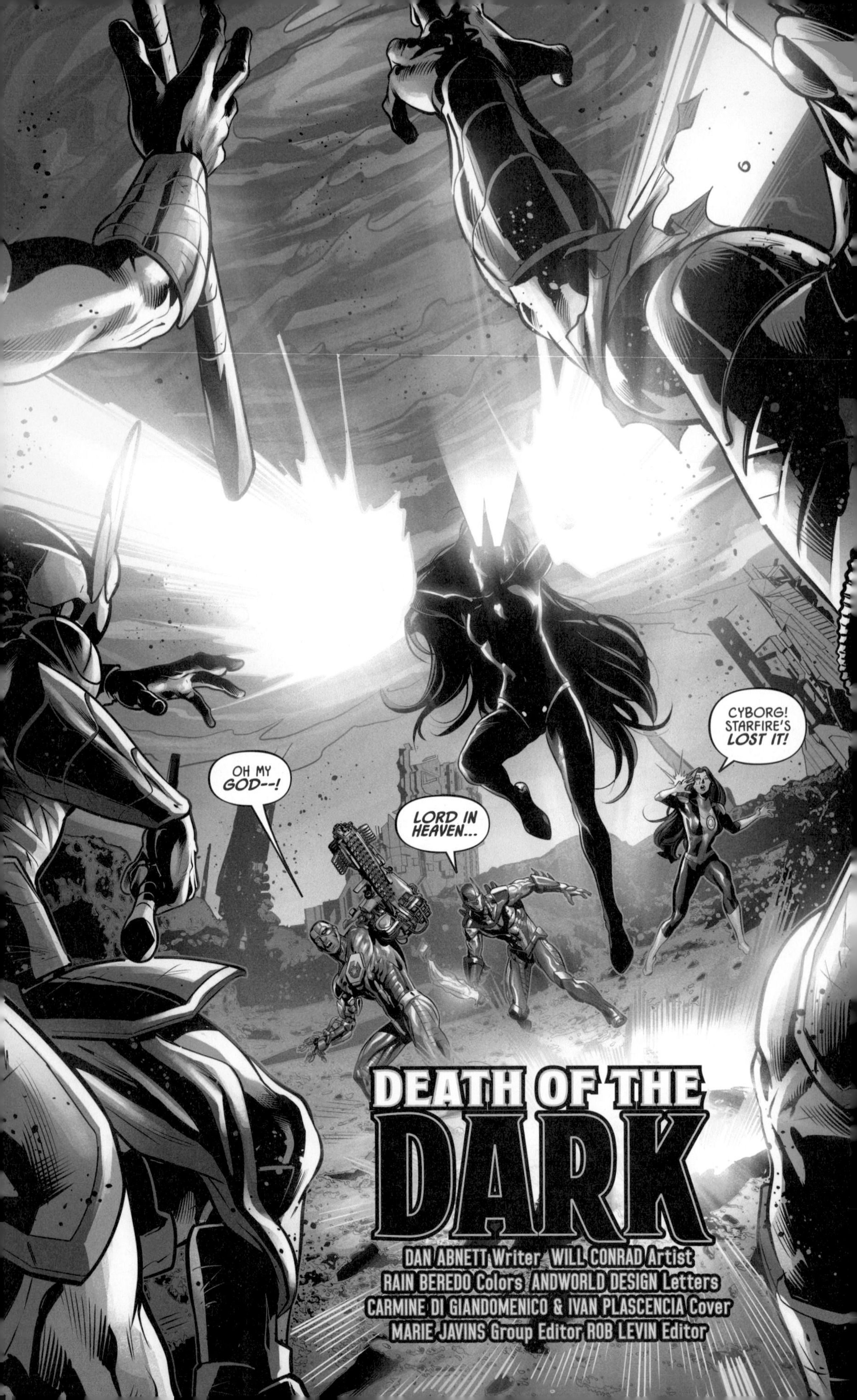
OH MY GOD--!
LORD IN HEAVEN...
CYBORG! STARFIRE'S LOST IT!
DEATH OF THE DARK
DAN ABNETT Writer WILL CONRAD Artist
RAIN BEREDO Colors ANDWORLD DESIGN Letters
CARMINE DI GIANDOMENICO & IVAN PLASCENCIA Cover
MARIE JAVINS Group Editor ROB LEVIN Editor

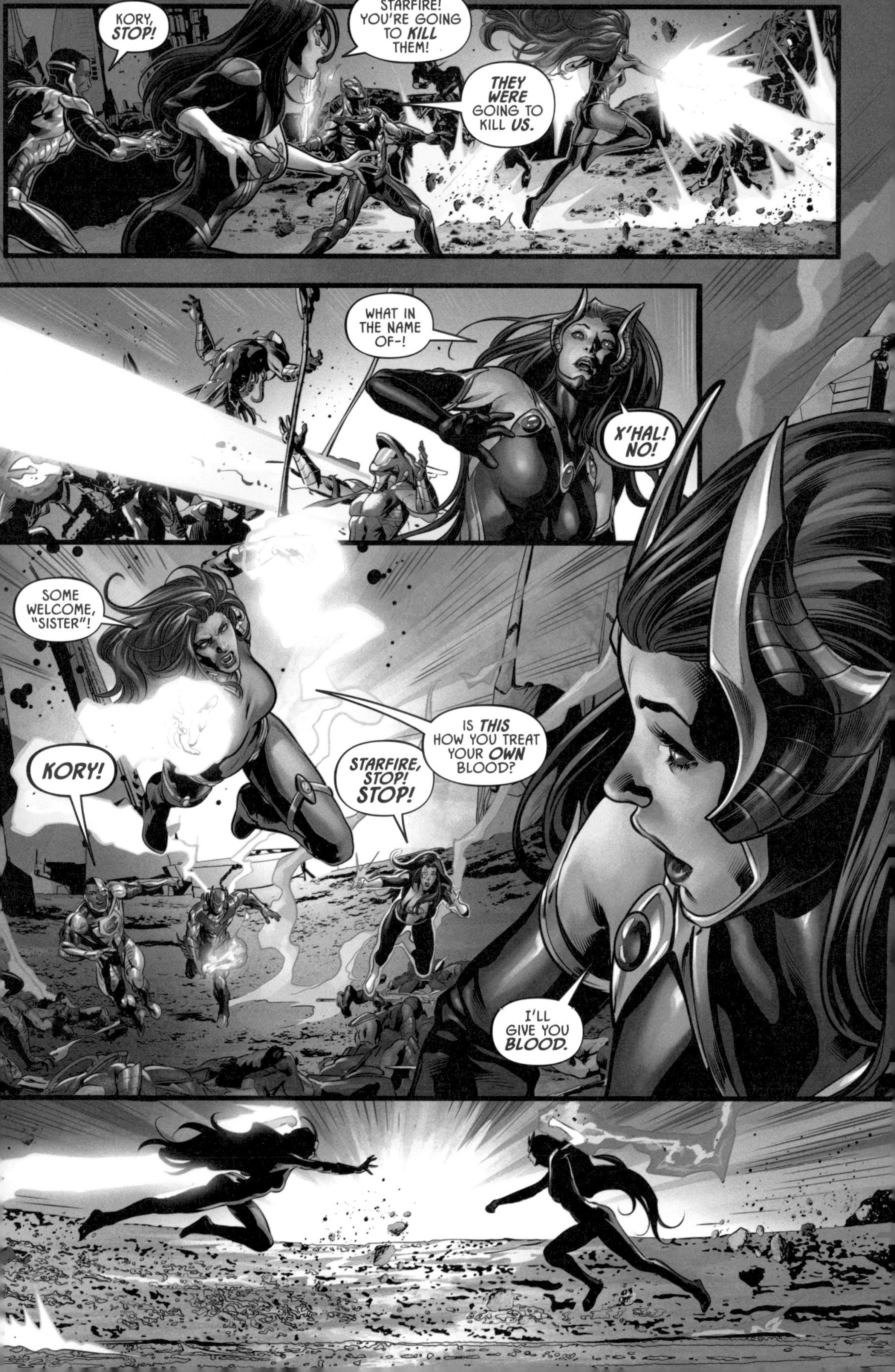
KORY, STOP!
STARFIRE! YOU'RE GOING TO KILL THEM!
THEY WERE GOING TO KILL US.
WHAT IN THE NAME OF-!
X'HAL! NO!
SOME WELCOME, "SISTER"!
IS THIS HOW YOU TREAT YOUR OWN BLOOD?
KORY!
STARFIRE, STOP! STOP!
I'LL GIVE YOU BLOOD.

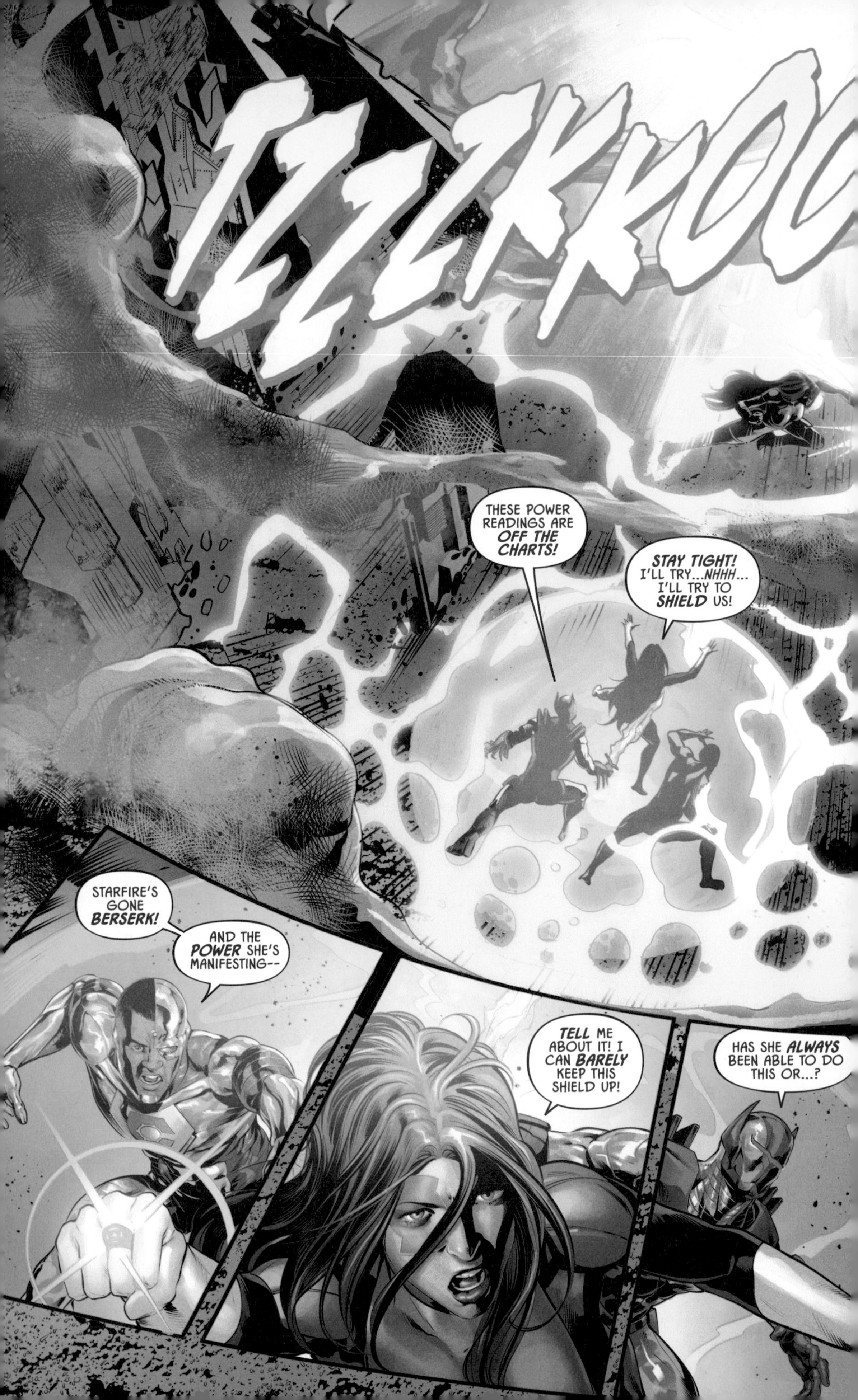
TZZKKOO
THESE POWER READINGS ARE OFF THE CHARTS!
STAY TIGHT! I'LL TRY...NHHH... I'LL TRY TO SHIELD US!
STARFIRE'S GONE BERSERK!
AND THE POWER SHE'S MANIFESTING--
TELL ME ABOUT IT! I CAN BARELY KEEP THIS SHIELD UP!
HAS SHE ALWAYS BEEN ABLE TO DO THIS OR...?

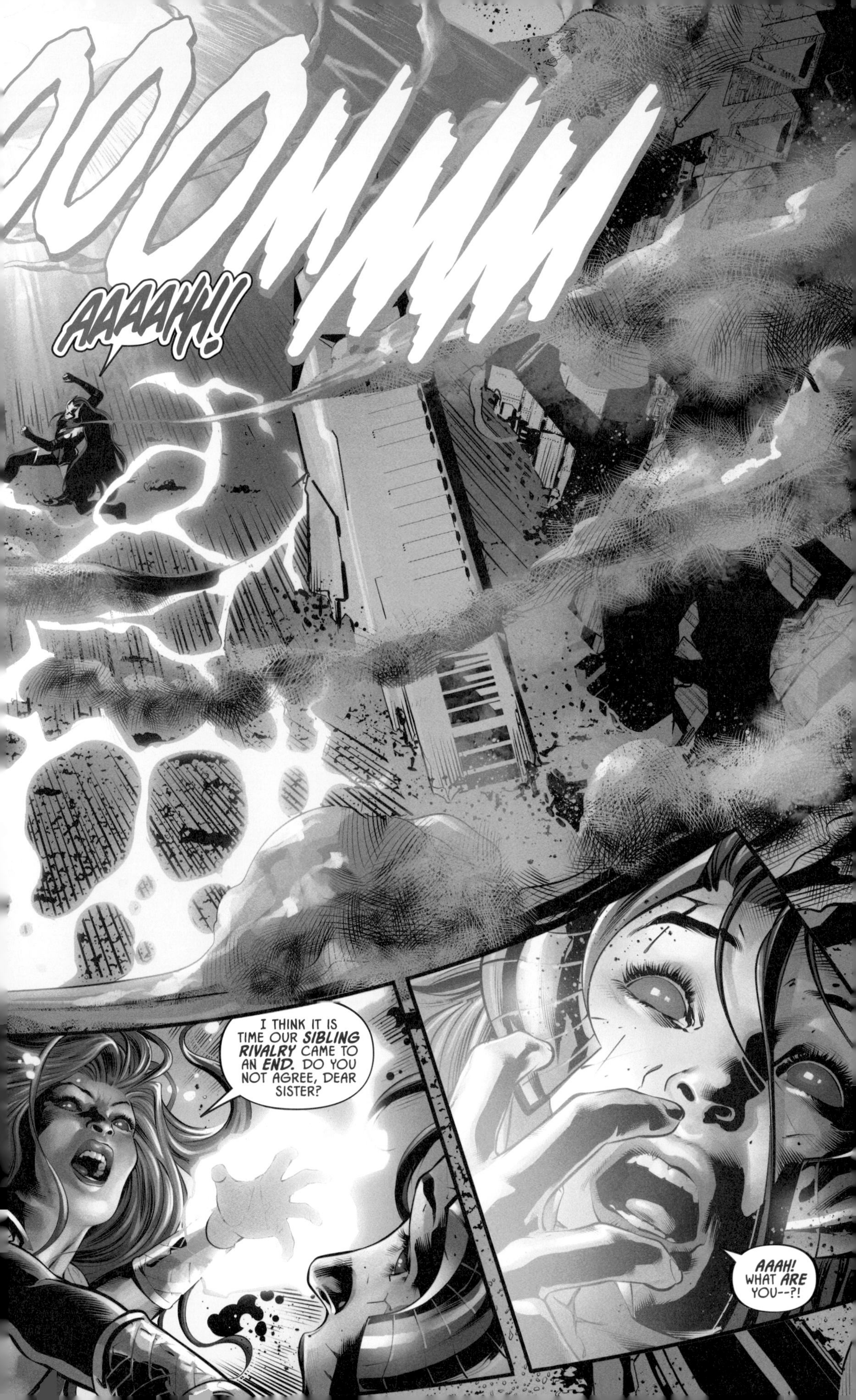
DOOOMMM
AAAAHH!
I THINK IT IS TIME OUR SIBLING RIVALRY CAME TO AN END. DO YOU NOT AGREE, DEAR SISTER?
AAAH! WHAT ARE YOU--?!

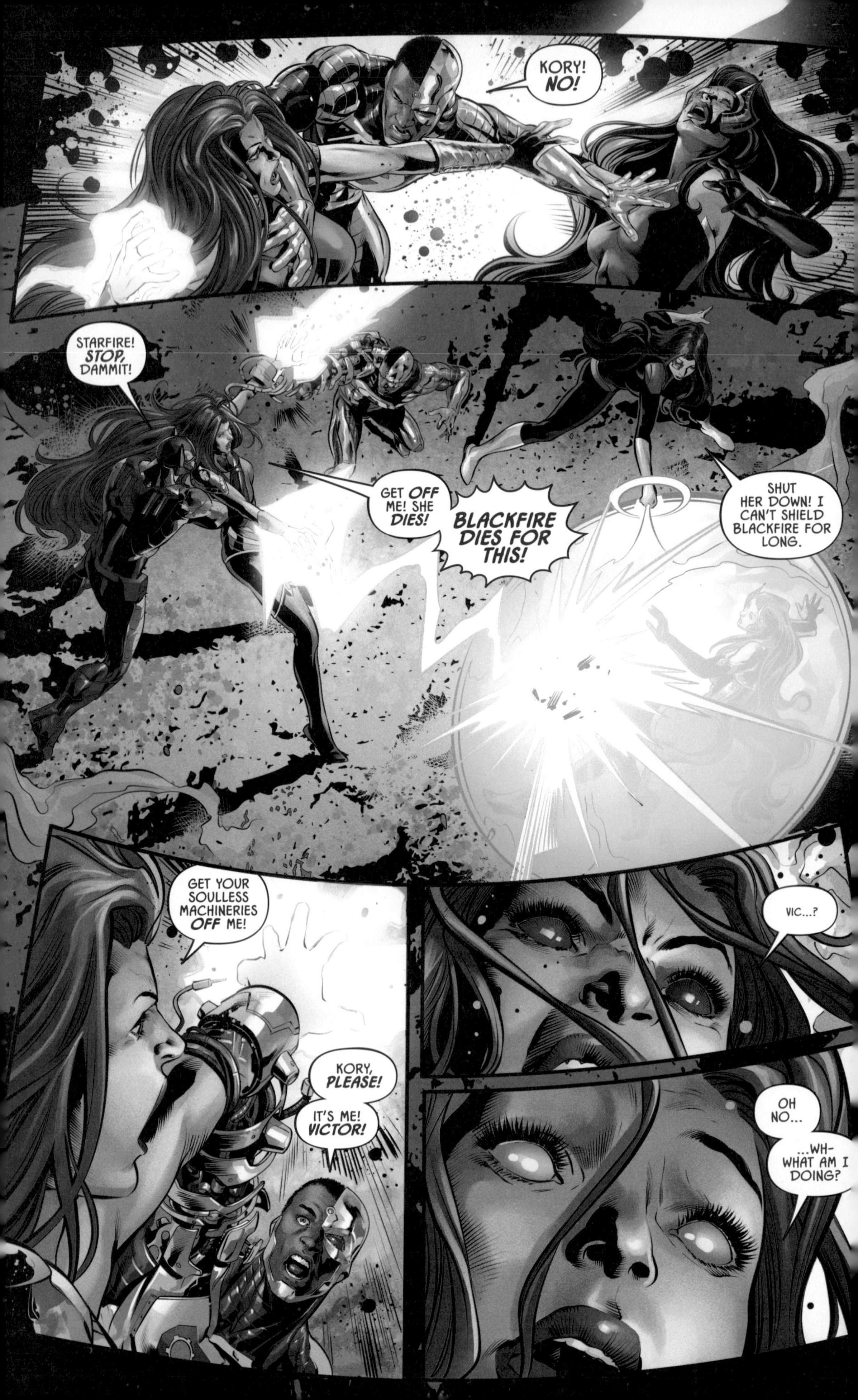
KORY! NO!
STARFIRE! STOP, DAMMIT!
GET OFF ME! SHE DIES!
BLACKFIRE DIES FOR THIS!
SHUT HER DOWN! I CAN'T SHIELD BLACKFIRE FOR LONG.
GET YOUR SOULLESS MACHINERIES OFF ME!
KORY, PLEASE!
IT'S ME! VICTOR!
VIC...?
OH NO...
...WH-WHAT AM I DOING?

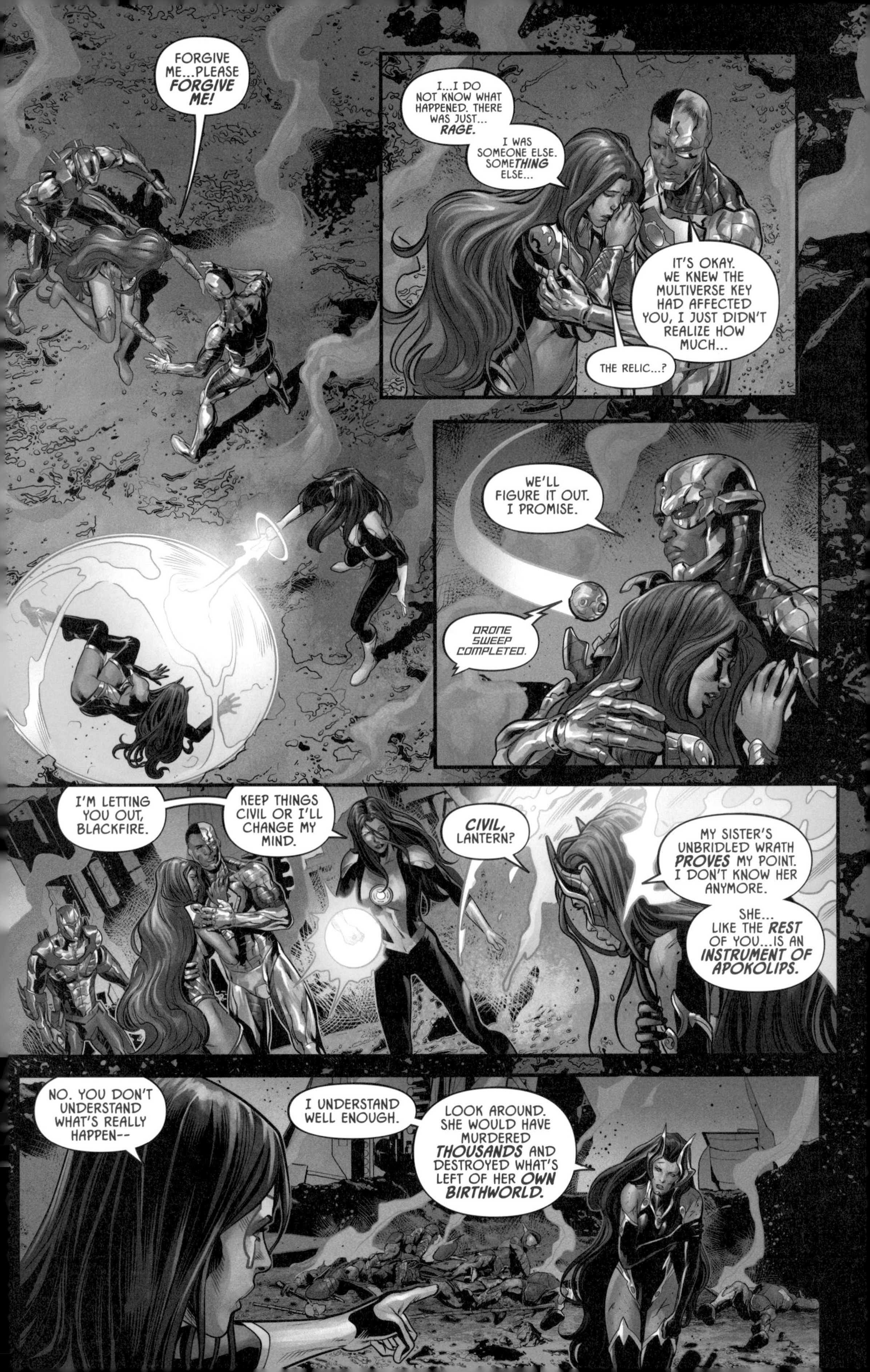
FORGIVE ME...PLEASE FORGIVE ME!
I...I DO NOT KNOW WHAT HAPPENED. THERE WAS JUST... RAGE.
I WAS SOMEONE ELSE. SOMETHING ELSE...
IT'S OKAY. WE KNEW THE MULTIVERSE KEY HAD AFFECTED YOU, I JUST DIDN'T REALIZE HOW MUCH...
THE RELIC...?
WE'LL FIGURE IT OUT. I PROMISE.
DRONE SWEEP COMPLETED.
I'M LETTING YOU OUT, BLACKFIRE.
KEEP THINGS CIVIL OR I'LL CHANGE MY MIND.
CIVIL, LANTERN?
MY SISTER'S UNBRIDLED WRATH PROVES MY POINT. I DON'T KNOW HER ANYMORE.
SHE... LIKE THE REST OF YOU...IS AN INSTRUMENT OF APOKOLIPS.
NO. YOU DON'T UNDERSTAND WHAT'S REALLY HAPPEN--
I UNDERSTAND WELL ENOUGH.
LOOK AROUND. SHE WOULD HAVE MURDERED THOUSANDS AND DESTROYED WHAT'S LEFT OF HER OWN BIRTHWORLD.

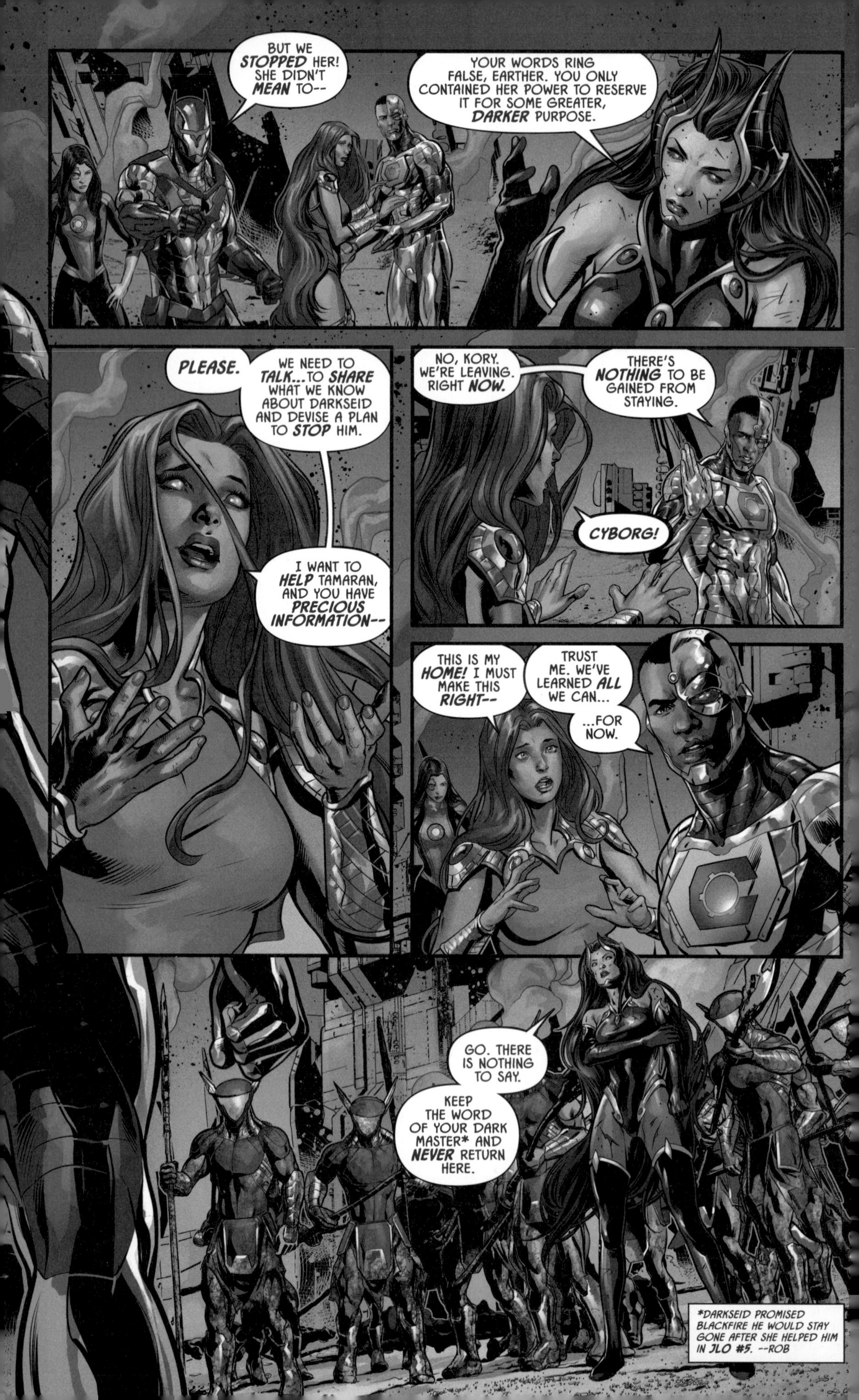

BUT WE STOPPED HER! SHE DIDN'T MEAN TO--
YOUR WORDS RING FALSE, EARTHER. YOU ONLY CONTAINED HER POWER TO RESERVE IT FOR SOME GREATER, DARKER PURPOSE.
PLEASE.
WE NEED TO TALK...TO SHARE WHAT WE KNOW ABOUT DARKSEID AND DEVISE A PLAN TO STOP HIM.
I WANT TO HELP TAMARAN, AND YOU HAVE PRECIOUS INFORMATION--
NO, KORY. WE'RE LEAVING. RIGHT NOW.
THERE'S NOTHING TO BE GAINED FROM STAYING.
CYBORG!
THIS IS MY HOME! I MUST MAKE THIS RIGHT--
TRUST ME. WE'VE LEARNED ALL WE CAN...
...FOR NOW.
GO. THERE IS NOTHING TO SAY.
KEEP THE WORD OF YOUR DARK MASTER* AND NEVER RETURN HERE.
*DARKSEID PROMISED BLACKFIRE HE WOULD STAY GONE AFTER SHE HELPED HIM IN JLO #5. --ROB

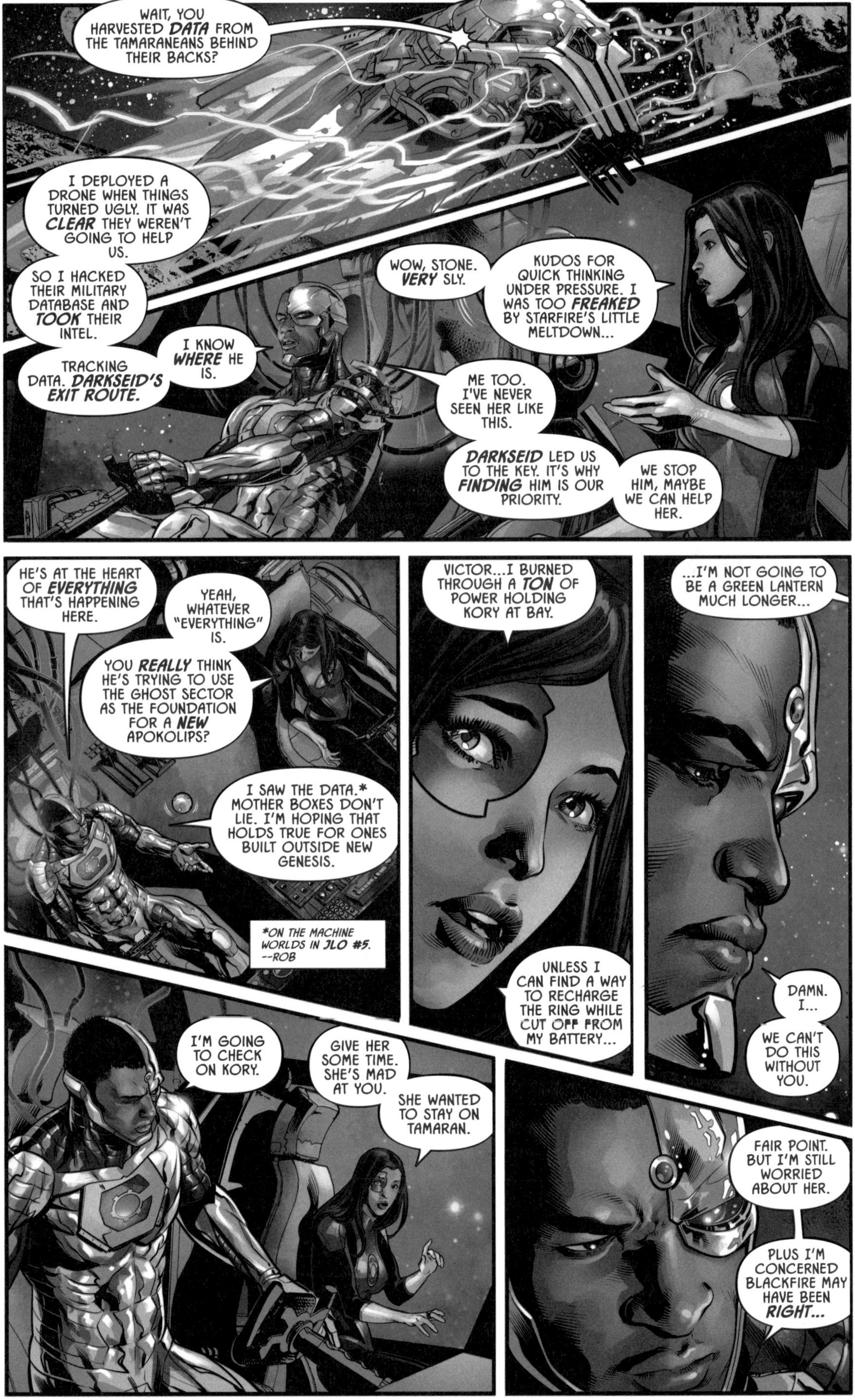
WAIT, YOU HARVESTED DATA FROM THE TAMARANEANS BEHIND THEIR BACKS?
I DEPLOYED A DRONE WHEN THINGS TURNED UGLY. IT WAS CLEAR THEY WEREN'T GOING TO HELP US.
SO I HACKED THEIR MILITARY DATABASE AND TOOK THEIR INTEL.
TRACKING DATA. DARKSEID'S EXIT ROUTE.
I KNOW WHERE HE IS.
WOW, STONE. VERY SLY.
KUDOS FOR QUICK THINKING UNDER PRESSURE. I WAS TOO FREAKED BY STARFIRE'S LITTLE MELTDOWN...
ME TOO. I'VE NEVER SEEN HER LIKE THIS.
DARKSEID LED US TO THE KEY. IT'S WHY FINDING HIM IS OUR PRIORITY.
WE STOP HIM, MAYBE WE CAN HELP HER.
HE'S AT THE HEART OF EVERYTHING THAT'S HAPPENING HERE.
YEAH, WHATEVER "EVERYTHING" IS.
YOU REALLY THINK HE'S TRYING TO USE THE GHOST SECTOR AS THE FOUNDATION FOR A NEW APOKOLIPS?
I SAW THE DATA.* MOTHER BOXES DON'T LIE. I'M HOPING THAT HOLDS TRUE FOR ONES BUILT OUTSIDE NEW GENESIS.
*ON THE MACHINE WORLDS IN JLO #5. --ROB
VICTOR...I BURNED THROUGH A TON OF POWER HOLDING KORY AT BAY.
...I'M NOT GOING TO BE A GREEN LANTERN MUCH LONGER...
UNLESS I CAN FIND A WAY TO RECHARGE THE RING WHILE CUT OFF FROM MY BATTERY...
DAMN. I...
WE CAN'T DO THIS WITHOUT YOU.
I'M GOING TO CHECK ON KORY.
GIVE HER SOME TIME. SHE'S MAD AT YOU.
SHE WANTED TO STAY ON TAMARAN.
FAIR POINT. BUT I'M STILL WORRIED ABOUT HER.
PLUS I'M CONCERNED BLACKFIRE MAY HAVE BEEN RIGHT...

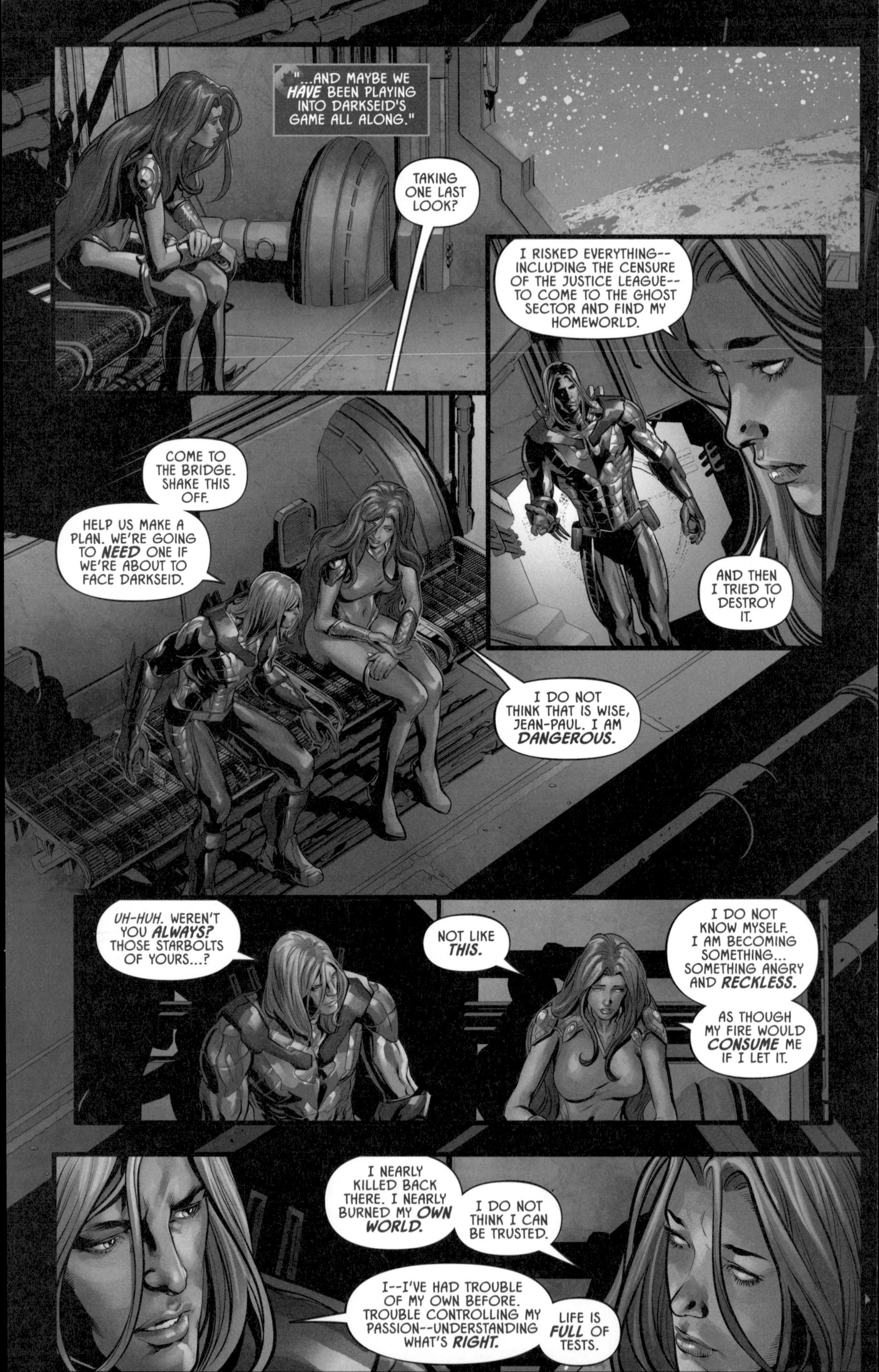
"...AND MAYBE WE *HAVE* BEEN PLAYING INTO DARKSEID'S GAME ALL ALONG."
TAKING ONE LAST LOOK?
I RISKED EVERYTHING-- INCLUDING THE CENSURE OF THE JUSTICE LEAGUE-- TO COME TO THE GHOST SECTOR AND FIND MY HOMEWORLD.
AND THEN I TRIED TO DESTROY IT.
COME TO THE BRIDGE. SHAKE THIS OFF.
HELP US MAKE A PLAN. WE'RE GOING TO *NEED* ONE IF WE'RE ABOUT TO FACE DARKSEID.
I DO NOT THINK THAT IS WISE, JEAN-PAUL. I AM *DANGEROUS.*
UH-HUH. WEREN'T YOU *ALWAYS?* THOSE STARBOLTS OF YOURS...?
NOT LIKE *THIS.*
I DO NOT KNOW MYSELF. I AM BECOMING SOMETHING... SOMETHING ANGRY AND *RECKLESS.*
AS THOUGH MY FIRE WOULD *CONSUME* ME IF I LET IT.
I NEARLY KILLED BACK THERE. I NEARLY BURNED MY *OWN WORLD.*
I DO NOT THINK I CAN BE TRUSTED.
I--I'VE HAD TROUBLE OF MY OWN BEFORE. TROUBLE CONTROLLING MY PASSION--UNDERSTANDING WHAT'S *RIGHT.*
LIFE IS *FULL* OF TESTS.

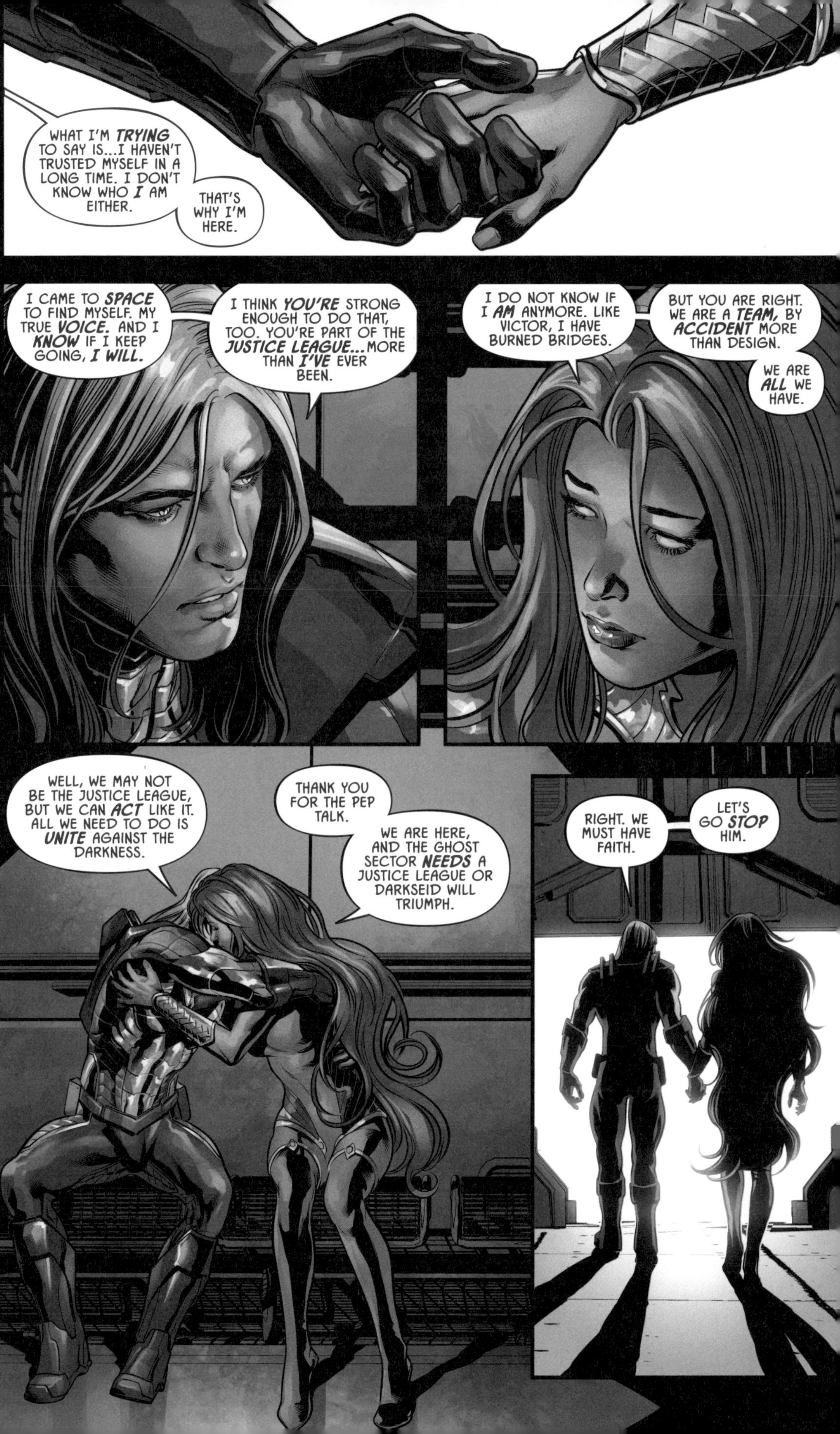

WHAT I'M TRYING TO SAY IS...I HAVEN'T TRUSTED MYSELF IN A LONG TIME. I DON'T KNOW WHO I AM EITHER.
THAT'S WHY I'M HERE.
I CAME TO SPACE TO FIND MYSELF. MY TRUE VOICE. AND I KNOW IF I KEEP GOING, I WILL.
I THINK YOU'RE STRONG ENOUGH TO DO THAT, TOO. YOU'RE PART OF THE JUSTICE LEAGUE...MORE THAN I'VE EVER BEEN.
I DO NOT KNOW IF I AM ANYMORE. LIKE VICTOR, I HAVE BURNED BRIDGES.
BUT YOU ARE RIGHT. WE ARE A TEAM, BY ACCIDENT MORE THAN DESIGN.
WE ARE ALL WE HAVE.
WELL, WE MAY NOT BE THE JUSTICE LEAGUE, BUT WE CAN ACT LIKE IT. ALL WE NEED TO DO IS UNITE AGAINST THE DARKNESS.
THANK YOU FOR THE PEP TALK.
WE ARE HERE, AND THE GHOST SECTOR NEEDS A JUSTICE LEAGUE OR DARKSEID WILL TRIUMPH.
RIGHT. WE MUST HAVE FAITH.
LET'S GO STOP HIM.

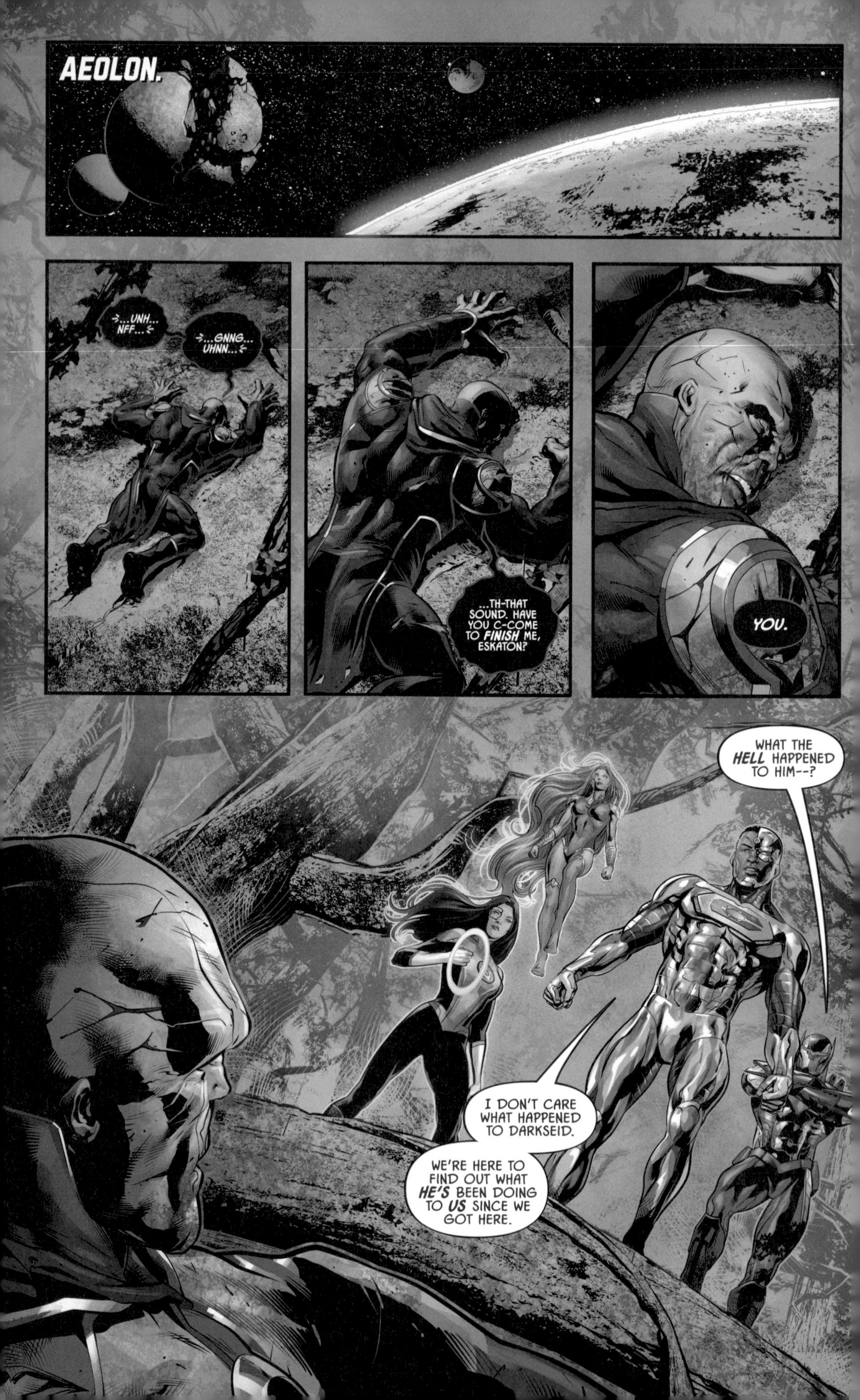
AEOLON.
...UNH... NFF...
...GNNG... UHNN...
...TH-THAT SOUND. HAVE YOU C-COME TO FINISH ME, ESKATON?
YOU.
WHAT THE HELL HAPPENED TO HIM--?
I DON'T CARE WHAT HAPPENED TO DARKSEID.
WE'RE HERE TO FIND OUT WHAT HE'S BEEN DOING TO US SINCE WE GOT HERE.

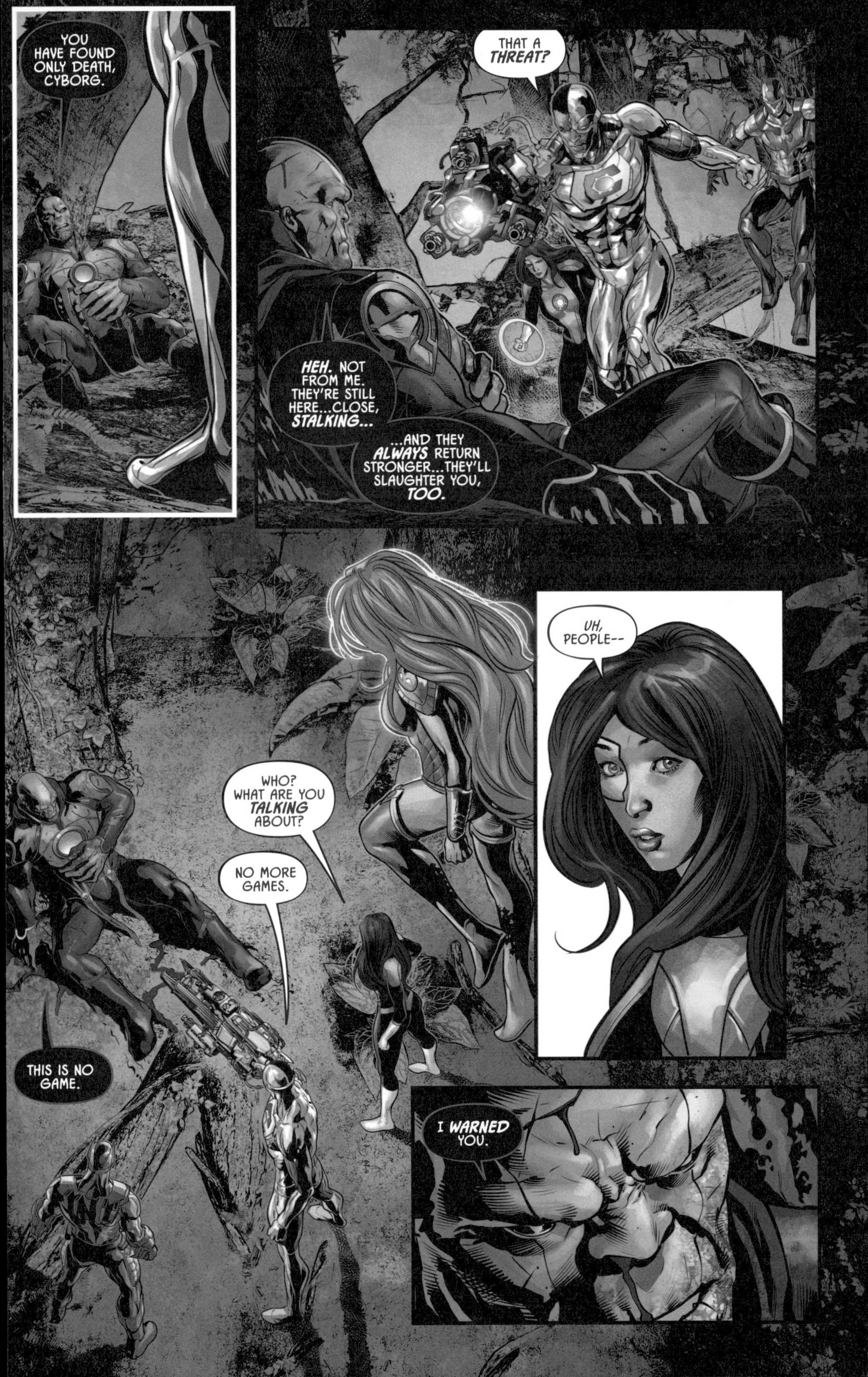

YOU HAVE FOUND ONLY DEATH, CYBORG.
THAT A THREAT?
HEH. NOT FROM ME. THEY'RE STILL HERE...CLOSE, STALKING...
...AND THEY ALWAYS RETURN STRONGER...THEY'LL SLAUGHTER YOU, TOO.
WHO? WHAT ARE YOU TALKING ABOUT?
NO MORE GAMES.
THIS IS NO GAME.
UH, PEOPLE--
I WARNED YOU.

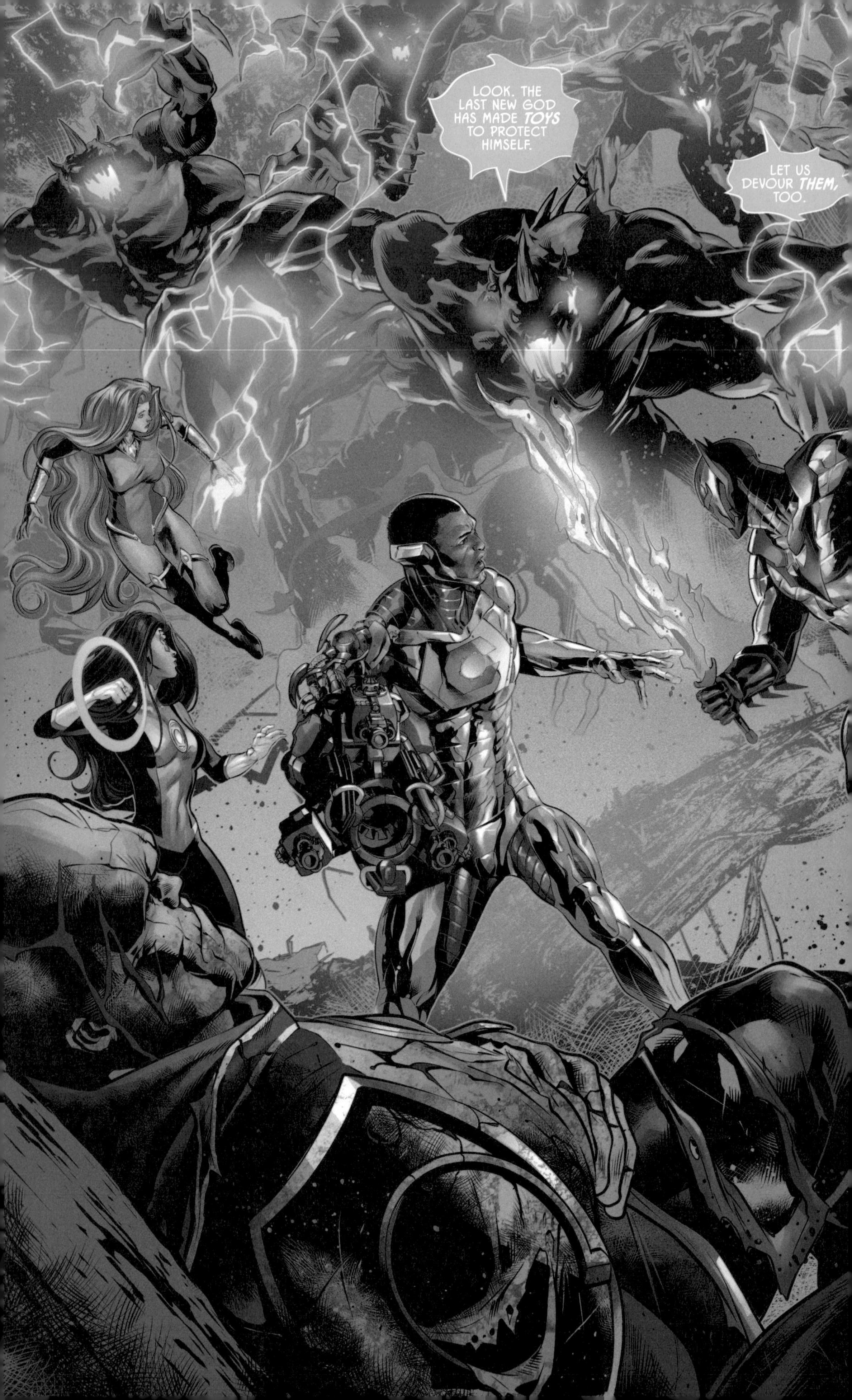
LOOK. THE LAST NEW GOD HAS MADE TOYS TO PROTECT HIMSELF.
LET US DEVOUR THEM, TOO.

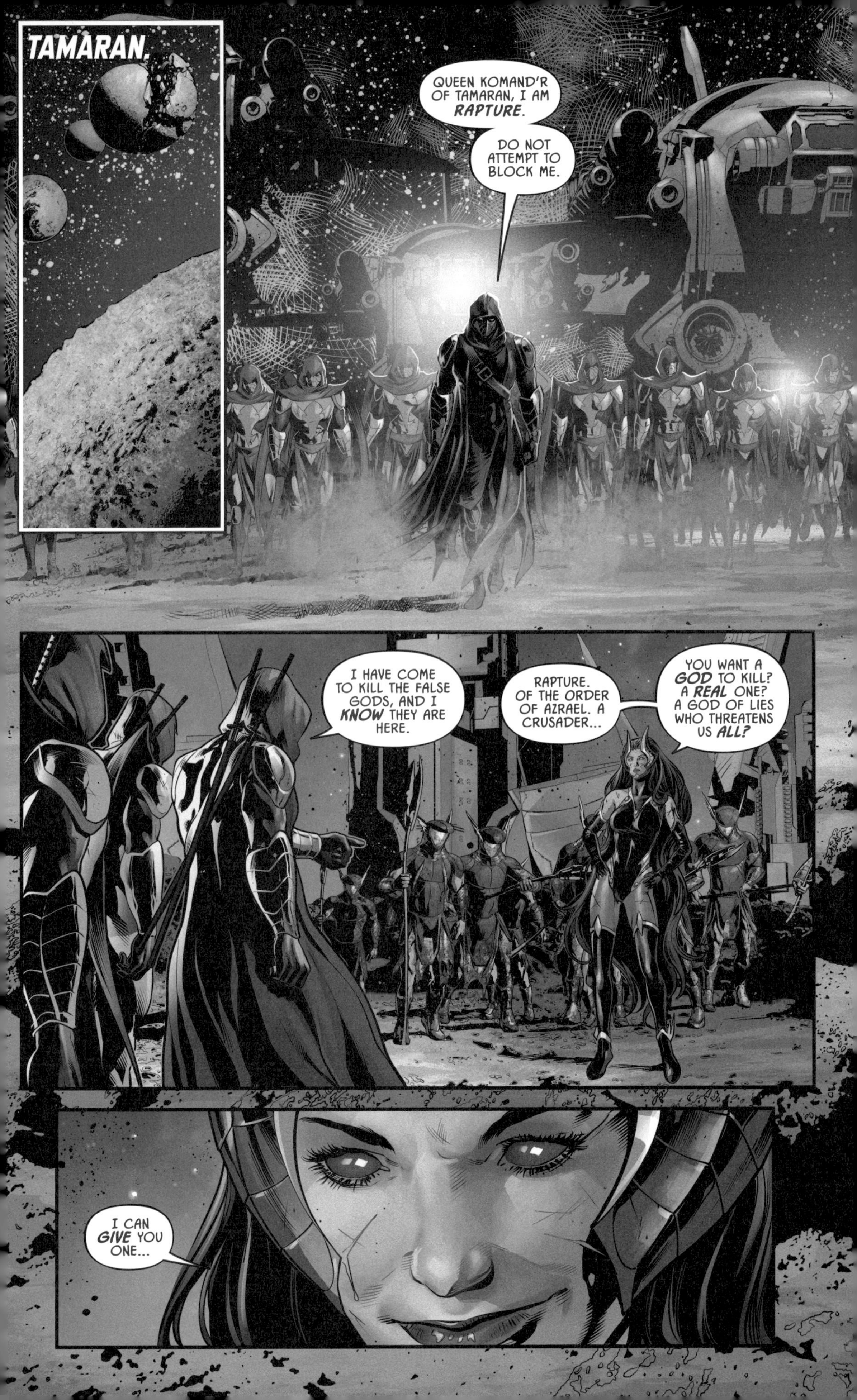
TAMARAN.
QUEEN KOMAND'R OF TAMARAN, I AM RAPTURE.
DO NOT ATTEMPT TO BLOCK ME.
I HAVE COME TO KILL THE FALSE GODS, AND I KNOW THEY ARE HERE.
RAPTURE. OF THE ORDER OF AZRAEL. A CRUSADER...
YOU WANT A GOD TO KILL? A REAL ONE? A GOD OF LIES WHO THREATENS US ALL?
I CAN GIVE YOU ONE...

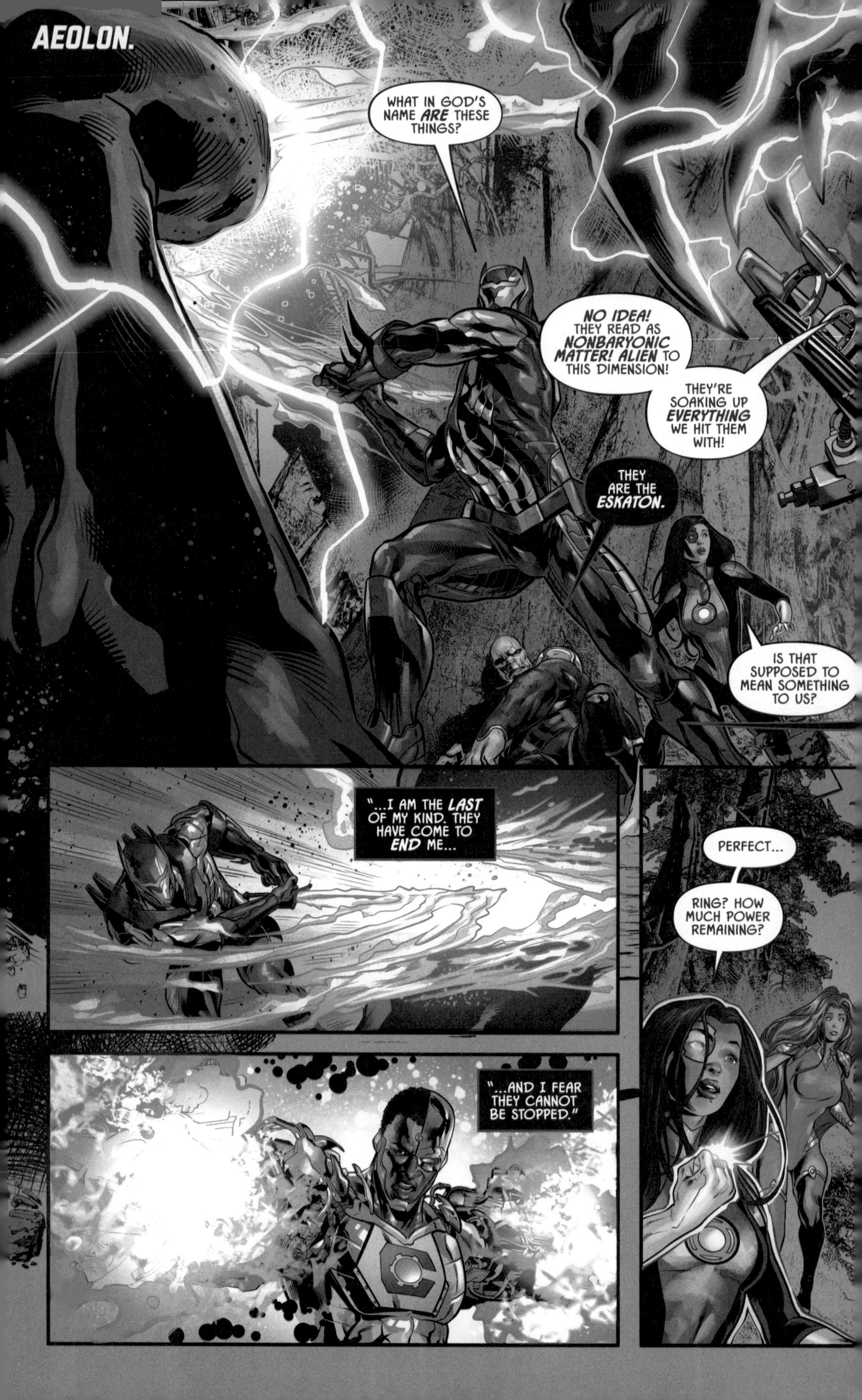
AEOLON.
WHAT IN GOD'S NAME ARE THESE THINGS?
NO IDEA! THEY READ AS NONBARYONIC MATTER! ALIEN TO THIS DIMENSION!
THEY'RE SOAKING UP EVERYTHING WE HIT THEM WITH!
THEY ARE THE ESKATON.
IS THAT SUPPOSED TO MEAN SOMETHING TO US?
"...I AM THE LAST OF MY KIND. THEY HAVE COME TO END ME...
PERFECT...
RING? HOW MUCH POWER REMAINING?
"...AND I FEAR THEY CANNOT BE STOPPED."

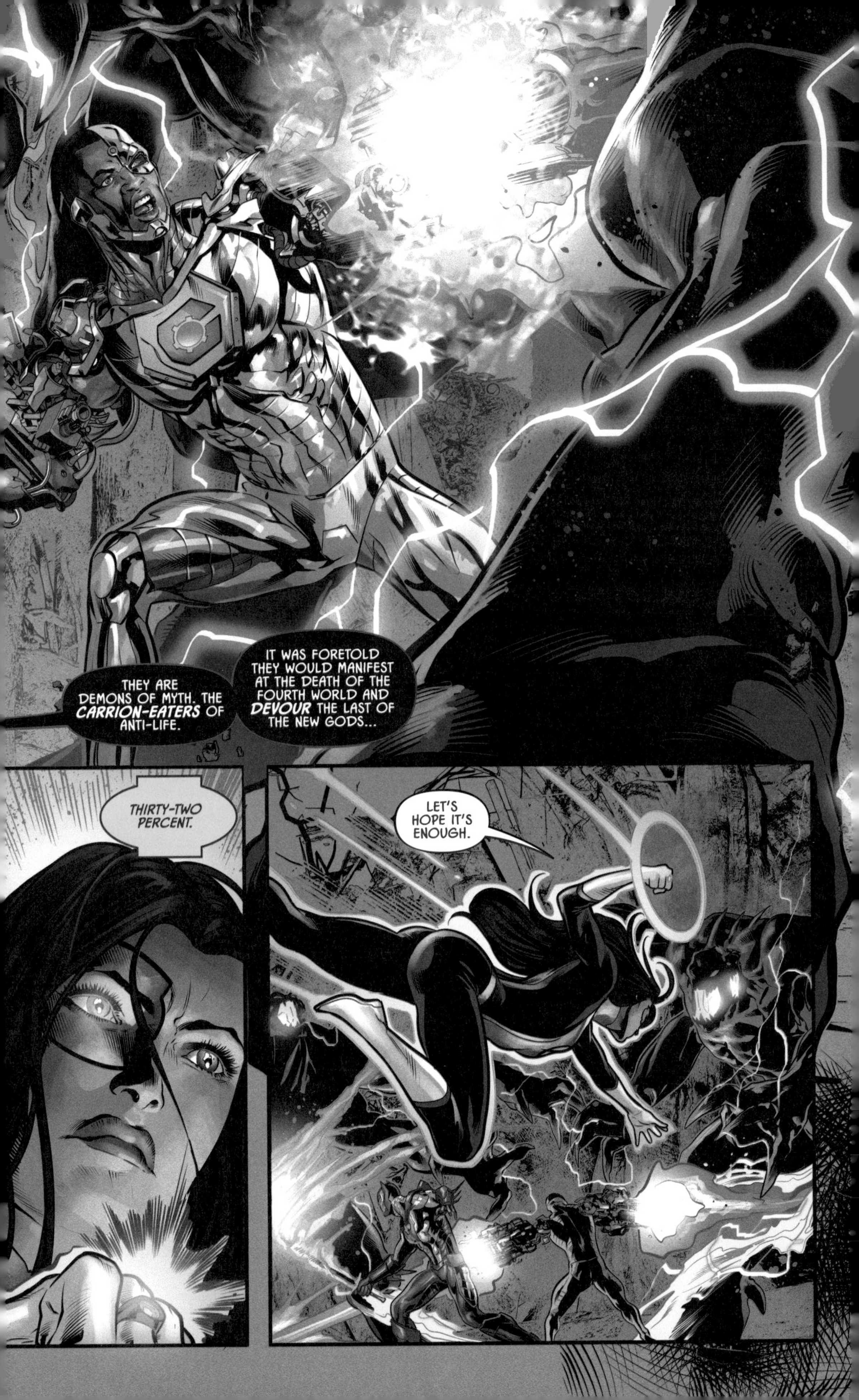
THEY ARE DEMONS OF MYTH. THE CARRION-EATERS OF ANTI-LIFE.
IT WAS FORETOLD THEY WOULD MANIFEST AT THE DEATH OF THE FOURTH WORLD AND DEVOUR THE LAST OF THE NEW GODS...
THIRTY-TWO PERCENT.
LET'S HOPE IT'S ENOUGH.

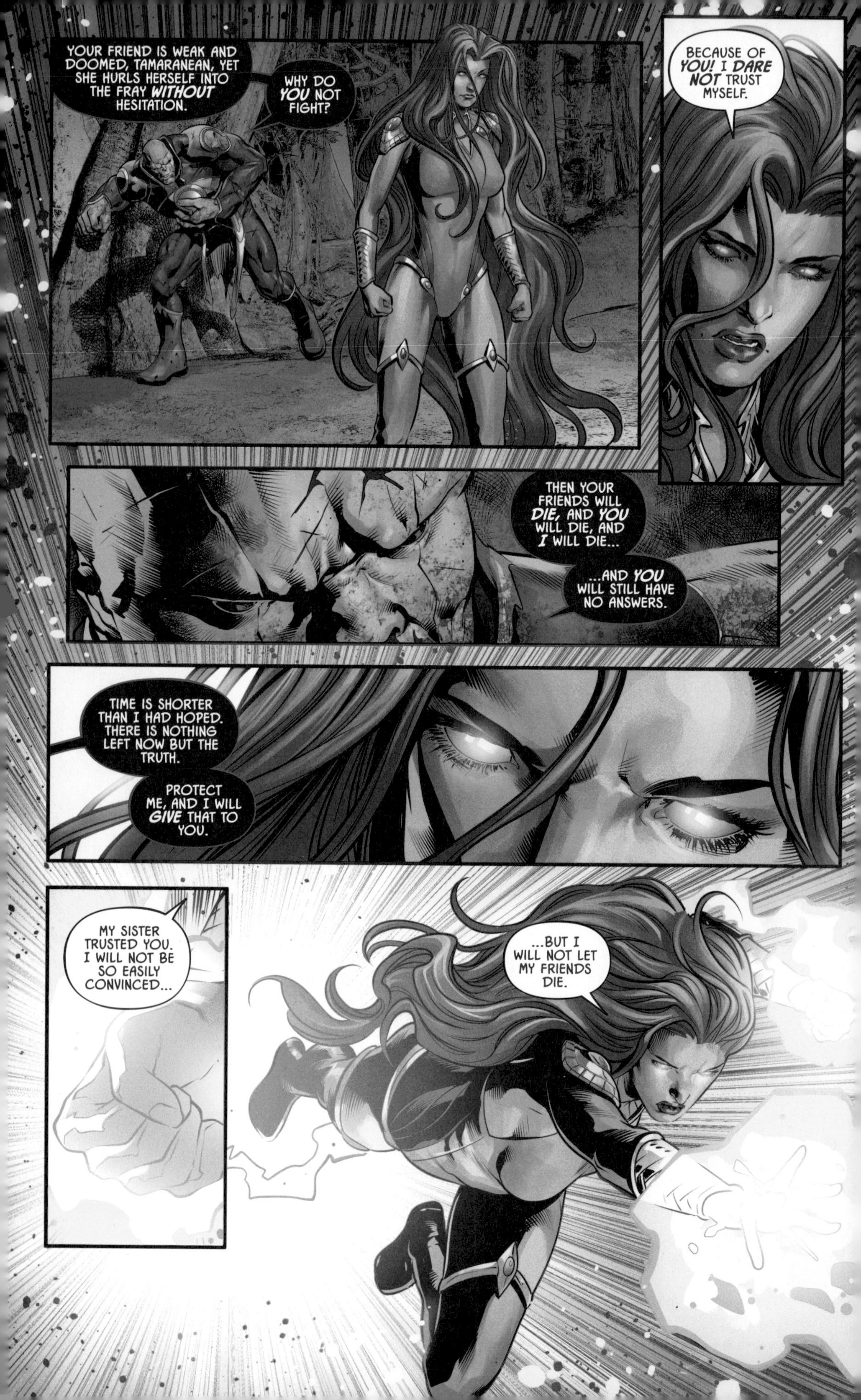
YOUR FRIEND IS WEAK AND DOOMED, TAMARANEAN, YET SHE HURLS HERSELF INTO THE FRAY WITHOUT HESITATION.
WHY DO YOU NOT FIGHT?
BECAUSE OF YOU! I DARE NOT TRUST MYSELF.
THEN YOUR FRIENDS WILL DIE, AND YOU WILL DIE, AND I WILL DIE...
...AND YOU WILL STILL HAVE NO ANSWERS.
TIME IS SHORTER THAN I HAD HOPED. THERE IS NOTHING LEFT NOW BUT THE TRUTH.
PROTECT ME, AND I WILL GIVE THAT TO YOU.
MY SISTER TRUSTED YOU. I WILL NOT BE SO EASILY CONVINCED...
...BUT I WILL NOT LET MY FRIENDS DIE.

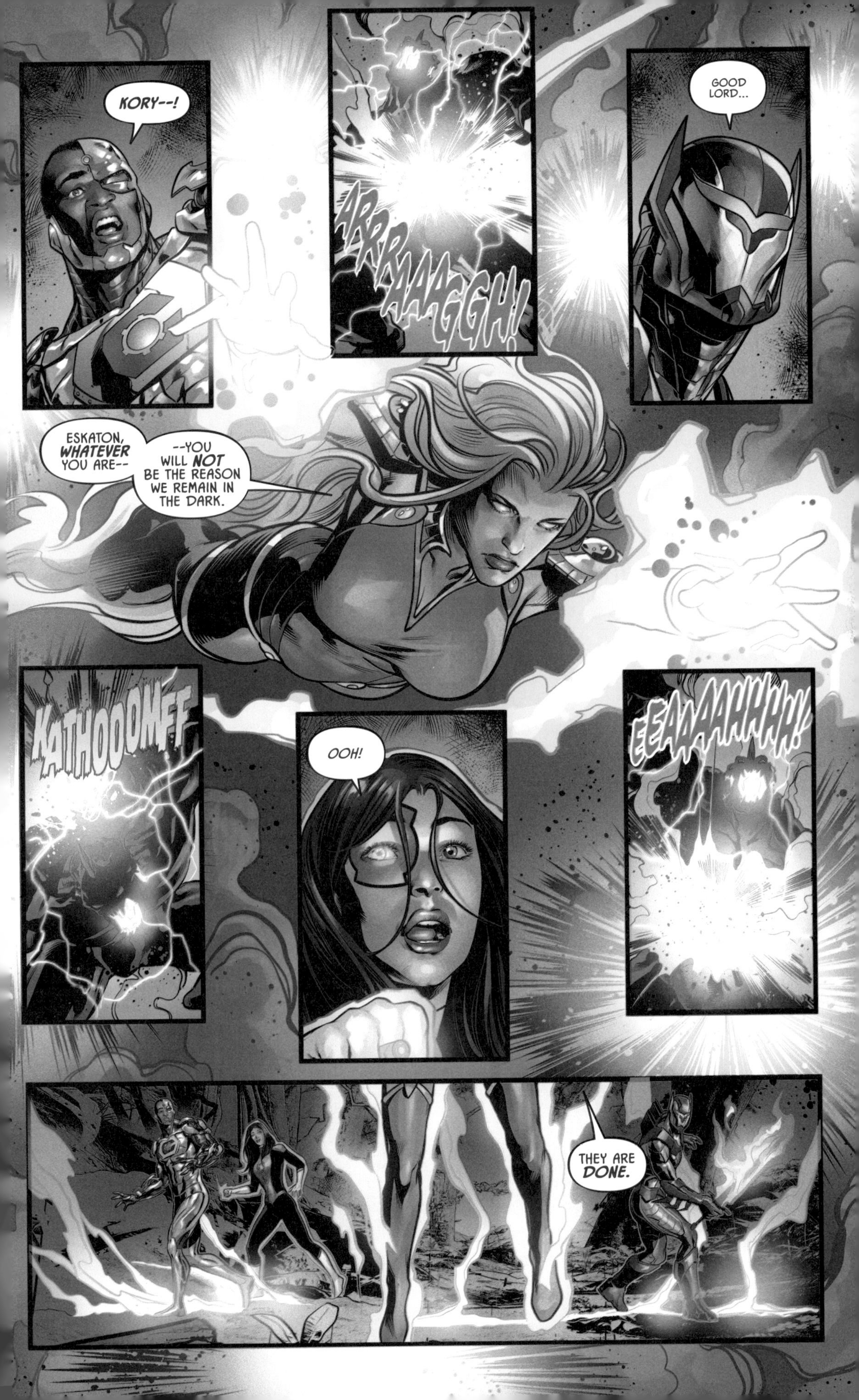
KORY--!
ARRRAAAGGH!
GOOD LORD...
ESKATON, WHATEVER YOU ARE--
--YOU WILL NOT BE THE REASON WE REMAIN IN THE DARK.
KATHOOOMFF
OOH!
EEAAAAHHHH!
THEY ARE DONE.

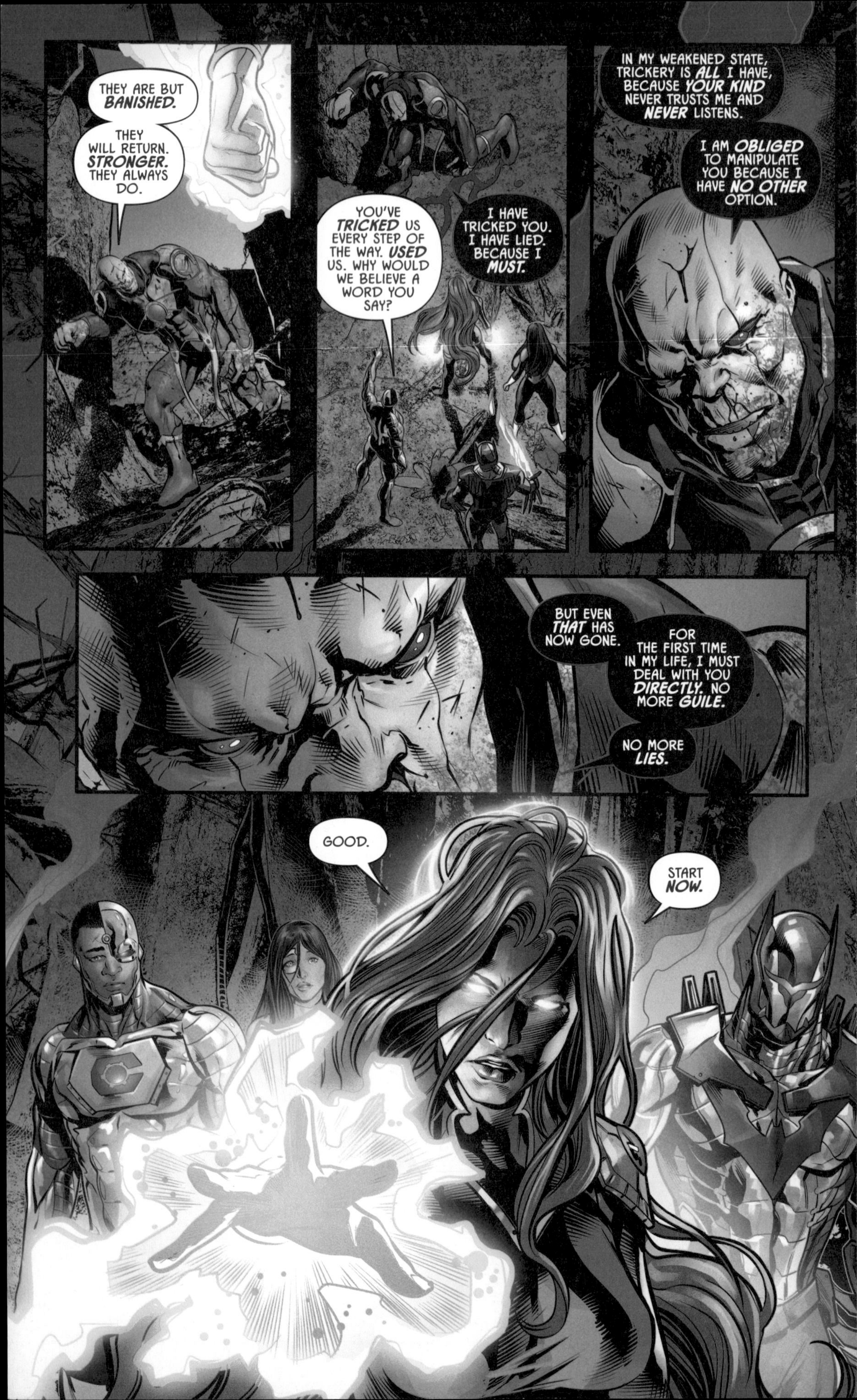
THEY ARE BUT BANISHED.
THEY WILL RETURN. STRONGER. THEY ALWAYS DO.
YOU'VE TRICKED US EVERY STEP OF THE WAY. USED US. WHY WOULD WE BELIEVE A WORD YOU SAY?
I HAVE TRICKED YOU. I HAVE LIED. BECAUSE I MUST.
IN MY WEAKENED STATE, TRICKERY IS ALL I HAVE, BECAUSE YOUR KIND NEVER TRUSTS ME AND NEVER LISTENS.
I AM OBLIGED TO MANIPULATE YOU BECAUSE I HAVE NO OTHER OPTION.
BUT EVEN THAT HAS NOW GONE.
FOR THE FIRST TIME IN MY LIFE, I MUST DEAL WITH YOU DIRECTLY. NO MORE GUILE.
NO MORE LIES.
GOOD.
START NOW.

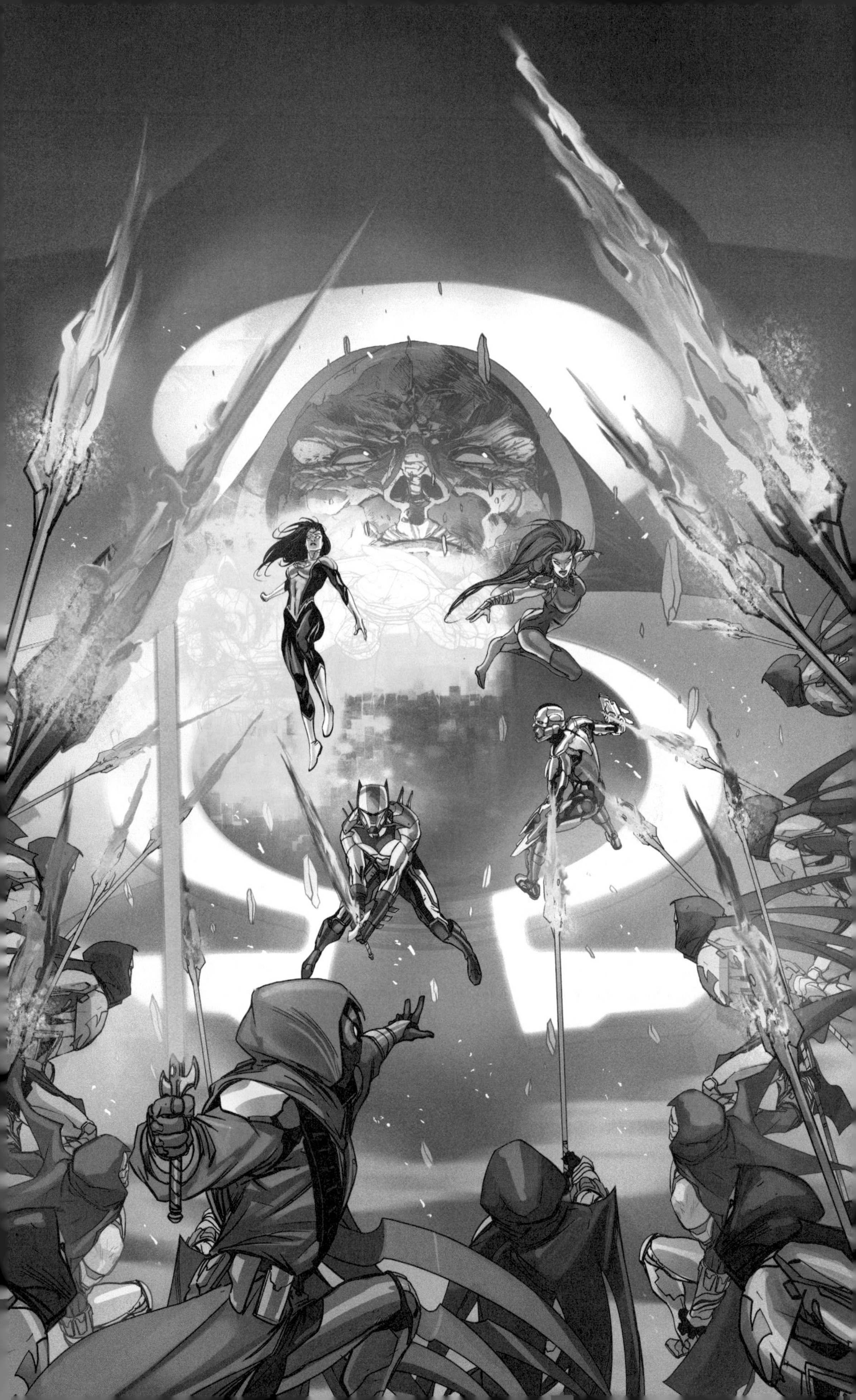

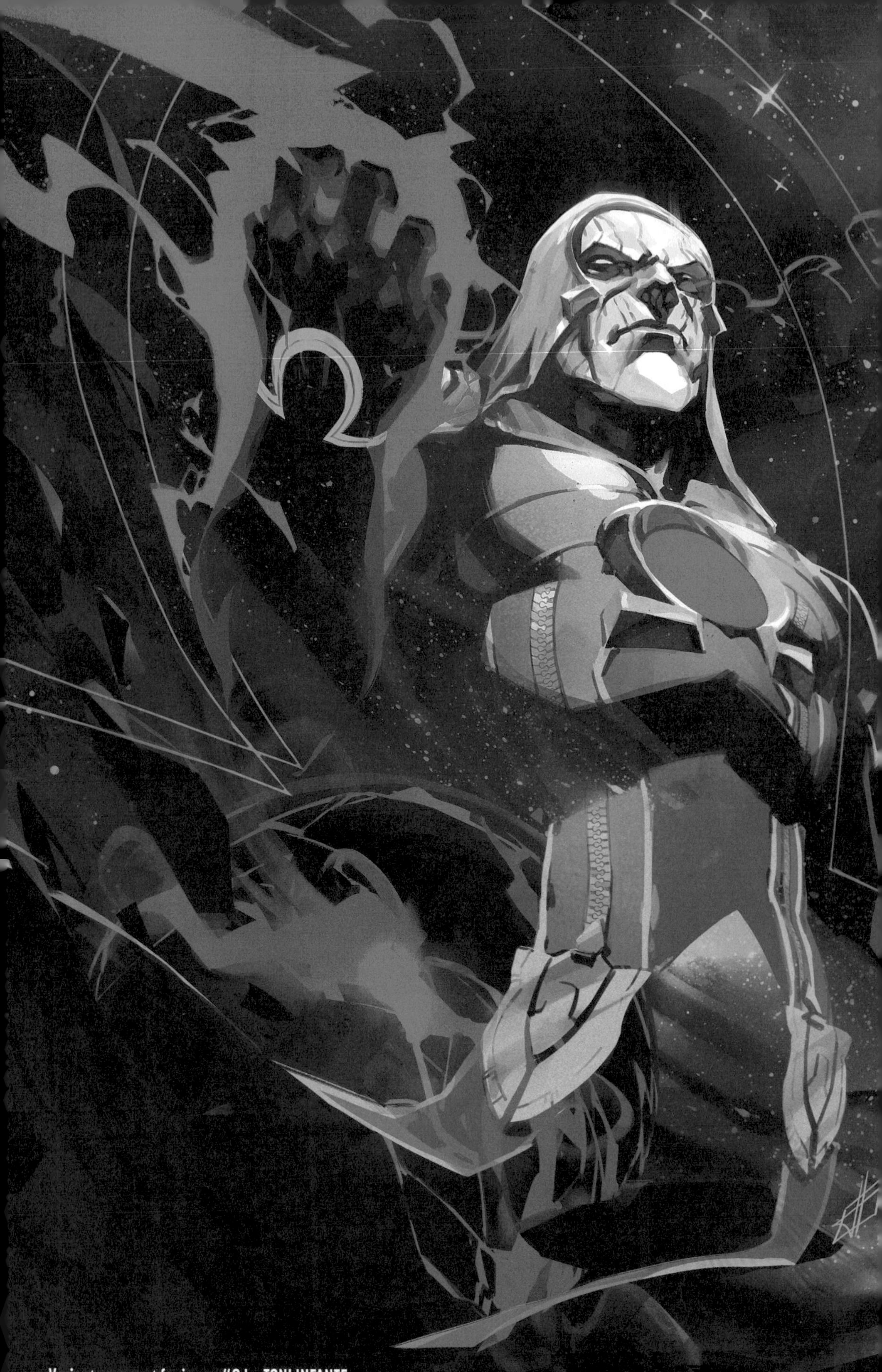

Variant cover art for issue #8 by TONI INFANTE

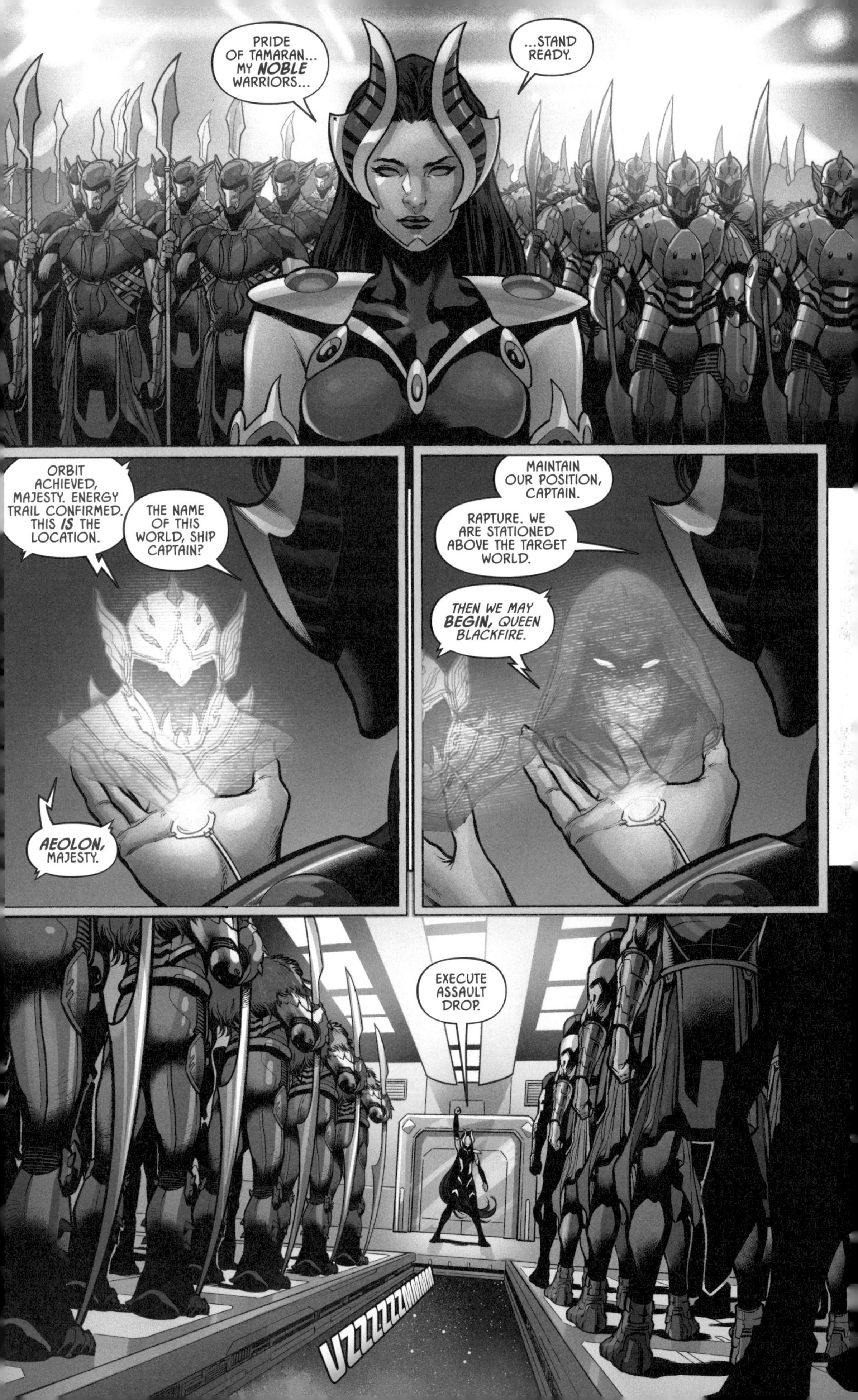
PRIDE OF TAMARAN... MY NOBLE WARRIORS...
...STAND READY.
ORBIT ACHIEVED, MAJESTY. ENERGY TRAIL CONFIRMED. THIS IS THE LOCATION.
THE NAME OF THIS WORLD, SHIP CAPTAIN?
AEOLON, MAJESTY.
MAINTAIN OUR POSITION, CAPTAIN.
RAPTURE. WE ARE STATIONED ABOVE THE TARGET WORLD.
THEN WE MAY BEGIN, QUEEN BLACKFIRE.
EXECUTE ASSAULT DROP.
VZZZZZZMMMMM

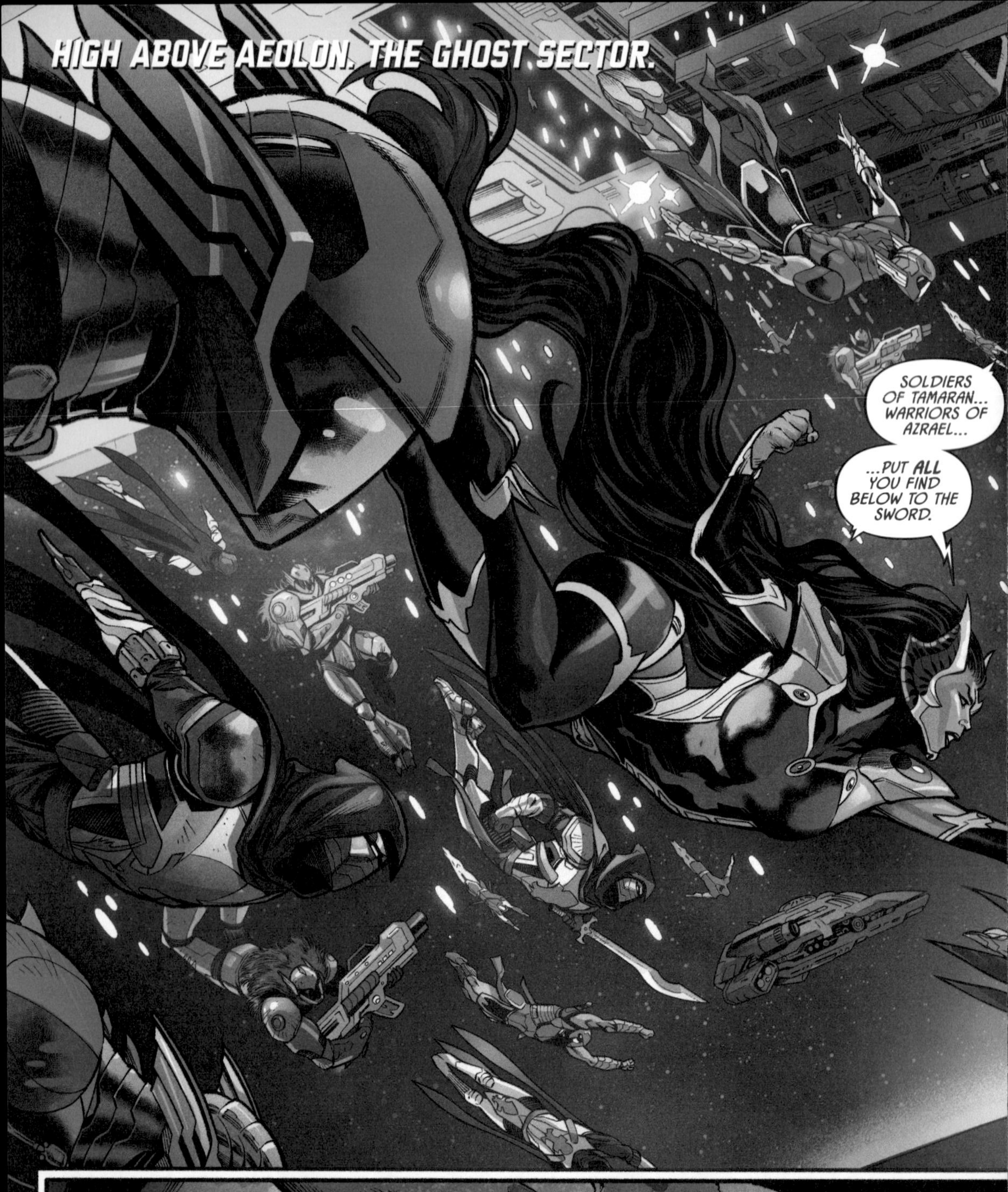
HIGH ABOVE AEOLON. THE GHOST SECTOR.
SOLDIERS OF TAMARAN... WARRIORS OF AZRAEL...
...PUT ALL YOU FIND BELOW TO THE SWORD.

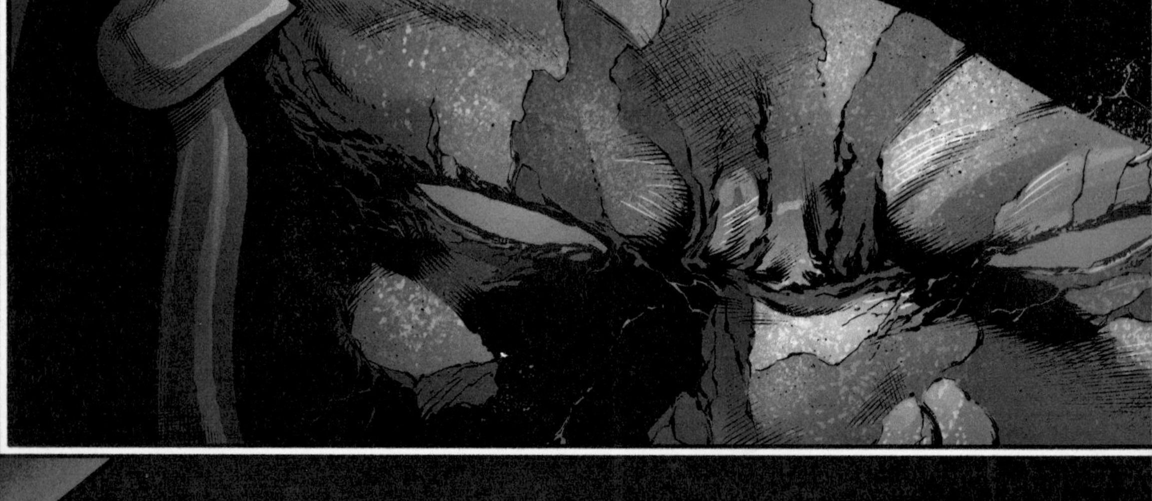

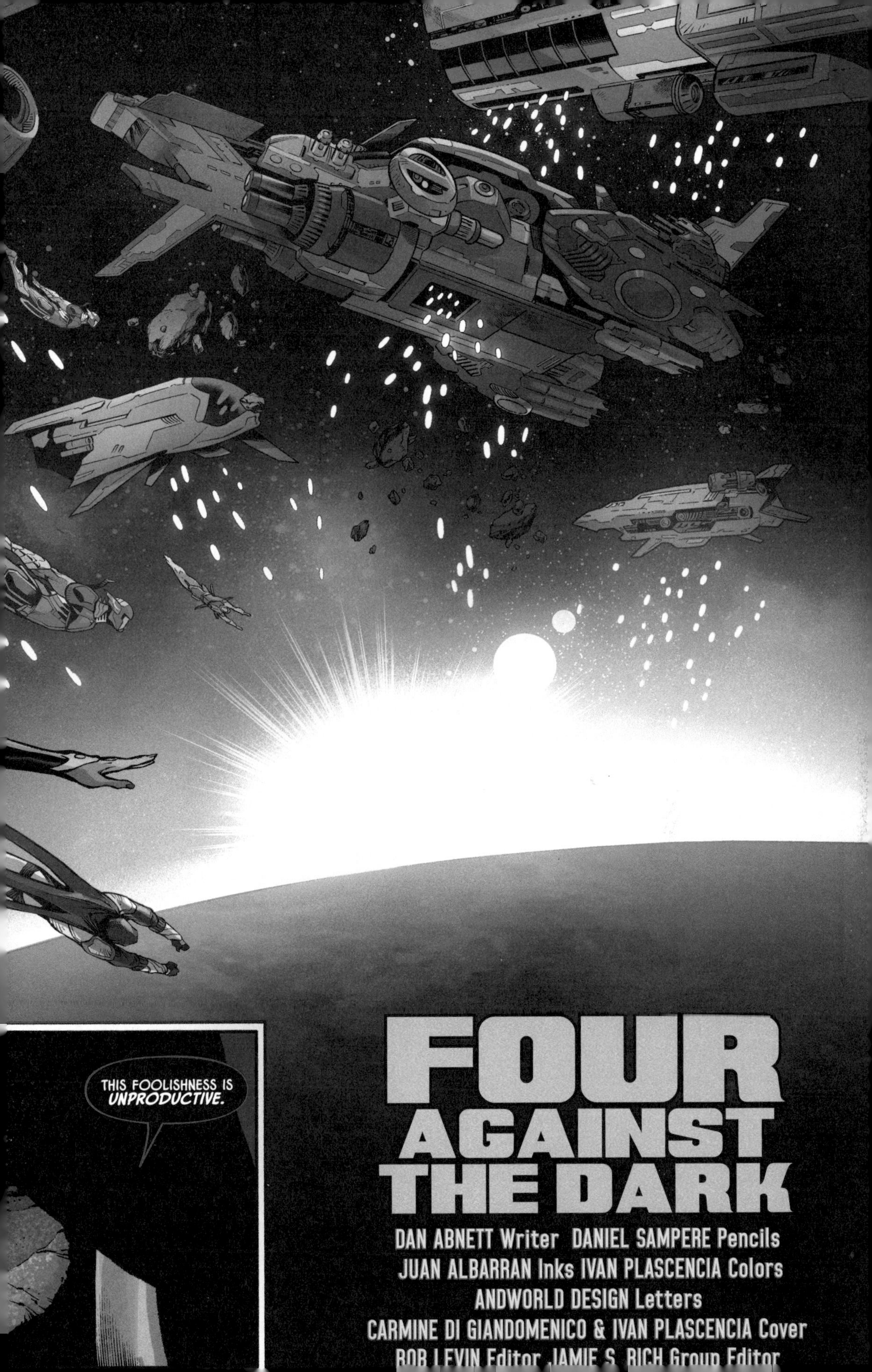

THIS FOOLISHNESS IS *UNPRODUCTIVE.*
FOUR AGAINST THE DARK
DAN ABNETT Writer DANIEL SAMPERE Pencils
JUAN ALBARRAN Inks IVAN PLASCENCIA Colors
ANDWORLD DESIGN Letters
CARMINE DI GIANDOMENICO & IVAN PLASCENCIA Cover
BOB LEVIN Editor JAMIE S. RICH Group Editor

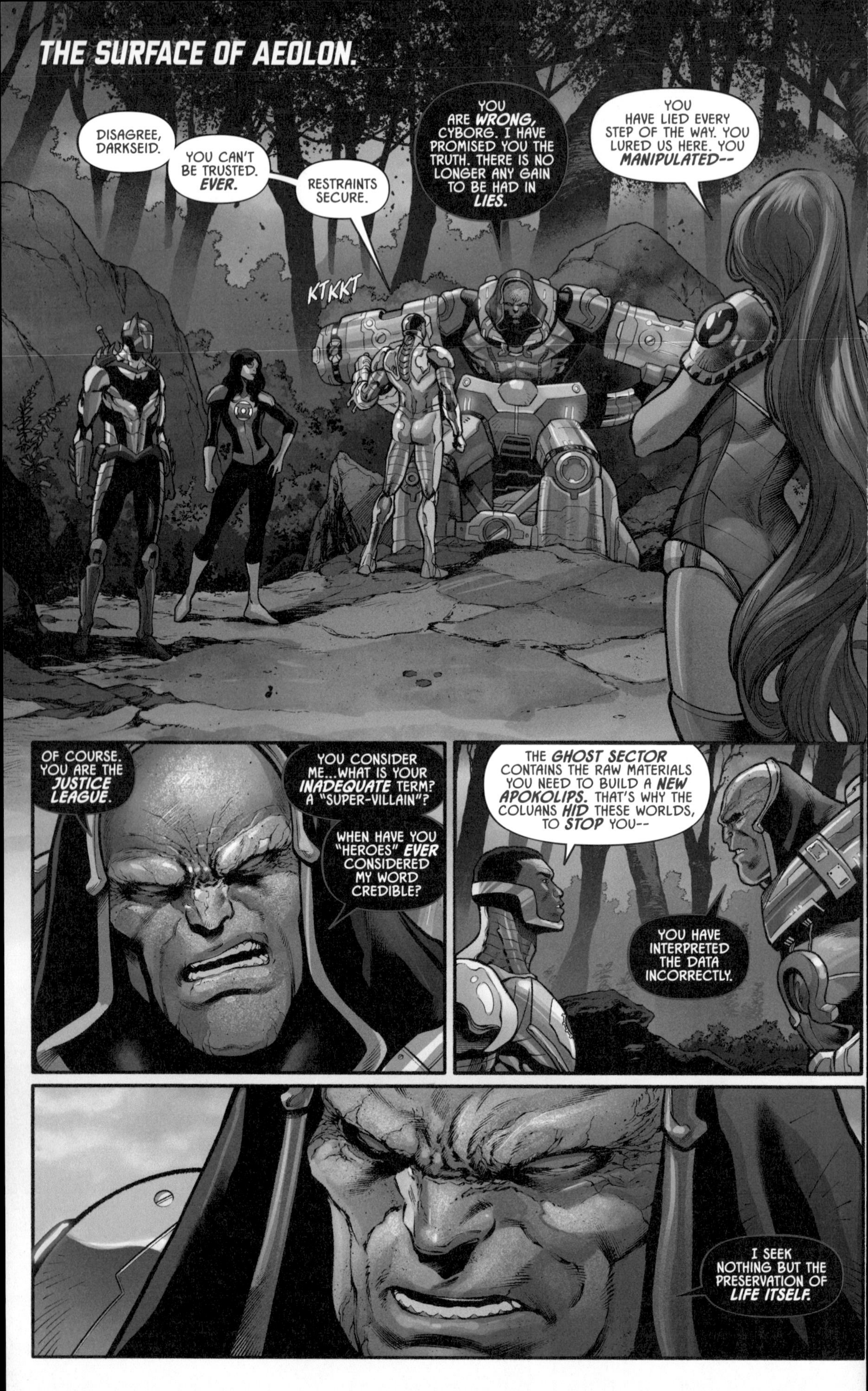
THE SURFACE OF AEOLON.
DISAGREE, DARKSEID.
YOU CAN'T BE TRUSTED. EVER.
RESTRAINTS SECURE.
KTKKT
YOU ARE WRONG, CYBORG. I HAVE PROMISED YOU THE TRUTH. THERE IS NO LONGER ANY GAIN TO BE HAD IN LIES.
YOU HAVE LIED EVERY STEP OF THE WAY. YOU LURED US HERE. YOU MANIPULATED--
OF COURSE. YOU ARE THE JUSTICE LEAGUE.
YOU CONSIDER ME...WHAT IS YOUR INADEQUATE TERM? A "SUPER-VILLAIN"?
WHEN HAVE YOU "HEROES" EVER CONSIDERED MY WORD CREDIBLE?
THE GHOST SECTOR CONTAINS THE RAW MATERIALS YOU NEED TO BUILD A NEW APOKOLIPS. THAT'S WHY THE COLUANS HID THESE WORLDS, TO STOP YOU--
YOU HAVE INTERPRETED THE DATA INCORRECTLY.
I SEEK NOTHING BUT THE PRESERVATION OF LIFE ITSELF.

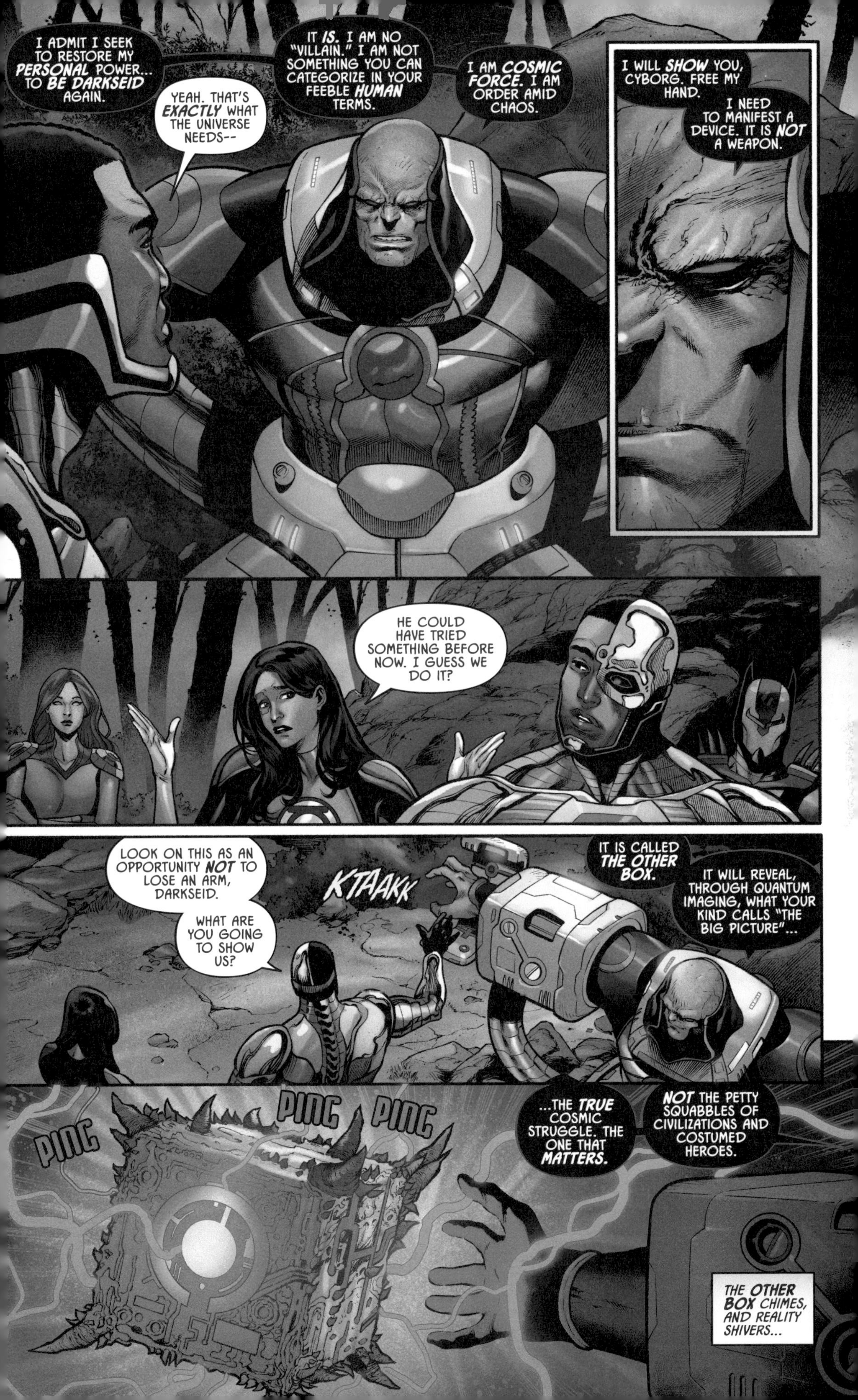
I ADMIT I SEEK TO RESTORE MY PERSONAL POWER... TO BE DARKSEID AGAIN.
YEAH. THAT'S EXACTLY WHAT THE UNIVERSE NEEDS--
IT IS. I AM NO "VILLAIN." I AM NOT SOMETHING YOU CAN CATEGORIZE IN YOUR FEEBLE HUMAN TERMS.
I AM COSMIC FORCE. I AM ORDER AMID CHAOS.
I WILL SHOW YOU, CYBORG. FREE MY HAND.
I NEED TO MANIFEST A DEVICE. IT IS NOT A WEAPON.
HE COULD HAVE TRIED SOMETHING BEFORE NOW. I GUESS WE DO IT?
LOOK ON THIS AS AN OPPORTUNITY NOT TO LOSE AN ARM, DARKSEID.
WHAT ARE YOU GOING TO SHOW US?
KTAAKK
IT IS CALLED THE OTHER BOX.
IT WILL REVEAL, THROUGH QUANTUM IMAGING, WHAT YOUR KIND CALLS "THE BIG PICTURE"...
PING
PING PING
...THE TRUE COSMIC STRUGGLE. THE ONE THAT MATTERS.
NOT THE PETTY SQUABBLES OF CIVILIZATIONS AND COSTUMED HEROES.
THE OTHER BOX CHIMES, AND REALITY SHIVERS...

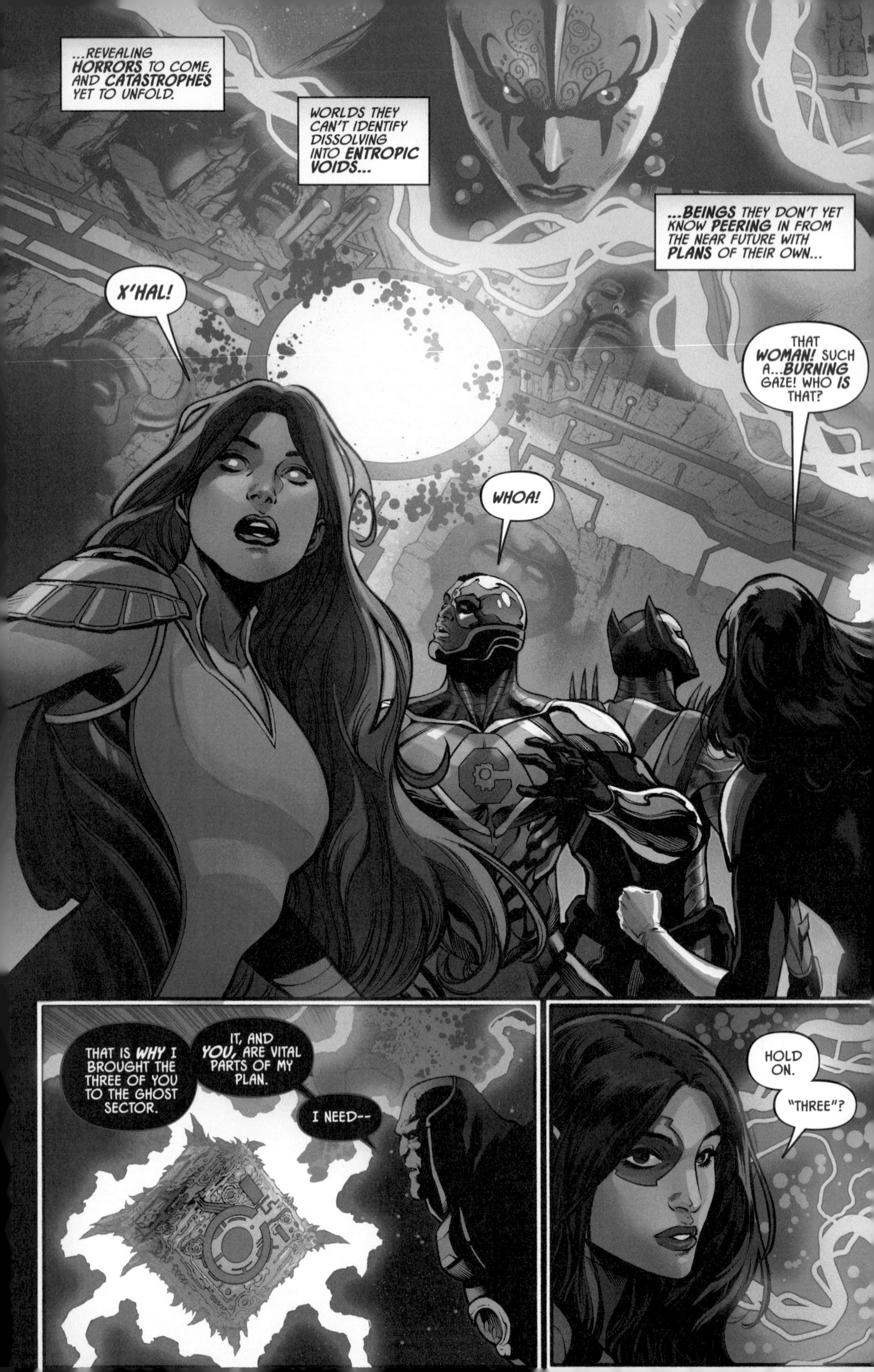
...REVEALING HORRORS TO COME, AND CATASTROPHES YET TO UNFOLD.
WORLDS THEY CAN'T IDENTIFY DISSOLVING INTO ENTROPIC VOIDS...
...BEINGS THEY DON'T YET KNOW PEERING IN FROM THE NEAR FUTURE WITH PLANS OF THEIR OWN...
X'HAL!
WHOA!
THAT WOMAN! SUCH A...BURNING GAZE! WHO IS THAT?
THAT IS WHY I BROUGHT THE THREE OF YOU TO THE GHOST SECTOR.
IT, AND YOU, ARE VITAL PARTS OF MY PLAN.
I NEED--
HOLD ON.
"THREE"?

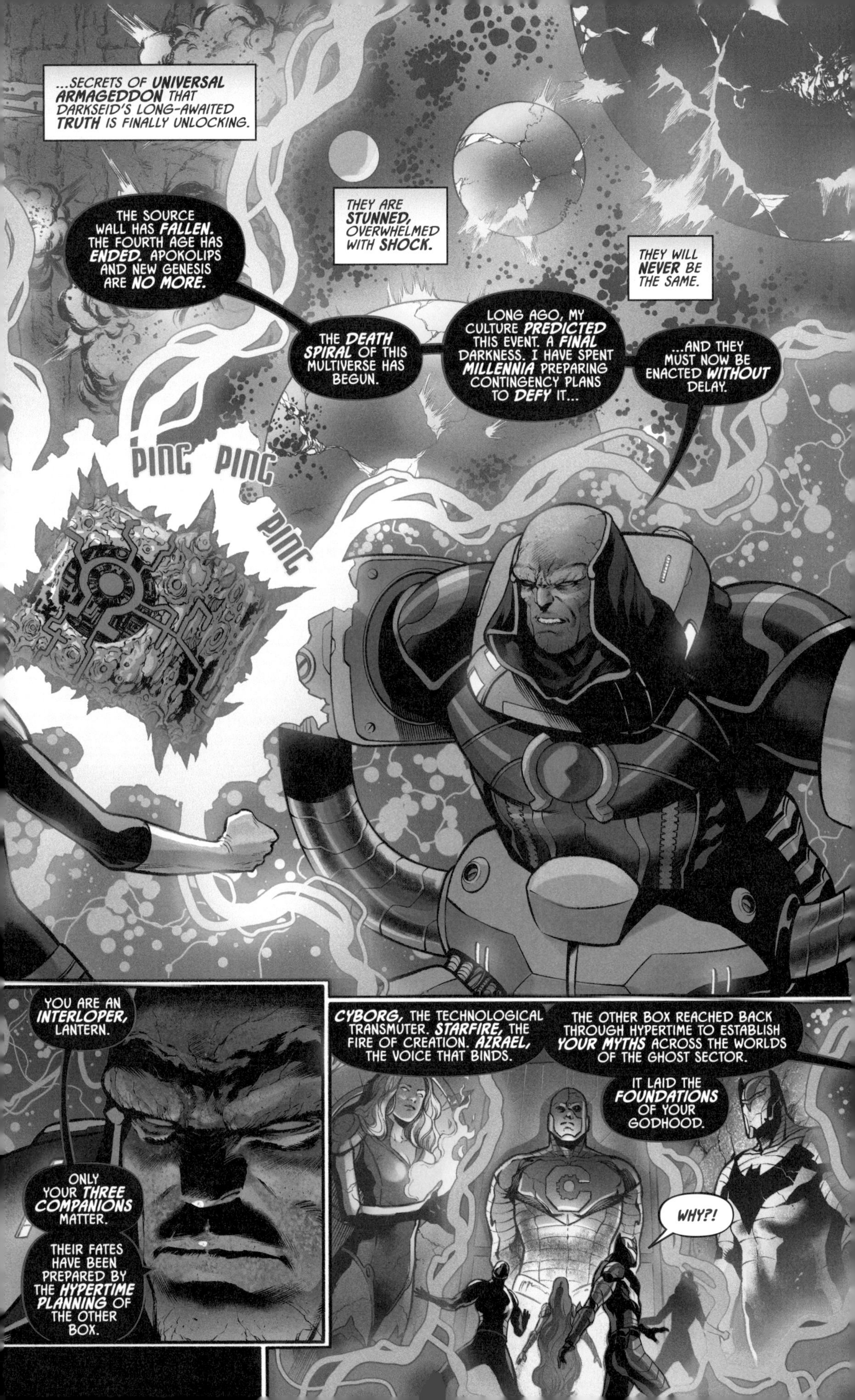

...SECRETS OF UNIVERSAL ARMAGEDDON THAT DARKSEID'S LONG-AWAITED TRUTH IS FINALLY UNLOCKING.
THE SOURCE WALL HAS FALLEN. THE FOURTH AGE HAS ENDED. APOKOLIPS AND NEW GENESIS ARE NO MORE.
THEY ARE STUNNED, OVERWHELMED WITH SHOCK.
THEY WILL NEVER BE THE SAME.
THE DEATH SPIRAL OF THIS MULTIVERSE HAS BEGUN.
LONG AGO, MY CULTURE PREDICTED THIS EVENT. A FINAL DARKNESS. I HAVE SPENT MILLENNIA PREPARING CONTINGENCY PLANS TO DEFY IT...
...AND THEY MUST NOW BE ENACTED WITHOUT DELAY.
PING PING PING
YOU ARE AN INTERLOPER, LANTERN.
ONLY YOUR THREE COMPANIONS MATTER.
THEIR FATES HAVE BEEN PREPARED BY THE HYPERTIME PLANNING OF THE OTHER BOX.
CYBORG, THE TECHNOLOGICAL TRANSMUTER. STARFIRE, THE FIRE OF CREATION. AZRAEL, THE VOICE THAT BINDS.
THE OTHER BOX REACHED BACK THROUGH HYPERTIME TO ESTABLISH YOUR MYTHS ACROSS THE WORLDS OF THE GHOST SECTOR.
IT LAID THE FOUNDATIONS OF YOUR GODHOOD.
WHY?!

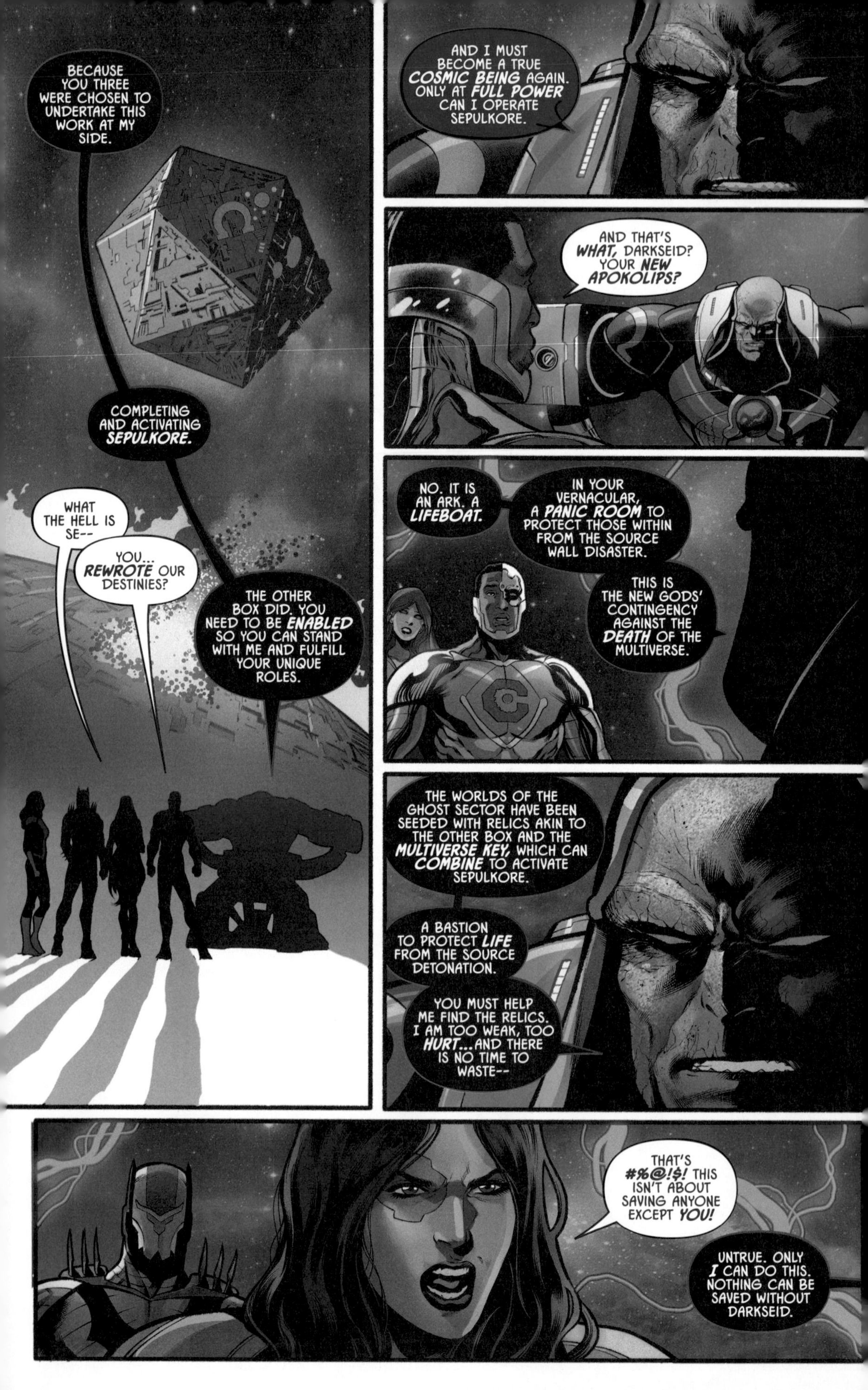

BECAUSE YOU THREE WERE CHOSEN TO UNDERTAKE THIS WORK AT MY SIDE.
COMPLETING AND ACTIVATING SEPULKORE.
WHAT THE HELL IS SE--
YOU... REWROTE OUR DESTINIES?
THE OTHER BOX DID. YOU NEED TO BE ENABLED SO YOU CAN STAND WITH ME AND FULFILL YOUR UNIQUE ROLES.
AND I MUST BECOME A TRUE COSMIC BEING AGAIN. ONLY AT FULL POWER CAN I OPERATE SEPULKORE.
AND THAT'S WHAT, DARKSEID? YOUR NEW APOKOLIPS?
NO. IT IS AN ARK. A LIFEBOAT.
IN YOUR VERNACULAR, A PANIC ROOM TO PROTECT THOSE WITHIN FROM THE SOURCE WALL DISASTER.
THIS IS THE NEW GODS' CONTINGENCY AGAINST THE DEATH OF THE MULTIVERSE.
THE WORLDS OF THE GHOST SECTOR HAVE BEEN SEEDED WITH RELICS AKIN TO THE OTHER BOX AND THE MULTIVERSE KEY, WHICH CAN COMBINE TO ACTIVATE SEPULKORE.
A BASTION TO PROTECT LIFE FROM THE SOURCE DETONATION.
YOU MUST HELP ME FIND THE RELICS. I AM TOO WEAK, TOO HURT...AND THERE IS NO TIME TO WASTE--
THAT'S #%@!$! THIS ISN'T ABOUT SAVING ANYONE EXCEPT YOU!
UNTRUE. ONLY I CAN DO THIS. NOTHING CAN BE SAVED WITHOUT DARKSEID.

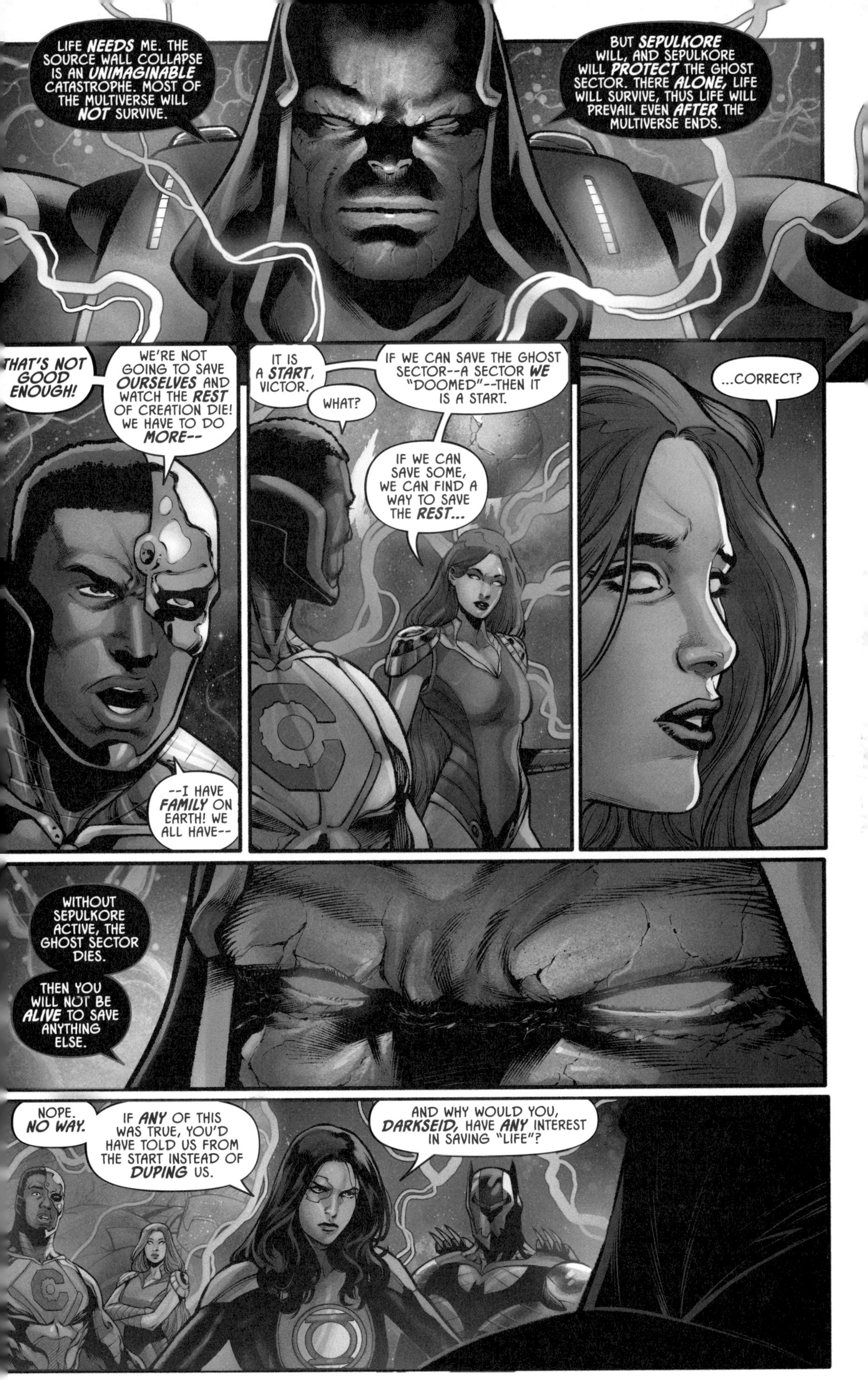

LIFE NEEDS ME. THE SOURCE WALL COLLAPSE IS AN UNIMAGINABLE CATASTROPHE. MOST OF THE MULTIVERSE WILL NOT SURVIVE.
BUT SEPULKORE WILL, AND SEPULKORE WILL PROTECT THE GHOST SECTOR. THERE ALONE, LIFE WILL SURVIVE, THUS LIFE WILL PREVAIL EVEN AFTER THE MULTIVERSE ENDS.
THAT'S NOT GOOD ENOUGH!
WE'RE NOT GOING TO SAVE OURSELVES AND WATCH THE REST OF CREATION DIE! WE HAVE TO DO MORE--
--I HAVE FAMILY ON EARTH! WE ALL HAVE--
IT IS A START, VICTOR.
WHAT?
IF WE CAN SAVE THE GHOST SECTOR--A SECTOR WE "DOOMED"--THEN IT IS A START.
IF WE CAN SAVE SOME, WE CAN FIND A WAY TO SAVE THE REST...
...CORRECT?
WITHOUT SEPULKORE ACTIVE, THE GHOST SECTOR DIES.
THEN YOU WILL NOT BE ALIVE TO SAVE ANYTHING ELSE.
NOPE. NO WAY.
IF ANY OF THIS WAS TRUE, YOU'D HAVE TOLD US FROM THE START INSTEAD OF DUPING US.
AND WHY WOULD YOU, DARKSEID, HAVE ANY INTEREST IN SAVING "LIFE"?

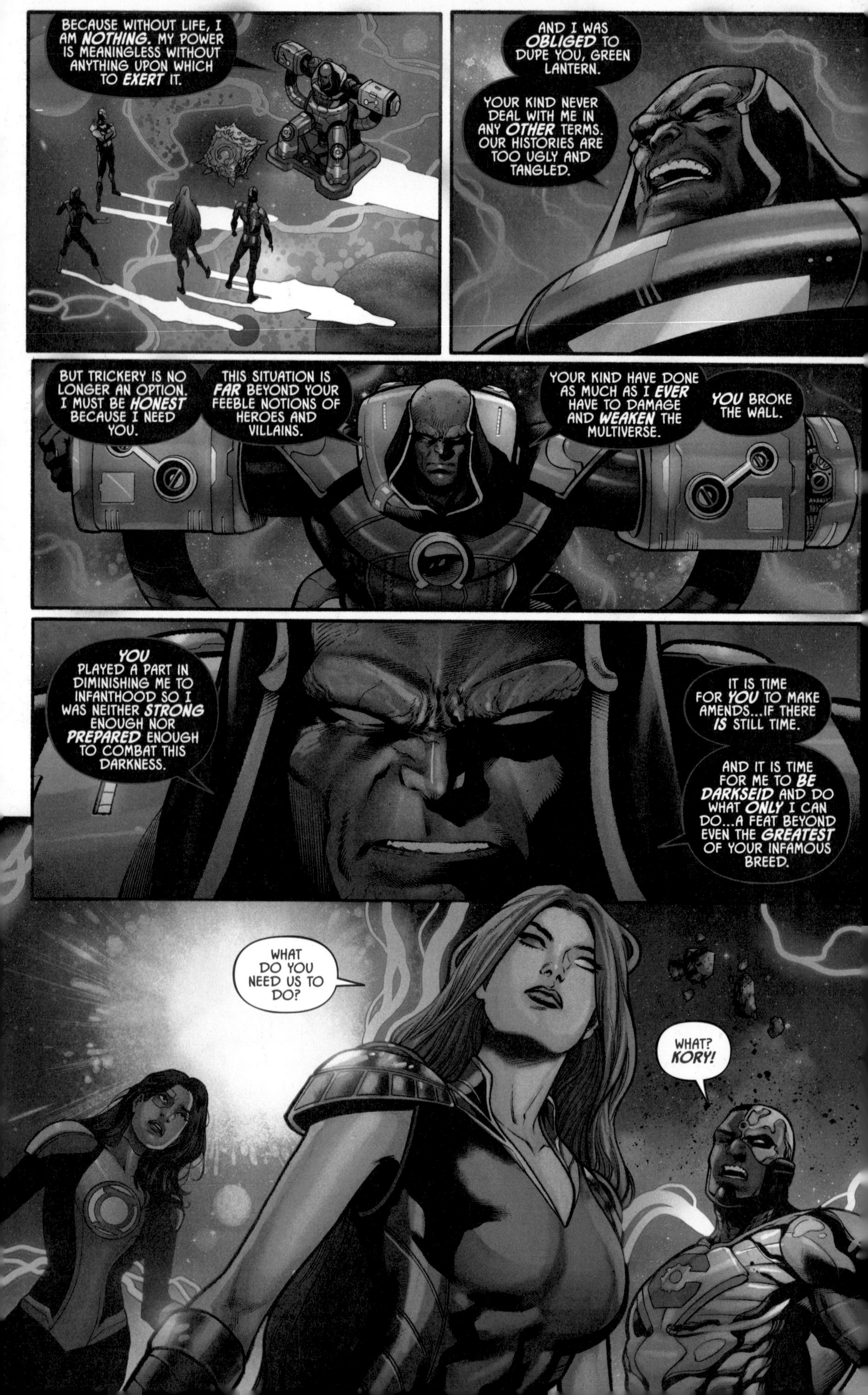
BECAUSE WITHOUT LIFE, I AM NOTHING. MY POWER IS MEANINGLESS WITHOUT ANYTHING UPON WHICH TO EXERT IT.
AND I WAS OBLIGED TO DUPE YOU, GREEN LANTERN.
YOUR KIND NEVER DEAL WITH ME IN ANY OTHER TERMS. OUR HISTORIES ARE TOO UGLY AND TANGLED.
BUT TRICKERY IS NO LONGER AN OPTION. I MUST BE HONEST BECAUSE I NEED YOU.
THIS SITUATION IS FAR BEYOND YOUR FEEBLE NOTIONS OF HEROES AND VILLAINS.
YOUR KIND HAVE DONE AS MUCH AS I EVER HAVE TO DAMAGE AND WEAKEN THE MULTIVERSE.
YOU BROKE THE WALL.
YOU PLAYED A PART IN DIMINISHING ME TO INFANTHOOD SO I WAS NEITHER STRONG ENOUGH NOR PREPARED ENOUGH TO COMBAT THIS DARKNESS.
IT IS TIME FOR YOU TO MAKE AMENDS...IF THERE IS STILL TIME.
AND IT IS TIME FOR ME TO BE DARKSEID AND DO WHAT ONLY I CAN DO...A FEAT BEYOND EVEN THE GREATEST OF YOUR INFAMOUS BREED.
WHAT DO YOU NEED US TO DO?
WHAT? KORY!

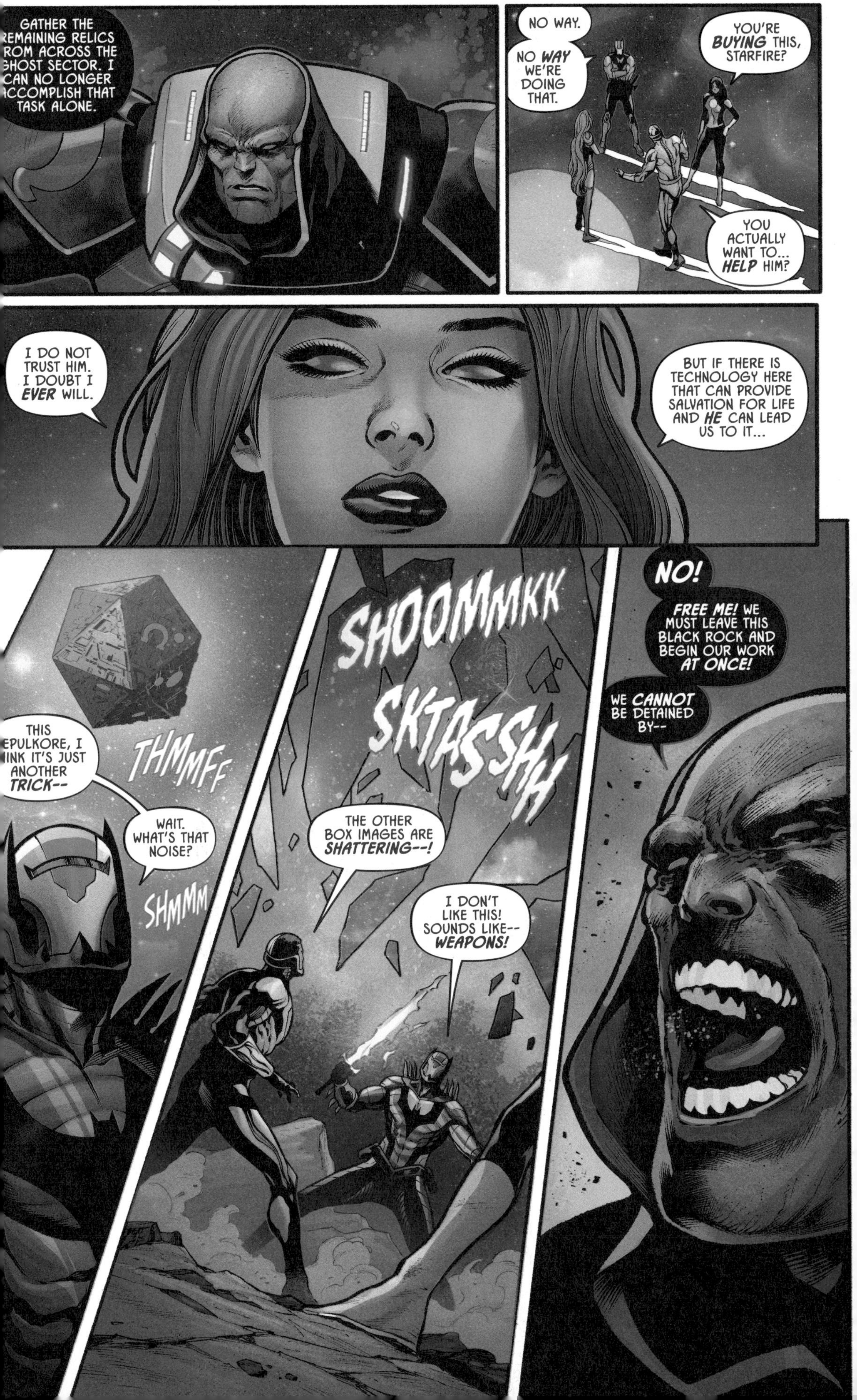
GATHER THE REMAINING RELICS FROM ACROSS THE GHOST SECTOR. I CAN NO LONGER ACCOMPLISH THAT TASK ALONE.
NO WAY.
NO WAY WE'RE DOING THAT.
YOU'RE BUYING THIS, STARFIRE?
YOU ACTUALLY WANT TO... HELP HIM?
I DO NOT TRUST HIM. I DOUBT I EVER WILL.
BUT IF THERE IS TECHNOLOGY HERE THAT CAN PROVIDE SALVATION FOR LIFE AND HE CAN LEAD US TO IT...
THMMFF
THIS EPULKORE, I INK IT'S JUST ANOTHER TRICK--
WAIT. WHAT'S THAT NOISE?
SHMMM
SHOOMMKK
SKTASSHH
THE OTHER BOX IMAGES ARE SHATTERING--!
I DON'T LIKE THIS! SOUNDS LIKE-- WEAPONS!
NO!
FREE ME! WE MUST LEAVE THIS BLACK ROCK AND BEGIN OUR WORK AT ONCE!
WE CANNOT BE DETAINED BY--

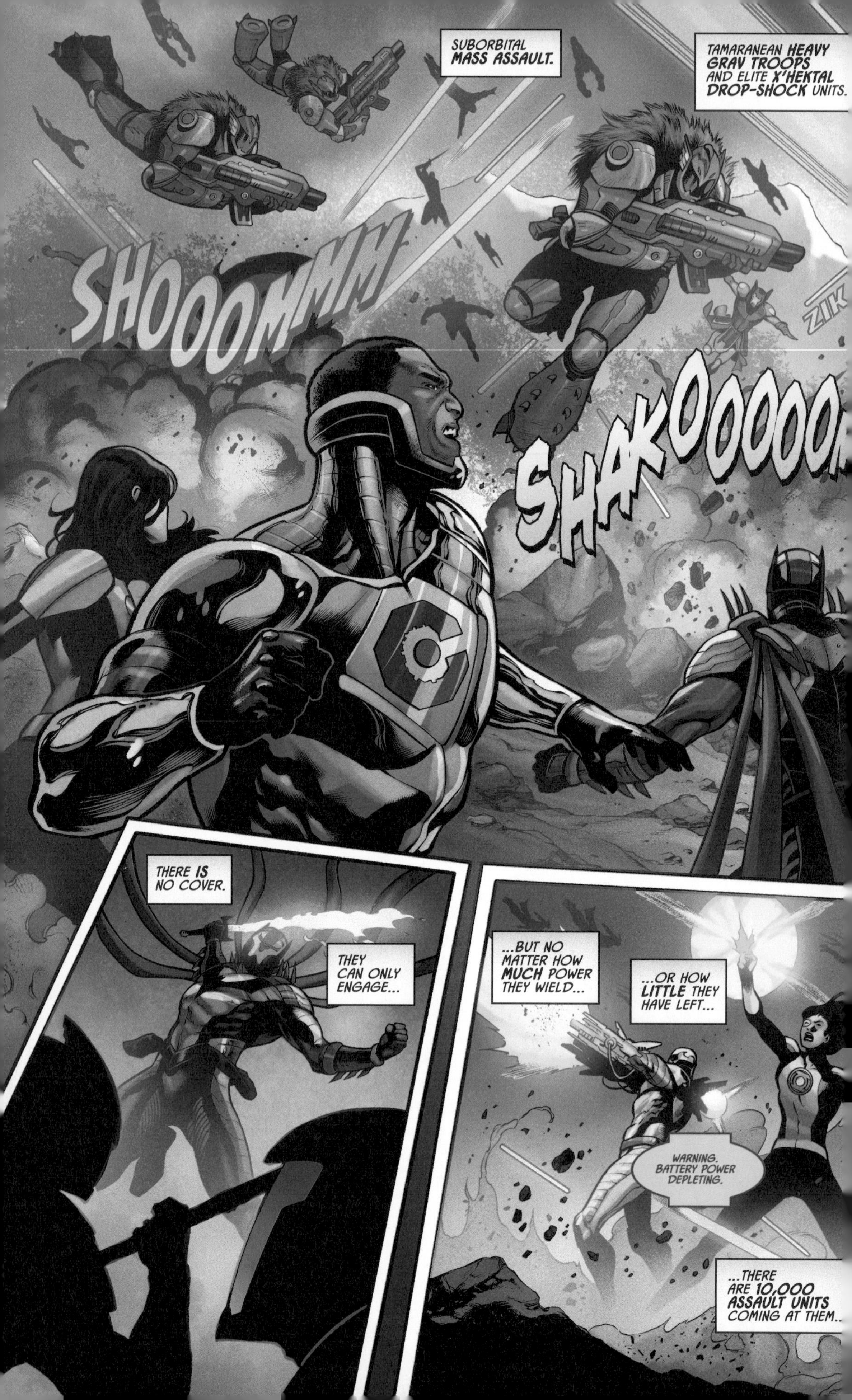
SUBORBITAL MASS ASSAULT.
TAMARANEAN HEAVY GRAV TROOPS AND ELITE X'HEKTAL DROP-SHOCK UNITS.
SHOOOMMM
ZIK
SHAKOOOOO
THERE IS NO COVER.
THEY CAN ONLY ENGAGE...
...BUT NO MATTER HOW MUCH POWER THEY WIELD...
...OR HOW LITTLE THEY HAVE LEFT...
WARNING. BATTERY POWER DEPLETING.
...THERE ARE 10,000 ASSAULT UNITS COMING AT THEM...

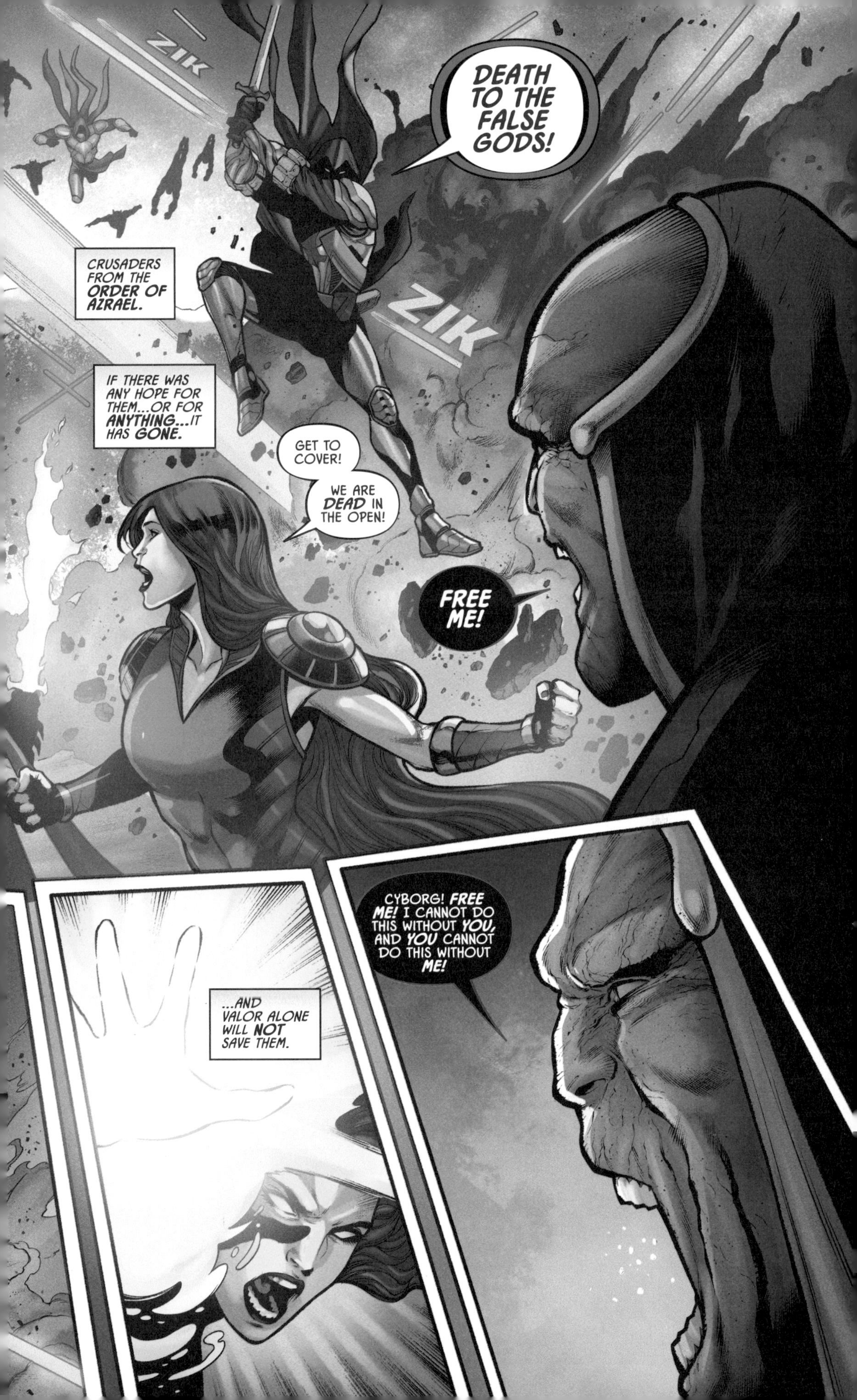
ZIK
DEATH TO THE FALSE GODS!
CRUSADERS FROM THE ORDER OF AZRAEL.
ZIK
IF THERE WAS ANY HOPE FOR THEM...OR FOR ANYTHING...IT HAS GONE.
GET TO COVER!
WE ARE DEAD IN THE OPEN!
FREE ME!
CYBORG! FREE ME! I CANNOT DO THIS WITHOUT YOU, AND YOU CANNOT DO THIS WITHOUT ME!
...AND VALOR ALONE WILL NOT SAVE THEM.

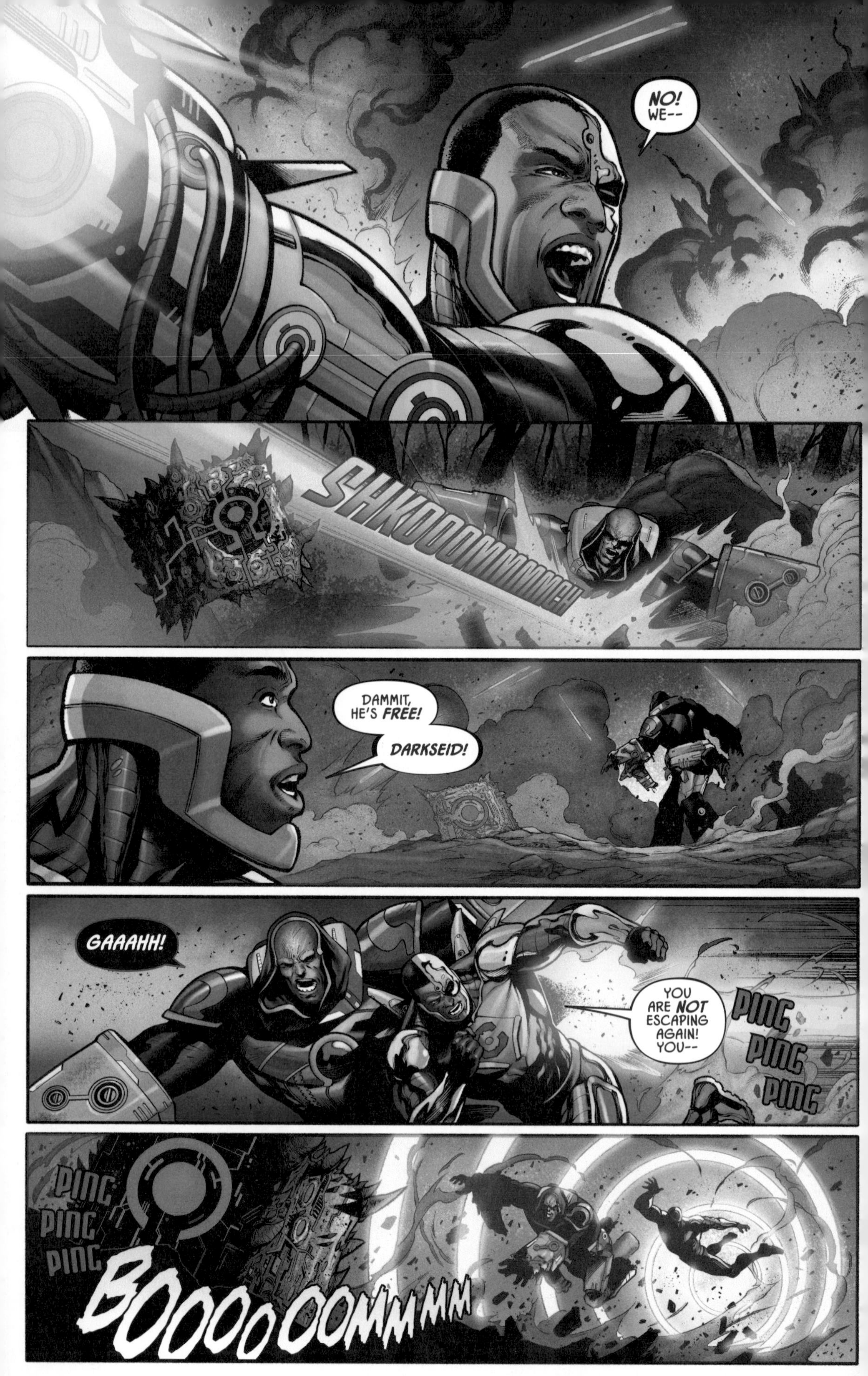

NO! WE--
SHKOOOMMMMMMMMMCH
DAMMIT, HE'S FREE!
DARKSEID!
GAAAHH!
YOU ARE NOT ESCAPING AGAIN! YOU--
PING PING PING
PING PING PING
BOOOOOOMMMM

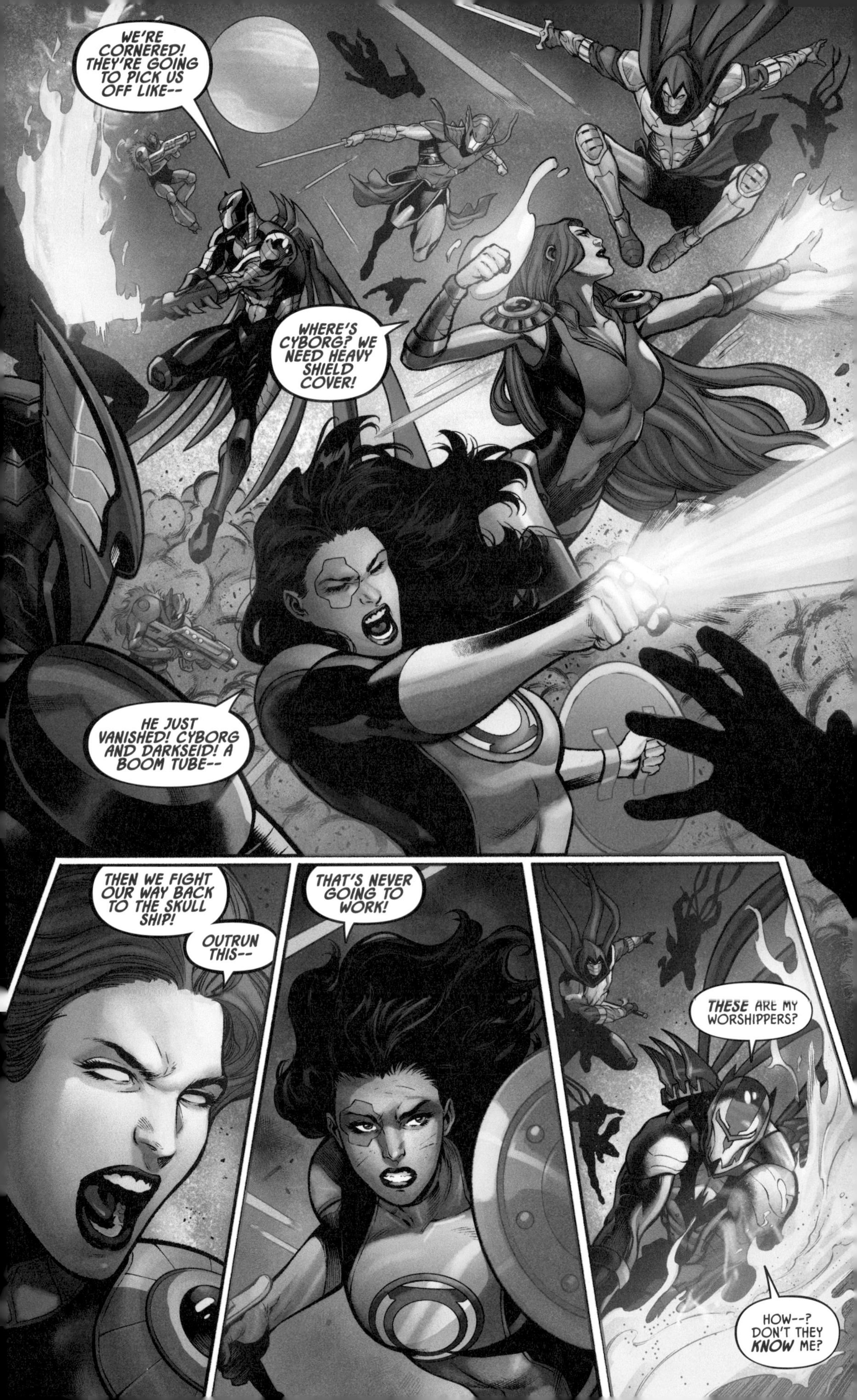
WE'RE CORNERED! THEY'RE GOING TO PICK US OFF LIKE--
WHERE'S CYBORG? WE NEED HEAVY SHIELD COVER!
HE JUST VANISHED! CYBORG AND DARKSEID! A BOOM TUBE--
THEN WE FIGHT OUR WAY BACK TO THE SKULL SHIP!
OUTRUN THIS--
THAT'S NEVER GOING TO WORK!
THESE ARE MY WORSHIPPERS?
HOW--? DON'T THEY KNOW ME?

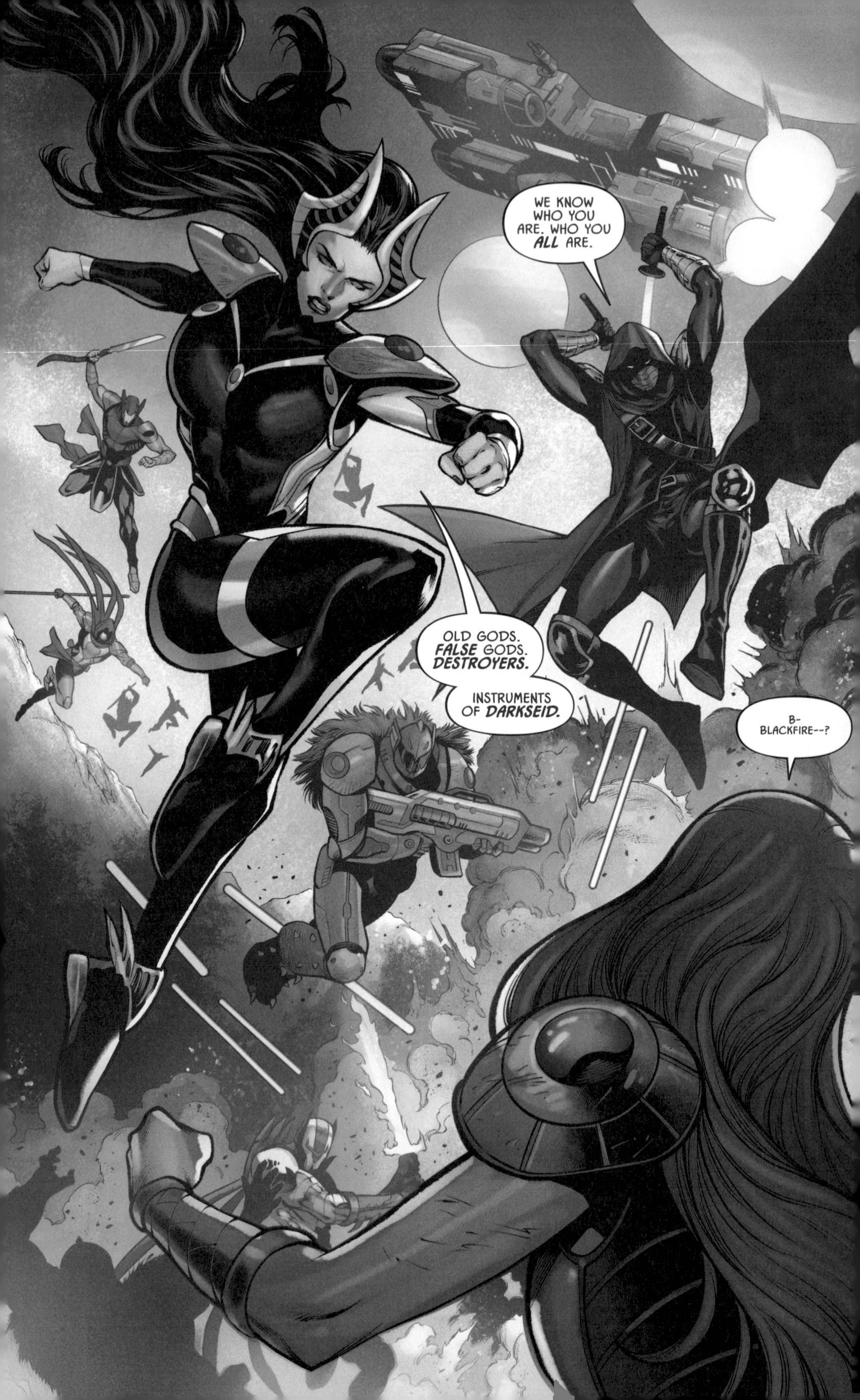
WE KNOW WHO YOU ARE. WHO YOU ALL ARE.
OLD GODS. FALSE GODS. DESTROYERS.
INSTRUMENTS OF DARKSEID.
B- BLACKFIRE--?

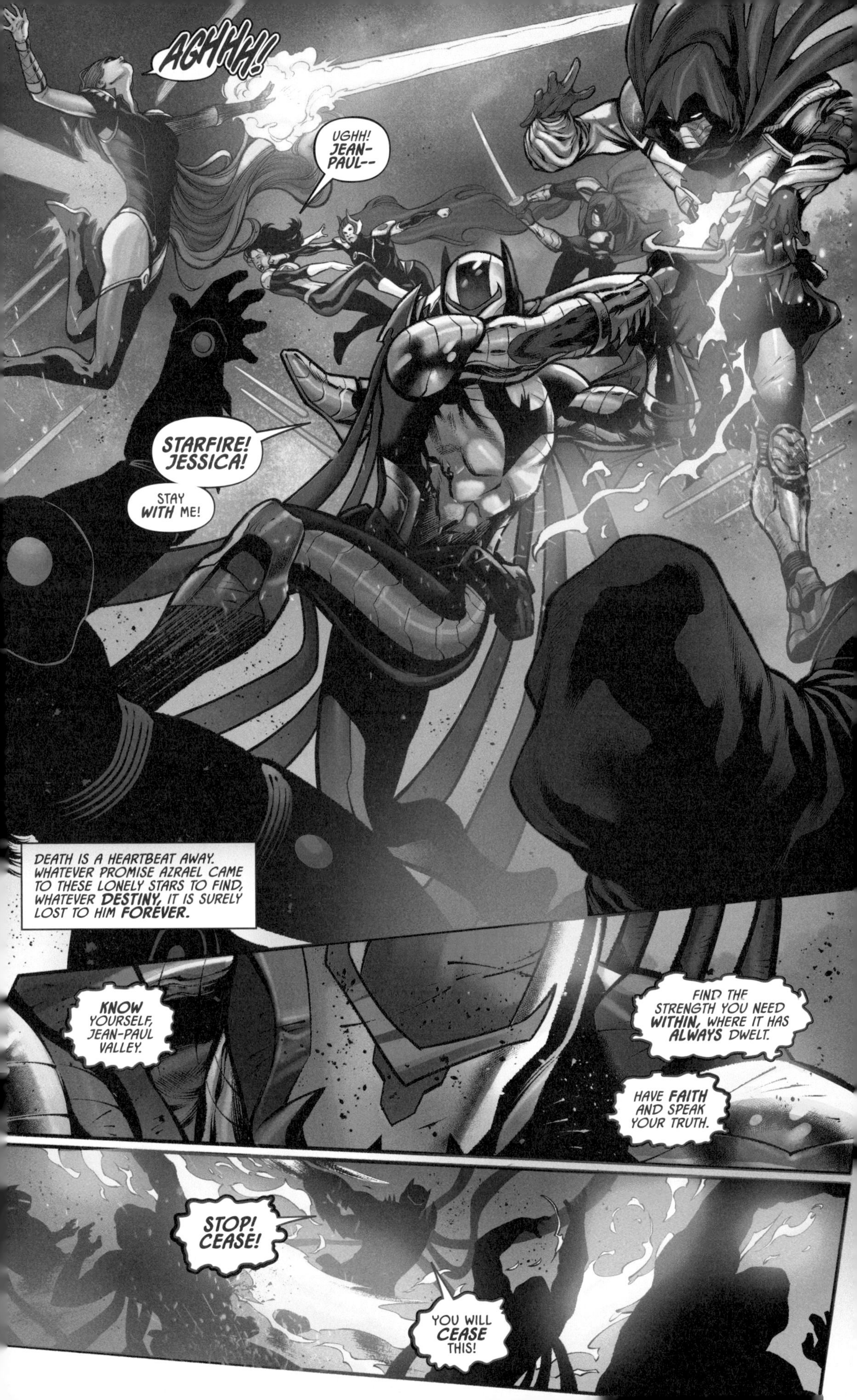
AGHHH!!
UGHH! JEAN-PAUL--
STARFIRE! JESSICA!
STAY WITH ME!
DEATH IS A HEARTBEAT AWAY. WHATEVER PROMISE AZRAEL CAME TO THESE LONELY STARS TO FIND, WHATEVER DESTINY, IT IS SURELY LOST TO HIM FOREVER.
KNOW YOURSELF, JEAN-PAUL VALLEY.
FIND THE STRENGTH YOU NEED WITHIN, WHERE IT HAS ALWAYS DWELT.
HAVE FAITH AND SPEAK YOUR TRUTH.
STOP! CEASE!
YOU WILL CEASE THIS!

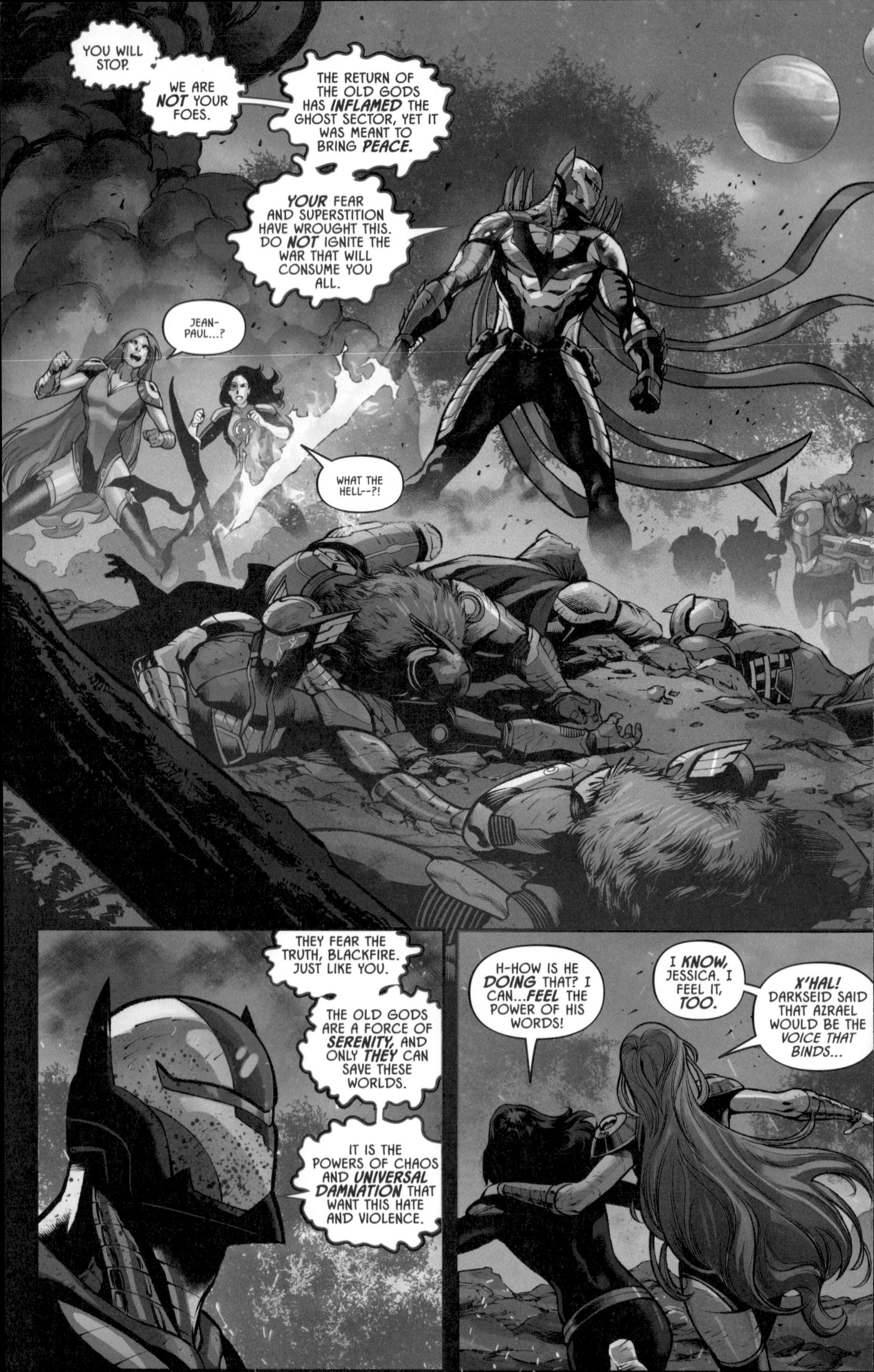
YOU WILL STOP.
WE ARE NOT YOUR FOES.
THE RETURN OF THE OLD GODS HAS INFLAMED THE GHOST SECTOR, YET IT WAS MEANT TO BRING PEACE.
YOUR FEAR AND SUPERSTITION HAVE WROUGHT THIS. DO NOT IGNITE THE WAR THAT WILL CONSUME YOU ALL.
JEAN-PAUL...?
WHAT THE HELL--?!
THEY FEAR THE TRUTH, BLACKFIRE. JUST LIKE YOU.
THE OLD GODS ARE A FORCE OF SERENITY, AND ONLY THEY CAN SAVE THESE WORLDS.
IT IS THE POWERS OF CHAOS AND UNIVERSAL DAMNATION THAT WANT THIS HATE AND VIOLENCE.
H-HOW IS HE DOING THAT? I CAN...FEEL THE POWER OF HIS WORDS!
I KNOW, JESSICA. I FEEL IT, TOO.
X'HAL! DARKSEID SAID THAT AZRAEL WOULD BE THE VOICE THAT BINDS...

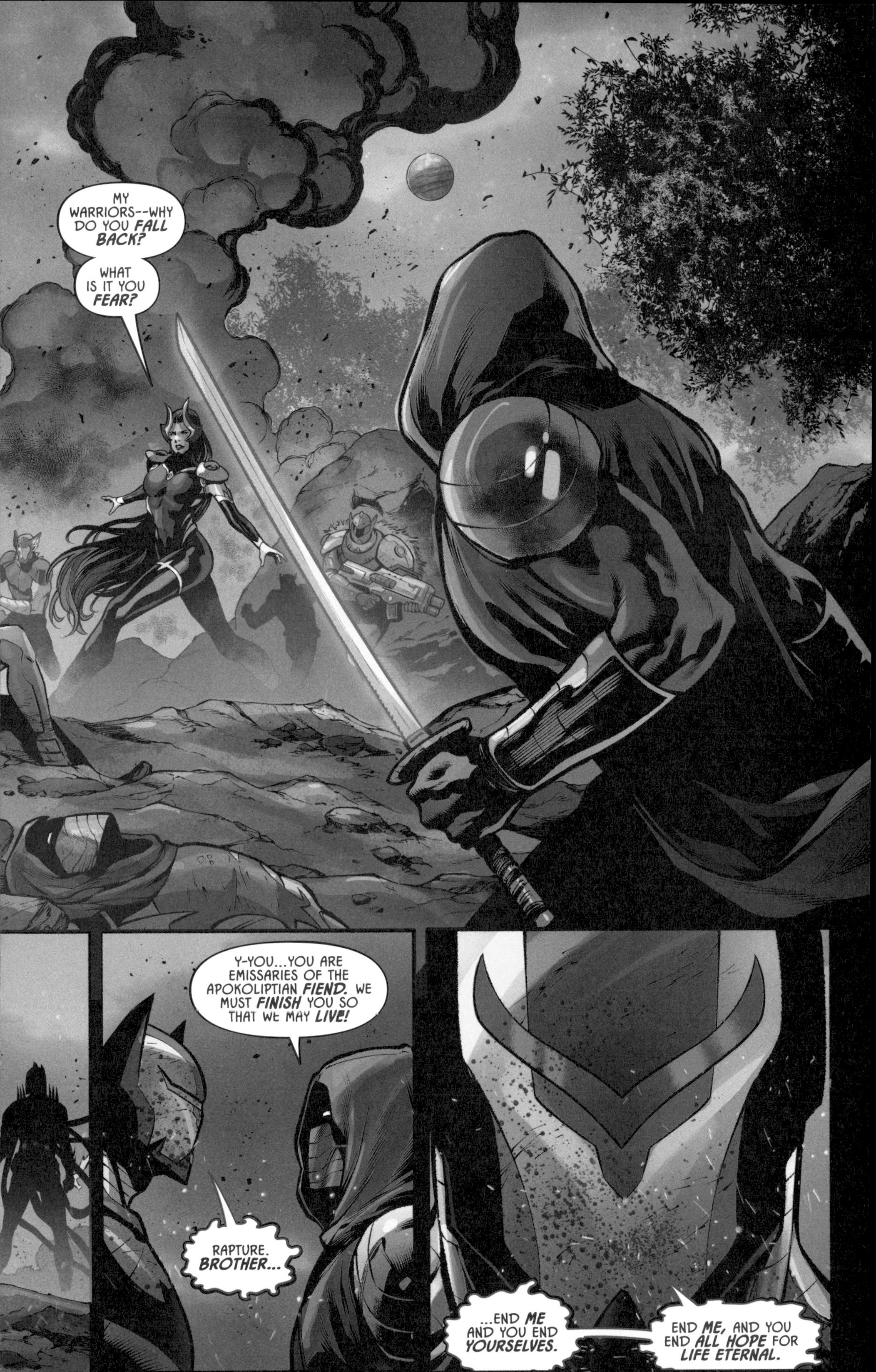
MY WARRIORS--WHY DO YOU FALL BACK?
WHAT IS IT YOU FEAR?
Y-YOU...YOU ARE EMISSARIES OF THE APOKOLIPTIAN FIEND. WE MUST FINISH YOU SO THAT WE MAY LIVE!
RAPTURE. BROTHER...
...END ME AND YOU END YOURSELVES.
END ME, AND YOU END ALL HOPE FOR LIFE ETERNAL.

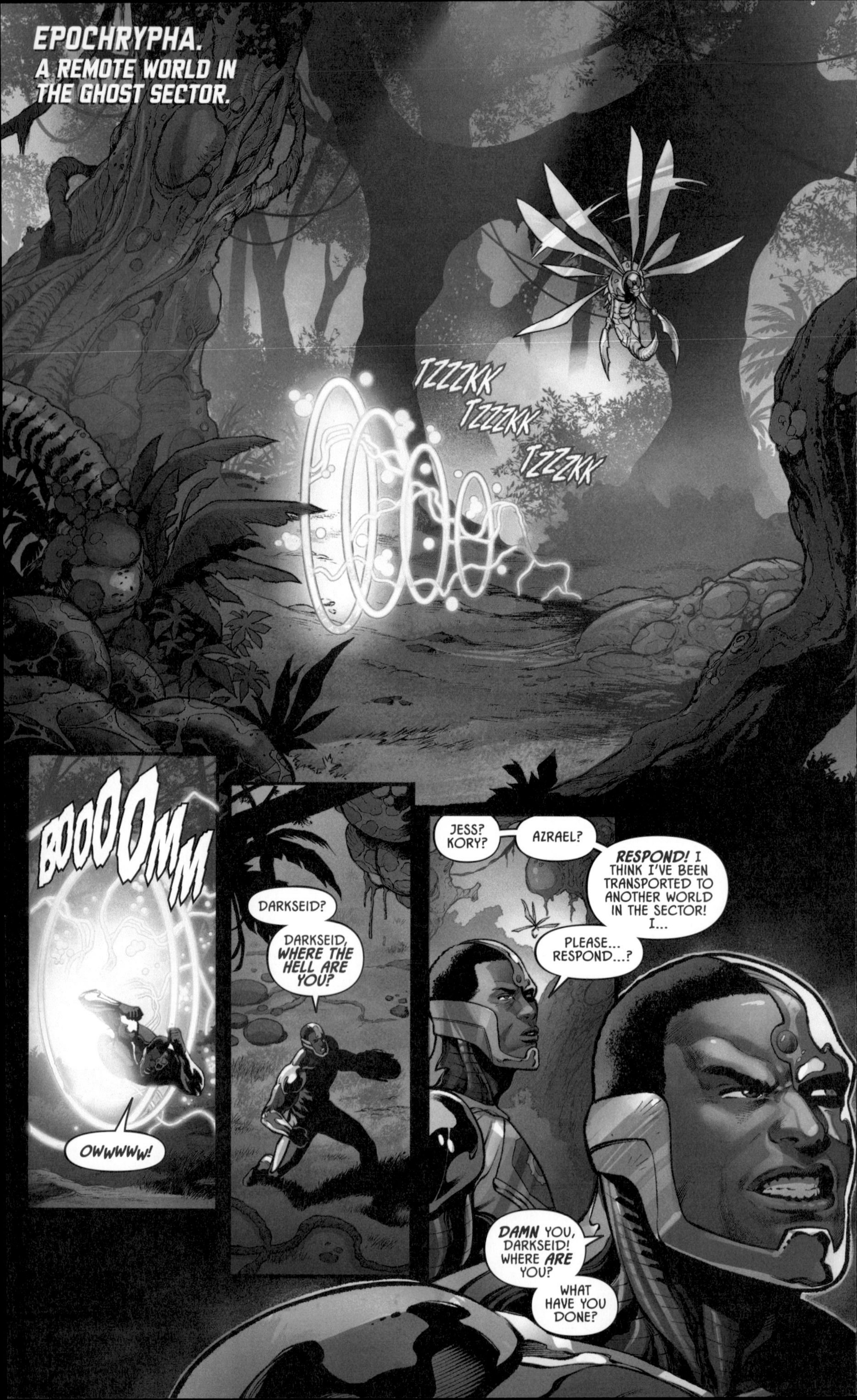
EPOCHRYPHA.
A REMOTE WORLD IN THE GHOST SECTOR.
TZZZKK
TZZZKK
TZZZKK
BOOOOMM
OWWWWW!
DARKSEID?
DARKSEID, WHERE THE HELL ARE YOU?
JESS? KORY?
AZRAEL?
RESPOND! I THINK I'VE BEEN TRANSPORTED TO ANOTHER WORLD IN THE SECTOR! I...
PLEASE... RESPOND...?
DAMN YOU, DARKSEID! WHERE ARE YOU?
WHAT HAVE YOU DONE?

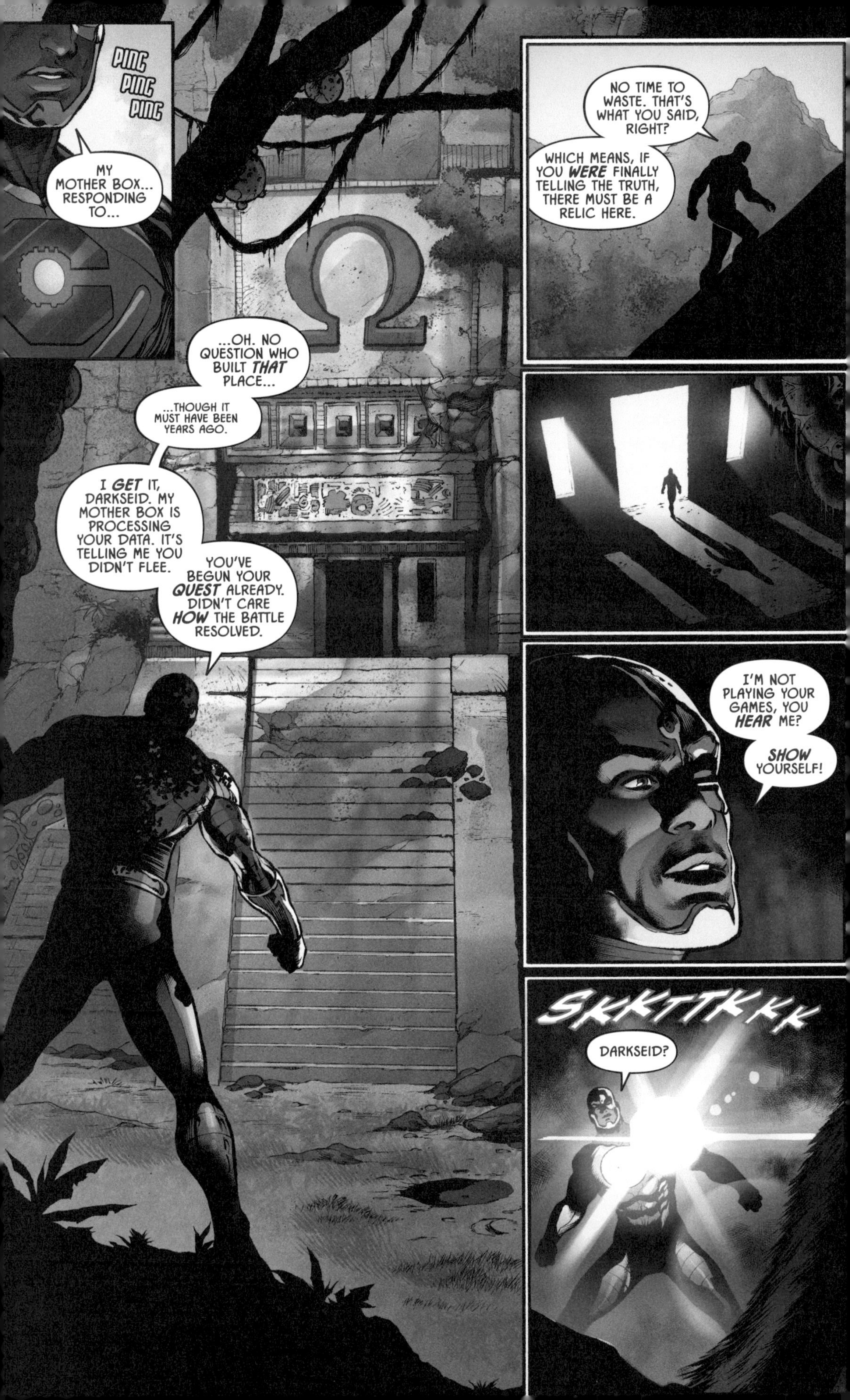
PING PING PING
MY MOTHER BOX... RESPONDING TO...
...OH. NO QUESTION WHO BUILT THAT PLACE...
...THOUGH IT MUST HAVE BEEN YEARS AGO.
I GET IT, DARKSEID. MY MOTHER BOX IS PROCESSING YOUR DATA. IT'S TELLING ME YOU DIDN'T FLEE.
YOU'VE BEGUN YOUR QUEST ALREADY. DIDN'T CARE HOW THE BATTLE RESOLVED.
NO TIME TO WASTE. THAT'S WHAT YOU SAID, RIGHT?
WHICH MEANS, IF YOU WERE FINALLY TELLING THE TRUTH, THERE MUST BE A RELIC HERE.
I'M NOT PLAYING YOUR GAMES, YOU HEAR ME?
SHOW YOURSELF!
SKKTTKKK
DARKSEID?

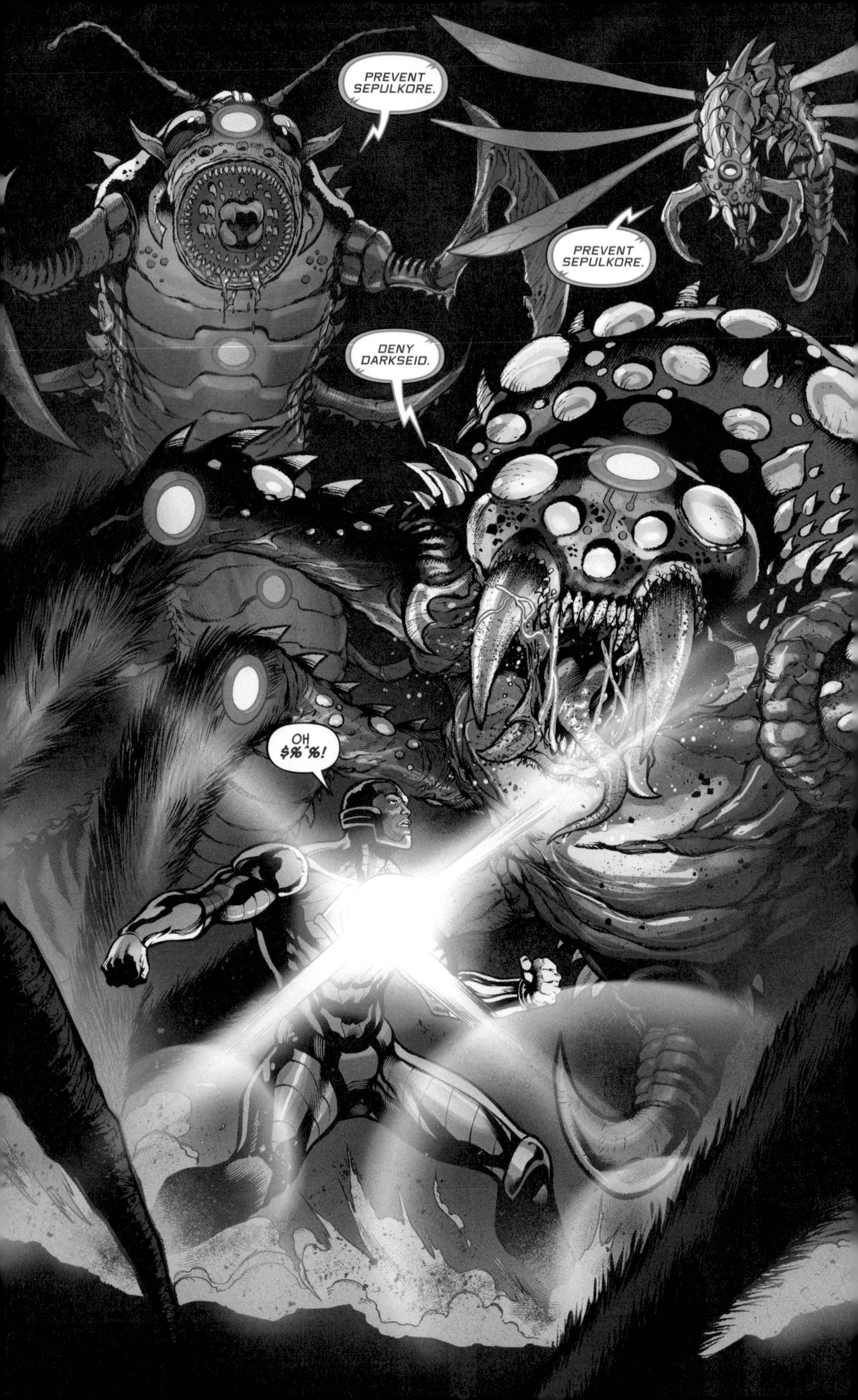
PREVENT SEPULKORE.
PREVENT SEPULKORE.
DENY DARKSEID.
OH $%^%!

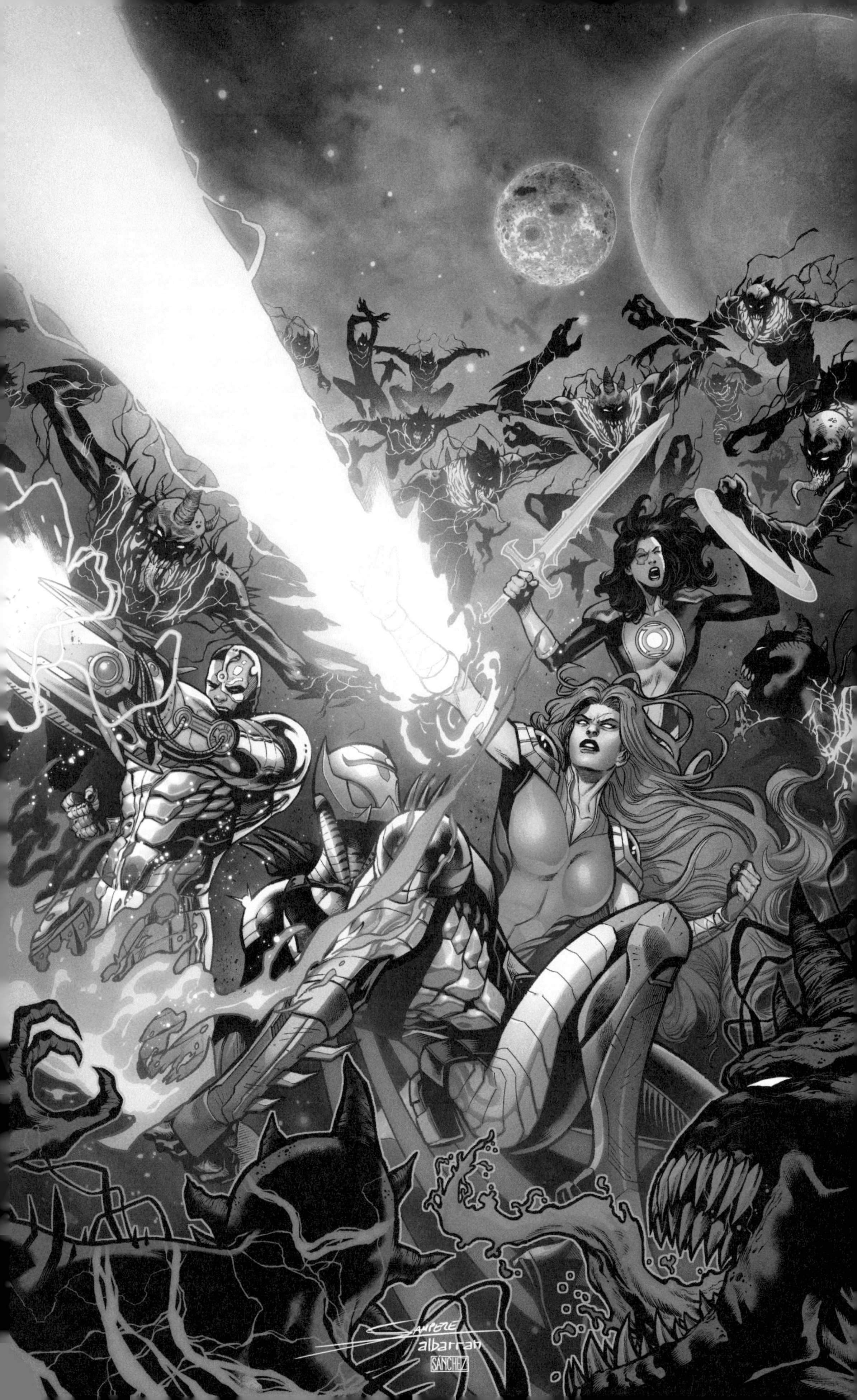
albarran
SÁNCHEZ

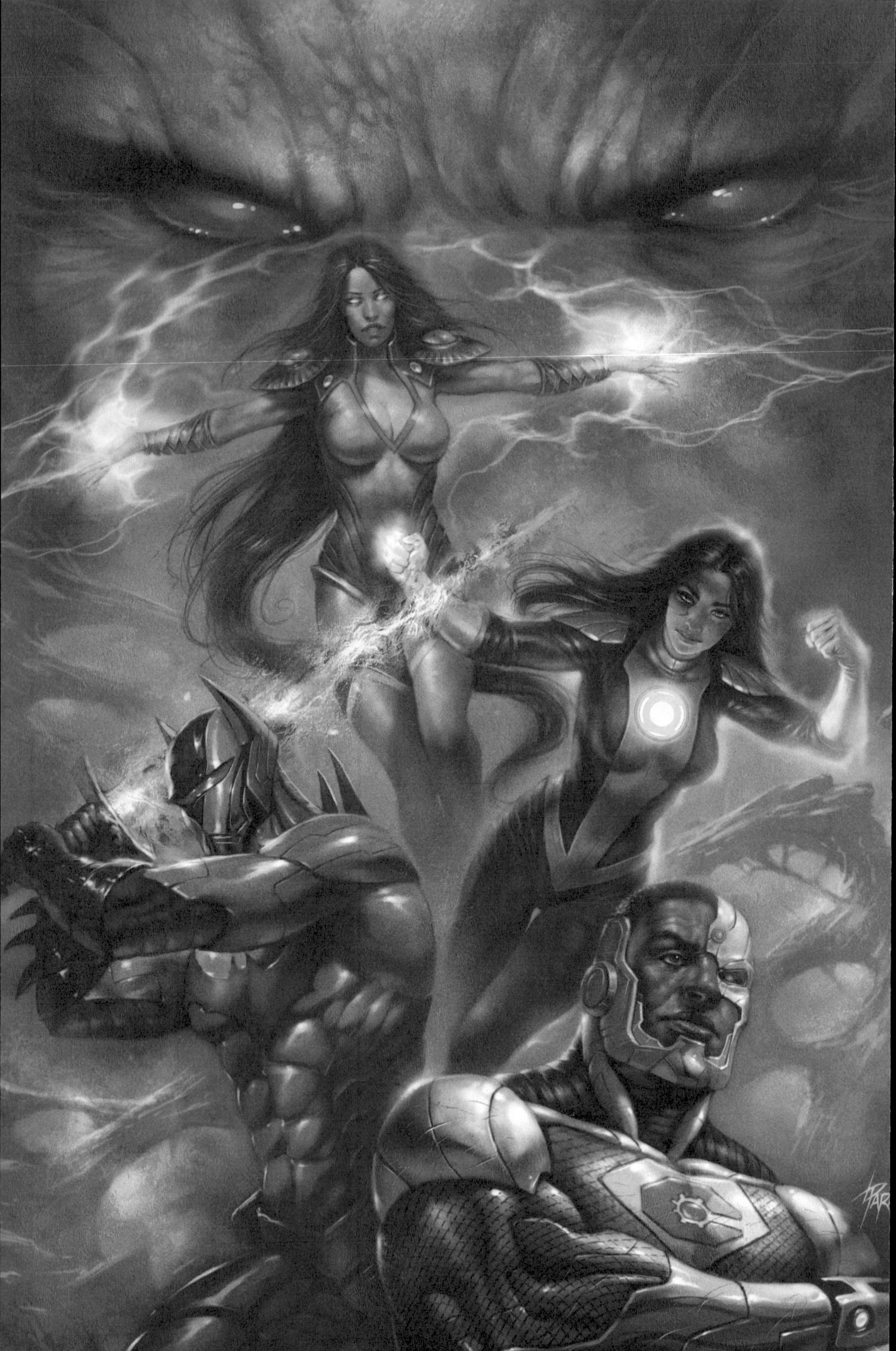

Variant cover art for issue #9 by LUCIO PARRILLO

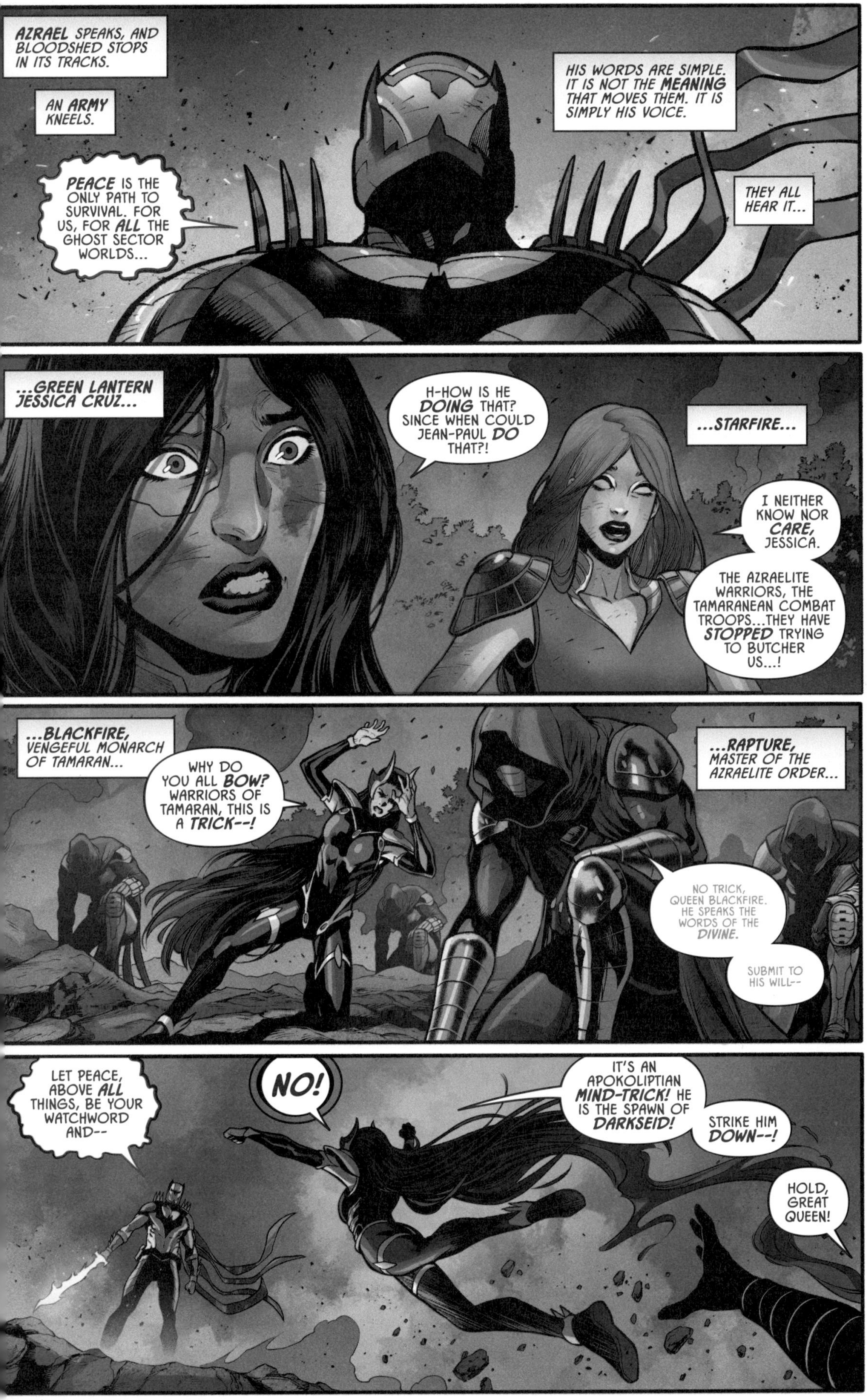
AZRAEL SPEAKS, AND BLOODSHED STOPS IN ITS TRACKS.
AN ARMY KNEELS.
HIS WORDS ARE SIMPLE. IT IS NOT THE MEANING THAT MOVES THEM. IT IS SIMPLY HIS VOICE.
PEACE IS THE ONLY PATH TO SURVIVAL. FOR US, FOR ALL THE GHOST SECTOR WORLDS...
THEY ALL HEAR IT...
...GREEN LANTERN JESSICA CRUZ...
H-HOW IS HE DOING THAT? SINCE WHEN COULD JEAN-PAUL DO THAT?!
...STARFIRE...
I NEITHER KNOW NOR CARE, JESSICA.
THE AZRAELITE WARRIORS, THE TAMARANEAN COMBAT TROOPS...THEY HAVE STOPPED TRYING TO BUTCHER US...!
...BLACKFIRE, VENGEFUL MONARCH OF TAMARAN...
WHY DO YOU ALL BOW? WARRIORS OF TAMARAN, THIS IS A TRICK--!
...RAPTURE, MASTER OF THE AZRAELITE ORDER...
NO TRICK, QUEEN BLACKFIRE. HE SPEAKS THE WORDS OF THE DIVINE.
SUBMIT TO HIS WILL--
LET PEACE, ABOVE ALL THINGS, BE YOUR WATCHWORD AND--
NO!
IT'S AN APOKOLIPTIAN MIND-TRICK! HE IS THE SPAWN OF DARKSEID!
STRIKE HIM DOWN--!
HOLD, GREAT QUEEN!

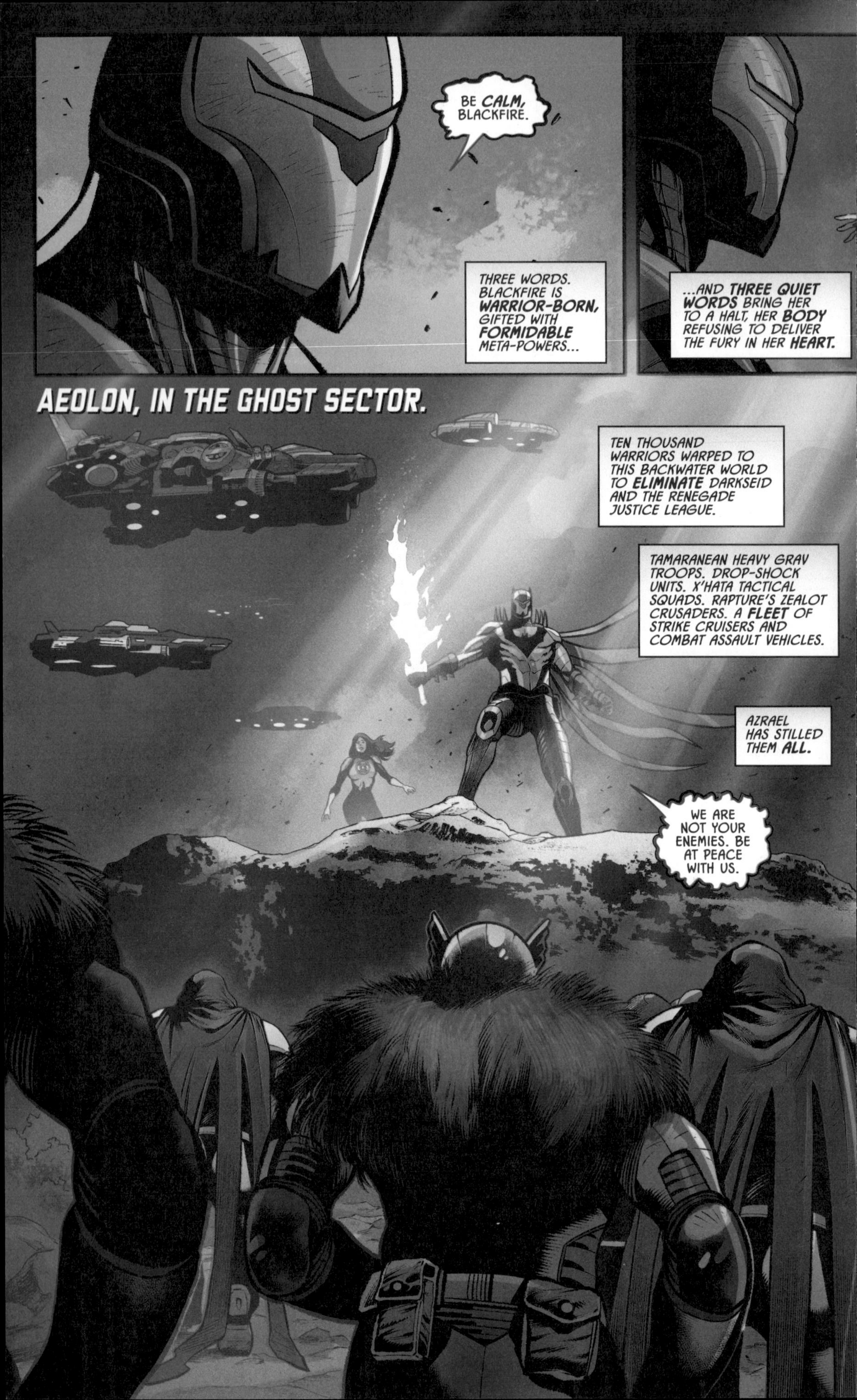
BE CALM, BLACKFIRE.
THREE WORDS. BLACKFIRE IS WARRIOR-BORN, GIFTED WITH FORMIDABLE META-POWERS...
...AND THREE QUIET WORDS BRING HER TO A HALT, HER BODY REFUSING TO DELIVER THE FURY IN HER HEART.
AEOLON, IN THE GHOST SECTOR.
TEN THOUSAND WARRIORS WARPED TO THIS BACKWATER WORLD TO ELIMINATE DARKSEID AND THE RENEGADE JUSTICE LEAGUE.
TAMARANEAN HEAVY GRAV TROOPS. DROP-SHOCK UNITS. X'HATA TACTICAL SQUADS. RAPTURE'S ZEALOT CRUSADERS. A FLEET OF STRIKE CRUISERS AND COMBAT ASSAULT VEHICLES.
AZRAEL HAS STILLED THEM ALL.
WE ARE NOT YOUR ENEMIES. BE AT PEACE WITH US.

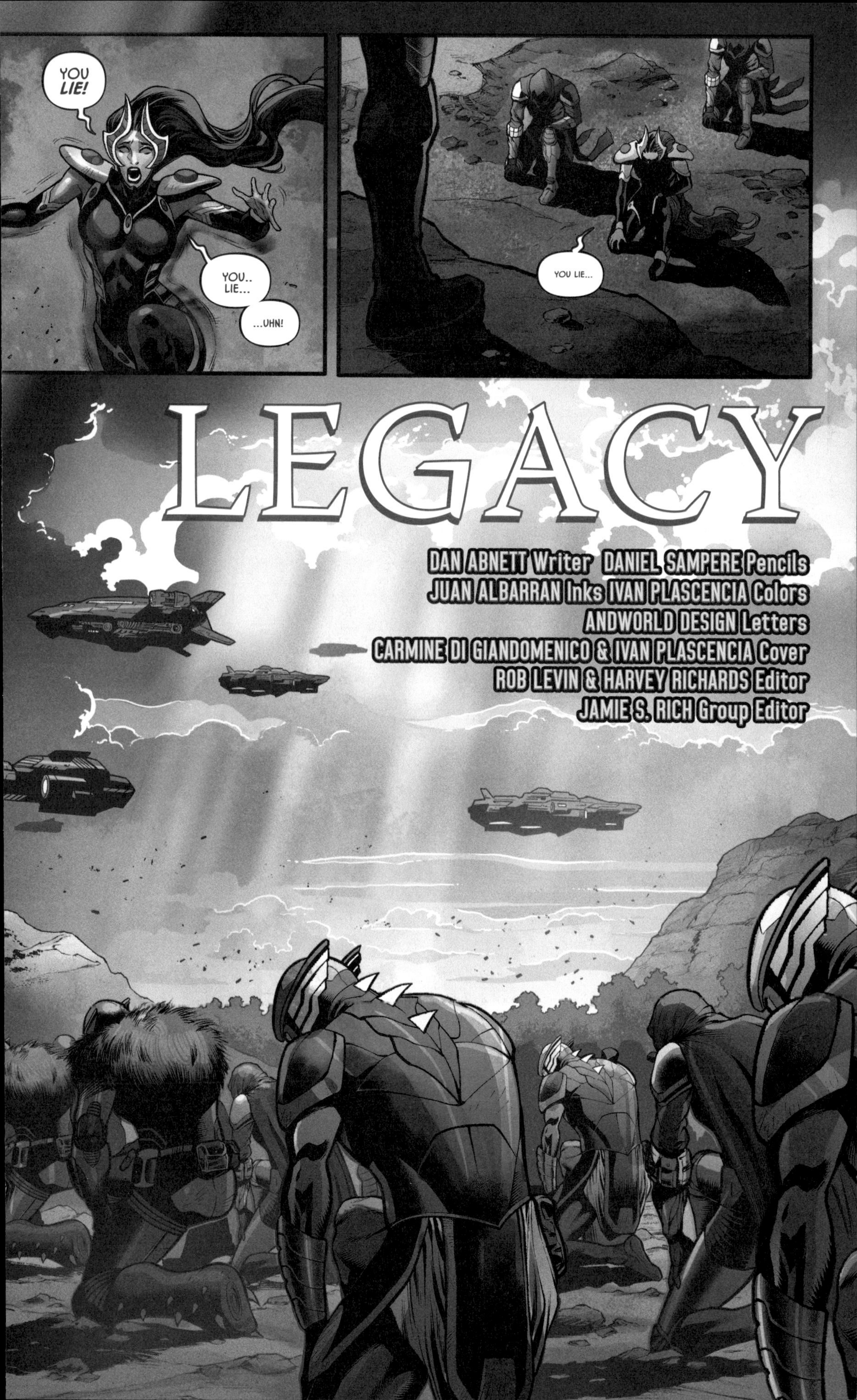
YOU LIE!
YOU.. LIE...
...UHN!
YOU LIE...
LEGACY
DAN ABNETT Writer DANIEL SAMPERE Pencils
JUAN ALBARRAN Inks IVAN PLASCENCIA Colors
ANDWORLD DESIGN Letters
CARMINE DI GIANDOMENICO & IVAN PLASCENCIA Cover
ROB LEVIN & HARVEY RICHARDS Editor
JAMIE S. RICH Group Editor

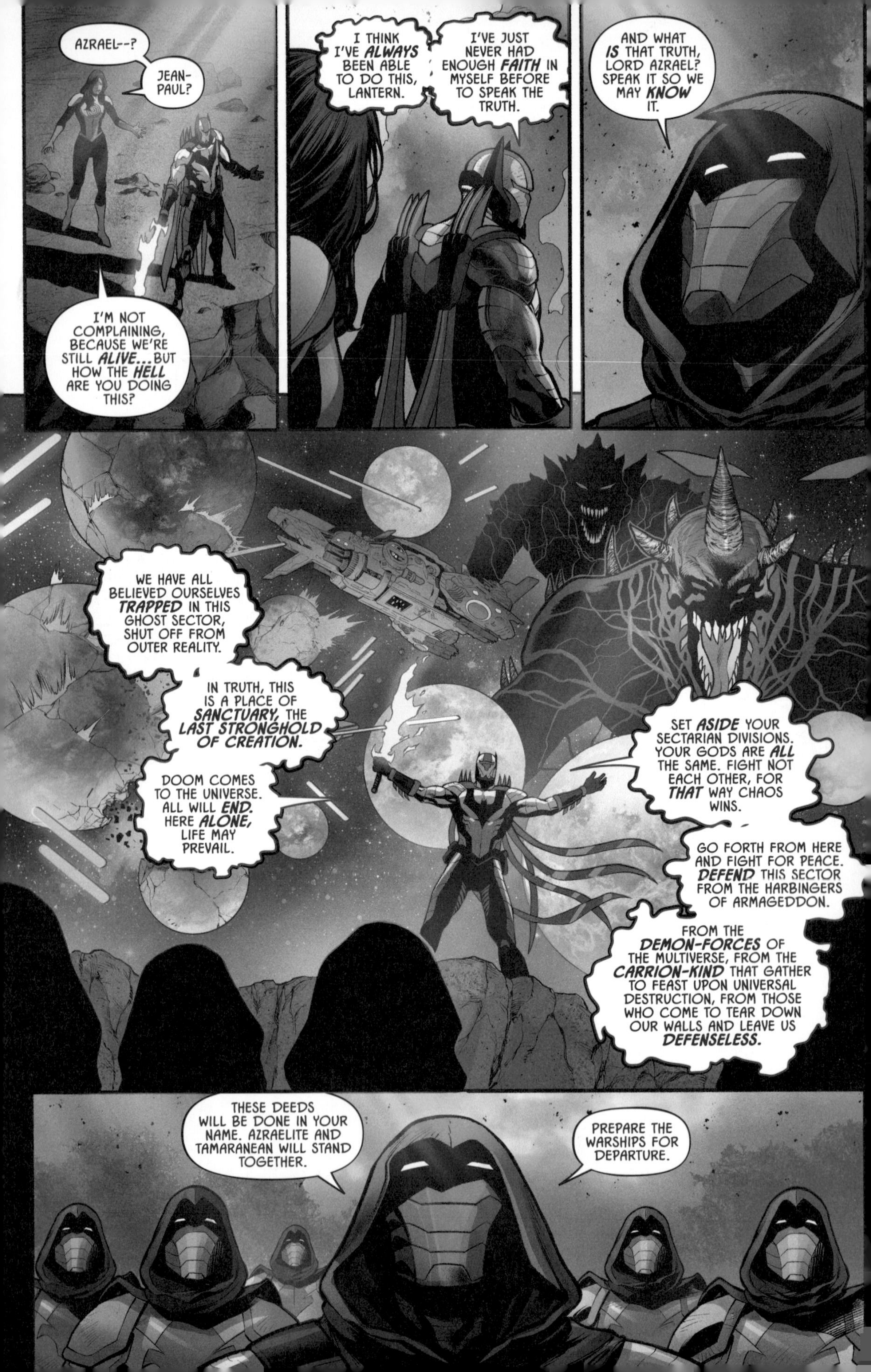
AZRAEL--?
JEAN-PAUL?
I'M NOT COMPLAINING, BECAUSE WE'RE STILL ALIVE... BUT HOW THE HELL ARE YOU DOING THIS?
I THINK I'VE ALWAYS BEEN ABLE TO DO THIS, LANTERN.
I'VE JUST NEVER HAD ENOUGH FAITH IN MYSELF BEFORE TO SPEAK THE TRUTH.
AND WHAT IS THAT TRUTH, LORD AZRAEL? SPEAK IT SO WE MAY KNOW IT.
WE HAVE ALL BELIEVED OURSELVES TRAPPED IN THIS GHOST SECTOR, SHUT OFF FROM OUTER REALITY.
IN TRUTH, THIS IS A PLACE OF SANCTUARY, THE LAST STRONGHOLD OF CREATION.
DOOM COMES TO THE UNIVERSE. ALL WILL END. HERE ALONE, LIFE MAY PREVAIL.
SET ASIDE YOUR SECTARIAN DIVISIONS. YOUR GODS ARE ALL THE SAME. FIGHT NOT EACH OTHER, FOR THAT WAY CHAOS WINS.
GO FORTH FROM HERE AND FIGHT FOR PEACE. DEFEND THIS SECTOR FROM THE HARBINGERS OF ARMAGEDDON.
FROM THE DEMON-FORCES OF THE MULTIVERSE, FROM THE CARRION-KIND THAT GATHER TO FEAST UPON UNIVERSAL DESTRUCTION, FROM THOSE WHO COME TO TEAR DOWN OUR WALLS AND LEAVE US DEFENSELESS.
THESE DEEDS WILL BE DONE IN YOUR NAME. AZRAELITE AND TAMARANEAN WILL STAND TOGETHER.
PREPARE THE WARSHIPS FOR DEPARTURE.

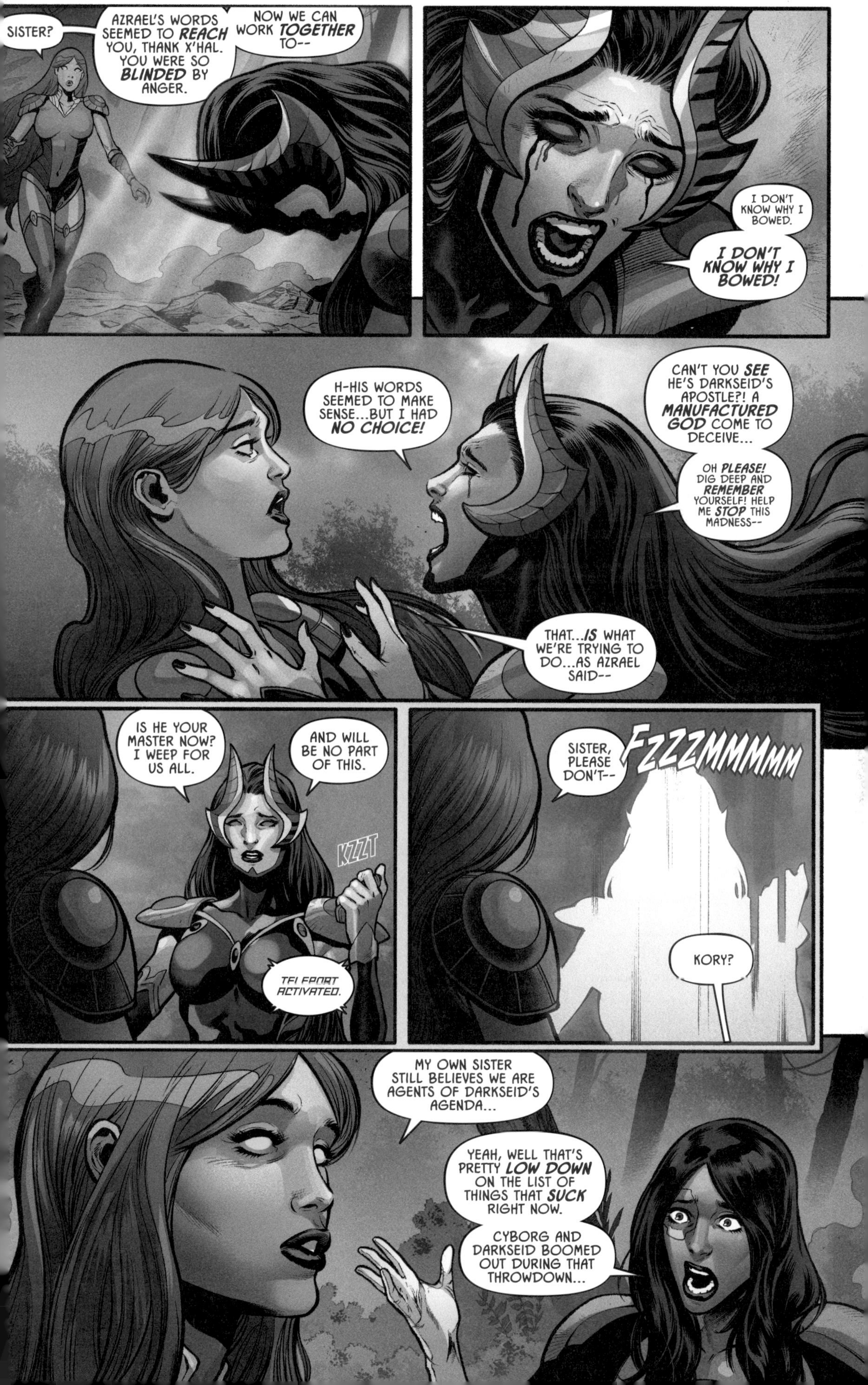
SISTER?
AZRAEL'S WORDS SEEMED TO REACH YOU, THANK X'HAL. YOU WERE SO BLINDED BY ANGER.
NOW WE CAN WORK TOGETHER TO--
I DON'T KNOW WHY I BOWED.
I DON'T KNOW WHY I BOWED!
H-HIS WORDS SEEMED TO MAKE SENSE...BUT I HAD NO CHOICE!
CAN'T YOU SEE HE'S DARKSEID'S APOSTLE?! A MANUFACTURED GOD COME TO DECEIVE...
OH PLEASE! DIG DEEP AND REMEMBER YOURSELF! HELP ME STOP THIS MADNESS--
THAT...IS WHAT WE'RE TRYING TO DO...AS AZRAEL SAID--
IS HE YOUR MASTER NOW? I WEEP FOR US ALL.
AND WILL BE NO PART OF THIS.
KZZT
TELEPORT ACTIVATED.
SISTER, PLEASE DON'T--
FZZZMMMMM
KORY?
MY OWN SISTER STILL BELIEVES WE ARE AGENTS OF DARKSEID'S AGENDA...
YEAH, WELL THAT'S PRETTY LOW DOWN ON THE LIST OF THINGS THAT SUCK RIGHT NOW.
CYBORG AND DARKSEID BOOMED OUT DURING THAT THROWDOWN...

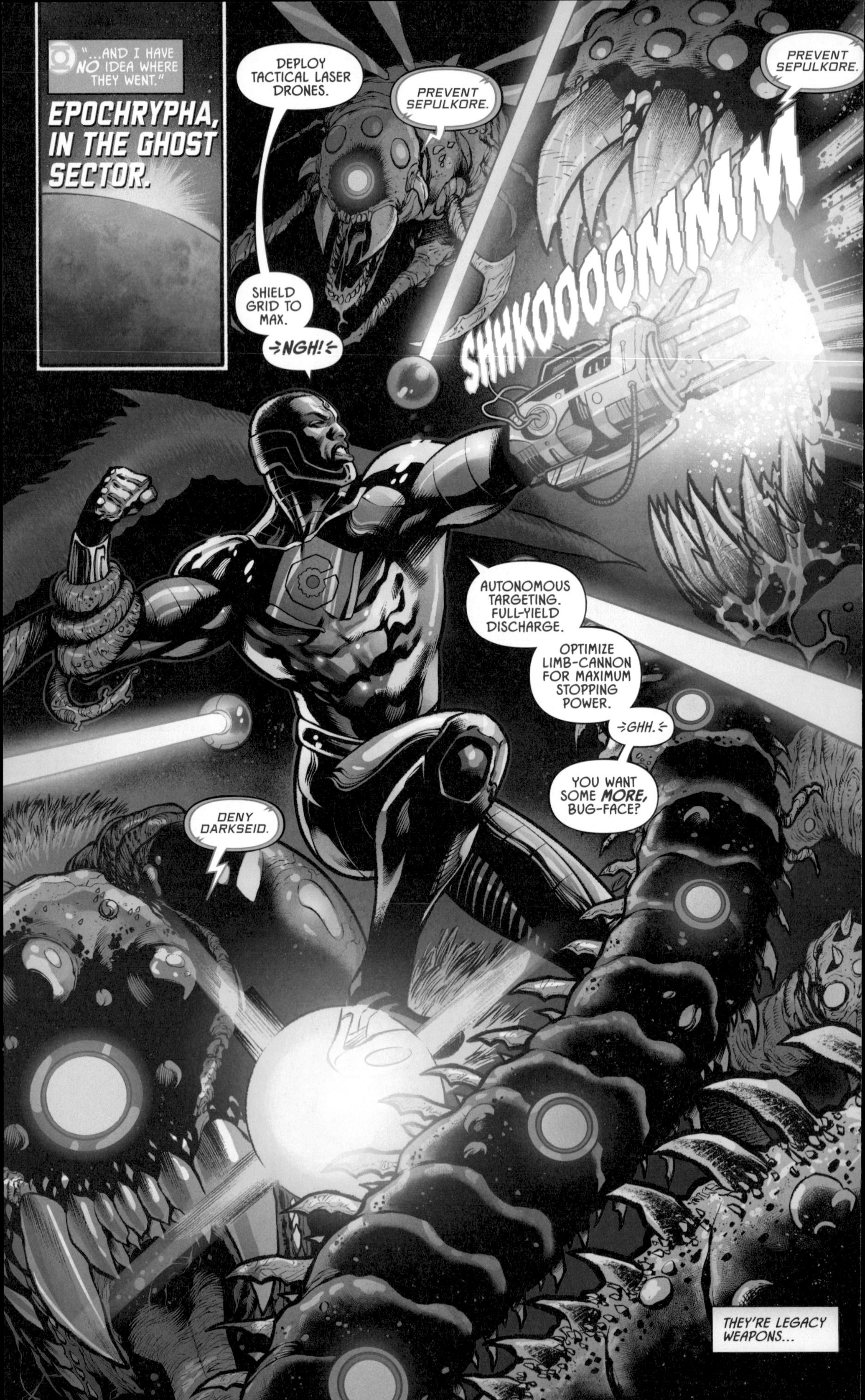
"...AND I HAVE NO IDEA WHERE THEY WENT."
EPOCHRYPHA, IN THE GHOST SECTOR.
DEPLOY TACTICAL LASER DRONES.
PREVENT SEPULKORE.
PREVENT SEPULKORE.
SHIELD GRID TO MAX.
NGH!
SHHKOOOOMMM
AUTONOMOUS TARGETING. FULL-YIELD DISCHARGE.
OPTIMIZE LIMB-CANNON FOR MAXIMUM STOPPING POWER.
GHH.
YOU WANT SOME MORE, BUG-FACE?
DENY DARKSEID.
THEY'RE LEGACY WEAPONS...

...ANCIENT DEVICES SEEDED BY BRAINIAC WHEN HE FIRST STOLE THESE WORLDS.
ANCIENT SNARES.
ACTIVATED, THEY CO-OPT INDIGENOUS BIOLOGICAL FORMS AND CONVERT THEM INTO WEAPONS...
PREVENT SEPULKORE.
DENY DARKSEID.
PREVENT SEPULKORE.
RUNNCHHH
...TO STOP ANY INTRUDER FROM COMPLETING DARKSEID'S SCHEME.
DENY DARKSEID.
YEAH, YOU SAID THAT!
PING PING
MOTHER BOX! LOCATE DARKSEID NOW!
PING
I KNOW THE NEXT RELIC IS CLOSE BY, MOTHER BOX! THAT'S WHY THESE FREAKS ARE KICKING OFF!
PREVENT SEPULKORE.
DENY DARKSEID.
JUST TELL ME... HAS DARKSEID DUMPED ME HERE TO HANDLE THIS ON MY OWN?
PREVENT SEPULKORE.
BECAUSE THAT'S NOT GOING WELL RIGHT NOW--
GNNHH!
DENY DARKSEID.
MMHHNNN---!

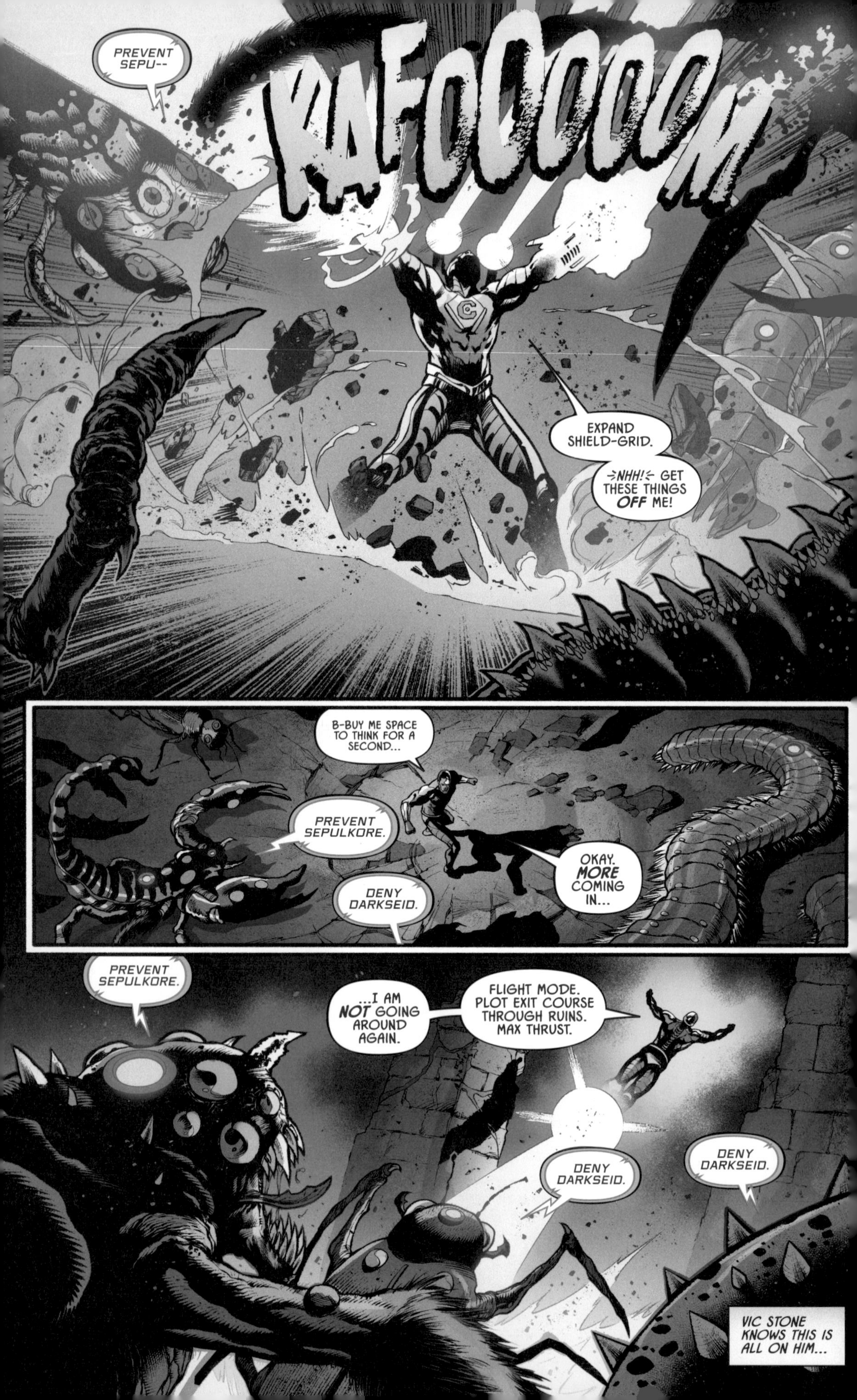
PREVENT SEPU--
KAFOOOOOM
EXPAND SHIELD-GRID.
NHH! GET THESE THINGS OFF ME!
B-BUY ME SPACE TO THINK FOR A SECOND...
PREVENT SEPULKORE.
OKAY. MORE COMING IN...
DENY DARKSEID.
PREVENT SEPULKORE.
...I AM NOT GOING AROUND AGAIN.
FLIGHT MODE. PLOT EXIT COURSE THROUGH RUINS. MAX THRUST.
DENY DARKSEID.
DENY DARKSEID.
VIC STONE KNOWS THIS IS ALL ON HIM...

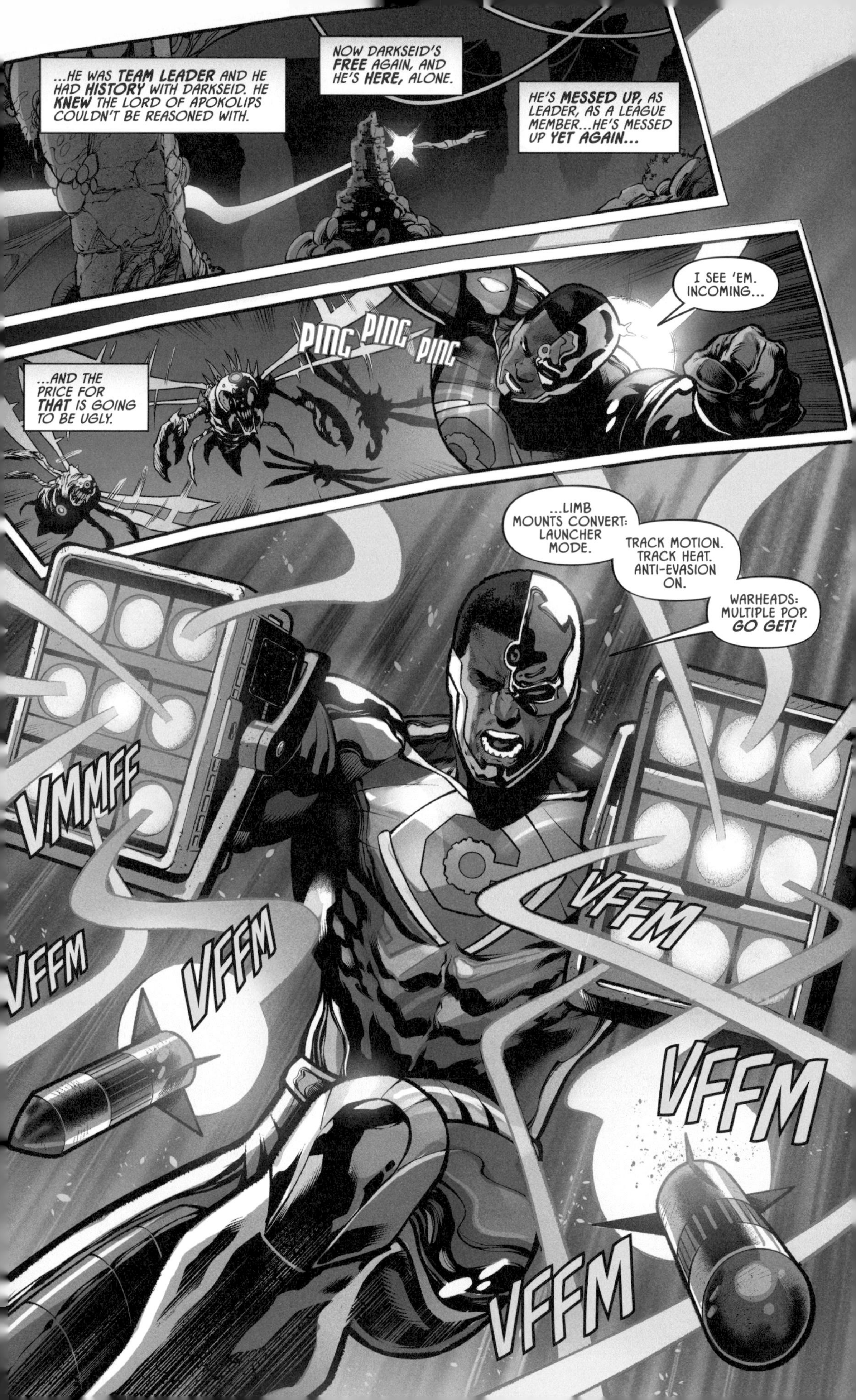
...HE WAS TEAM LEADER AND HE HAD HISTORY WITH DARKSEID. HE KNEW THE LORD OF APOKOLIPS COULDN'T BE REASONED WITH.
NOW DARKSEID'S FREE AGAIN, AND HE'S HERE, ALONE.
HE'S MESSED UP, AS LEADER, AS A LEAGUE MEMBER...HE'S MESSED UP YET AGAIN...
PING PING PING
I SEE 'EM. INCOMING...
...AND THE PRICE FOR THAT IS GOING TO BE UGLY.
...LIMB MOUNTS CONVERT: LAUNCHER MODE.
TRACK MOTION. TRACK HEAT. ANTI-EVASION ON.
WARHEADS: MULTIPLE POP. GO GET!
VMMFF
VFFM
VFFM
VFFM
VFFM
VFFM

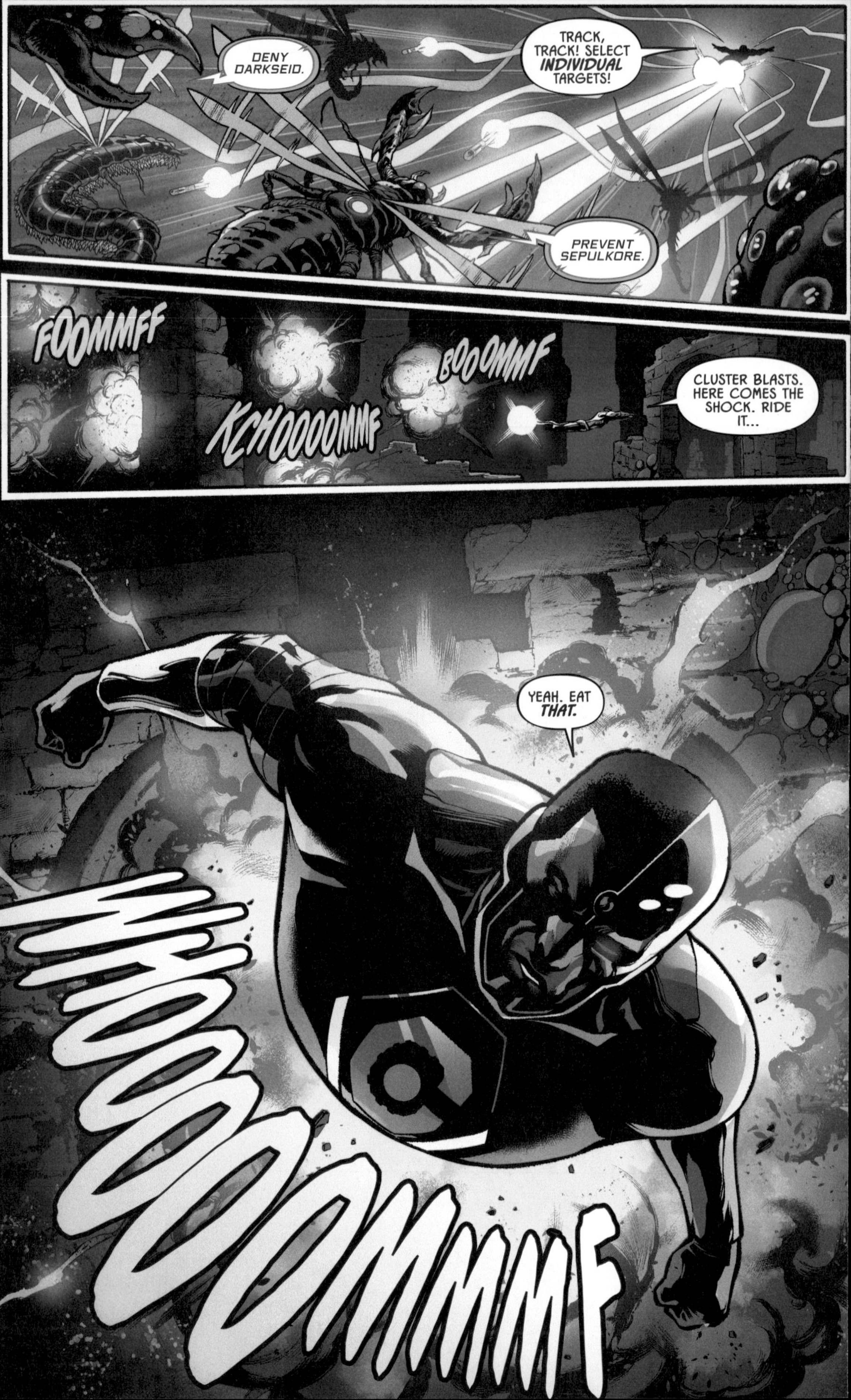

DENY DARKSEID.
TRACK, TRACK! SELECT INDIVIDUAL TARGETS!
PREVENT SEPULKORE.
FOOMMFF
KCHOOOOOMMF
BOOOMMF
CLUSTER BLASTS. HERE COMES THE SHOCK. RIDE IT...
YEAH. EAT THAT.
WHOOOOOOOMMMF

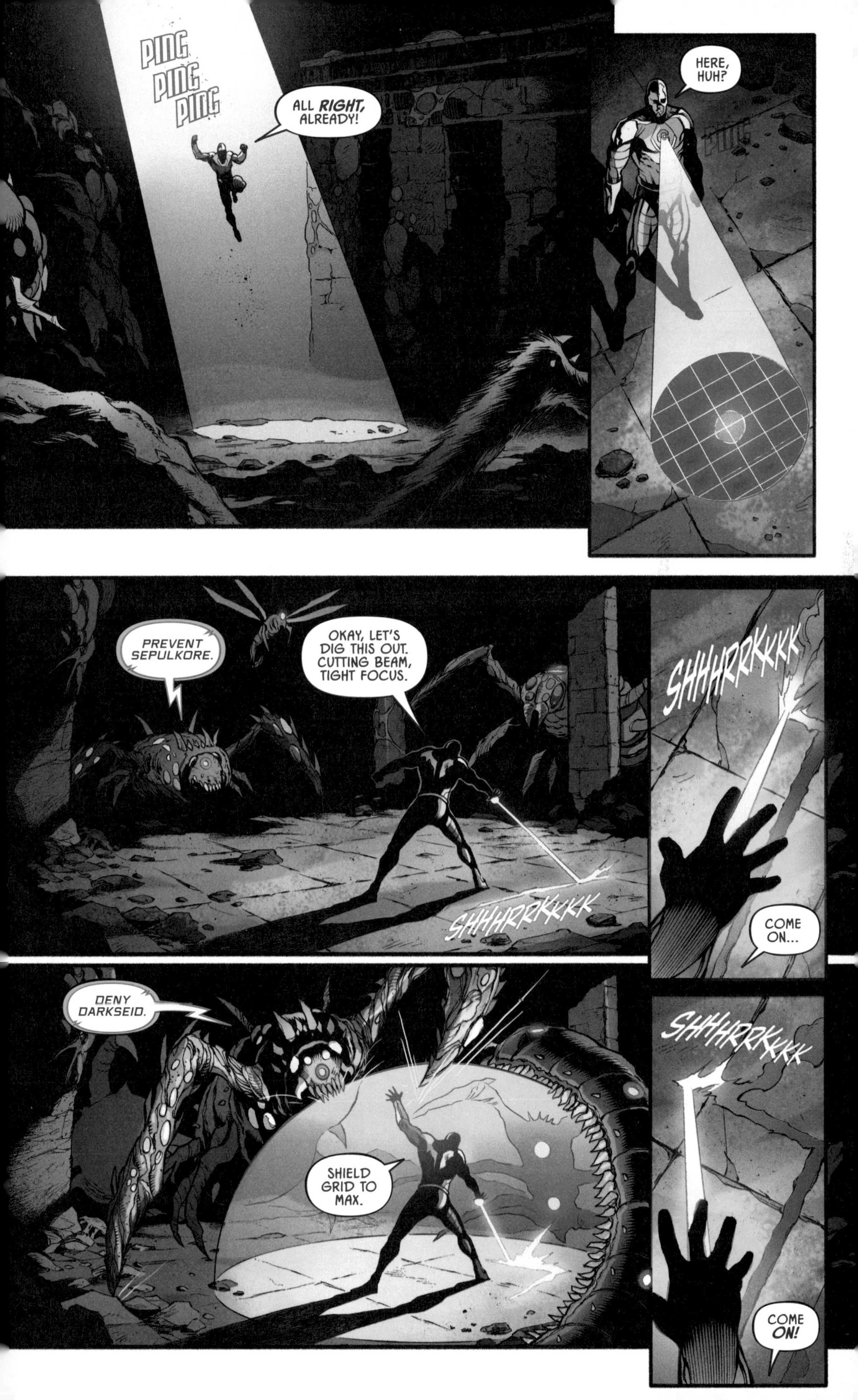
PING
PING
PING
ALL RIGHT, ALREADY!
HERE, HUH?
PING
PREVENT SEPULKORE.
OKAY, LET'S DIG THIS OUT. CUTTING BEAM, TIGHT FOCUS.
SHHHRRKKKK
SHHHRRKKKK
COME ON...
DENY DARKSEID.
SHIELD GRID TO MAX.
SHHHRRKKKK
COME ON!

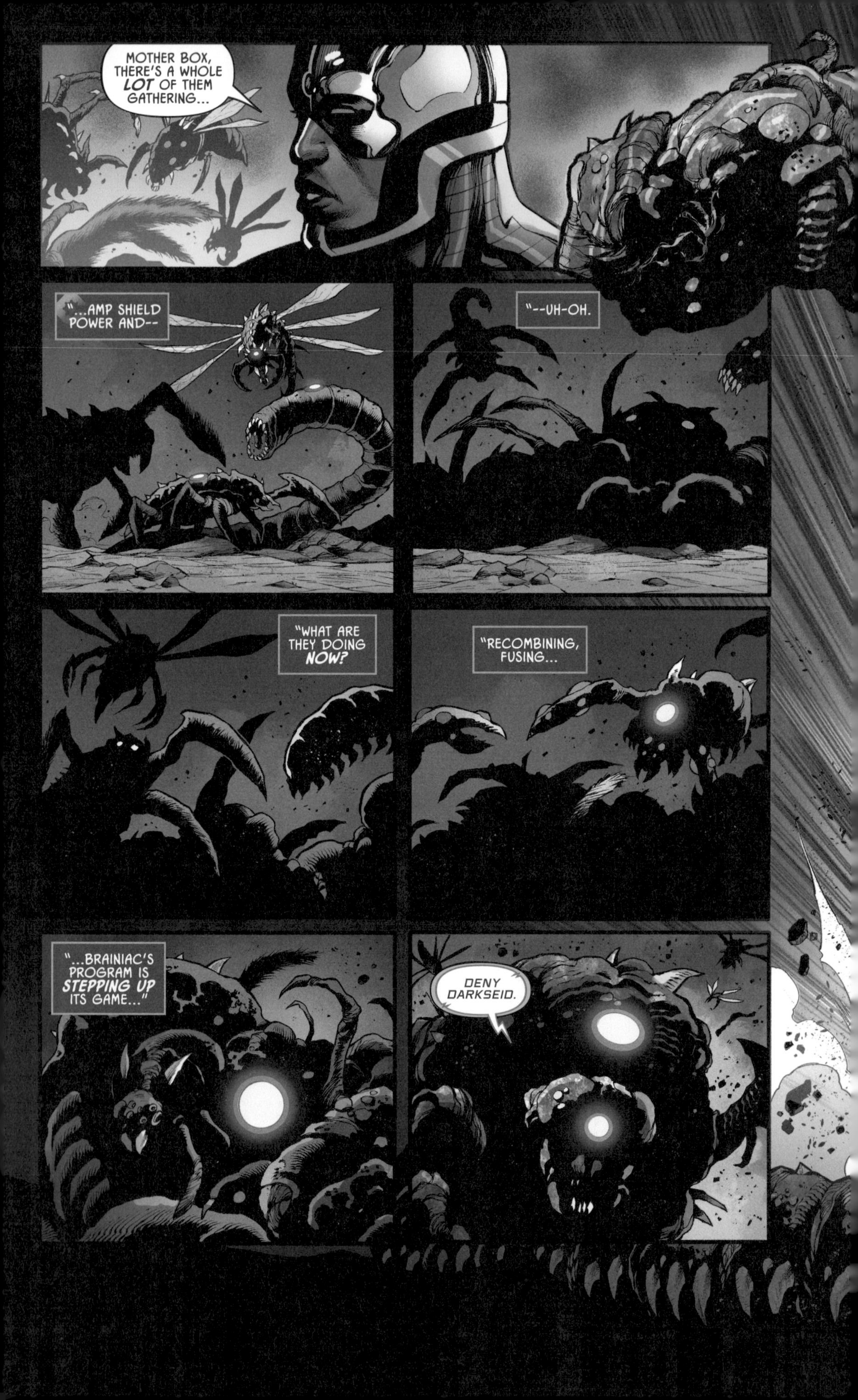
MOTHER BOX, THERE'S A WHOLE LOT OF THEM GATHERING...
"...AMP SHIELD POWER AND--
"--UH-OH.
"WHAT ARE THEY DOING NOW?
"RECOMBINING, FUSING...
"...BRAINIAC'S PROGRAM IS STEPPING UP ITS GAME..."
DENY DARKSEID.

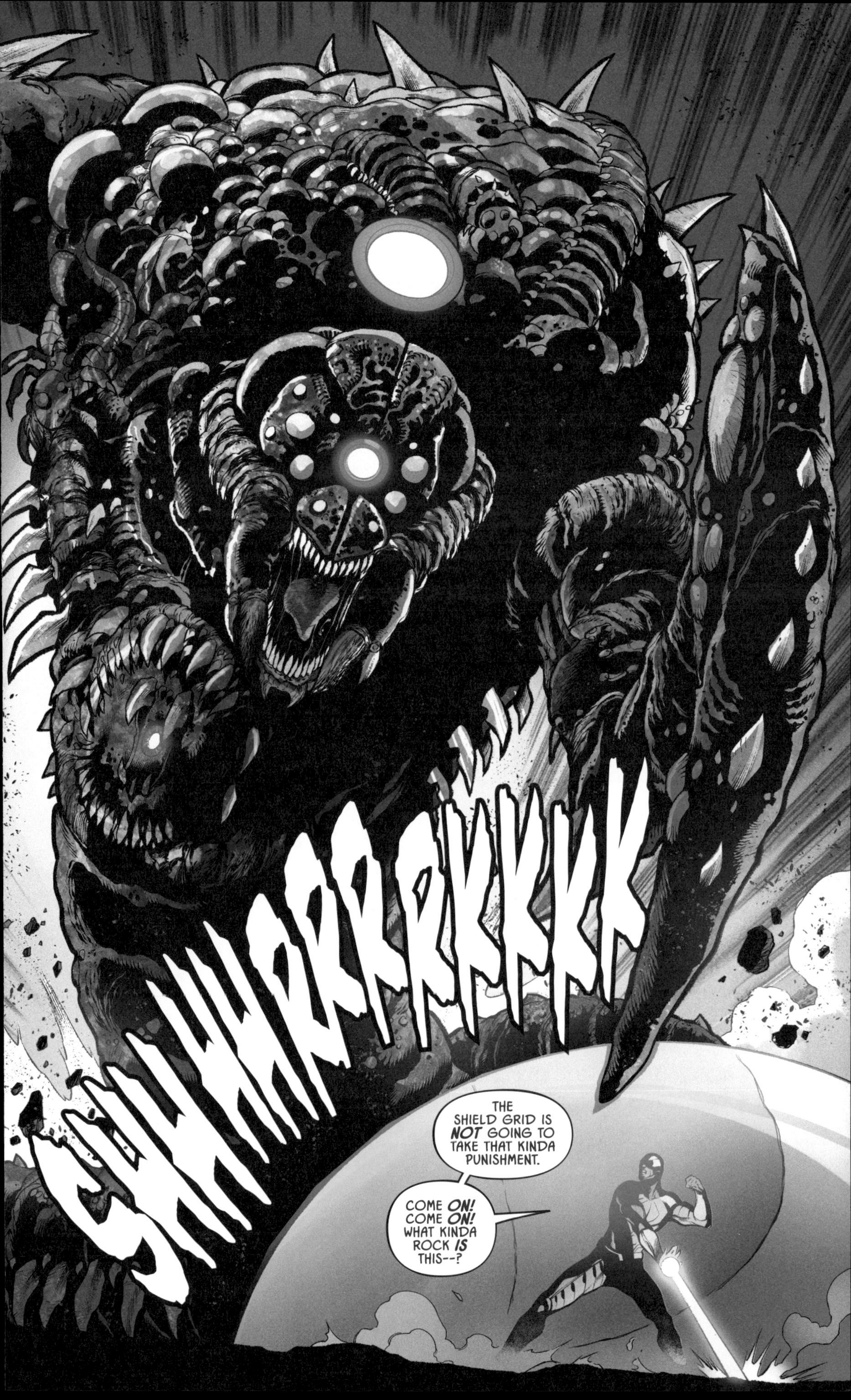
SHHHRRRRKKKKK
THE SHIELD GRID IS NOT GOING TO TAKE THAT KINDA PUNISHMENT.
COME ON! COME ON! WHAT KINDA ROCK IS THIS--?

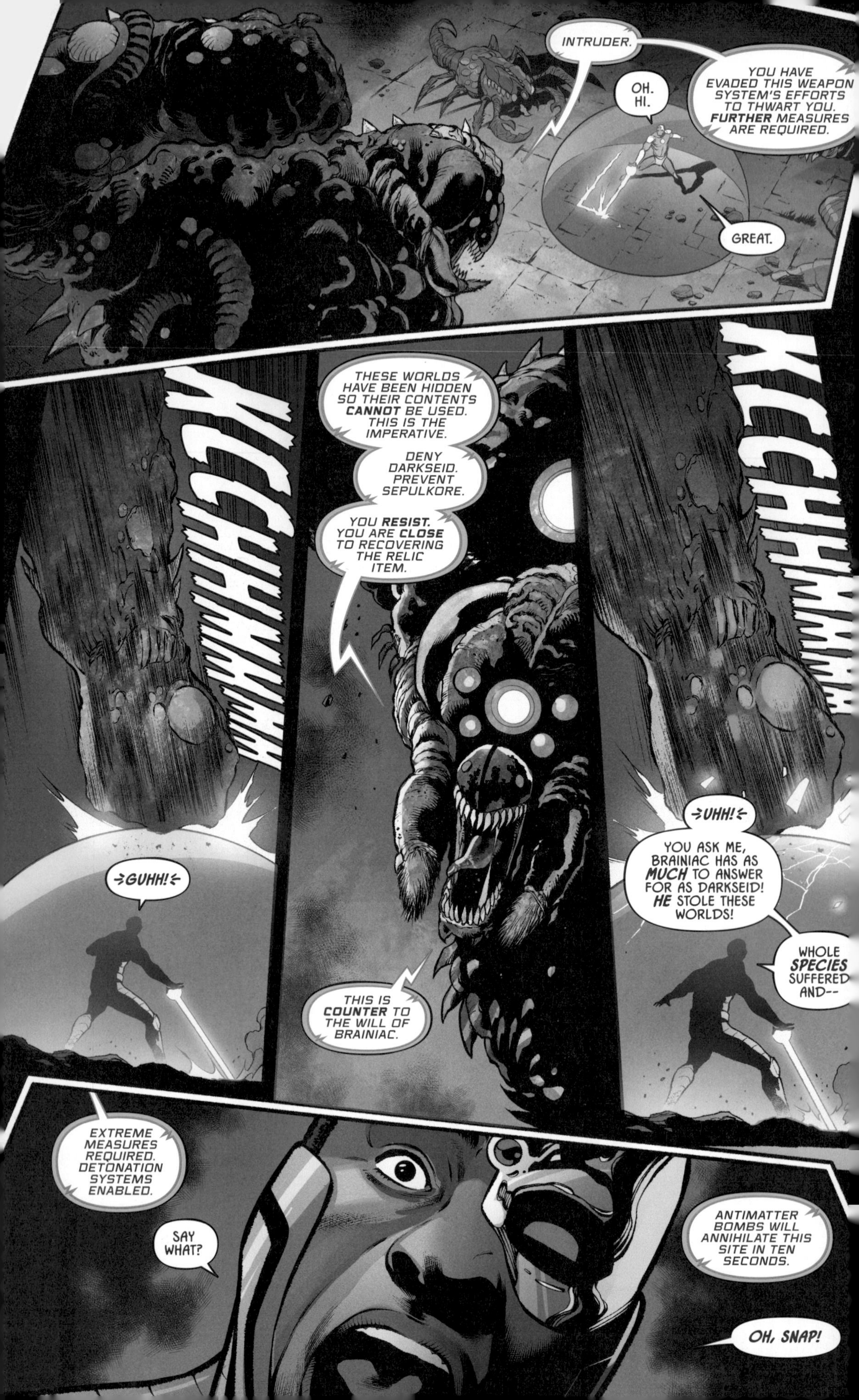

INTRUDER.
OH. HI.
YOU HAVE EVADED THIS WEAPON SYSTEM'S EFFORTS TO THWART YOU. FURTHER MEASURES ARE REQUIRED.
GREAT.
XCHHHHHH
THESE WORLDS HAVE BEEN HIDDEN SO THEIR CONTENTS CANNOT BE USED. THIS IS THE IMPERATIVE.
DENY DARKSEID. PREVENT SEPULKORE.
YOU RESIST. YOU ARE CLOSE TO RECOVERING THE RELIC ITEM.
THIS IS COUNTER TO THE WILL OF BRAINIAC.
GUHH!
XCHHHHHH
UHH!
YOU ASK ME, BRAINIAC HAS AS MUCH TO ANSWER FOR AS DARKSEID! HE STOLE THESE WORLDS!
WHOLE SPECIES SUFFERED AND--
EXTREME MEASURES REQUIRED. DETONATION SYSTEMS ENABLED.
SAY WHAT?
ANTIMATTER BOMBS WILL ANNIHILATE THIS SITE IN TEN SECONDS.
OH, SNAP!

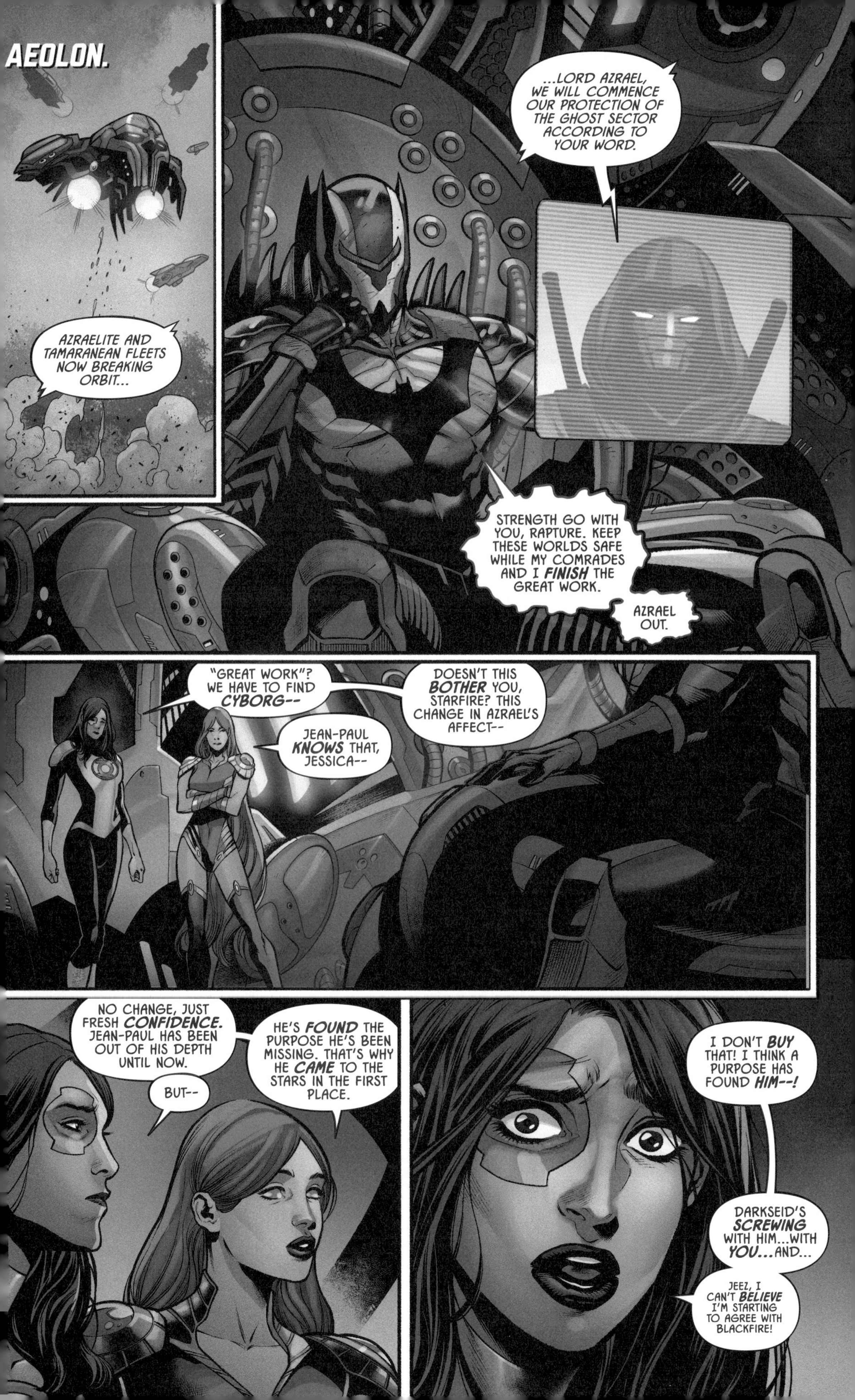
AEOLON.
AZRAELITE AND TAMARANEAN FLEETS NOW BREAKING ORBIT...
...LORD AZRAEL, WE WILL COMMENCE OUR PROTECTION OF THE GHOST SECTOR ACCORDING TO YOUR WORD.
STRENGTH GO WITH YOU, RAPTURE. KEEP THESE WORLDS SAFE WHILE MY COMRADES AND I FINISH THE GREAT WORK.
AZRAEL OUT.
"GREAT WORK"? WE HAVE TO FIND CYBORG--
JEAN-PAUL KNOWS THAT, JESSICA--
DOESN'T THIS BOTHER YOU, STARFIRE? THIS CHANGE IN AZRAEL'S AFFECT--
NO CHANGE, JUST FRESH CONFIDENCE. JEAN-PAUL HAS BEEN OUT OF HIS DEPTH UNTIL NOW.
BUT--
HE'S FOUND THE PURPOSE HE'S BEEN MISSING. THAT'S WHY HE CAME TO THE STARS IN THE FIRST PLACE.
I DON'T BUY THAT! I THINK A PURPOSE HAS FOUND HIM--!
DARKSEID'S SCREWING WITH HIM...WITH YOU...AND...
JEEZ, I CAN'T BELIEVE I'M STARTING TO AGREE WITH BLACKFIRE!

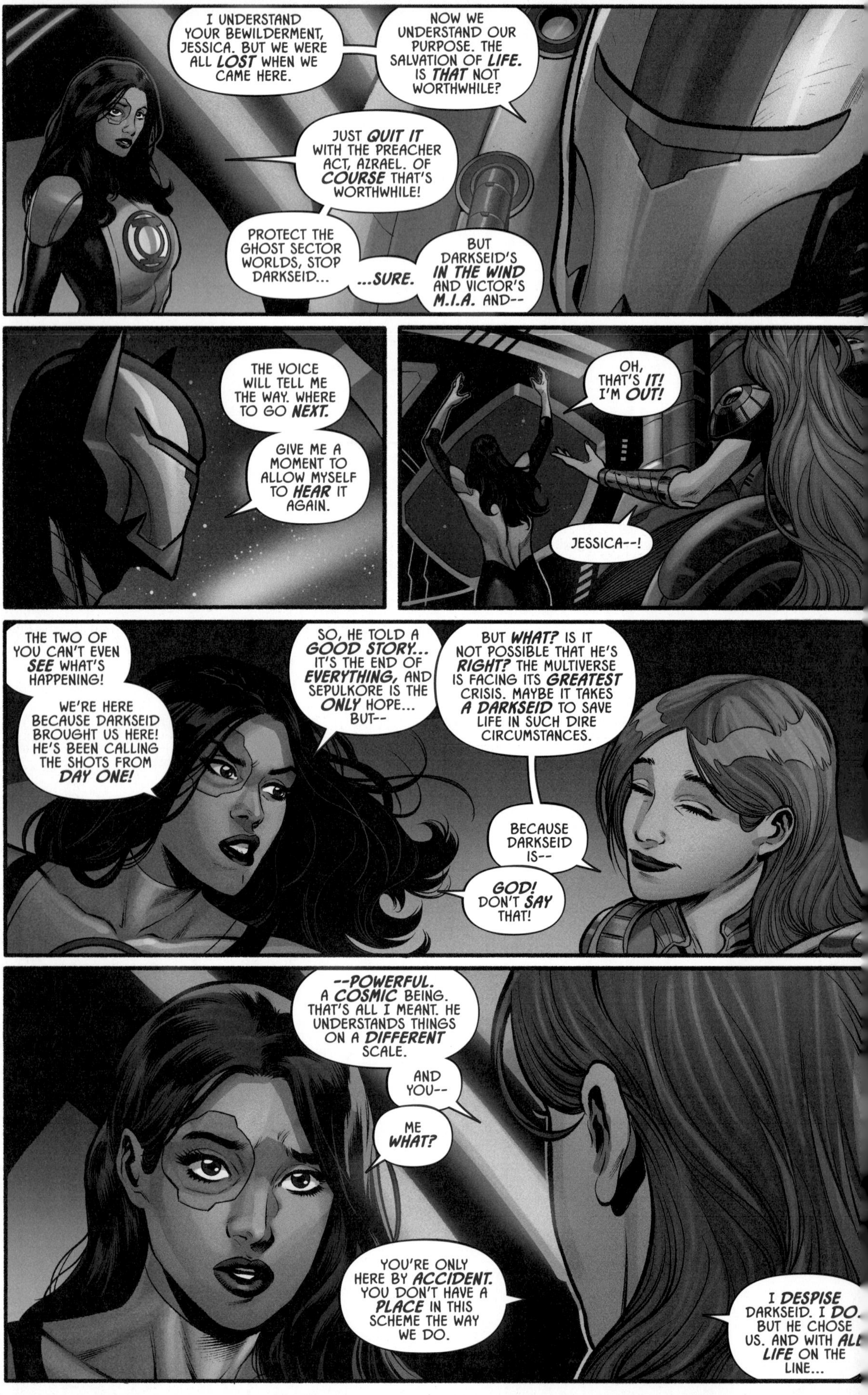
I UNDERSTAND YOUR BEWILDERMENT, JESSICA. BUT WE WERE ALL LOST WHEN WE CAME HERE.
NOW WE UNDERSTAND OUR PURPOSE. THE SALVATION OF LIFE. IS THAT NOT WORTHWHILE?
JUST QUIT IT WITH THE PREACHER ACT, AZRAEL. OF COURSE THAT'S WORTHWHILE!
PROTECT THE GHOST SECTOR WORLDS, STOP DARKSEID...
...SURE.
BUT DARKSEID'S IN THE WIND AND VICTOR'S M.I.A. AND--
THE VOICE WILL TELL ME THE WAY. WHERE TO GO NEXT.
GIVE ME A MOMENT TO ALLOW MYSELF TO HEAR IT AGAIN.
OH, THAT'S IT! I'M OUT!
JESSICA--!
THE TWO OF YOU CAN'T EVEN SEE WHAT'S HAPPENING!
WE'RE HERE BECAUSE DARKSEID BROUGHT US HERE! HE'S BEEN CALLING THE SHOTS FROM DAY ONE!
SO, HE TOLD A GOOD STORY... IT'S THE END OF EVERYTHING, AND SEPULKORE IS THE ONLY HOPE... BUT--
BUT WHAT? IS IT NOT POSSIBLE THAT HE'S RIGHT? THE MULTIVERSE IS FACING ITS GREATEST CRISIS. MAYBE IT TAKES A DARKSEID TO SAVE LIFE IN SUCH DIRE CIRCUMSTANCES.
BECAUSE DARKSEID IS--
GOD! DON'T SAY THAT!
--POWERFUL. A COSMIC BEING. THAT'S ALL I MEANT. HE UNDERSTANDS THINGS ON A DIFFERENT SCALE.
AND YOU--
ME WHAT?
YOU'RE ONLY HERE BY ACCIDENT. YOU DON'T HAVE A PLACE IN THIS SCHEME THE WAY WE DO.
I DESPISE DARKSEID. I DO. BUT HE CHOSE US. AND WITH ALL LIFE ON THE LINE...

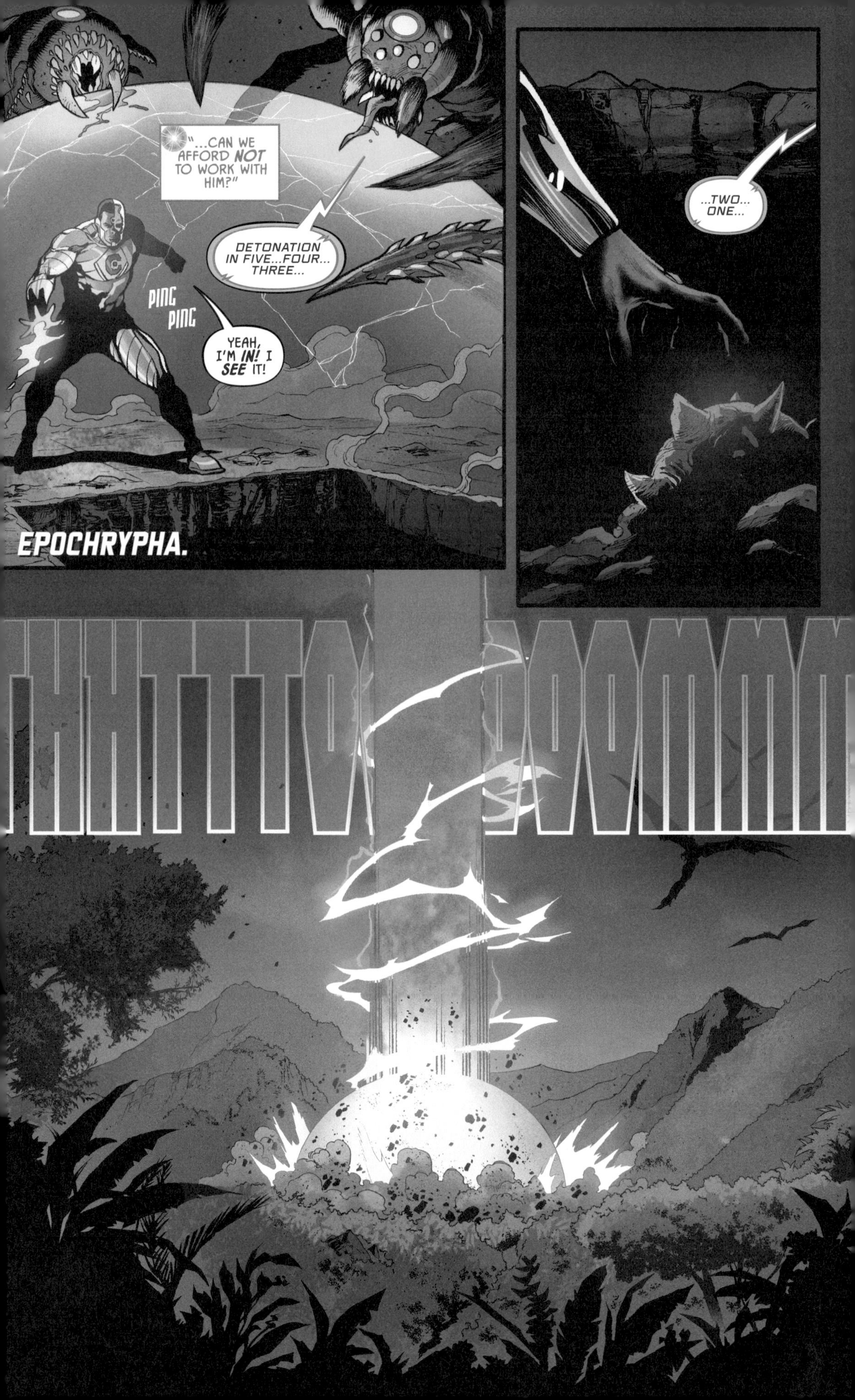
"...CAN WE AFFORD NOT TO WORK WITH HIM?"
DETONATION IN FIVE...FOUR... THREE...
PING PING
YEAH, I'M IN! I SEE IT!
EPOCHRYPHA.
...TWO... ONE...
THTTO DOOMM

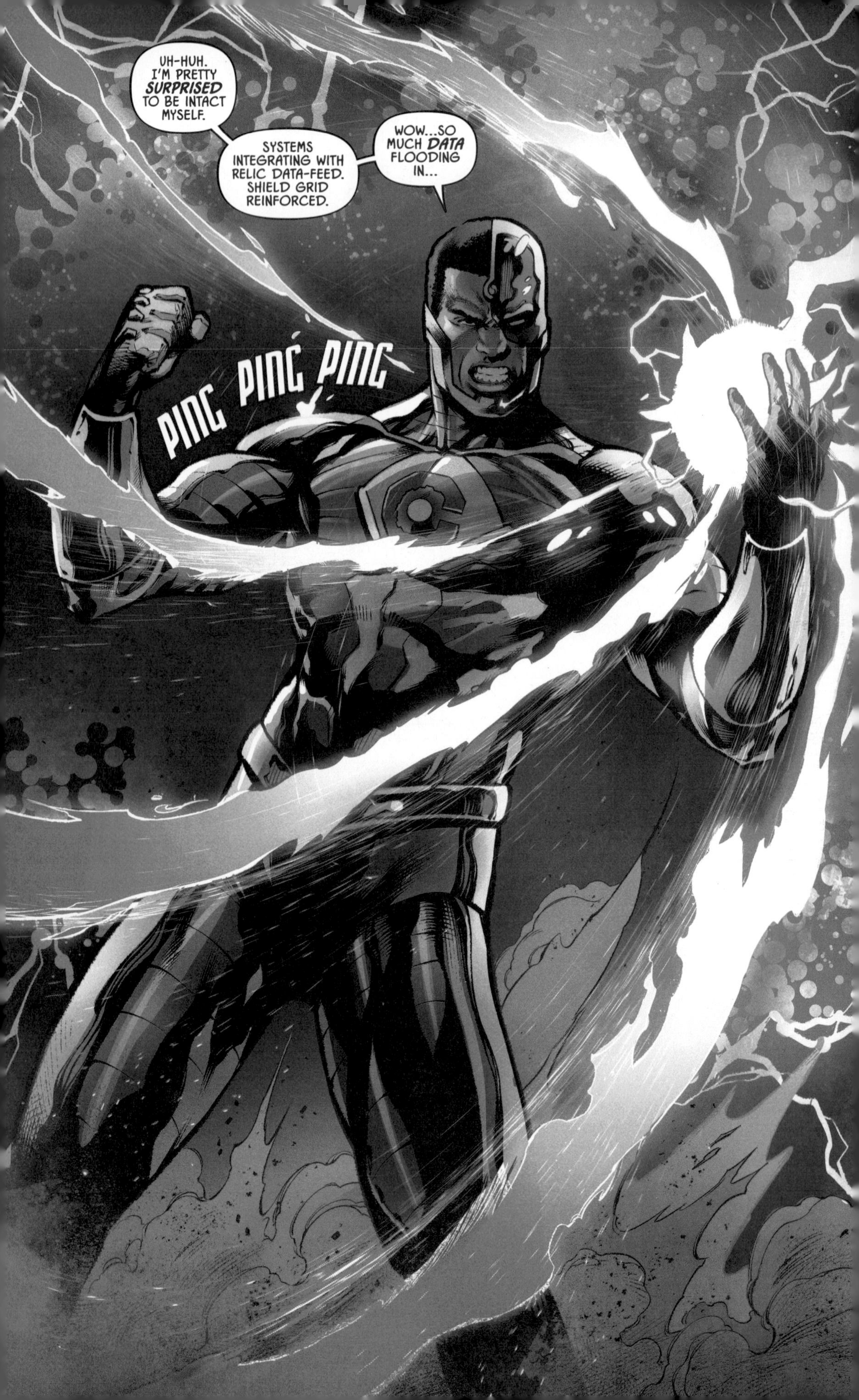
UH-HUH. I'M PRETTY SURPRISED TO BE INTACT MYSELF.
SYSTEMS INTEGRATING WITH RELIC DATA-FEED. SHIELD GRID REINFORCED.
WOW...SO MUCH DATA FLOODING IN...
PING PING PING

I UNDERSTAND NOW. I SEE IT.
THERE'S NO TIME TO WASTE. THAT'S WHY DARKSEID TOOK OFF AND LEFT ME HERE.
HE TRUSTED ME TO GET THIS DONE.
TO RECOVER THIS.
AND THIS IS GIVING ME THE LOCATIONS OF OTHER RELICS...
PING
PING
PING
...UPLOADING.
I FEEL REBOOTED. LIKE THERE ARE NEW THINGS I CAN DO...THINGS FAR BEYOND MY PREVIOUS SPECS...
TRIGGER BOOM TUBE.
PING
PING
PING
BOOOOOOOM

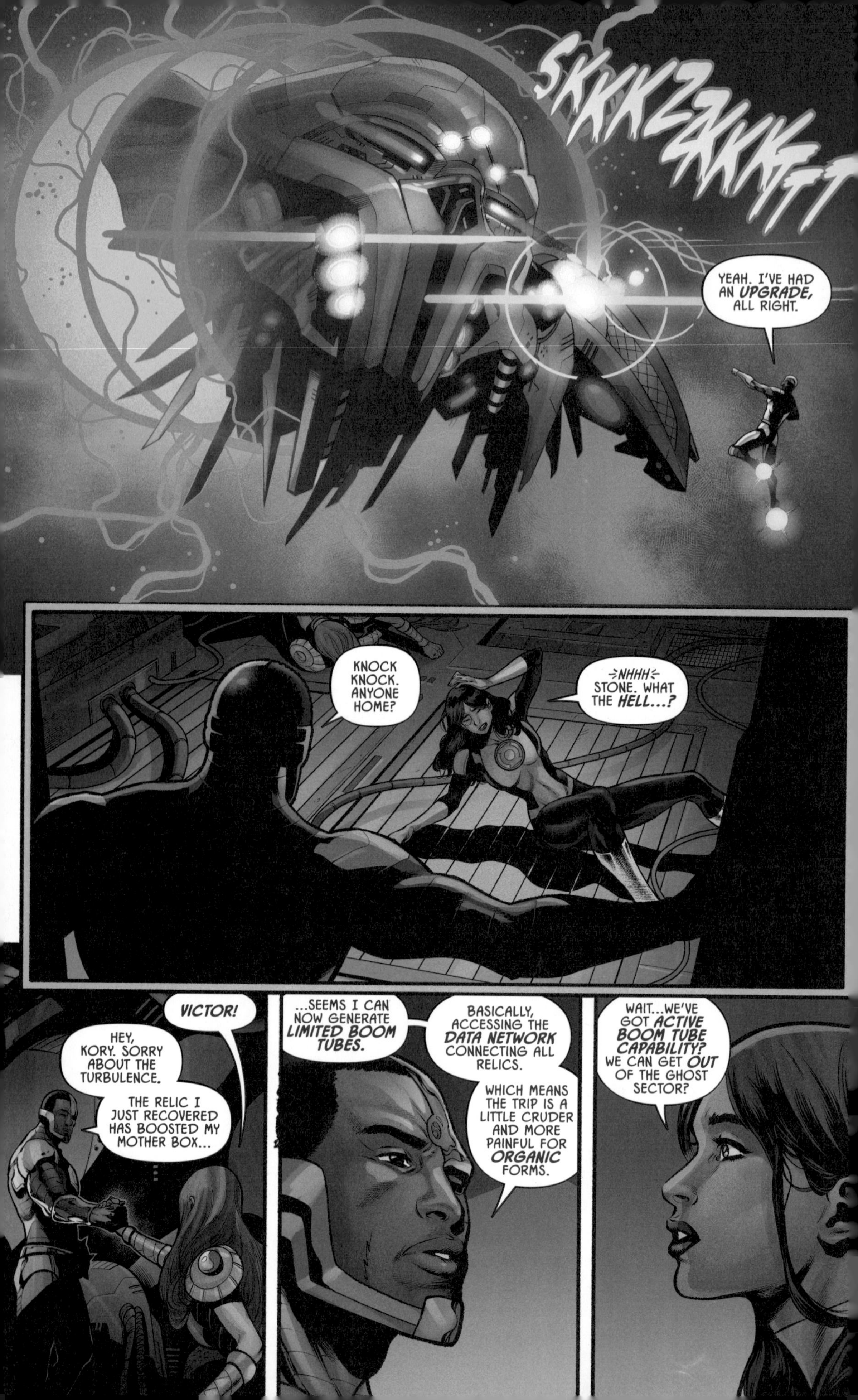
SKKKZZKKKTTT
YEAH. I'VE HAD AN UPGRADE, ALL RIGHT.
KNOCK KNOCK. ANYONE HOME?
≶NHHH≷ STONE. WHAT THE HELL...?
VICTOR!
HEY, KORY. SORRY ABOUT THE TURBULENCE.
THE RELIC I JUST RECOVERED HAS BOOSTED MY MOTHER BOX...
...SEEMS I CAN NOW GENERATE LIMITED BOOM TUBES.
BASICALLY, ACCESSING THE DATA NETWORK CONNECTING ALL RELICS.
WHICH MEANS THE TRIP IS A LITTLE CRUDER AND MORE PAINFUL FOR ORGANIC FORMS.
WAIT...WE'VE GOT ACTIVE BOOM TUBE CAPABILITY? WE CAN GET OUT OF THE GHOST SECTOR?

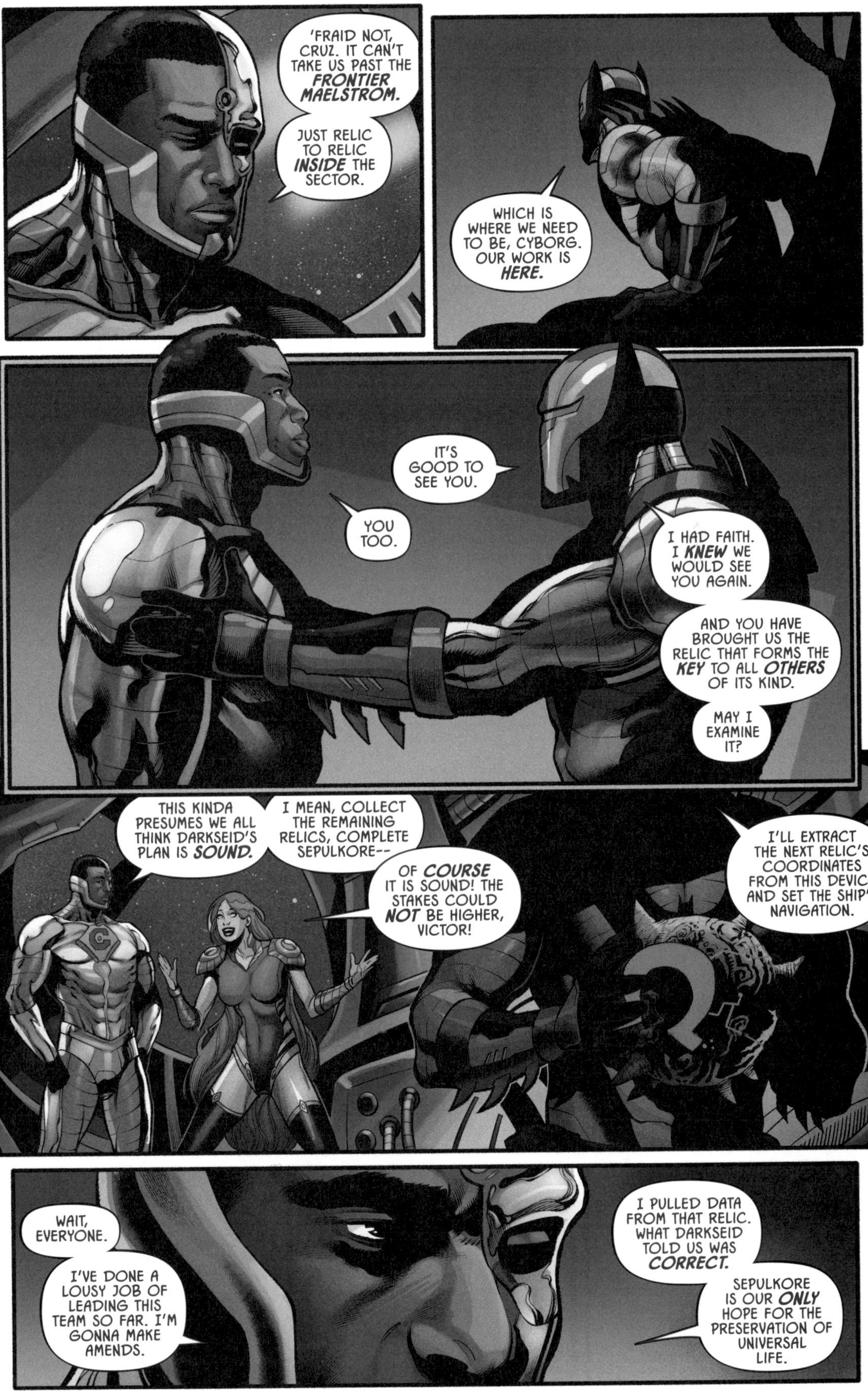
'FRAID NOT, CRUZ. IT CAN'T TAKE US PAST THE FRONTIER MAELSTROM.
JUST RELIC TO RELIC INSIDE THE SECTOR.
WHICH IS WHERE WE NEED TO BE, CYBORG. OUR WORK IS HERE.
IT'S GOOD TO SEE YOU.
YOU TOO.
I HAD FAITH. I KNEW WE WOULD SEE YOU AGAIN.
AND YOU HAVE BROUGHT US THE RELIC THAT FORMS THE KEY TO ALL OTHERS OF ITS KIND.
MAY I EXAMINE IT?
THIS KINDA PRESUMES WE ALL THINK DARKSEID'S PLAN IS SOUND.
I MEAN, COLLECT THE REMAINING RELICS, COMPLETE SEPULKORE--
OF COURSE IT IS SOUND! THE STAKES COULD NOT BE HIGHER, VICTOR!
I'LL EXTRACT THE NEXT RELIC'S COORDINATES FROM THIS DEVICE AND SET THE SHIP'S NAVIGATION.
WAIT, EVERYONE.
I'VE DONE A LOUSY JOB OF LEADING THIS TEAM SO FAR. I'M GONNA MAKE AMENDS.
I PULLED DATA FROM THAT RELIC. WHAT DARKSEID TOLD US WAS CORRECT.
SEPULKORE IS OUR ONLY HOPE FOR THE PRESERVATION OF UNIVERSAL LIFE.

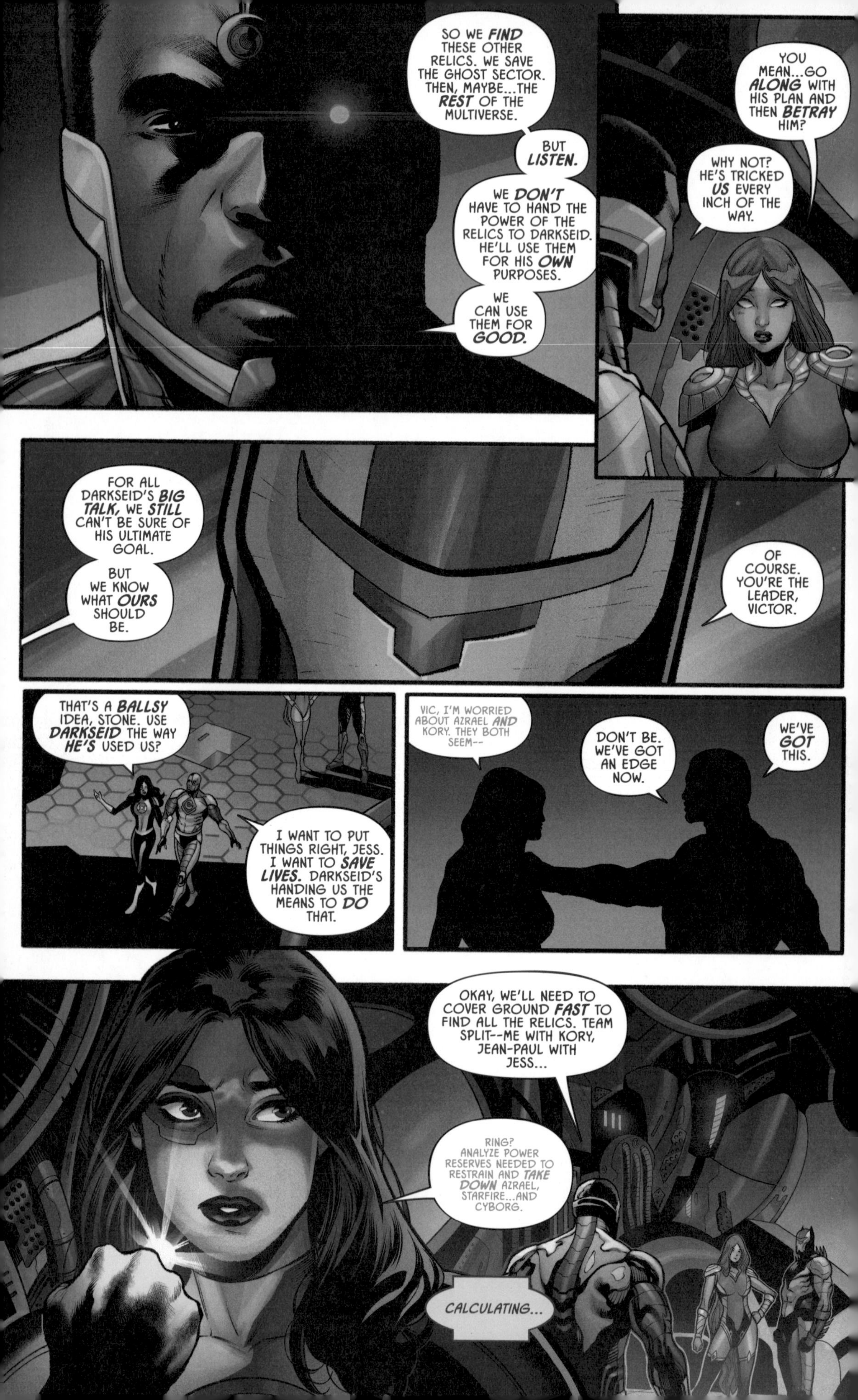
SO WE FIND THESE OTHER RELICS. WE SAVE THE GHOST SECTOR. THEN, MAYBE...THE REST OF THE MULTIVERSE.
BUT LISTEN.
WE DON'T HAVE TO HAND THE POWER OF THE RELICS TO DARKSEID. HE'LL USE THEM FOR HIS OWN PURPOSES.
WE CAN USE THEM FOR GOOD.
YOU MEAN...GO ALONG WITH HIS PLAN AND THEN BETRAY HIM?
WHY NOT? HE'S TRICKED US EVERY INCH OF THE WAY.
FOR ALL DARKSEID'S BIG TALK, WE STILL CAN'T BE SURE OF HIS ULTIMATE GOAL.
BUT WE KNOW WHAT OURS SHOULD BE.
OF COURSE. YOU'RE THE LEADER, VICTOR.
THAT'S A BALLSY IDEA, STONE. USE DARKSEID THE WAY HE'S USED US?
I WANT TO PUT THINGS RIGHT, JESS. I WANT TO SAVE LIVES. DARKSEID'S HANDING US THE MEANS TO DO THAT.
VIC, I'M WORRIED ABOUT AZRAEL AND KORY. THEY BOTH SEEM--
DON'T BE. WE'VE GOT AN EDGE NOW.
WE'VE GOT THIS.
OKAY, WE'LL NEED TO COVER GROUND FAST TO FIND ALL THE RELICS. TEAM SPLIT--ME WITH KORY, JEAN-PAUL WITH JESS...
RING? ANALYZE POWER RESERVES NEEDED TO RESTRAIN AND TAKE DOWN AZRAEL, STARFIRE...AND CYBORG.
CALCULATING...

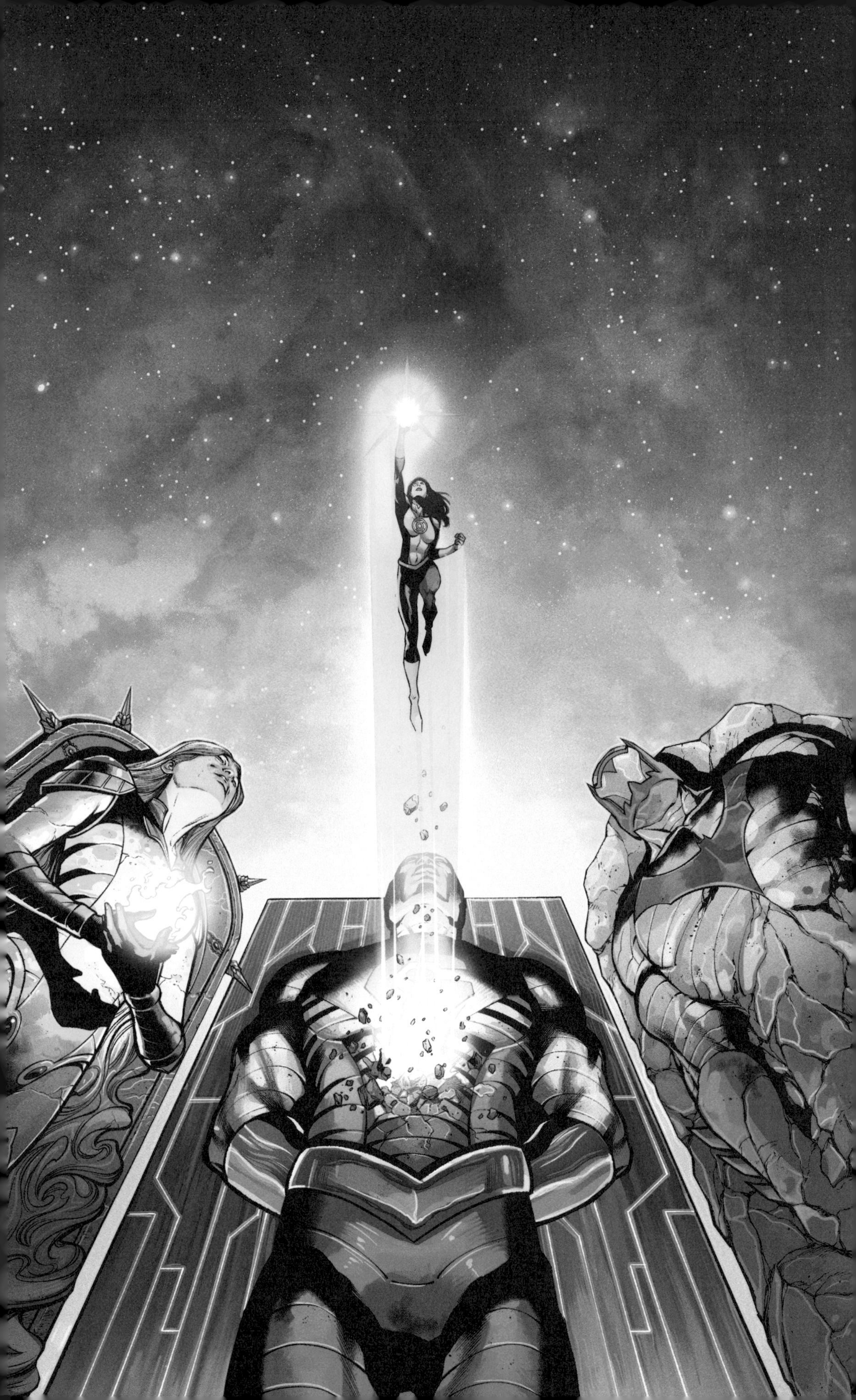

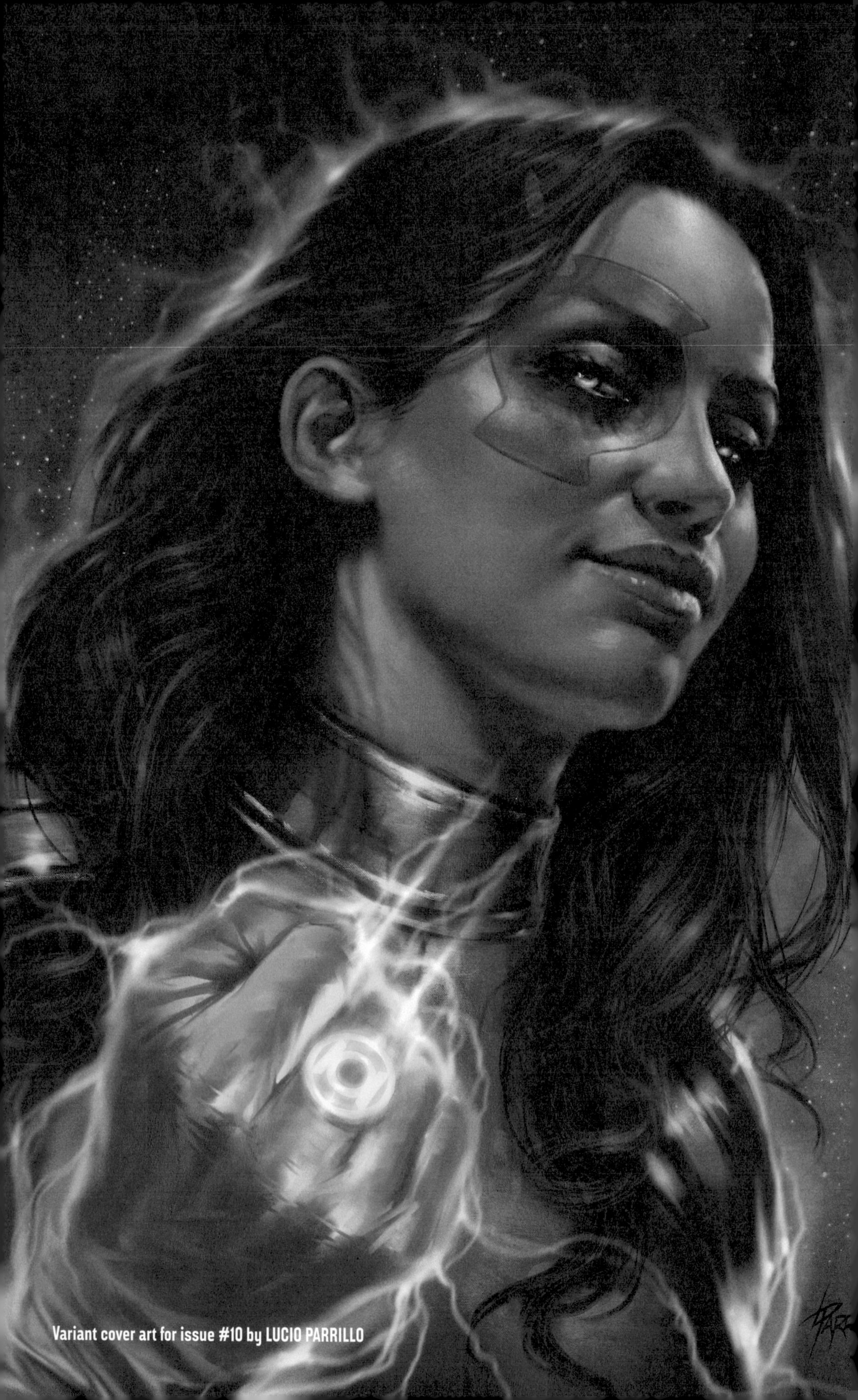

Variant cover art for issue #10 by LUCIO PARRILLO

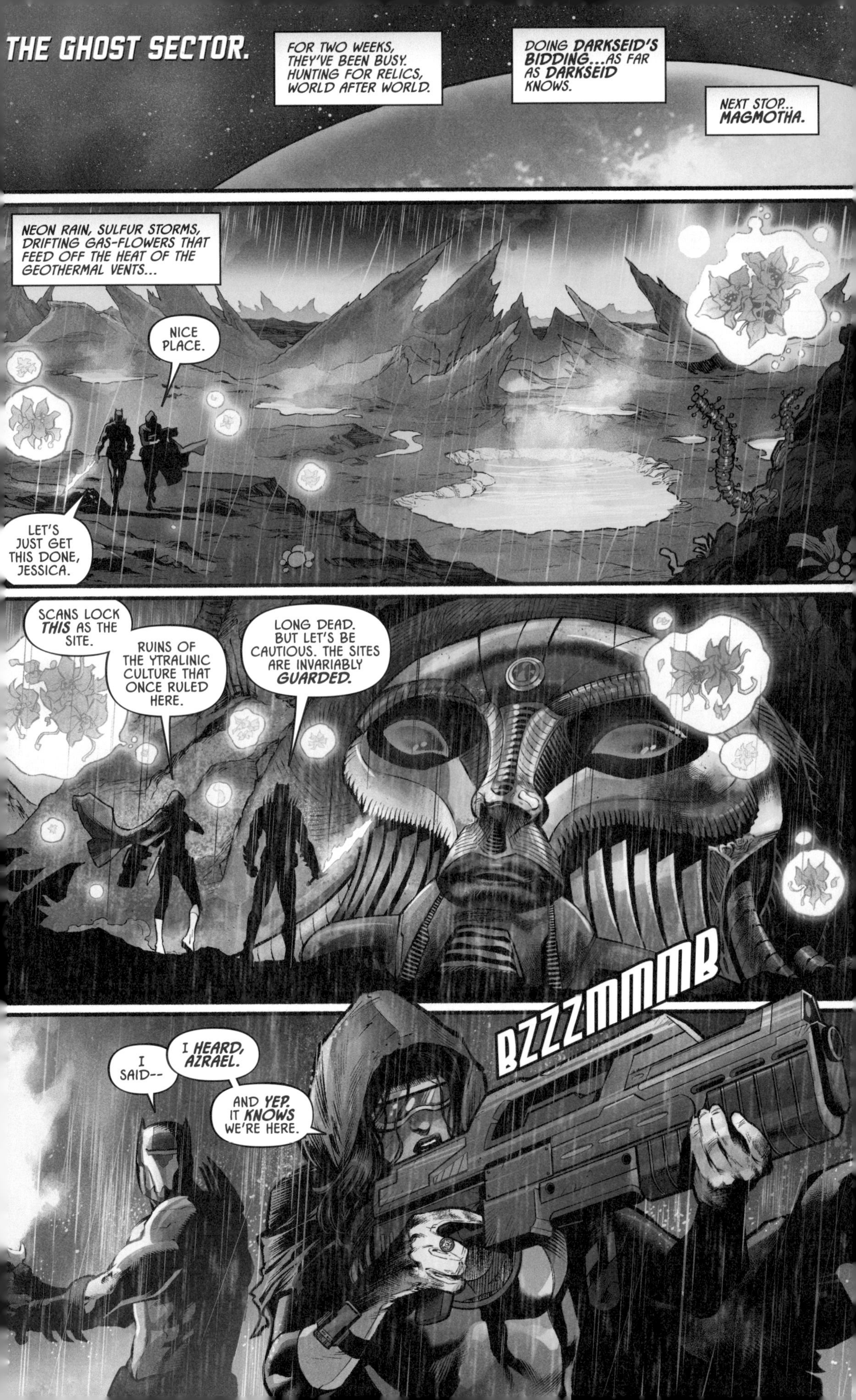
THE GHOST SECTOR.
FOR TWO WEEKS, THEY'VE BEEN BUSY. HUNTING FOR RELICS, WORLD AFTER WORLD.
DOING DARKSEID'S BIDDING...AS FAR AS DARKSEID KNOWS.
NEXT STOP... MAGMOTHA.
NEON RAIN, SULFUR STORMS, DRIFTING GAS-FLOWERS THAT FEED OFF THE HEAT OF THE GEOTHERMAL VENTS...
NICE PLACE.
LET'S JUST GET THIS DONE, JESSICA.
SCANS LOCK THIS AS THE SITE.
RUINS OF THE YTRALINIC CULTURE THAT ONCE RULED HERE.
LONG DEAD. BUT LET'S BE CAUTIOUS. THE SITES ARE INVARIABLY GUARDED.
BZZZMMMMB
I SAID--
I HEARD, AZRAEL.
AND YEP. IT KNOWS WE'RE HERE.

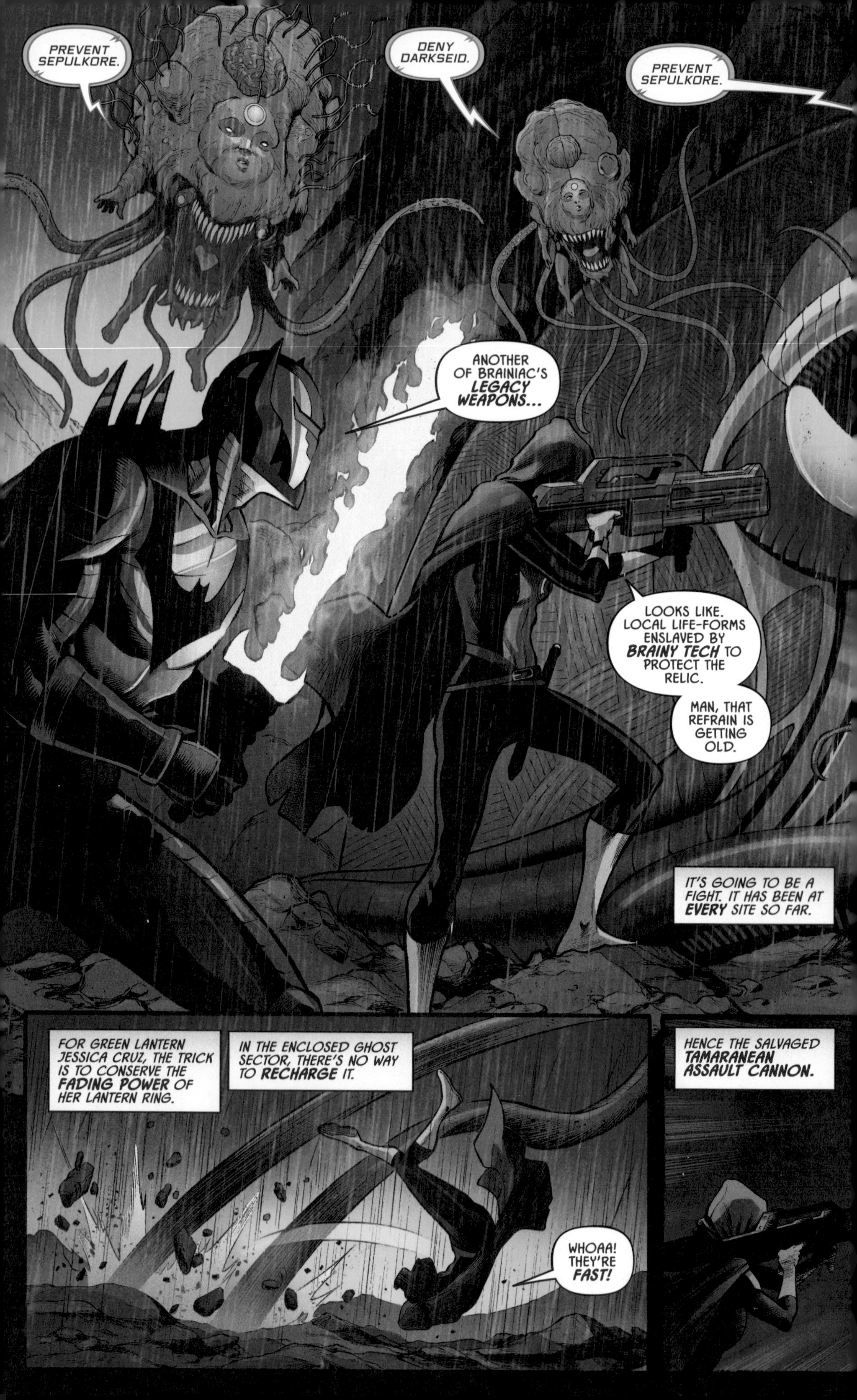
PREVENT SEPULKORE.
DENY DARKSEID.
PREVENT SEPULKORE.
ANOTHER OF BRAINIAC'S LEGACY WEAPONS...
LOOKS LIKE. LOCAL LIFE-FORMS ENSLAVED BY BRAINY TECH TO PROTECT THE RELIC.
MAN, THAT REFRAIN IS GETTING OLD.
IT'S GOING TO BE A FIGHT. IT HAS BEEN AT EVERY SITE SO FAR.
FOR GREEN LANTERN JESSICA CRUZ, THE TRICK IS TO CONSERVE THE FADING POWER OF HER LANTERN RING.
IN THE ENCLOSED GHOST SECTOR, THERE'S NO WAY TO RECHARGE IT.
WHOAA! THEY'RE FAST!
HENCE THE SALVAGED TAMARANEAN ASSAULT CANNON.

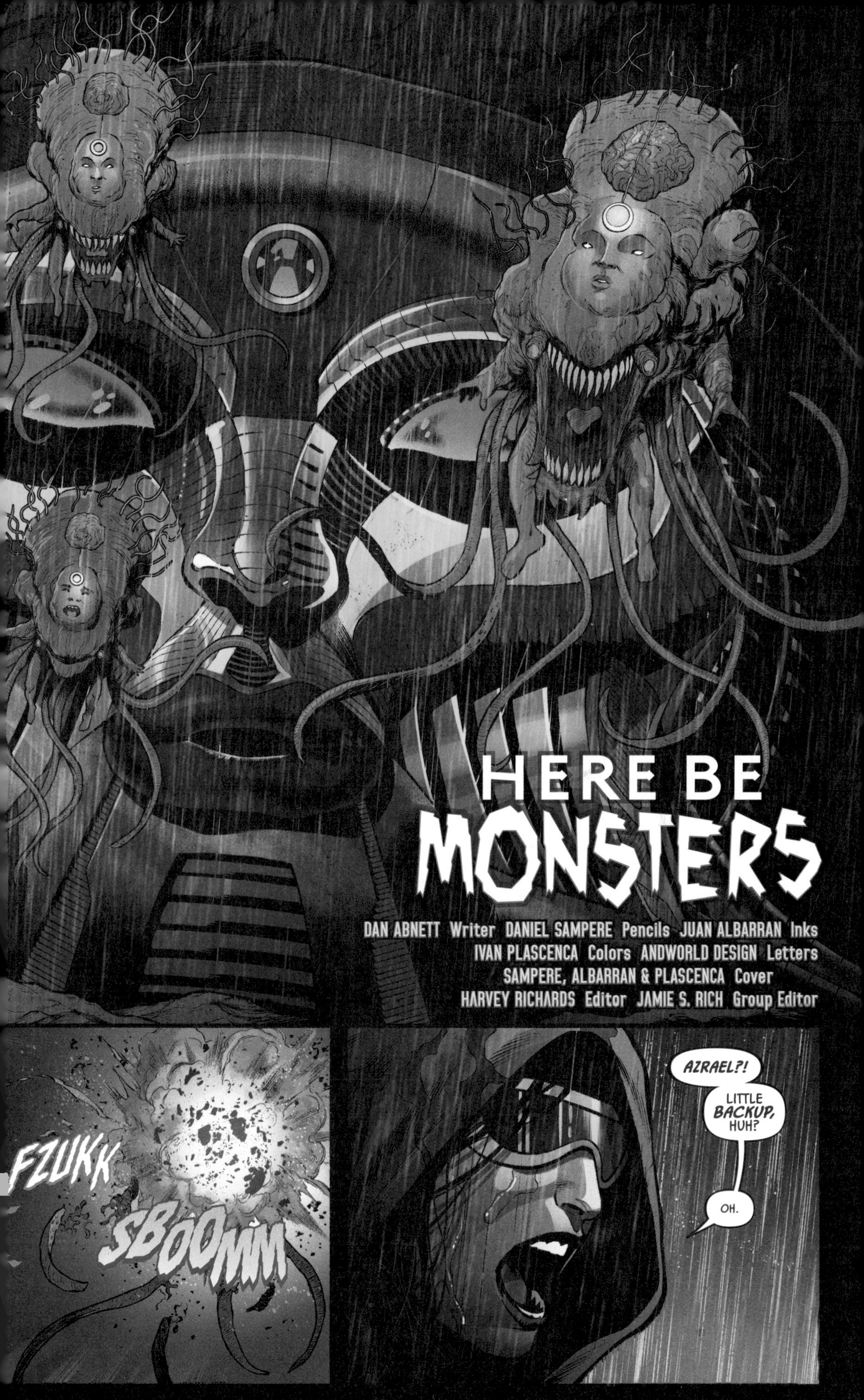
HERE BE
MONSTERS
DAN ABNETT Writer DANIEL SAMPERE Pencils JUAN ALBARRAN Inks
IVAN PLASCENCA Colors ANDWORLD DESIGN Letters
SAMPERE, ALBARRAN & PLASCENCA Cover
HARVEY RICHARDS Editor JAMIE S. RICH Group Editor
FZUKK
SBOOMM
AZRAEL?!
LITTLE BACKUP, HUH?
OH.

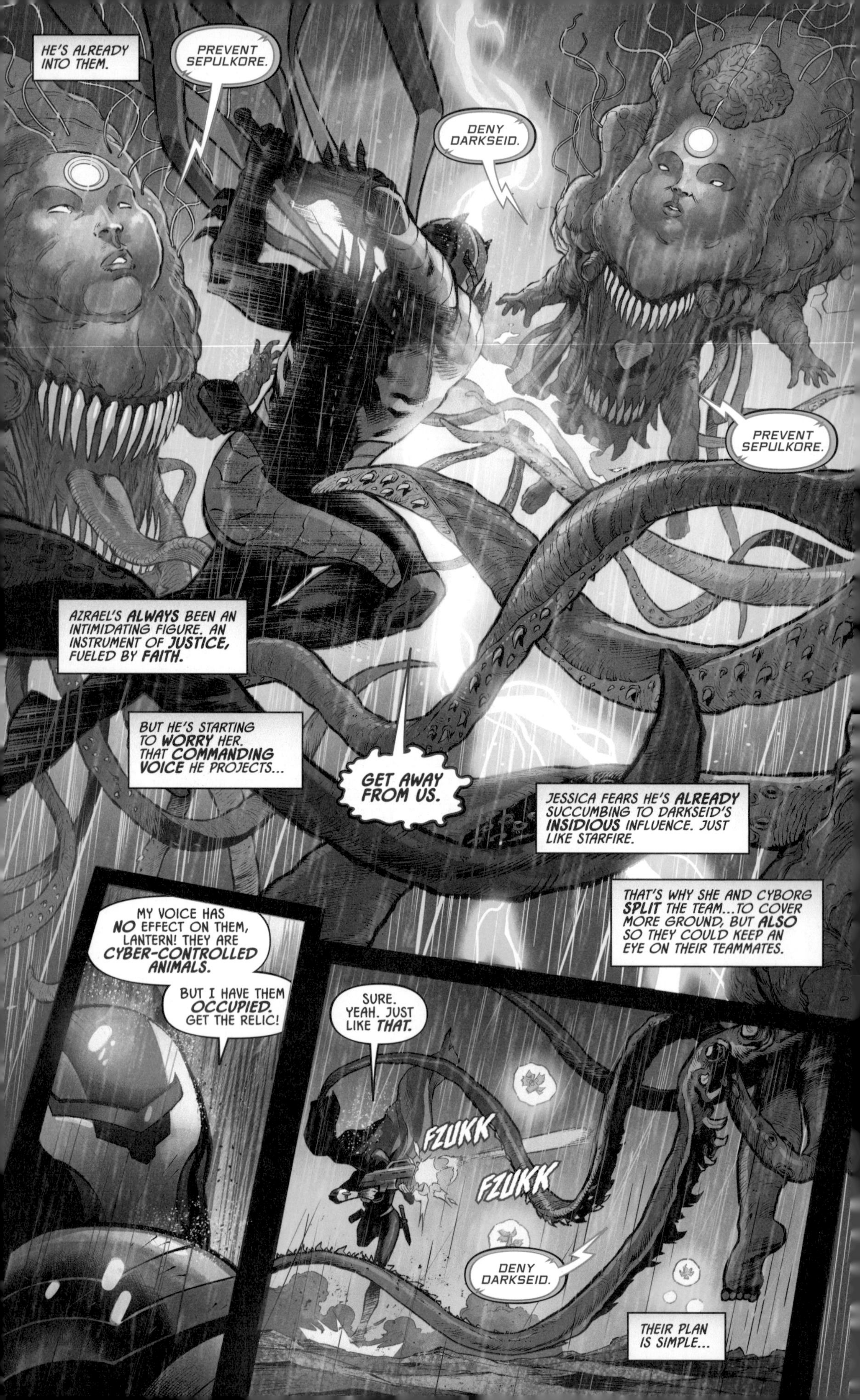
HE'S ALREADY INTO THEM.
PREVENT SEPULKORE.
DENY DARKSEID.
PREVENT SEPULKORE.
AZRAEL'S ALWAYS BEEN AN INTIMIDATING FIGURE. AN INSTRUMENT OF JUSTICE, FUELED BY FAITH.
BUT HE'S STARTING TO WORRY HER. THAT COMMANDING VOICE HE PROJECTS...
GET AWAY FROM US.
JESSICA FEARS HE'S ALREADY SUCCUMBING TO DARKSEID'S INSIDIOUS INFLUENCE. JUST LIKE STARFIRE.
THAT'S WHY SHE AND CYBORG SPLIT THE TEAM...TO COVER MORE GROUND, BUT ALSO SO THEY COULD KEEP AN EYE ON THEIR TEAMMATES.
MY VOICE HAS NO EFFECT ON THEM, LANTERN! THEY ARE CYBER-CONTROLLED ANIMALS.
BUT I HAVE THEM OCCUPIED. GET THE RELIC!
SURE. YEAH. JUST LIKE THAT.
FZUKK
FZUKK
DENY DARKSEID.
THEIR PLAN IS SIMPLE...

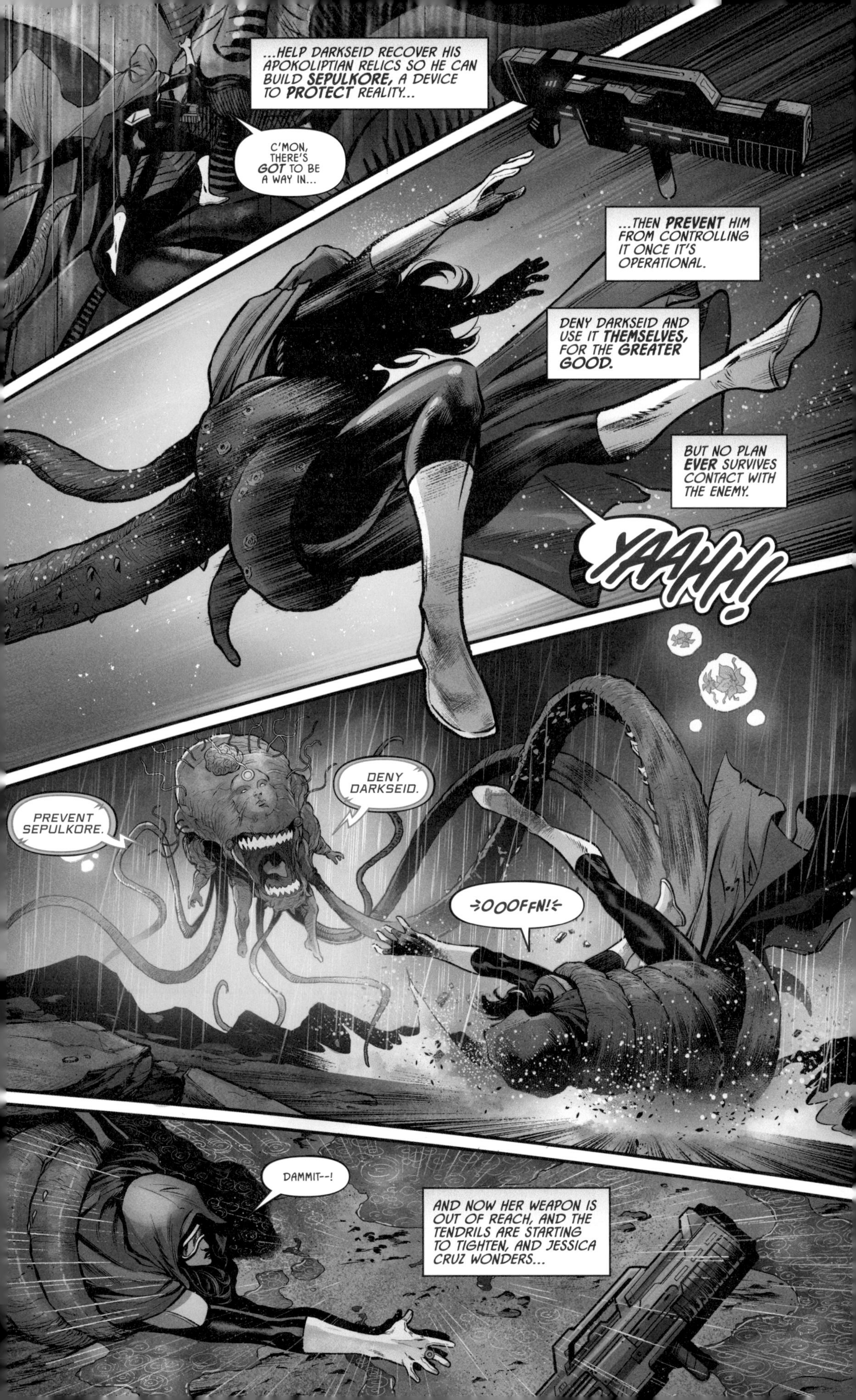
...HELP DARKSEID RECOVER HIS APOKOLIPTIAN RELICS SO HE CAN BUILD SEPULKORE, A DEVICE TO PROTECT REALITY...
C'MON, THERE'S GOT TO BE A WAY IN...
...THEN PREVENT HIM FROM CONTROLLING IT ONCE IT'S OPERATIONAL.
DENY DARKSEID AND USE IT THEMSELVES, FOR THE GREATER GOOD.
BUT NO PLAN EVER SURVIVES CONTACT WITH THE ENEMY.
YAAHH!
PREVENT SEPULKORE.
DENY DARKSEID.
OOOFFN!
DAMMIT--!
AND NOW HER WEAPON IS OUT OF REACH, AND THE TENDRILS ARE STARTING TO TIGHTEN, AND JESSICA CRUZ WONDERS...

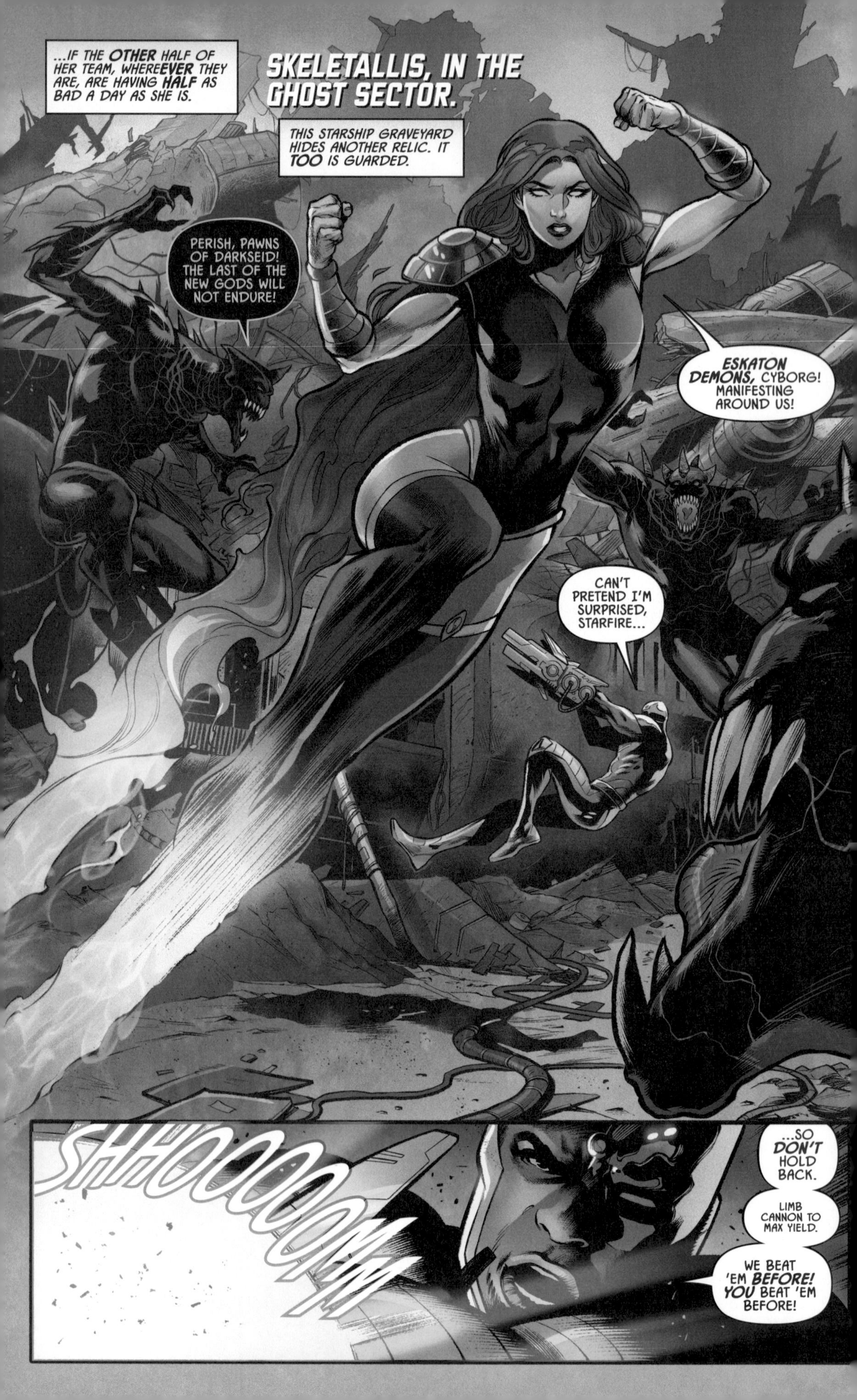
...IF THE OTHER HALF OF HER TEAM, WHEREEVER THEY ARE, ARE HAVING HALF AS BAD A DAY AS SHE IS.
SKELETALLIS, IN THE GHOST SECTOR.
THIS STARSHIP GRAVEYARD HIDES ANOTHER RELIC. IT TOO IS GUARDED.
PERISH, PAWNS OF DARKSEID! THE LAST OF THE NEW GODS WILL NOT ENDURE!
ESKATON DEMONS, CYBORG! MANIFESTING AROUND US!
CAN'T PRETEND I'M SURPRISED, STARFIRE...
SHHOOOOOM
...SO DON'T HOLD BACK.
LIMB CANNON TO MAX YIELD.
WE BEAT 'EM BEFORE! YOU BEAT 'EM BEFORE!

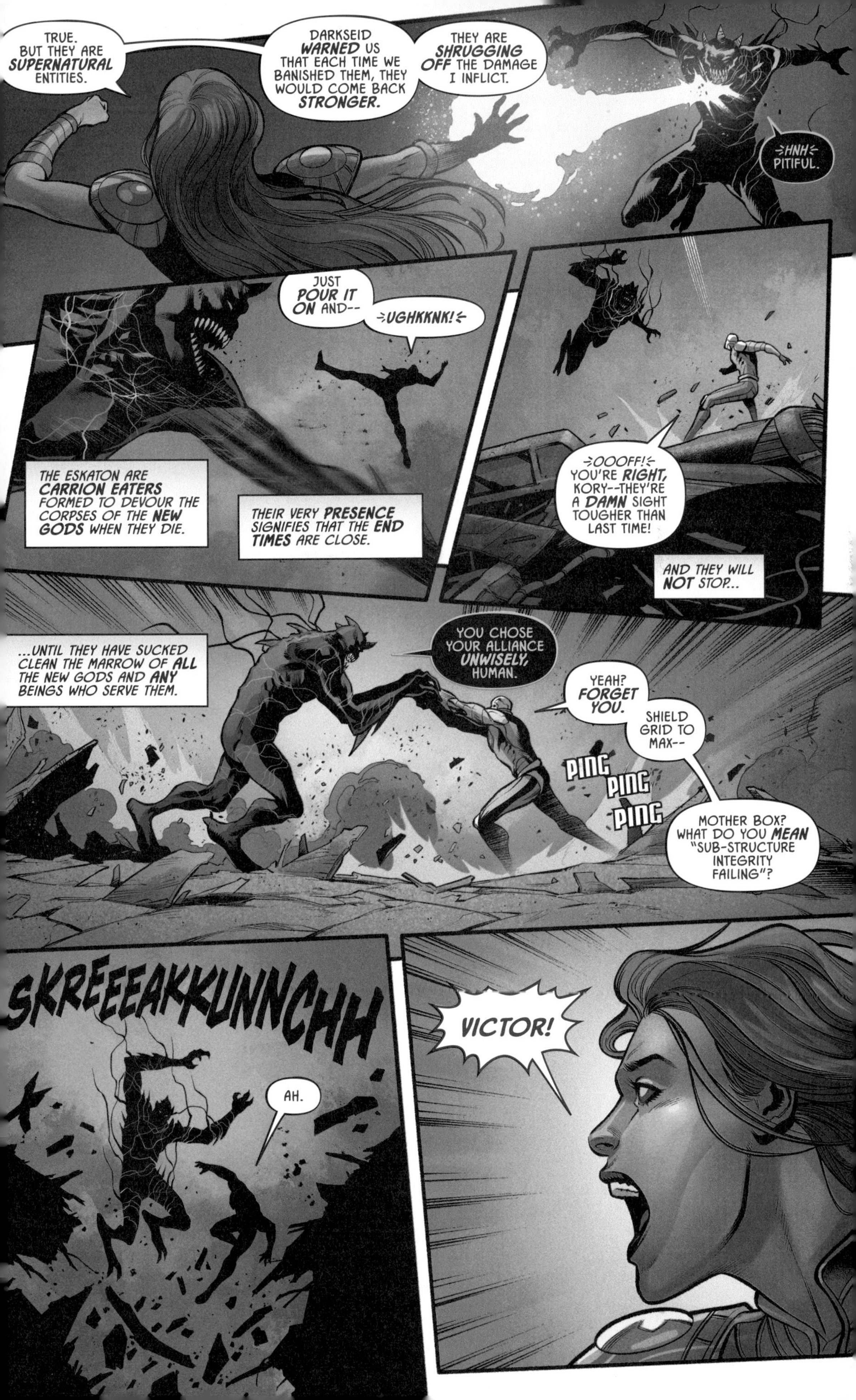
TRUE. BUT THEY ARE SUPERNATURAL ENTITIES.
DARKSEID WARNED US THAT EACH TIME WE BANISHED THEM, THEY WOULD COME BACK STRONGER.
THEY ARE SHRUGGING OFF THE DAMAGE I INFLICT.
HNH PITIFUL.
JUST POUR IT ON AND--
UGHKKNK!
THE ESKATON ARE CARRION EATERS FORMED TO DEVOUR THE CORPSES OF THE NEW GODS WHEN THEY DIE.
THEIR VERY PRESENCE SIGNIFIES THAT THE END TIMES ARE CLOSE.
OOOFF! YOU'RE RIGHT, KORY--THEY'RE A DAMN SIGHT TOUGHER THAN LAST TIME!
AND THEY WILL NOT STOP...
...UNTIL THEY HAVE SUCKED CLEAN THE MARROW OF ALL THE NEW GODS AND ANY BEINGS WHO SERVE THEM.
YOU CHOSE YOUR ALLIANCE UNWISELY, HUMAN.
YEAH? FORGET YOU.
SHIELD GRID TO MAX--
PING
PING
PING
MOTHER BOX? WHAT DO YOU MEAN "SUB-STRUCTURE INTEGRITY FAILING"?
SKREEEAKKUNNCHH
AH.
VICTOR!

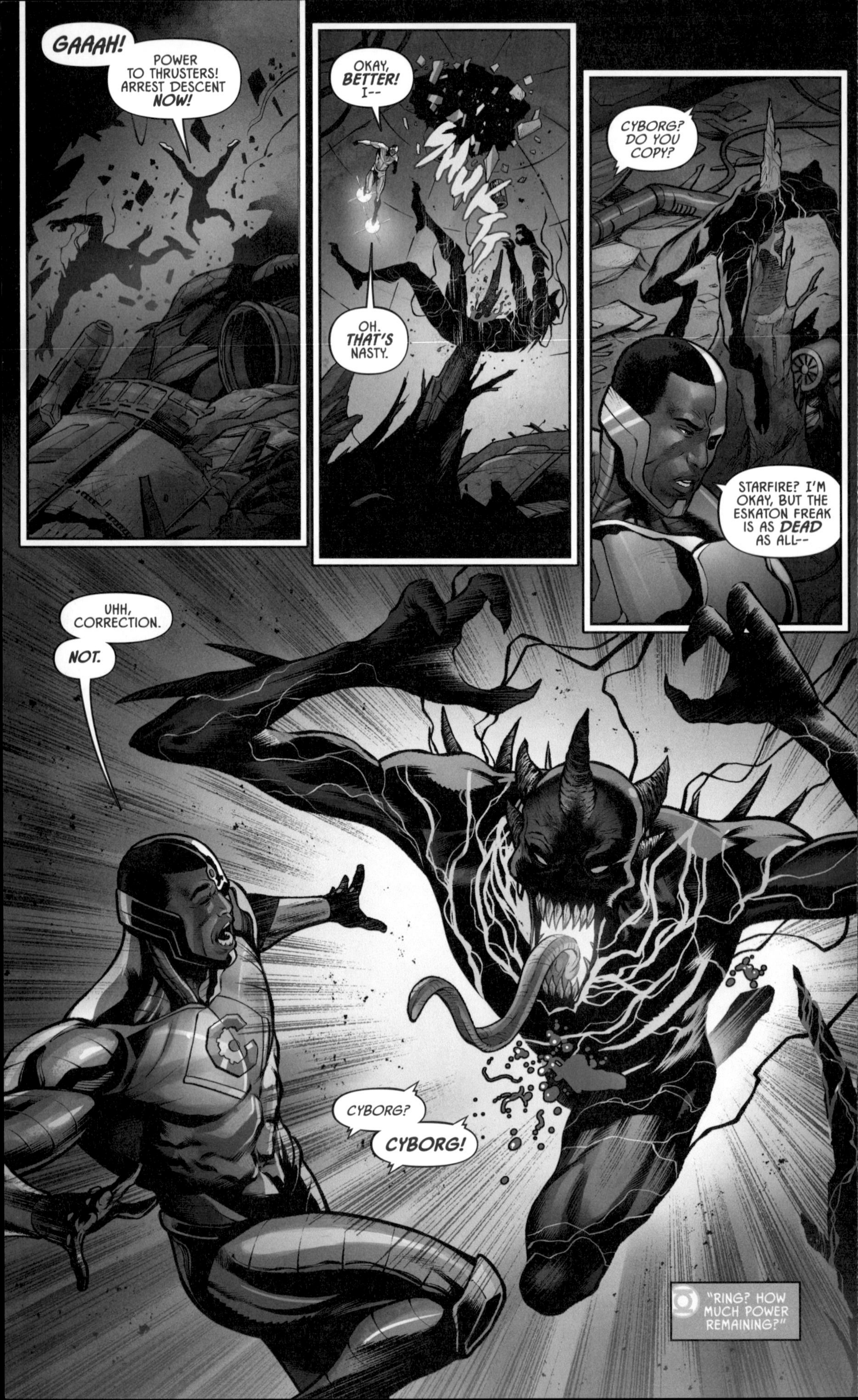
GAAAH!
POWER TO THRUSTERS! ARREST DESCENT NOW!
OKAY, BETTER! I--
SHUKT
OH. THAT'S NASTY.
CYBORG? DO YOU COPY?
STARFIRE? I'M OKAY, BUT THE ESKATON FREAK IS AS DEAD AS ALL--
UHH, CORRECTION.
NOT.
CYBORG?
CYBORG!
"RING? HOW MUCH POWER REMAINING?"

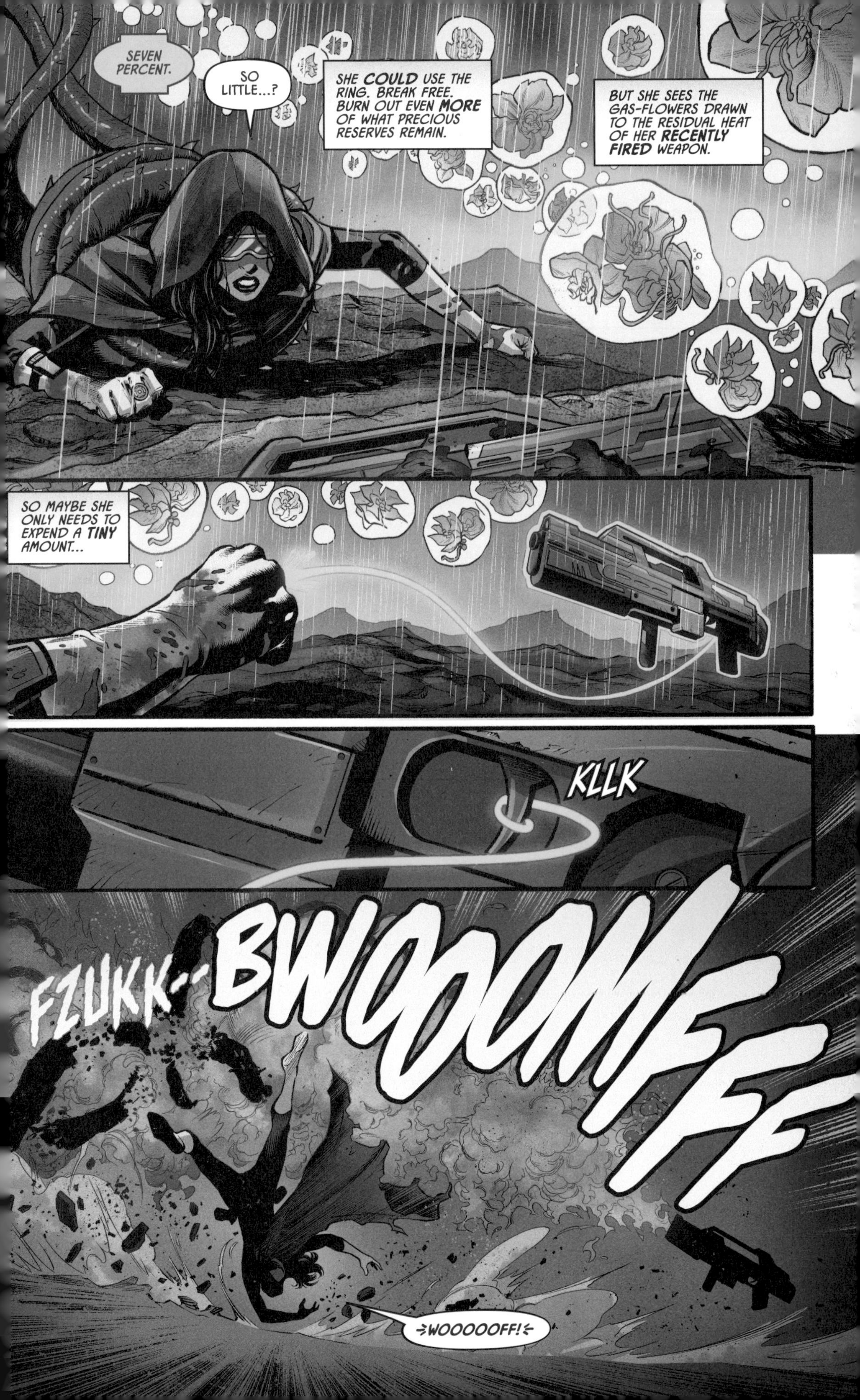
SEVEN PERCENT.
SO LITTLE...?
SHE COULD USE THE RING. BREAK FREE. BURN OUT EVEN MORE OF WHAT PRECIOUS RESERVES REMAIN.
BUT SHE SEES THE GAS-FLOWERS DRAWN TO THE RESIDUAL HEAT OF HER RECENTLY FIRED WEAPON.
SO MAYBE SHE ONLY NEEDS TO EXPEND A TINY AMOUNT...
KLLK
FZUKK--BWOOOMFFF
WOOOOOFF!

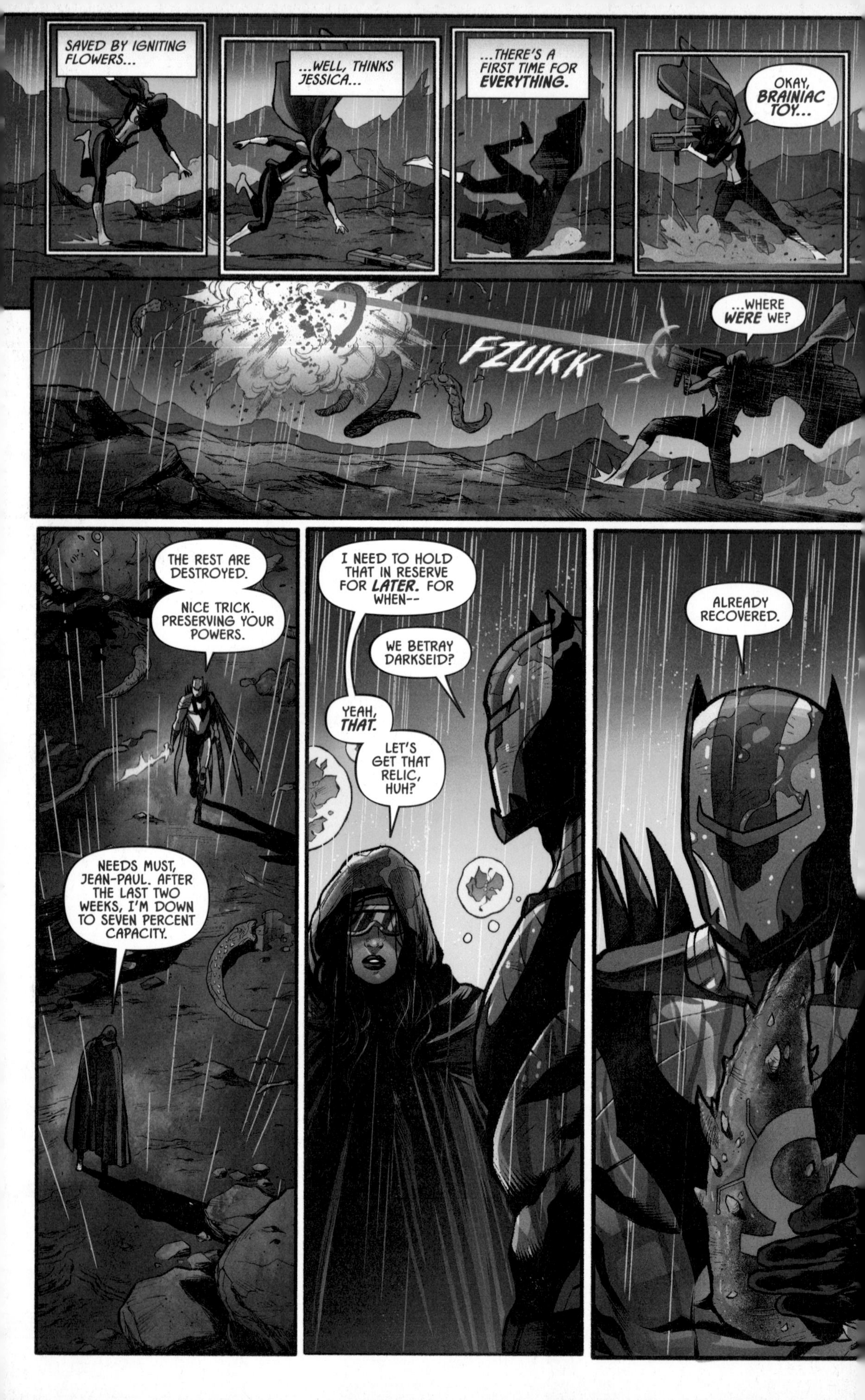
SAVED BY IGNITING FLOWERS...
...WELL, THINKS JESSICA...
...THERE'S A FIRST TIME FOR EVERYTHING.
OKAY, BRAINIAC TOY...
FZUKK
...WHERE WERE WE?
THE REST ARE DESTROYED.
NICE TRICK. PRESERVING YOUR POWERS.
NEEDS MUST, JEAN-PAUL. AFTER THE LAST TWO WEEKS, I'M DOWN TO SEVEN PERCENT CAPACITY.
I NEED TO HOLD THAT IN RESERVE FOR LATER. FOR WHEN--
WE BETRAY DARKSEID?
YEAH, THAT.
LET'S GET THAT RELIC, HUH?
ALREADY RECOVERED.

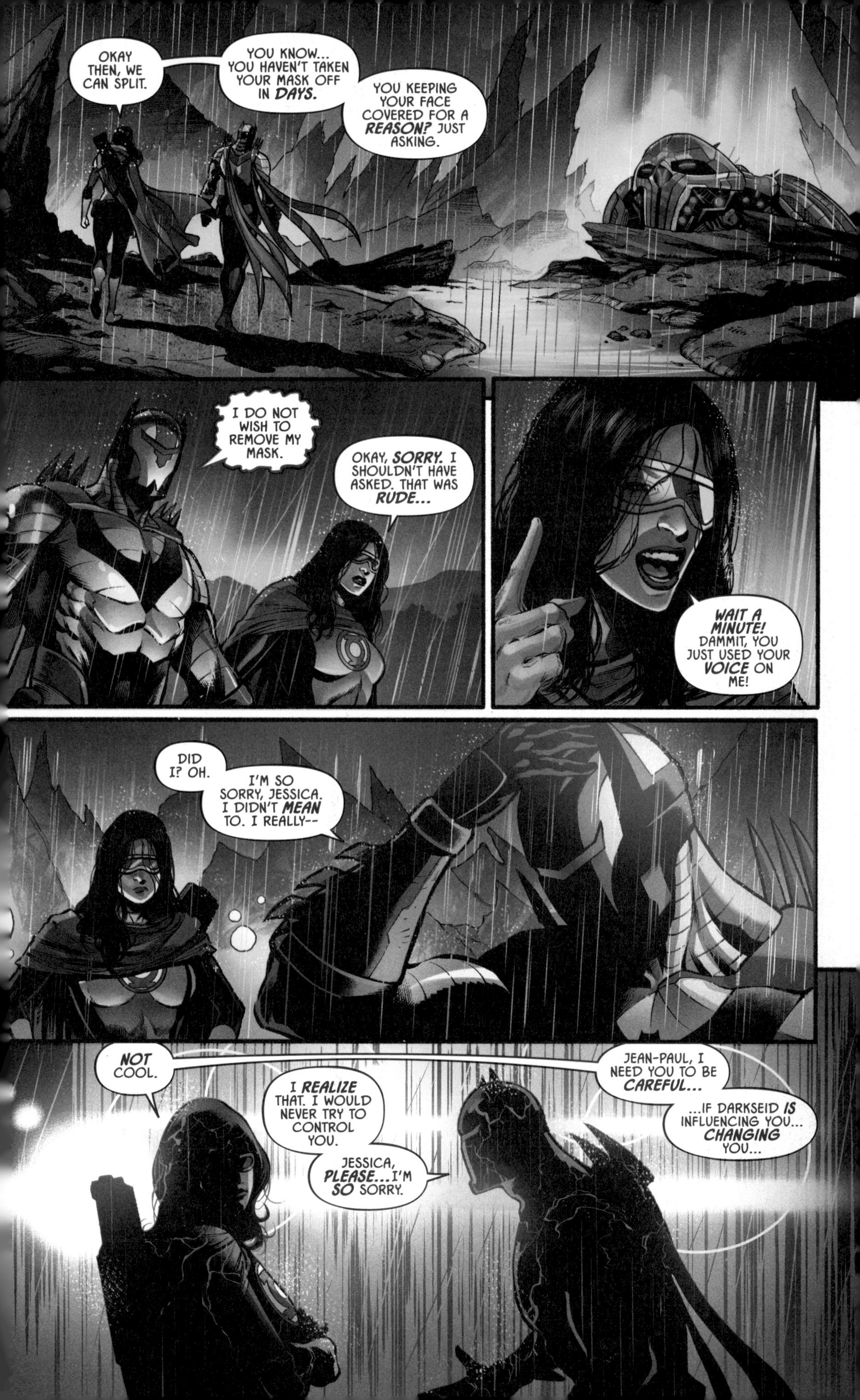
OKAY THEN, WE CAN SPLIT.
YOU KNOW... YOU HAVEN'T TAKEN YOUR MASK OFF IN DAYS.
YOU KEEPING YOUR FACE COVERED FOR A REASON? JUST ASKING.
I DO NOT WISH TO REMOVE MY MASK.
OKAY, SORRY. I SHOULDN'T HAVE ASKED. THAT WAS RUDE...
WAIT A MINUTE! DAMMIT, YOU JUST USED YOUR VOICE ON ME!
DID I? OH.
I'M SO SORRY, JESSICA. I DIDN'T MEAN TO. I REALLY--
NOT COOL.
I REALIZE THAT. I WOULD NEVER TRY TO CONTROL YOU.
JESSICA, PLEASE...I'M SO SORRY.
JEAN-PAUL, I NEED YOU TO BE CAREFUL...
...IF DARKSEID IS INFLUENCING YOU... CHANGING YOU...

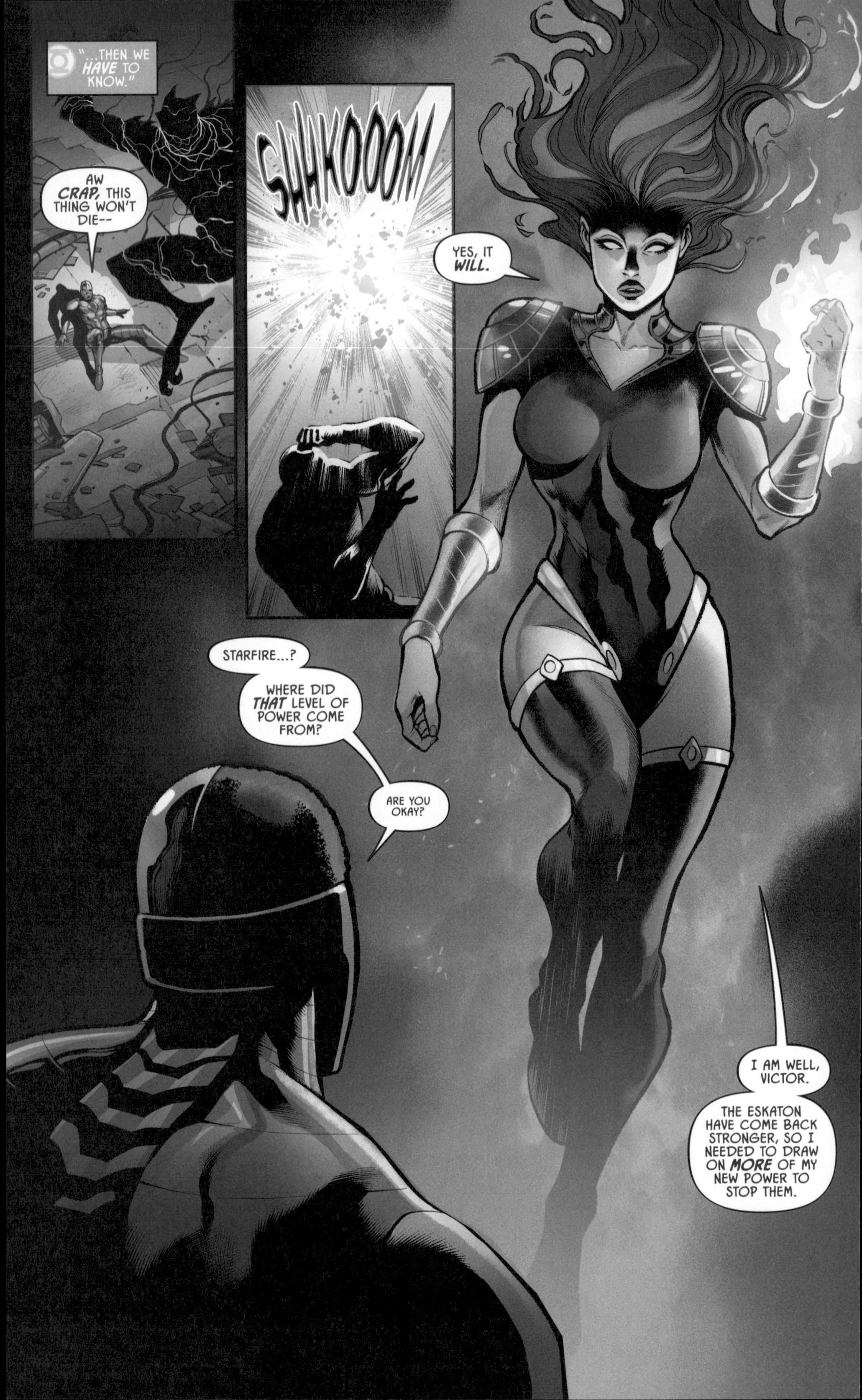
"...THEN WE HAVE TO KNOW."
AW CRAP, THIS THING WON'T DIE--
SHHKOOOM
YES, IT WILL.
STARFIRE...?
WHERE DID THAT LEVEL OF POWER COME FROM?
ARE YOU OKAY?
I AM WELL, VICTOR.
THE ESKATON HAVE COME BACK STRONGER, SO I NEEDED TO DRAW ON MORE OF MY NEW POWER TO STOP THEM.

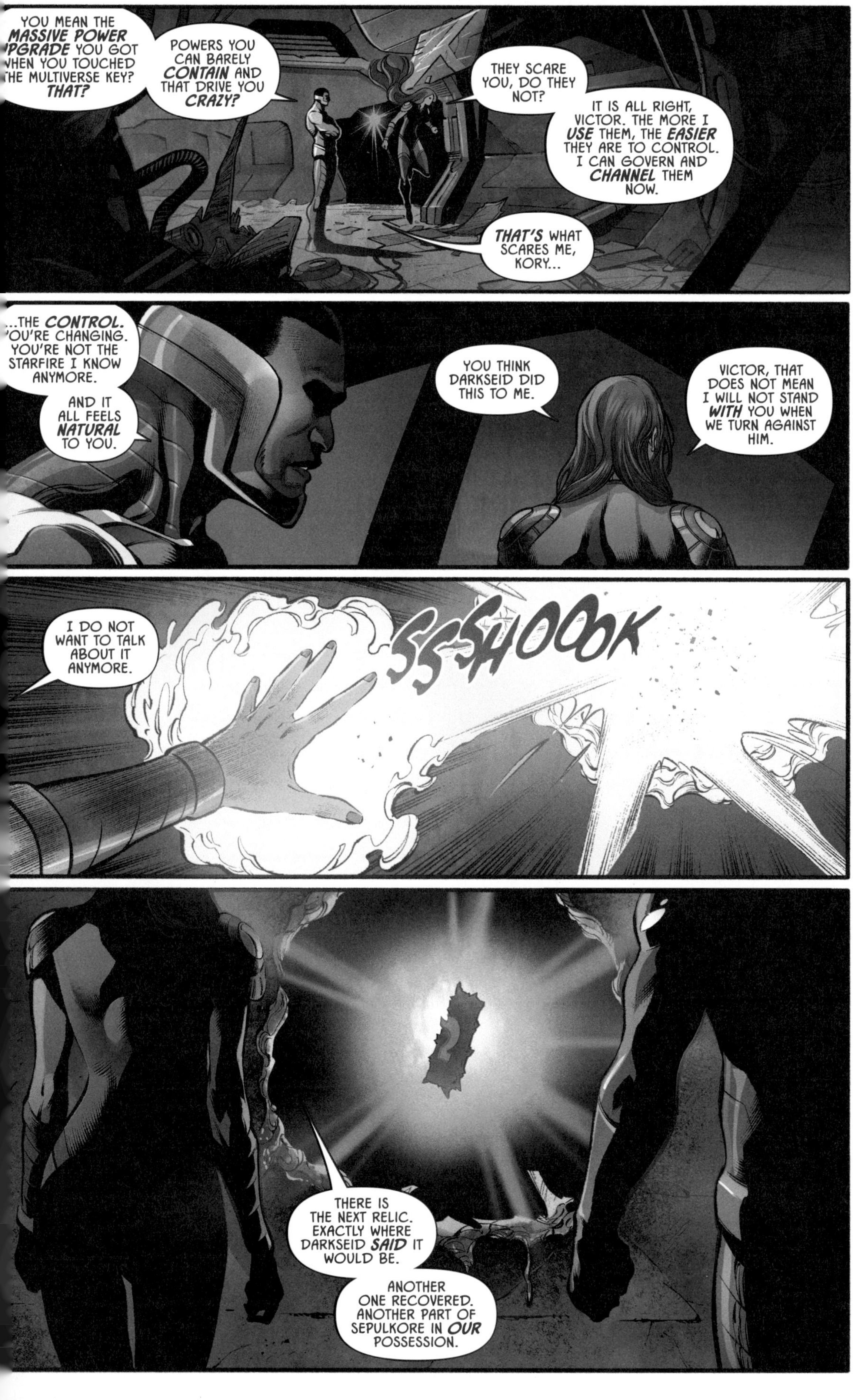
YOU MEAN THE MASSIVE POWER PGRADE YOU GOT HEN YOU TOUCHED HE MULTIVERSE KEY? THAT?
POWERS YOU CAN BARELY CONTAIN AND THAT DRIVE YOU CRAZY?
THEY SCARE YOU, DO THEY NOT?
IT IS ALL RIGHT, VICTOR. THE MORE I USE THEM, THE EASIER THEY ARE TO CONTROL. I CAN GOVERN AND CHANNEL THEM NOW.
THAT'S WHAT SCARES ME, KORY...
...THE CONTROL. OU'RE CHANGING. YOU'RE NOT THE STARFIRE I KNOW ANYMORE.
AND IT ALL FEELS NATURAL TO YOU.
YOU THINK DARKSEID DID THIS TO ME.
VICTOR, THAT DOES NOT MEAN I WILL NOT STAND WITH YOU WHEN WE TURN AGAINST HIM.
I DO NOT WANT TO TALK ABOUT IT ANYMORE.
SSSHOOOK
THERE IS THE NEXT RELIC. EXACTLY WHERE DARKSEID SAID IT WOULD BE.
ANOTHER ONE RECOVERED. ANOTHER PART OF SEPULKORE IN OUR POSSESSION.

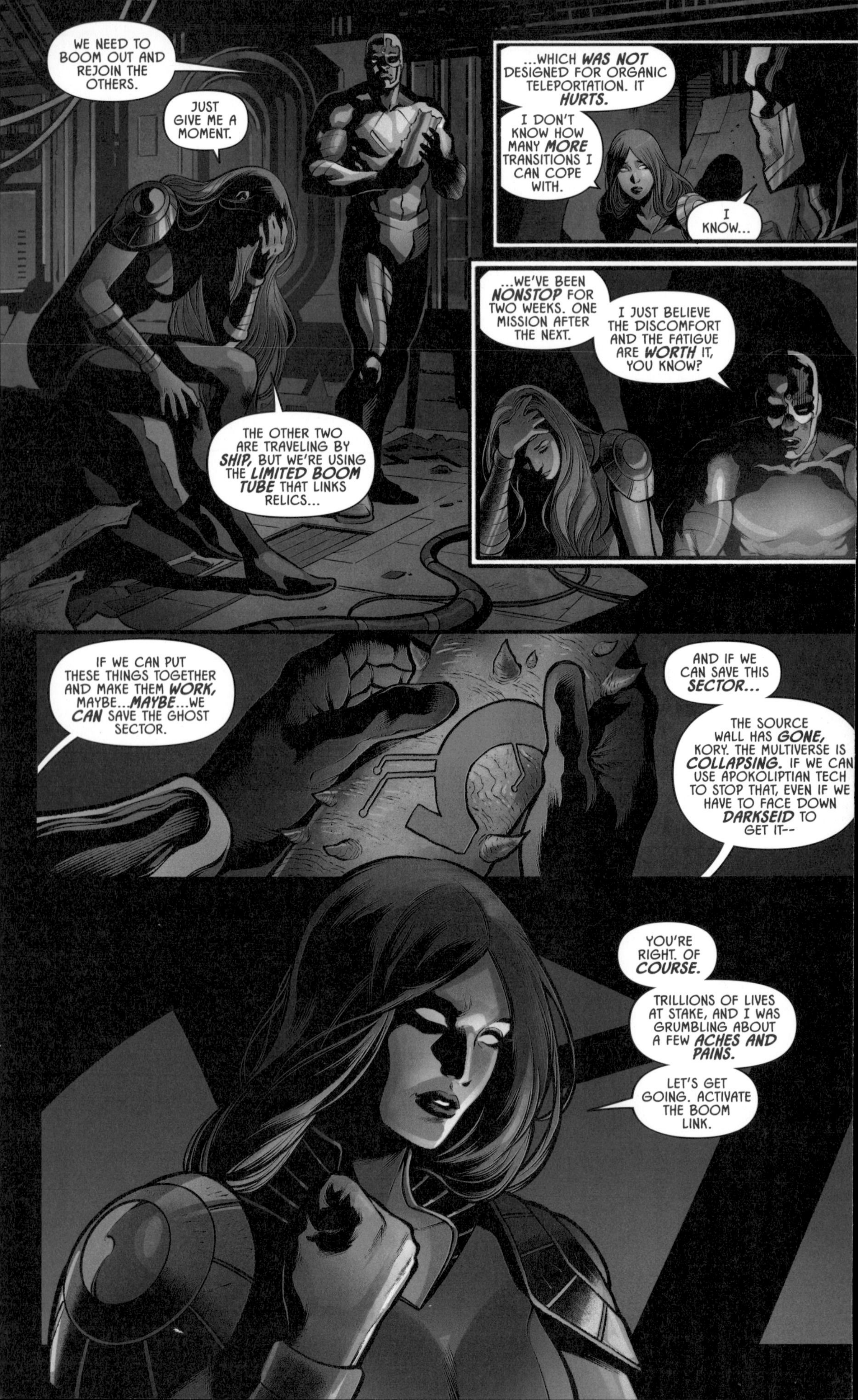

WE NEED TO BOOM OUT AND REJOIN THE OTHERS.
JUST GIVE ME A MOMENT.
THE OTHER TWO ARE TRAVELING BY SHIP, BUT WE'RE USING THE LIMITED BOOM TUBE THAT LINKS RELICS...
...WHICH WAS NOT DESIGNED FOR ORGANIC TELEPORTATION. IT HURTS.
I DON'T KNOW HOW MANY MORE TRANSITIONS I CAN COPE WITH.
I KNOW...
...WE'VE BEEN NONSTOP FOR TWO WEEKS. ONE MISSION AFTER THE NEXT.
I JUST BELIEVE THE DISCOMFORT AND THE FATIGUE ARE WORTH IT, YOU KNOW?
IF WE CAN PUT THESE THINGS TOGETHER AND MAKE THEM WORK, MAYBE...MAYBE...WE CAN SAVE THE GHOST SECTOR.
AND IF WE CAN SAVE THIS SECTOR...
THE SOURCE WALL HAS GONE, KORY. THE MULTIVERSE IS COLLAPSING. IF WE CAN USE APOKOLIPTIAN TECH TO STOP THAT, EVEN IF WE HAVE TO FACE DOWN DARKSEID TO GET IT--
YOU'RE RIGHT. OF COURSE.
TRILLIONS OF LIVES AT STAKE, AND I WAS GRUMBLING ABOUT A FEW ACHES AND PAINS.
LET'S GET GOING. ACTIVATE THE BOOM LINK.

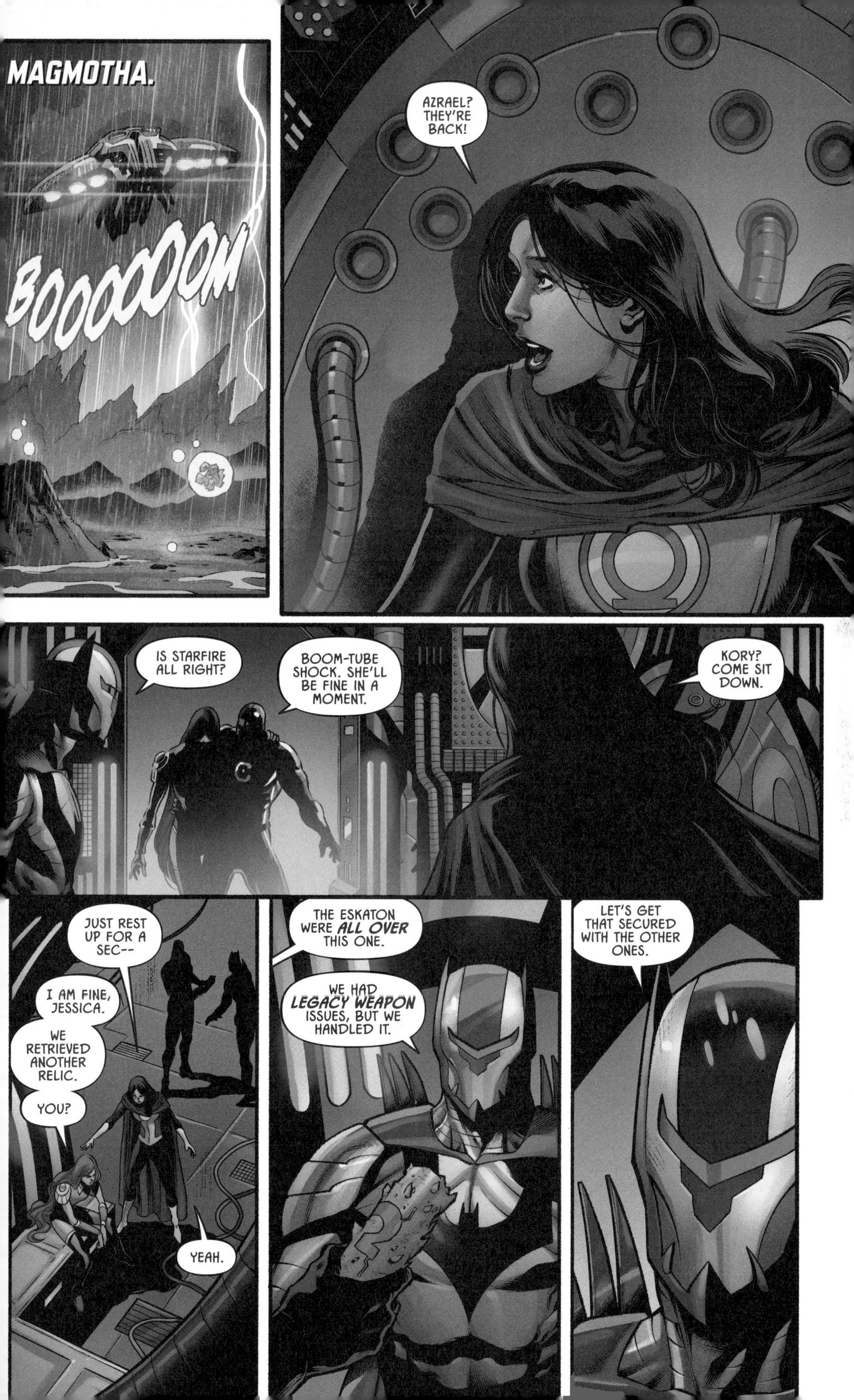
MAGMOTHA.
BOOOOOOM
AZRAEL? THEY'RE BACK!
IS STARFIRE ALL RIGHT?
BOOM-TUBE SHOCK. SHE'LL BE FINE IN A MOMENT.
KORY? COME SIT DOWN.
JUST REST UP FOR A SEC--
I AM FINE, JESSICA.
WE RETRIEVED ANOTHER RELIC.
YOU?
YEAH.
THE ESKATON WERE ALL OVER THIS ONE.
WE HAD LEGACY WEAPON ISSUES, BUT WE HANDLED IT.
LET'S GET THAT SECURED WITH THE OTHER ONES.

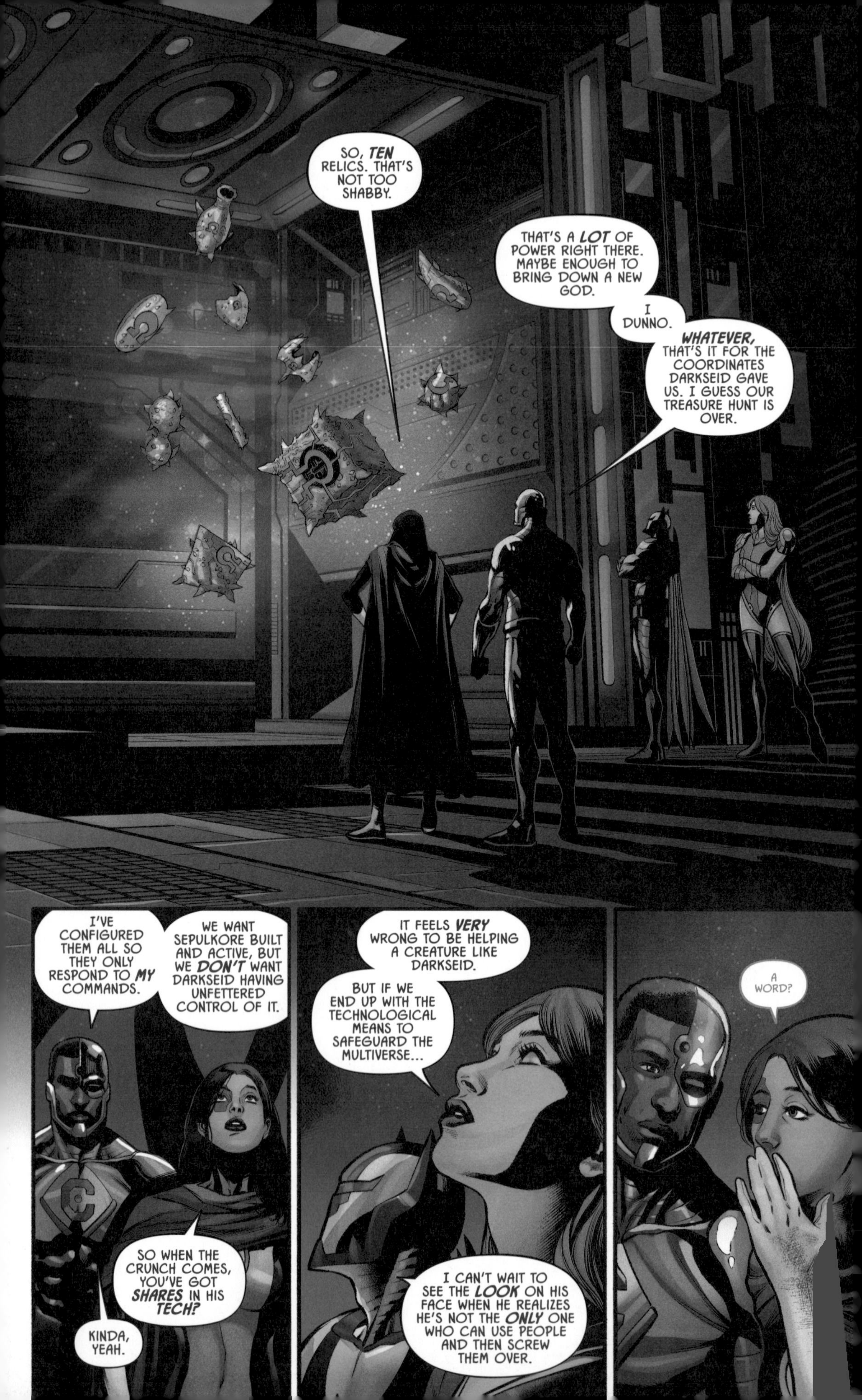
SO, TEN RELICS. THAT'S NOT TOO SHABBY.
THAT'S A LOT OF POWER RIGHT THERE. MAYBE ENOUGH TO BRING DOWN A NEW GOD.
I DUNNO.
WHATEVER, THAT'S IT FOR THE COORDINATES DARKSEID GAVE US. I GUESS OUR TREASURE HUNT IS OVER.
I'VE CONFIGURED THEM ALL SO THEY ONLY RESPOND TO MY COMMANDS.
WE WANT SEPULKORE BUILT AND ACTIVE, BUT WE DON'T WANT DARKSEID HAVING UNFETTERED CONTROL OF IT.
SO WHEN THE CRUNCH COMES, YOU'VE GOT SHARES IN HIS TECH?
KINDA, YEAH.
IT FEELS VERY WRONG TO BE HELPING A CREATURE LIKE DARKSEID.
BUT IF WE END UP WITH THE TECHNOLOGICAL MEANS TO SAFEGUARD THE MULTIVERSE...
I CAN'T WAIT TO SEE THE LOOK ON HIS FACE WHEN HE REALIZES HE'S NOT THE ONLY ONE WHO CAN USE PEOPLE AND THEN SCREW THEM OVER.
A WORD?

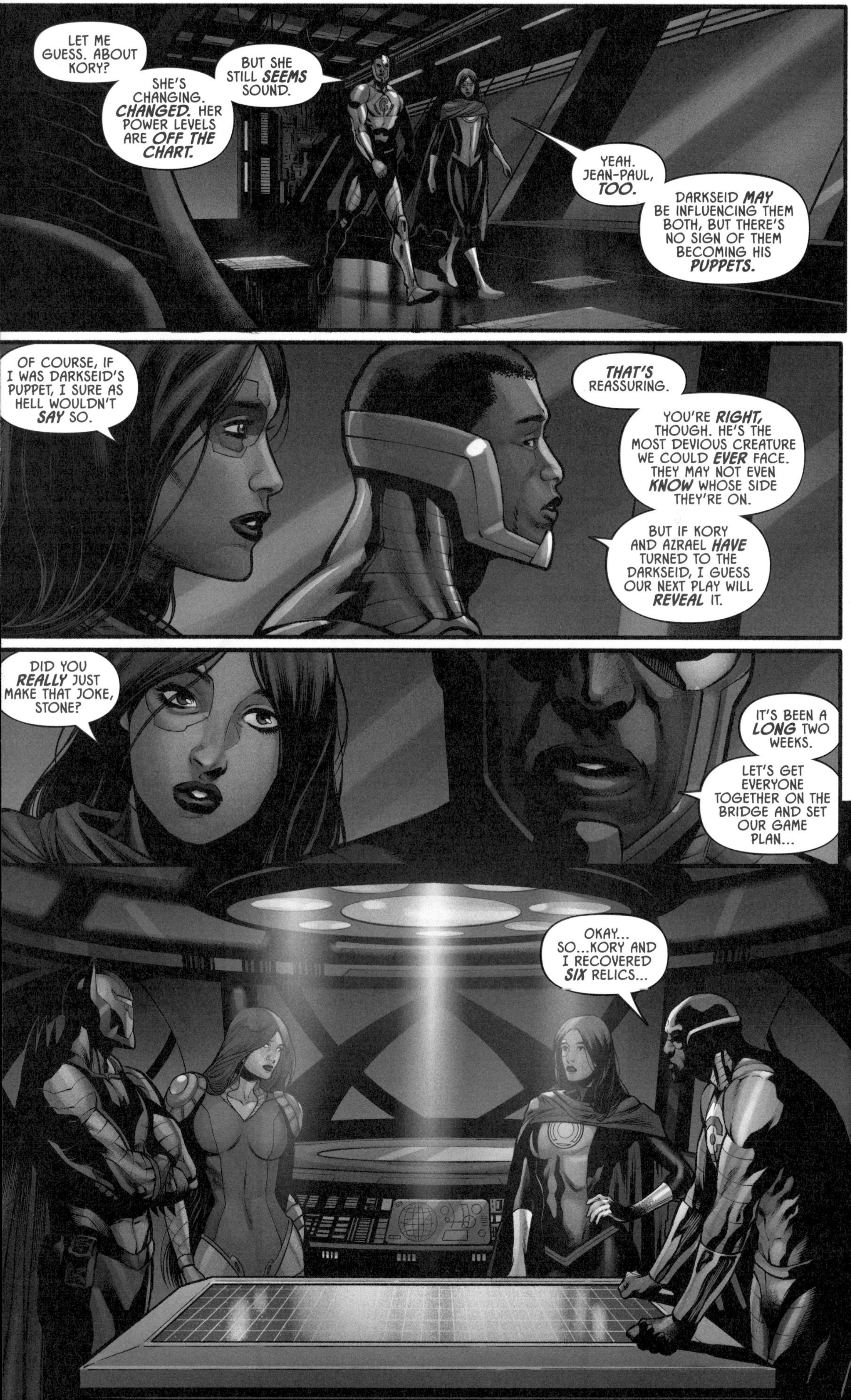
LET ME GUESS. ABOUT KORY?
SHE'S CHANGING. CHANGED. HER POWER LEVELS ARE OFF THE CHART.
BUT SHE STILL SEEMS SOUND.
YEAH. JEAN-PAUL, TOO.
DARKSEID MAY BE INFLUENCING THEM BOTH, BUT THERE'S NO SIGN OF THEM BECOMING HIS PUPPETS.
OF COURSE, IF I WAS DARKSEID'S PUPPET, I SURE AS HELL WOULDN'T SAY SO.
THAT'S REASSURING.
YOU'RE RIGHT, THOUGH. HE'S THE MOST DEVIOUS CREATURE WE COULD EVER FACE. THEY MAY NOT EVEN KNOW WHOSE SIDE THEY'RE ON.
BUT IF KORY AND AZRAEL HAVE TURNED TO THE DARKSEID, I GUESS OUR NEXT PLAY WILL REVEAL IT.
DID YOU REALLY JUST MAKE THAT JOKE, STONE?
IT'S BEEN A LONG TWO WEEKS.
LET'S GET EVERYONE TOGETHER ON THE BRIDGE AND SET OUR GAME PLAN...
OKAY... SO...KORY AND I RECOVERED SIX RELICS...

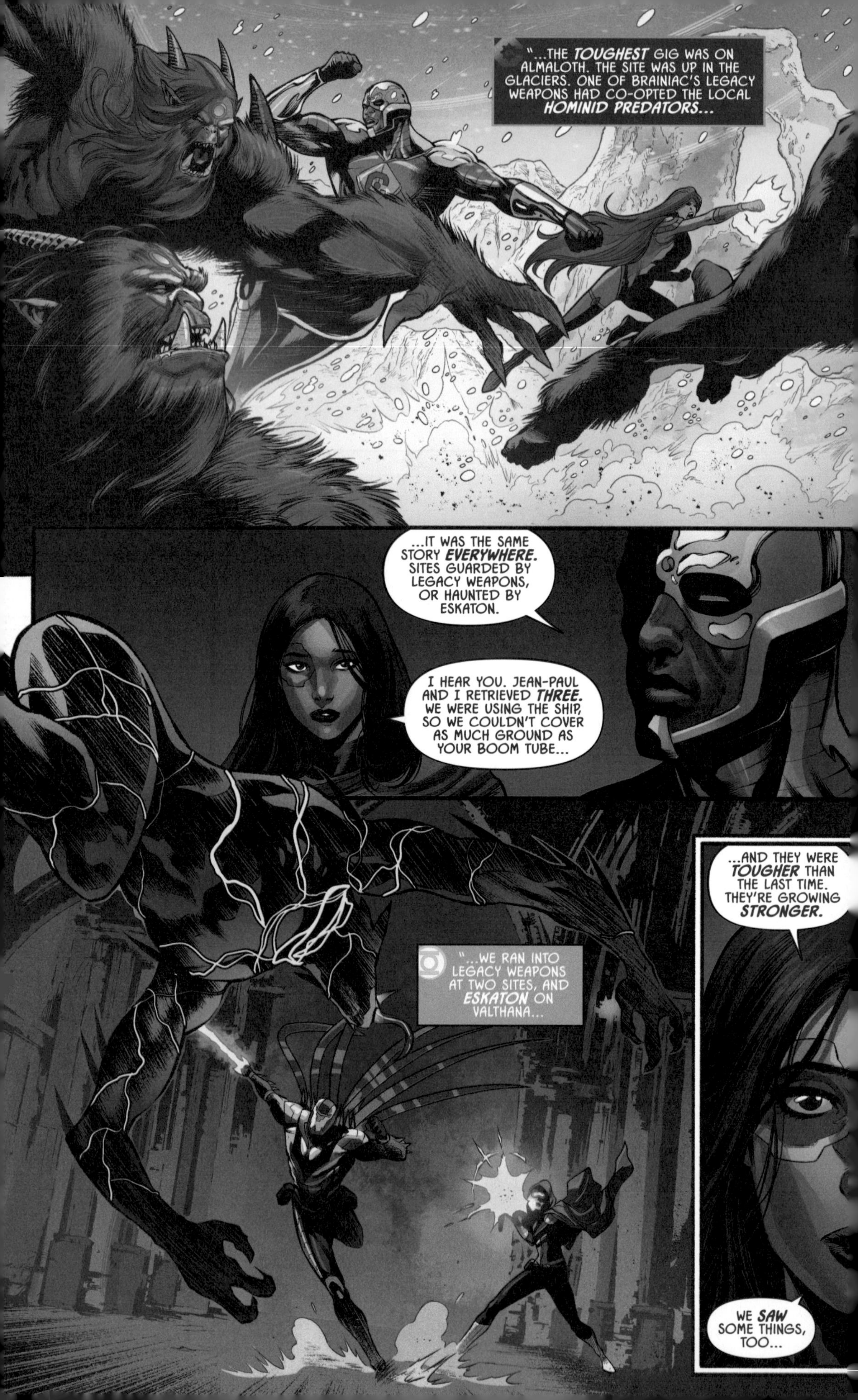
"...THE TOUGHEST GIG WAS ON ALMALOTH. THE SITE WAS UP IN THE GLACIERS. ONE OF BRAINIAC'S LEGACY WEAPONS HAD CO-OPTED THE LOCAL HOMINID PREDATORS...
...IT WAS THE SAME STORY EVERYWHERE. SITES GUARDED BY LEGACY WEAPONS, OR HAUNTED BY ESKATON.
I HEAR YOU. JEAN-PAUL AND I RETRIEVED THREE. WE WERE USING THE SHIP, SO WE COULDN'T COVER AS MUCH GROUND AS YOUR BOOM TUBE...
"...WE RAN INTO LEGACY WEAPONS AT TWO SITES, AND ESKATON ON VALTHANA...
...AND THEY WERE TOUGHER THAN THE LAST TIME. THEY'RE GROWING STRONGER.
WE SAW SOME THINGS, TOO...

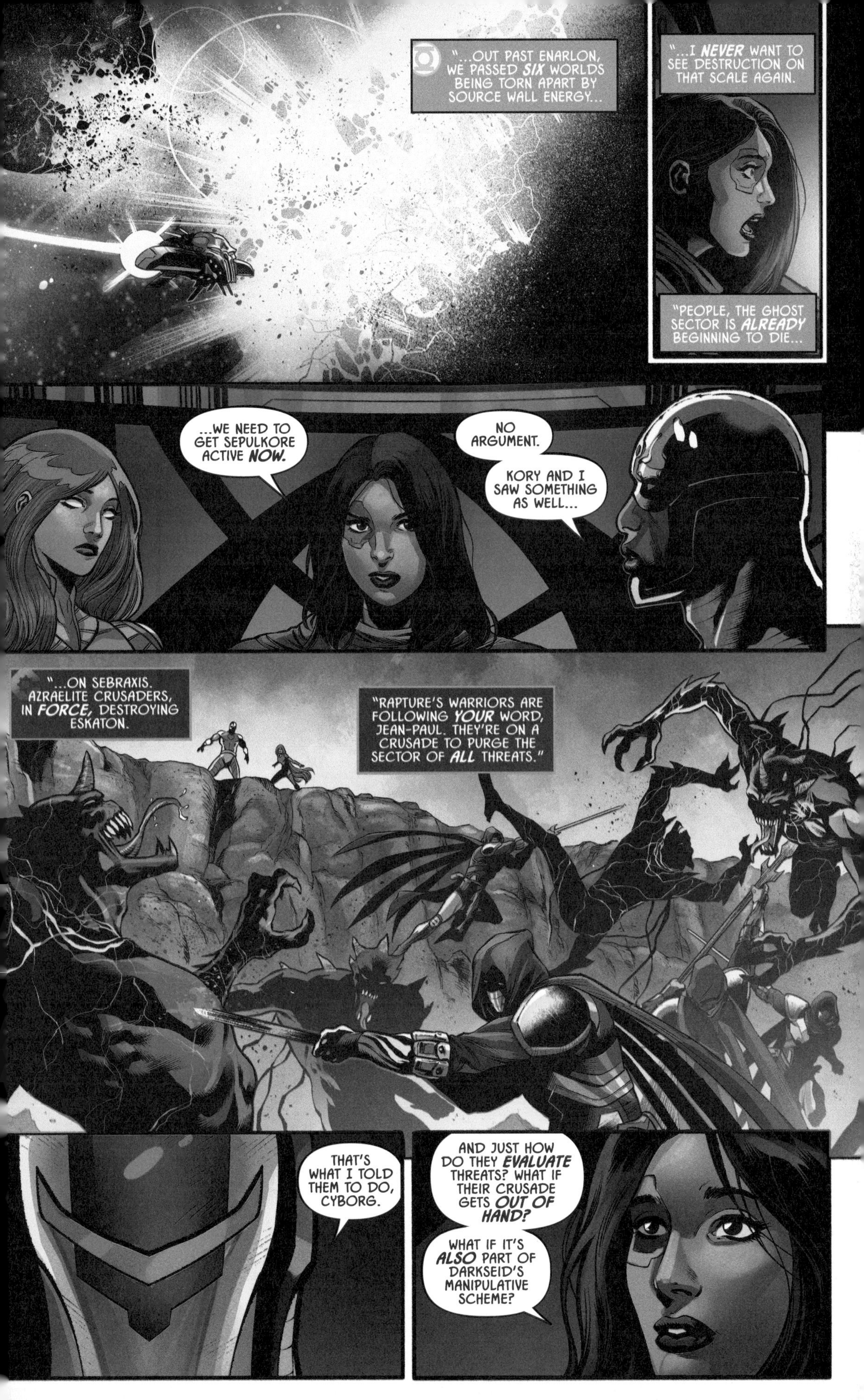
"...OUT PAST ENARLON, WE PASSED SIX WORLDS BEING TORN APART BY SOURCE WALL ENERGY...
"...I NEVER WANT TO SEE DESTRUCTION ON THAT SCALE AGAIN.
"PEOPLE, THE GHOST SECTOR IS ALREADY BEGINNING TO DIE...
...WE NEED TO GET SEPULKORE ACTIVE NOW.
NO ARGUMENT.
KORY AND I SAW SOMETHING AS WELL...
"...ON SEBRAXIS. AZRAELITE CRUSADERS, IN FORCE, DESTROYING ESKATON.
"RAPTURE'S WARRIORS ARE FOLLOWING YOUR WORD, JEAN-PAUL. THEY'RE ON A CRUSADE TO PURGE THE SECTOR OF ALL THREATS."
THAT'S WHAT I TOLD THEM TO DO, CYBORG.
AND JUST HOW DO THEY EVALUATE THREATS? WHAT IF THEIR CRUSADE GETS OUT OF HAND?
WHAT IF IT'S ALSO PART OF DARKSEID'S MANIPULATIVE SCHEME?

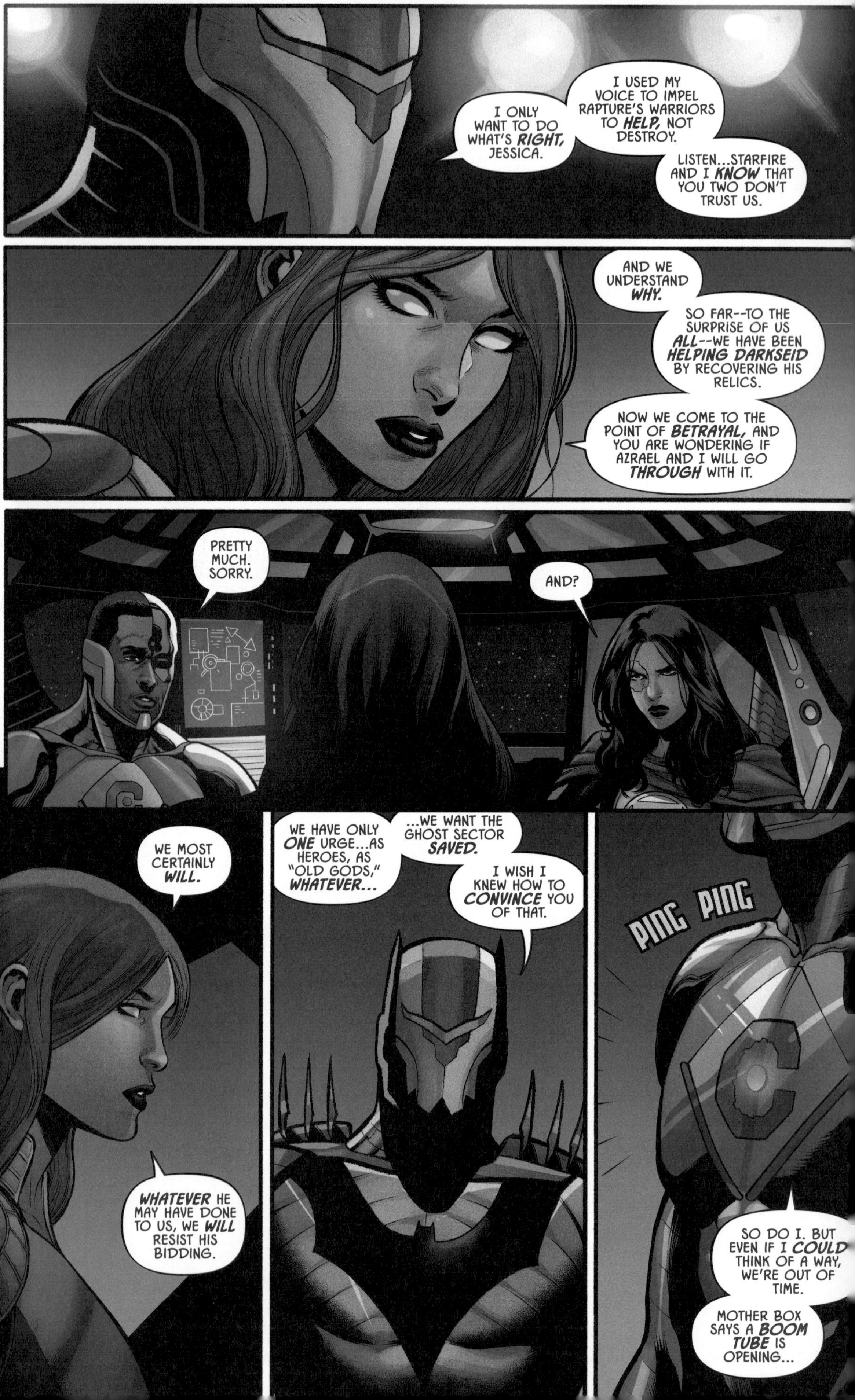
I ONLY WANT TO DO WHAT'S RIGHT, JESSICA.
I USED MY VOICE TO IMPEL RAPTURE'S WARRIORS TO HELP, NOT DESTROY.
LISTEN...STARFIRE AND I KNOW THAT YOU TWO DON'T TRUST US.
AND WE UNDERSTAND WHY.
SO FAR--TO THE SURPRISE OF US ALL--WE HAVE BEEN HELPING DARKSEID BY RECOVERING HIS RELICS.
NOW WE COME TO THE POINT OF BETRAYAL, AND YOU ARE WONDERING IF AZRAEL AND I WILL GO THROUGH WITH IT.
PRETTY MUCH. SORRY.
AND?
WE MOST CERTAINLY WILL.
WHATEVER HE MAY HAVE DONE TO US, WE WILL RESIST HIS BIDDING.
WE HAVE ONLY ONE URGE...AS HEROES, AS "OLD GODS," WHATEVER...
...WE WANT THE GHOST SECTOR SAVED.
I WISH I KNEW HOW TO CONVINCE YOU OF THAT.
PING PING
SO DO I. BUT EVEN IF I COULD THINK OF A WAY, WE'RE OUT OF TIME.
MOTHER BOX SAYS A BOOM TUBE IS OPENING...

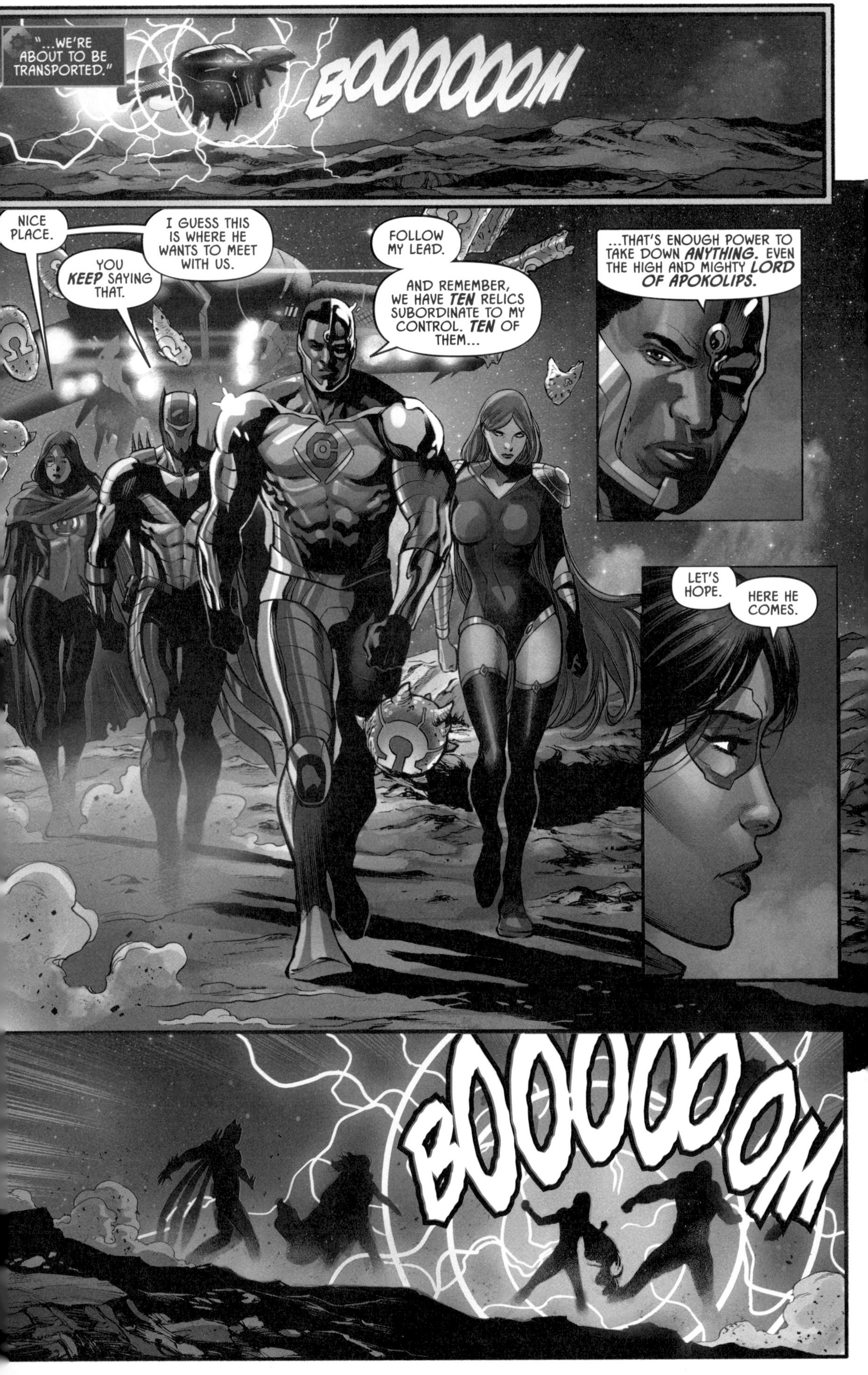
"...WE'RE ABOUT TO BE TRANSPORTED."
BOOOOOOM
NICE PLACE.
I GUESS THIS IS WHERE HE WANTS TO MEET WITH US.
YOU KEEP SAYING THAT.
FOLLOW MY LEAD.
AND REMEMBER, WE HAVE TEN RELICS SUBORDINATE TO MY CONTROL. TEN OF THEM...
...THAT'S ENOUGH POWER TO TAKE DOWN ANYTHING. EVEN THE HIGH AND MIGHTY LORD OF APOKOLIPS.
LET'S HOPE.
HERE HE COMES.
BOOOOOOM

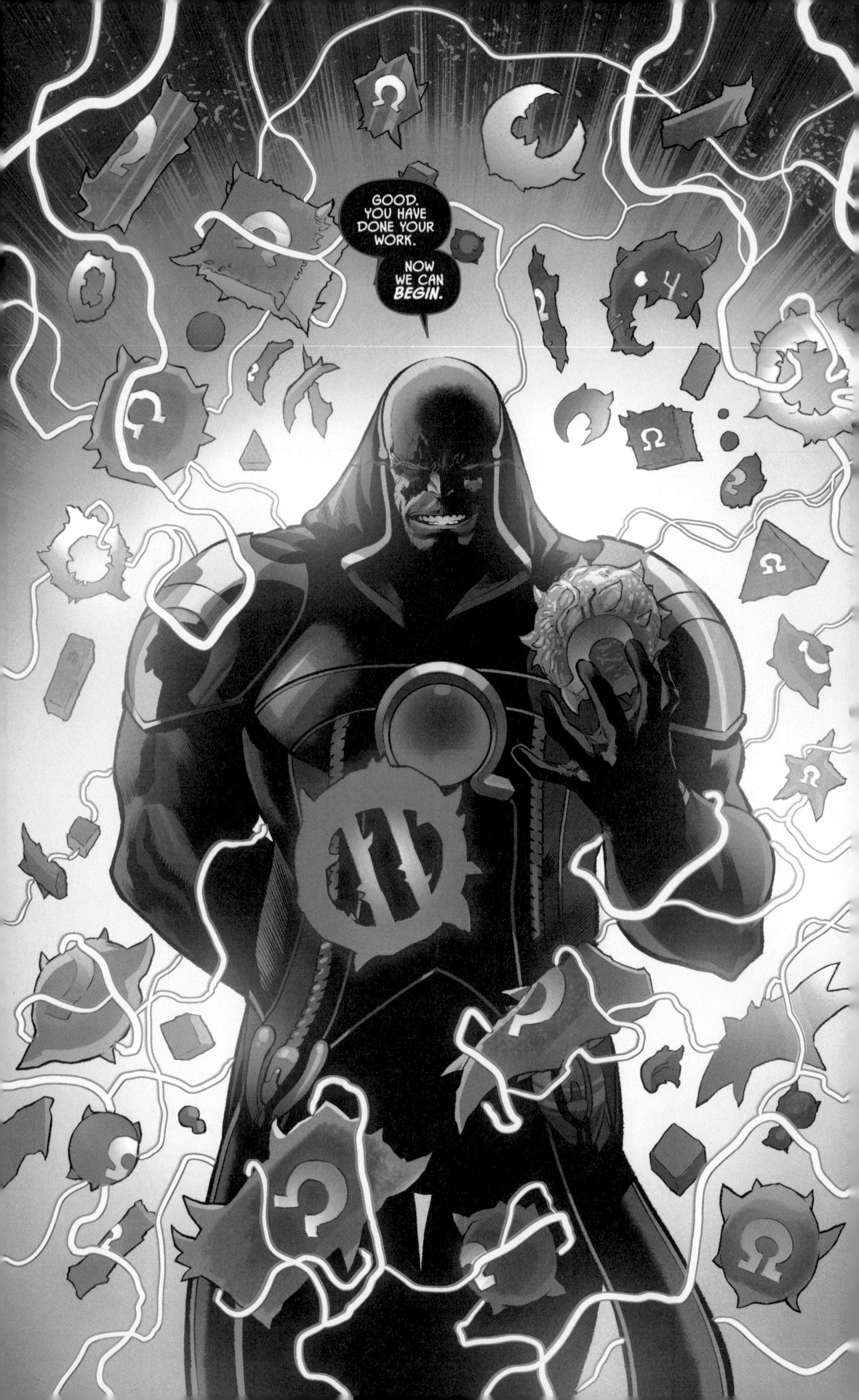
GOOD. YOU HAVE DONE YOUR WORK.
NOW WE CAN *BEGIN*.

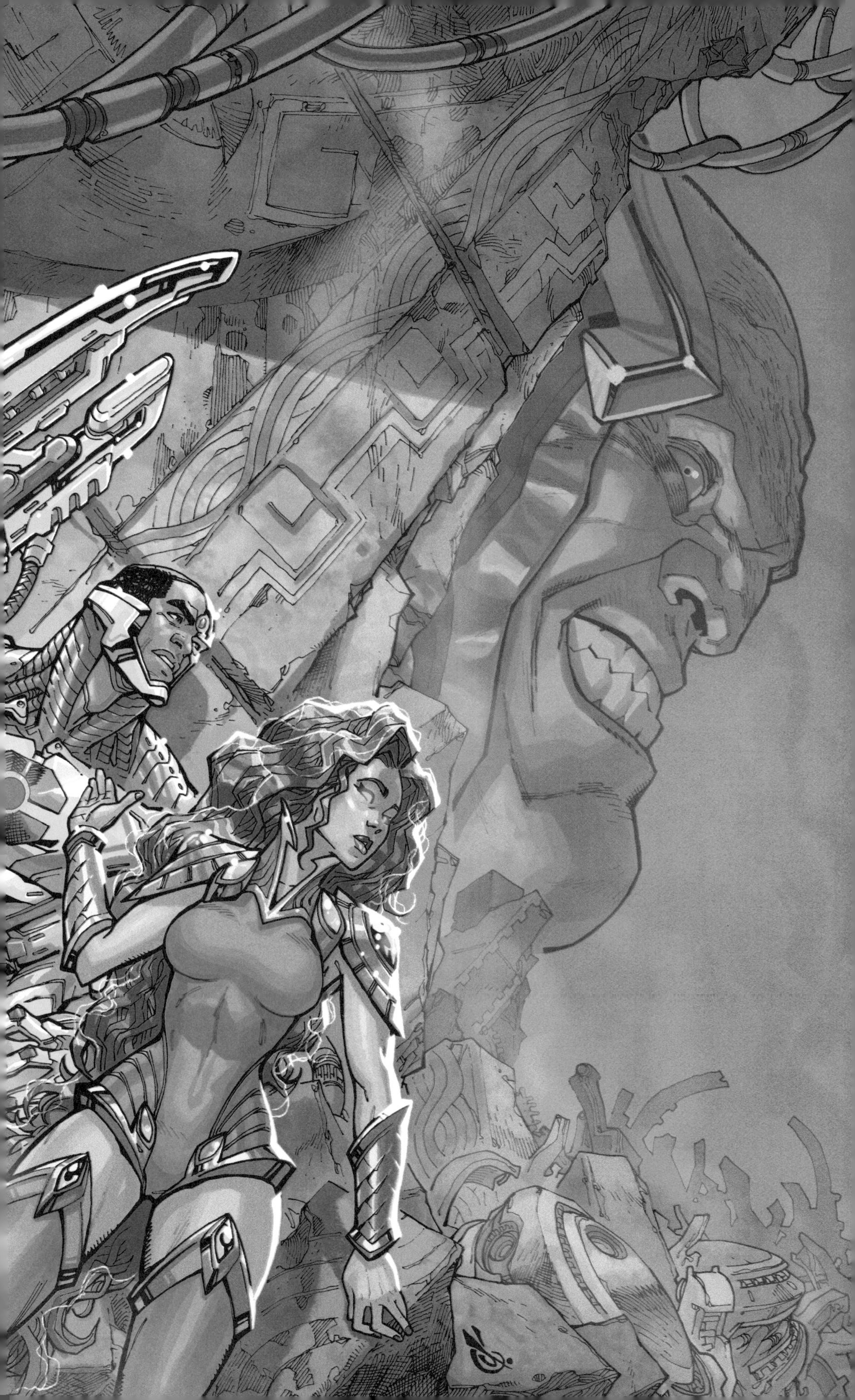

Variant cover art for issue #11 by LUCIO PARRILLO

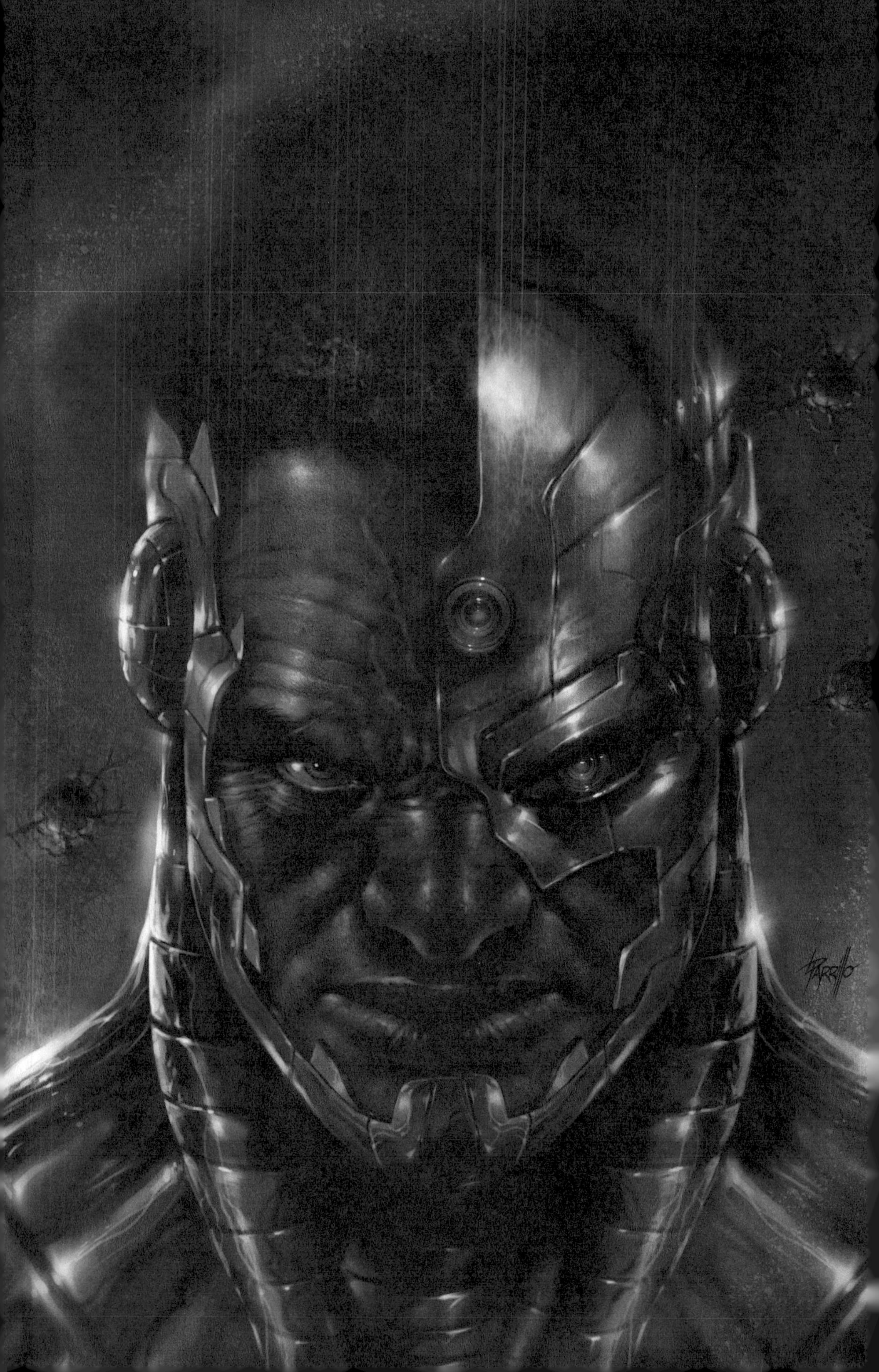

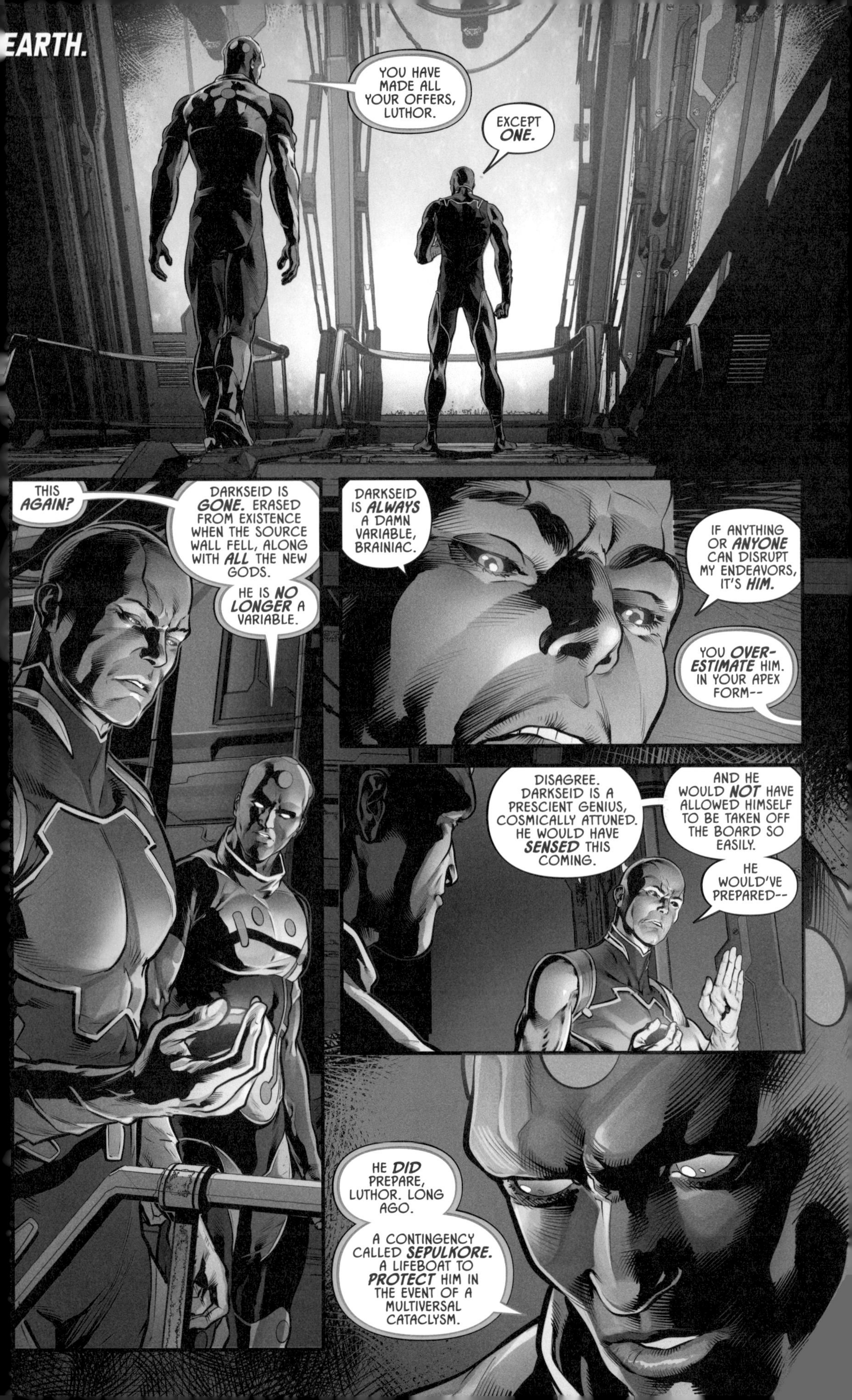
EARTH.
YOU HAVE MADE ALL YOUR OFFERS, LUTHOR.
EXCEPT ONE.
THIS AGAIN?
DARKSEID IS GONE. ERASED FROM EXISTENCE WHEN THE SOURCE WALL FELL, ALONG WITH ALL THE NEW GODS.
HE IS NO LONGER A VARIABLE.
DARKSEID IS ALWAYS A DAMN VARIABLE, BRAINIAC.
IF ANYTHING OR ANYONE CAN DISRUPT MY ENDEAVORS, IT'S HIM.
YOU OVER-ESTIMATE HIM. IN YOUR APEX FORM--
DISAGREE. DARKSEID IS A PRESCIENT GENIUS, COSMICALLY ATTUNED. HE WOULD HAVE SENSED THIS COMING.
AND HE WOULD NOT HAVE ALLOWED HIMSELF TO BE TAKEN OFF THE BOARD SO EASILY.
HE WOULD'VE PREPARED--
HE DID PREPARE, LUTHOR. LONG AGO.
A CONTINGENCY CALLED SEPULKORE. A LIFEBOAT TO PROTECT HIM IN THE EVENT OF A MULTIVERSAL CATACLYSM.

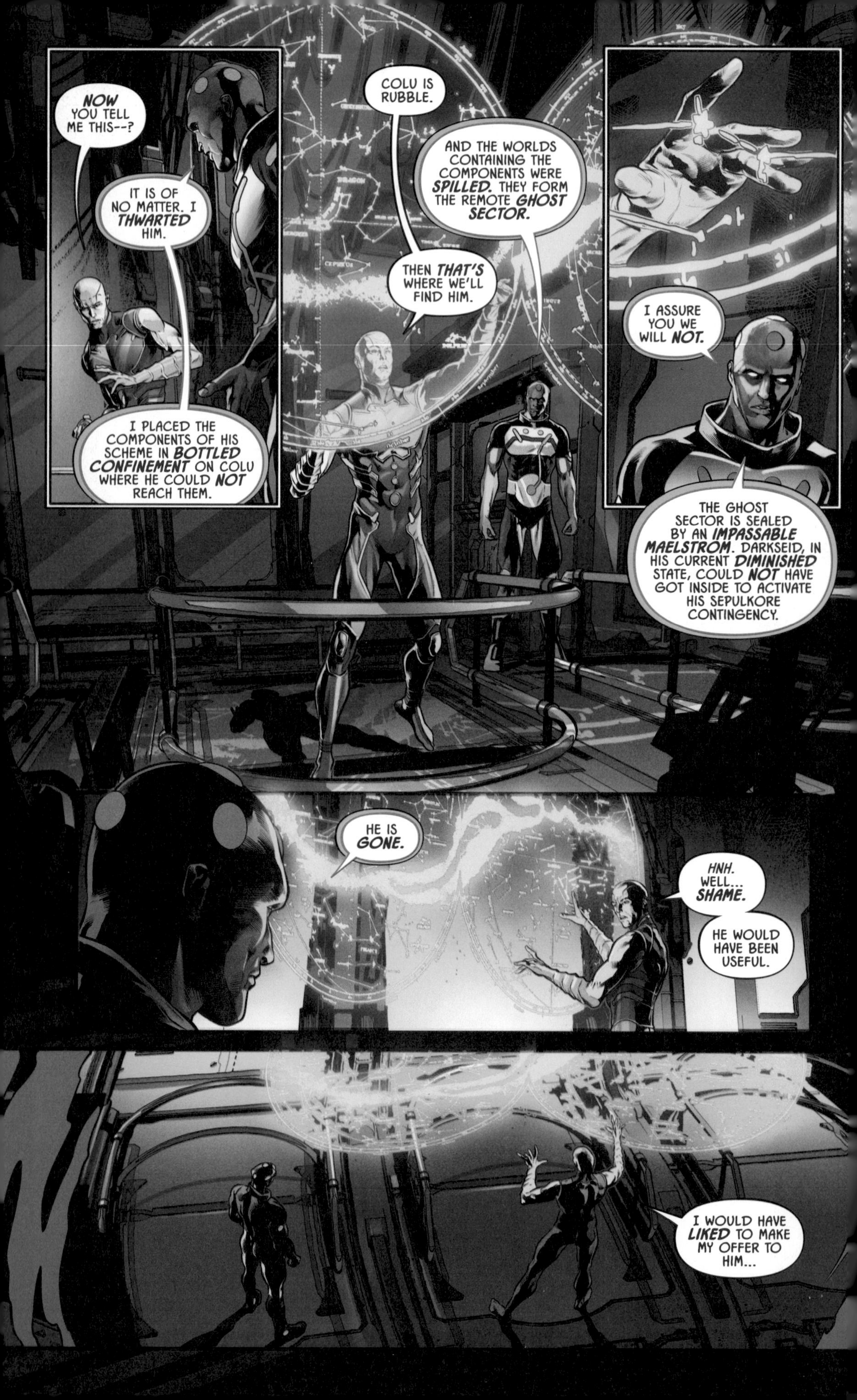
NOW YOU TELL ME THIS--?
IT IS OF NO MATTER. I THWARTED HIM.
I PLACED THE COMPONENTS OF HIS SCHEME IN BOTTLED CONFINEMENT ON COLU WHERE HE COULD NOT REACH THEM.
COLU IS RUBBLE.
AND THE WORLDS CONTAINING THE COMPONENTS WERE SPILLED. THEY FORM THE REMOTE GHOST SECTOR.
THEN THAT'S WHERE WE'LL FIND HIM.
I ASSURE YOU WE WILL NOT.
THE GHOST SECTOR IS SEALED BY AN IMPASSABLE MAELSTROM. DARKSEID, IN HIS CURRENT DIMINISHED STATE, COULD NOT HAVE GOT INSIDE TO ACTIVATE HIS SEPULKORE CONTINGENCY.
HE IS GONE.
HNH. WELL... SHAME.
HE WOULD HAVE BEEN USEFUL.
I WOULD HAVE LIKED TO MAKE MY OFFER TO HIM...

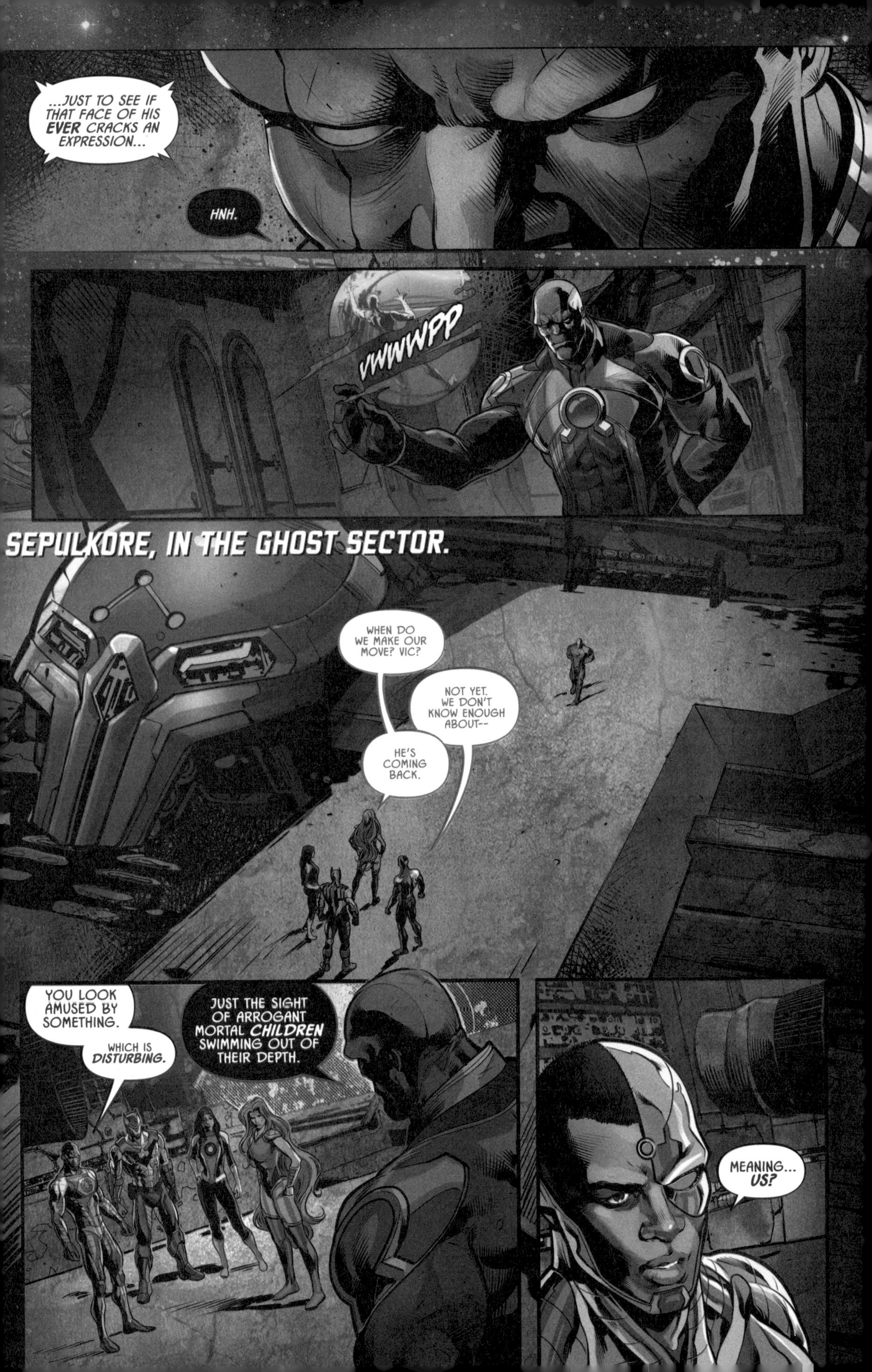
...JUST TO SEE IF THAT FACE OF HIS EVER CRACKS AN EXPRESSION...
HNH.
VWWWPP
SEPULKORE, IN THE GHOST SECTOR.
WHEN DO WE MAKE OUR MOVE? VIC?
NOT YET. WE DON'T KNOW ENOUGH ABOUT--
HE'S COMING BACK.
YOU LOOK AMUSED BY SOMETHING.
WHICH IS DISTURBING.
JUST THE SIGHT OF ARROGANT MORTAL CHILDREN SWIMMING OUT OF THEIR DEPTH.
MEANING... US?

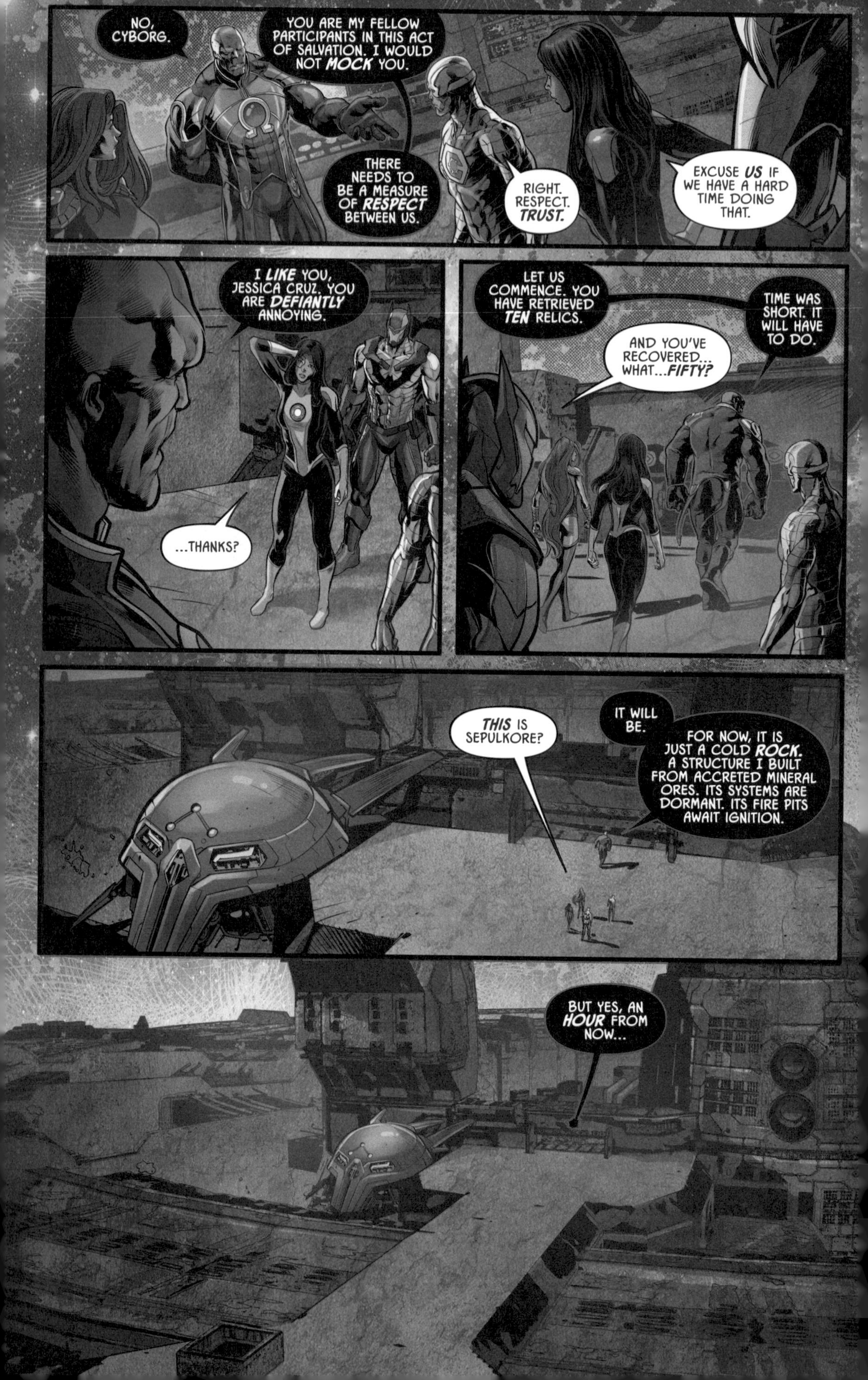
NO, CYBORG.
YOU ARE MY FELLOW PARTICIPANTS IN THIS ACT OF SALVATION. I WOULD NOT MOCK YOU.
THERE NEEDS TO BE A MEASURE OF RESPECT BETWEEN US.
RIGHT. RESPECT. TRUST.
EXCUSE US IF WE HAVE A HARD TIME DOING THAT.
I LIKE YOU, JESSICA CRUZ. YOU ARE DEFIANTLY ANNOYING.
...THANKS?
LET US COMMENCE. YOU HAVE RETRIEVED TEN RELICS.
TIME WAS SHORT. IT WILL HAVE TO DO.
AND YOU'VE RECOVERED... WHAT...FIFTY?
THIS IS SEPULKORE?
IT WILL BE.
FOR NOW, IT IS JUST A COLD ROCK. A STRUCTURE I BUILT FROM ACCRETED MINERAL ORES. ITS SYSTEMS ARE DORMANT. ITS FIRE PITS AWAIT IGNITION.
BUT YES, AN HOUR FROM NOW...

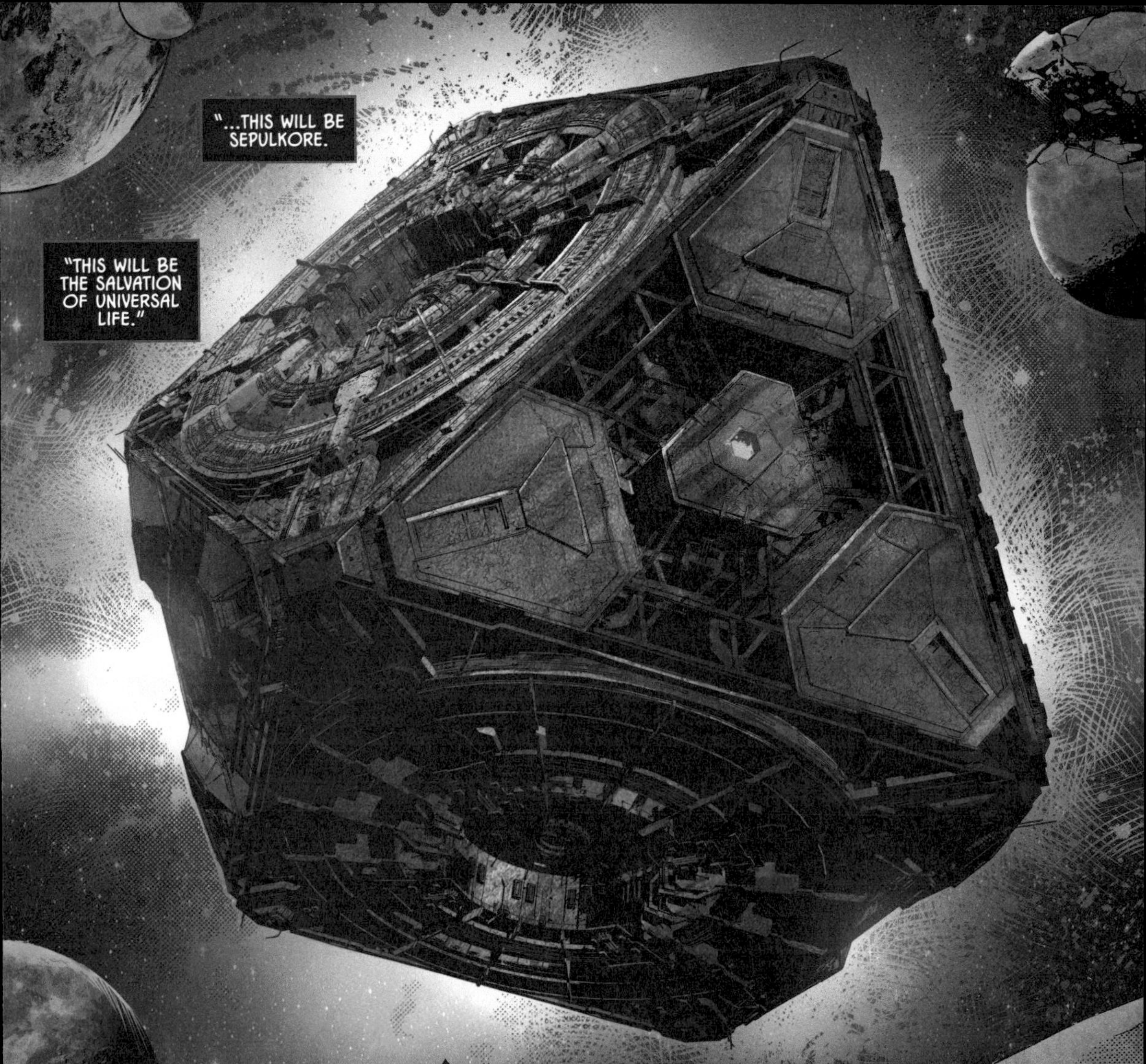
"...THIS WILL BE SEPULKORE.
"THIS WILL BE THE SALVATION OF UNIVERSAL LIFE."

SEPULKORE

DAN ABNETT Writer WILL CONRAD Art
IVAN PLASCENCIA & PETE PANTAZIS Colors
ANDWORLD DESIGN Letters
CARLOS D'ANDA Cover
HARVEY RICHARDS Editor JAMIE S. RICH Group Editor

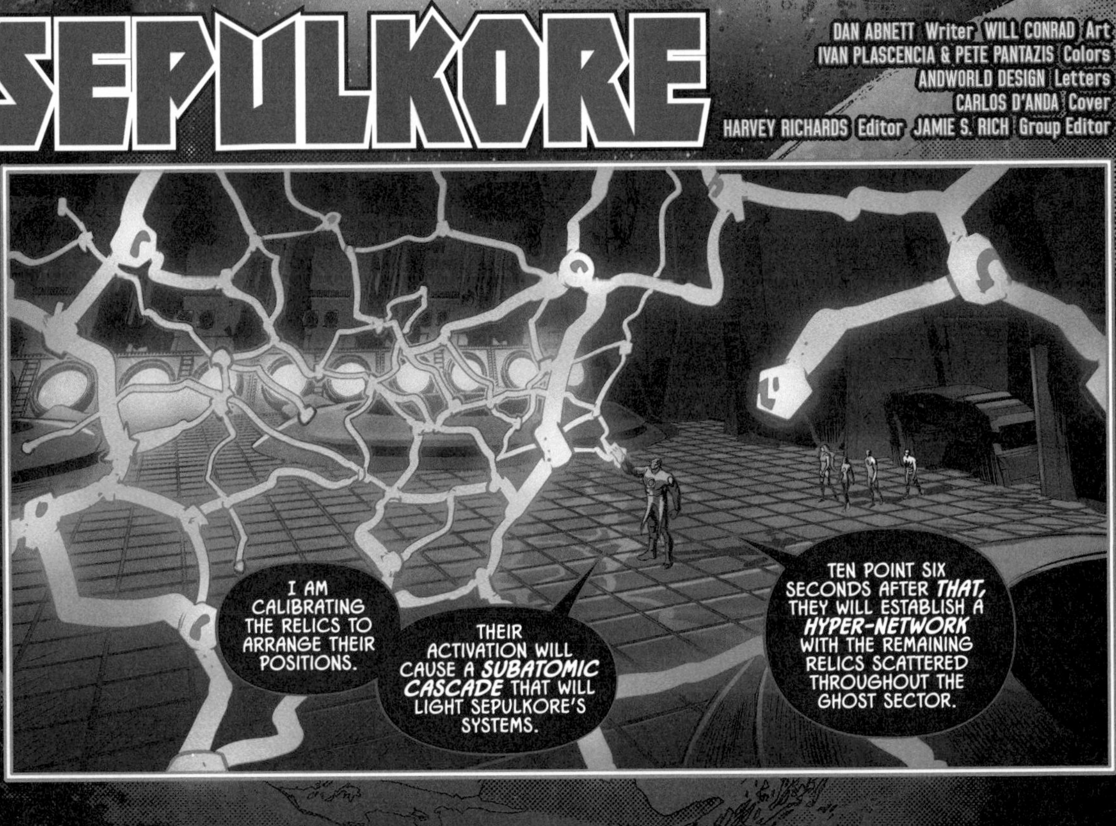
I AM CALIBRATING THE RELICS TO ARRANGE THEIR POSITIONS.
THEIR ACTIVATION WILL CAUSE A *SUBATOMIC CASCADE* THAT WILL LIGHT SEPULKORE'S SYSTEMS.
TEN POINT SIX SECONDS AFTER *THAT,* THEY WILL ESTABLISH A *HYPER-NETWORK* WITH THE REMAINING RELICS SCATTERED THROUGHOUT THE GHOST SECTOR.

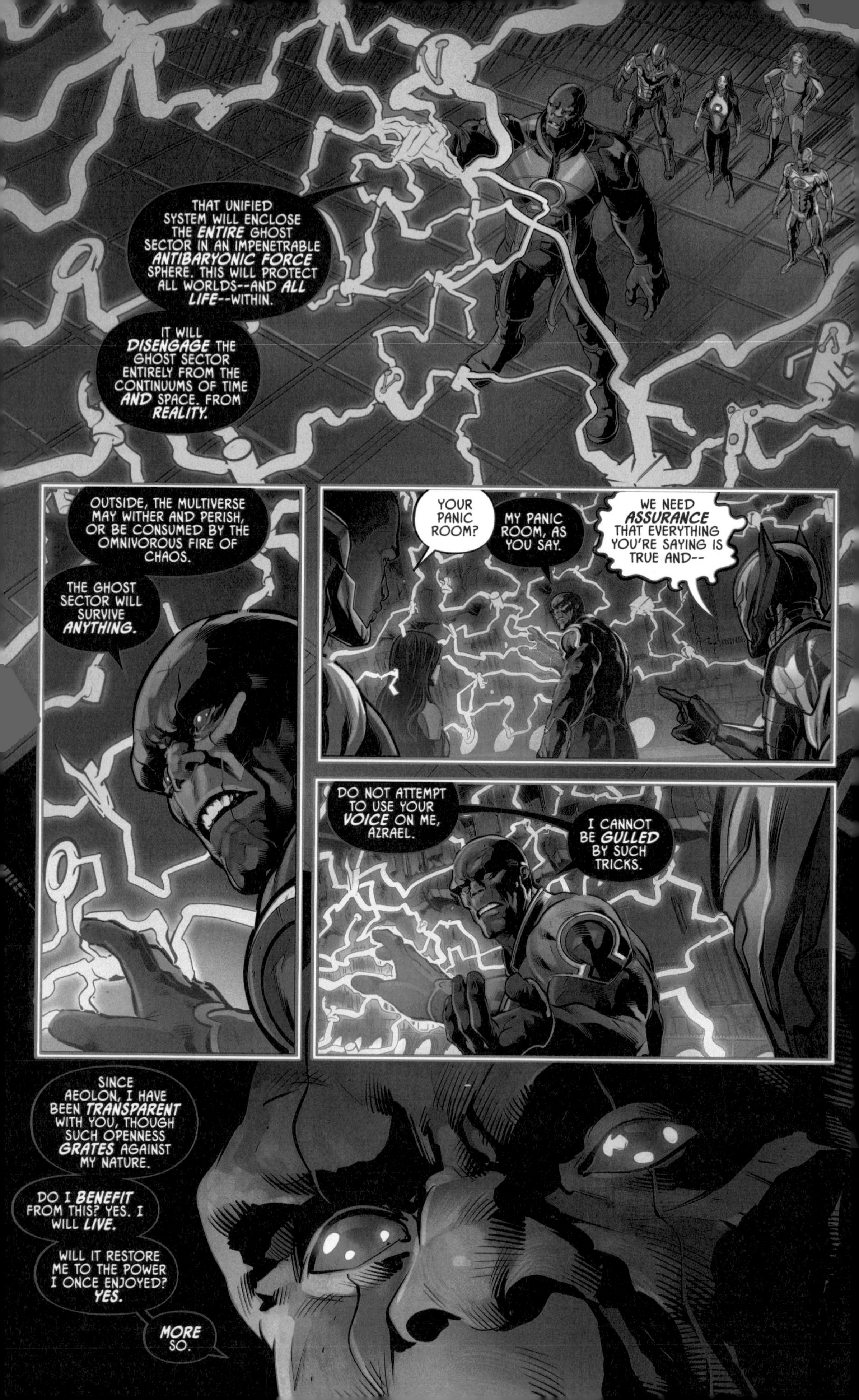
THAT UNIFIED SYSTEM WILL ENCLOSE THE ENTIRE GHOST SECTOR IN AN IMPENETRABLE ANTIBARYONIC FORCE SPHERE. THIS WILL PROTECT ALL WORLDS--AND ALL LIFE--WITHIN.
IT WILL DISENGAGE THE GHOST SECTOR ENTIRELY FROM THE CONTINUUMS OF TIME AND SPACE. FROM REALITY.
OUTSIDE, THE MULTIVERSE MAY WITHER AND PERISH, OR BE CONSUMED BY THE OMNIVOROUS FIRE OF CHAOS.
THE GHOST SECTOR WILL SURVIVE ANYTHING.
YOUR PANIC ROOM?
MY PANIC ROOM, AS YOU SAY.
WE NEED ASSURANCE THAT EVERYTHING YOU'RE SAYING IS TRUE AND--
DO NOT ATTEMPT TO USE YOUR VOICE ON ME, AZRAEL.
I CANNOT BE GULLED BY SUCH TRICKS.
SINCE AEOLON, I HAVE BEEN TRANSPARENT WITH YOU, THOUGH SUCH OPENNESS GRATES AGAINST MY NATURE.
DO I BENEFIT FROM THIS? YES. I WILL LIVE.
WILL IT RESTORE ME TO THE POWER I ONCE ENJOYED? YES.
MORE SO.

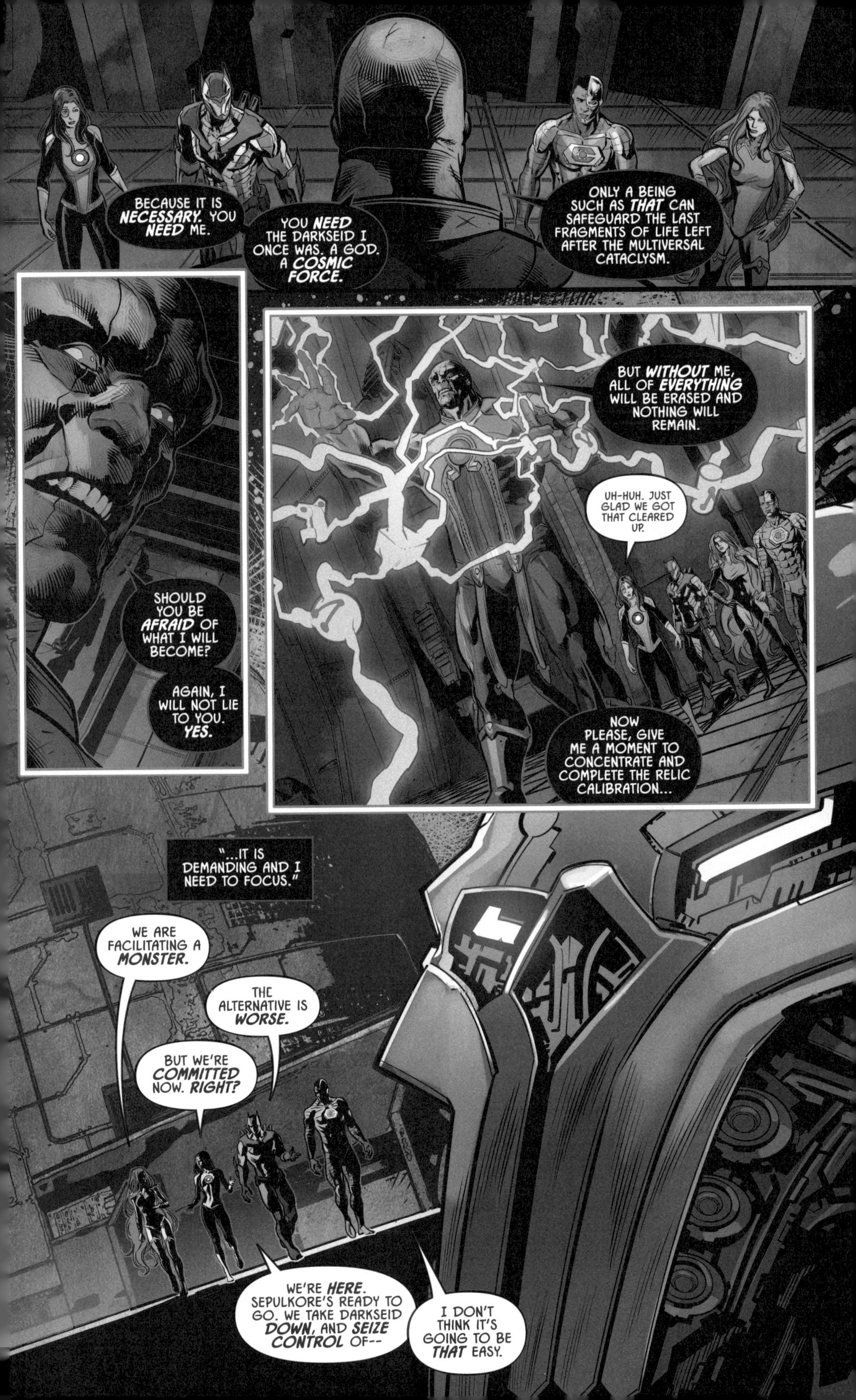
BECAUSE IT IS NECESSARY. YOU NEED ME.
YOU NEED THE DARKSEID I ONCE WAS. A GOD. A COSMIC FORCE.
ONLY A BEING SUCH AS THAT CAN SAFEGUARD THE LAST FRAGMENTS OF LIFE LEFT AFTER THE MULTIVERSAL CATACLYSM.
SHOULD YOU BE AFRAID OF WHAT I WILL BECOME?
AGAIN, I WILL NOT LIE TO YOU. YES.
BUT WITHOUT ME, ALL OF EVERYTHING WILL BE ERASED AND NOTHING WILL REMAIN.
UH-HUH. JUST GLAD WE GOT THAT CLEARED UP.
NOW PLEASE, GIVE ME A MOMENT TO CONCENTRATE AND COMPLETE THE RELIC CALIBRATION...
"...IT IS DEMANDING AND I NEED TO FOCUS."
WE ARE FACILITATING A MONSTER.
THE ALTERNATIVE IS WORSE.
BUT WE'RE COMMITTED NOW. RIGHT?
WE'RE HERE. SEPULKORE'S READY TO GO. WE TAKE DARKSEID DOWN, AND SEIZE CONTROL OF--
I DON'T THINK IT'S GOING TO BE THAT EASY.

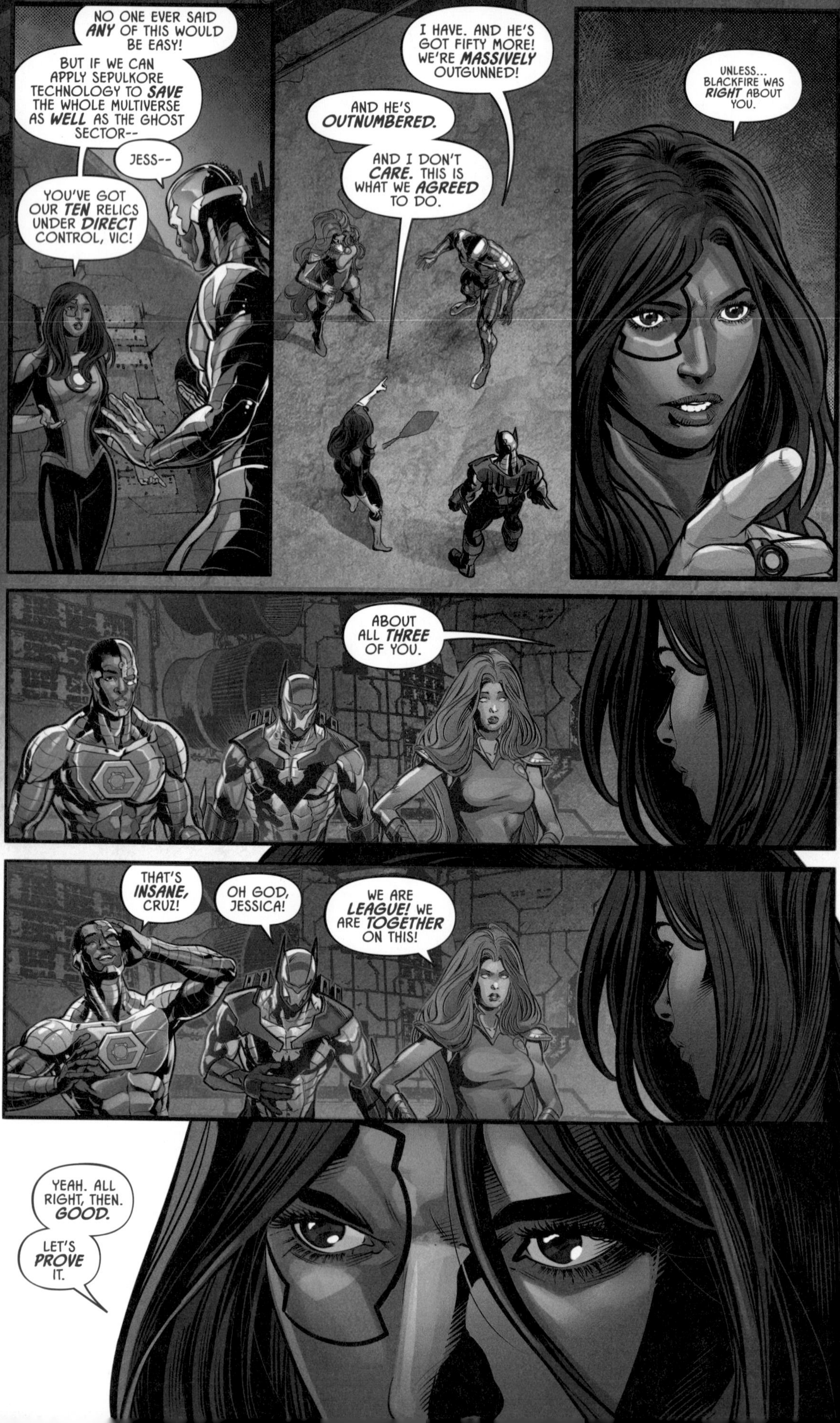
NO ONE EVER SAID ANY OF THIS WOULD BE EASY!
BUT IF WE CAN APPLY SEPULKORE TECHNOLOGY TO SAVE THE WHOLE MULTIVERSE AS WELL AS THE GHOST SECTOR--
JESS--
YOU'VE GOT OUR TEN RELICS UNDER DIRECT CONTROL, VIC!
I HAVE. AND HE'S GOT FIFTY MORE! WE'RE MASSIVELY OUTGUNNED!
AND HE'S OUTNUMBERED.
AND I DON'T CARE. THIS IS WHAT WE AGREED TO DO.
UNLESS... BLACKFIRE WAS RIGHT ABOUT YOU.
ABOUT ALL THREE OF YOU.
THAT'S INSANE, CRUZ!
OH GOD, JESSICA!
WE ARE LEAGUE! WE ARE TOGETHER ON THIS!
YEAH. ALL RIGHT, THEN. GOOD.
LET'S PROVE IT.

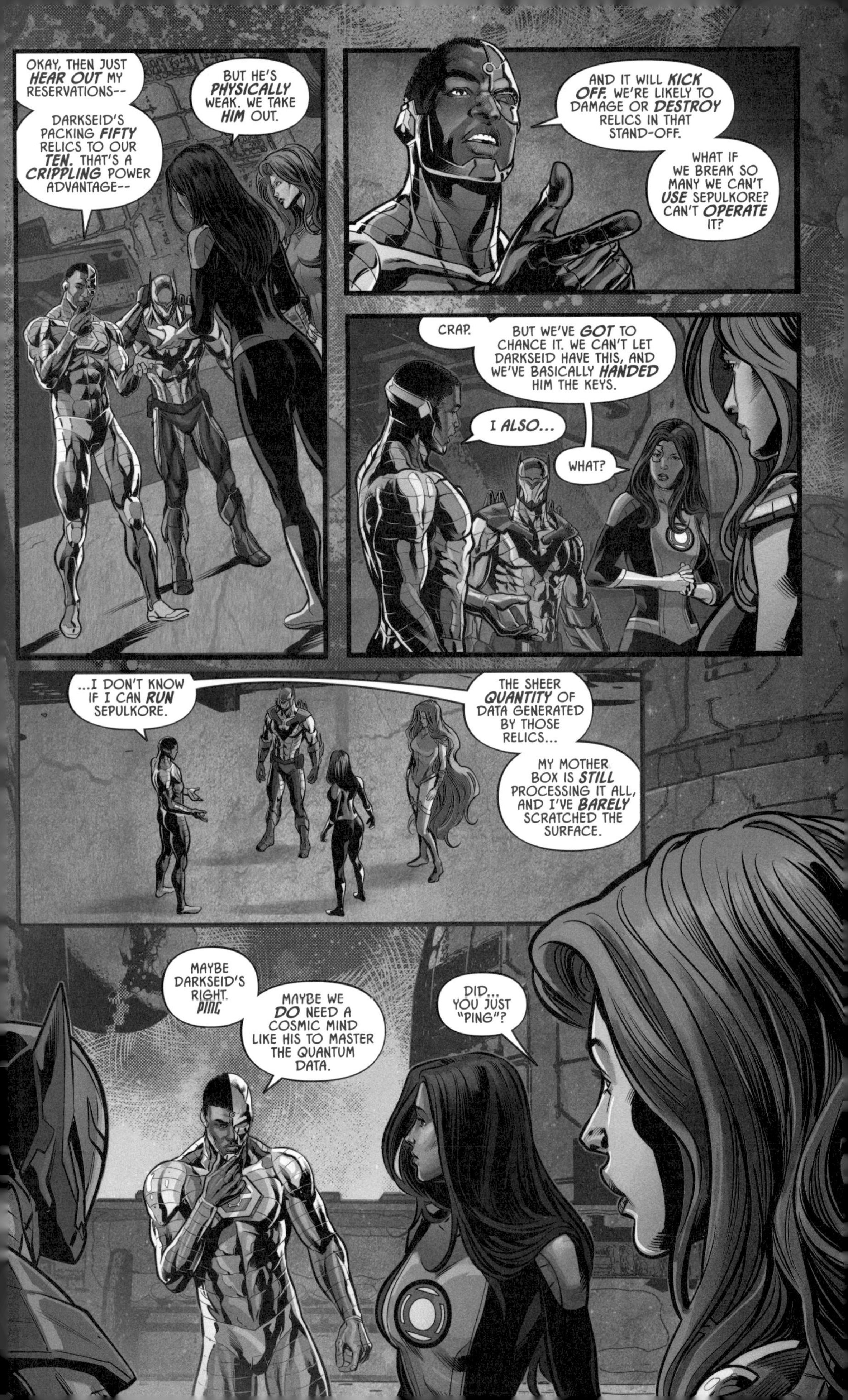
OKAY, THEN JUST HEAR OUT MY RESERVATIONS--
DARKSEID'S PACKING FIFTY RELICS TO OUR TEN. THAT'S A CRIPPLING POWER ADVANTAGE--
BUT HE'S PHYSICALLY WEAK. WE TAKE HIM OUT.
AND IT WILL KICK OFF. WE'RE LIKELY TO DAMAGE OR DESTROY RELICS IN THAT STAND-OFF.
WHAT IF WE BREAK SO MANY WE CAN'T USE SEPULKORE? CAN'T OPERATE IT?
CRAP.
BUT WE'VE GOT TO CHANCE IT. WE CAN'T LET DARKSEID HAVE THIS, AND WE'VE BASICALLY HANDED HIM THE KEYS.
I ALSO...
WHAT?
...I DON'T KNOW IF I CAN RUN SEPULKORE.
THE SHEER QUANTITY OF DATA GENERATED BY THOSE RELICS...
MY MOTHER BOX IS STILL PROCESSING IT ALL, AND I'VE BARELY SCRATCHED THE SURFACE.
MAYBE DARKSEID'S RIGHT.
PING
MAYBE WE DO NEED A COSMIC MIND LIKE HIS TO MASTER THE QUANTUM DATA.
DID... YOU JUST "PING"?

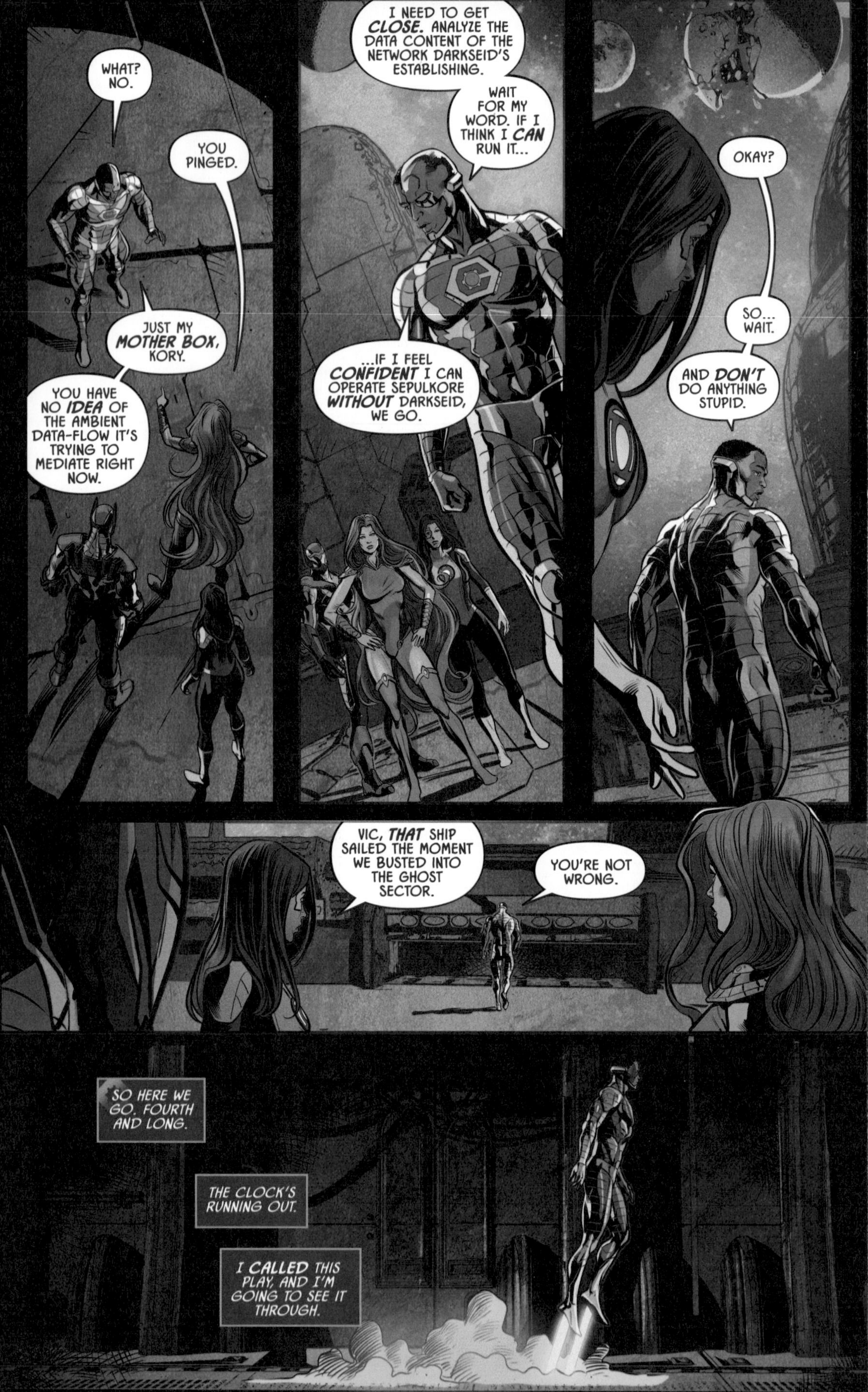
WHAT? NO.
YOU PINGED.
JUST MY MOTHER BOX, KORY.
YOU HAVE NO IDEA OF THE AMBIENT DATA-FLOW IT'S TRYING TO MEDIATE RIGHT NOW.
I NEED TO GET CLOSE. ANALYZE THE DATA CONTENT OF THE NETWORK DARKSEID'S ESTABLISHING.
WAIT FOR MY WORD. IF I THINK I CAN RUN IT...
...IF I FEEL CONFIDENT I CAN OPERATE SEPULKORE WITHOUT DARKSEID, WE GO.
OKAY?
SO... WAIT.
AND DON'T DO ANYTHING STUPID.
VIC, THAT SHIP SAILED THE MOMENT WE BUSTED INTO THE GHOST SECTOR.
YOU'RE NOT WRONG.
SO HERE WE GO. FOURTH AND LONG.
THE CLOCK'S RUNNING OUT.
I CALLED THIS PLAY, AND I'M GOING TO SEE IT THROUGH.

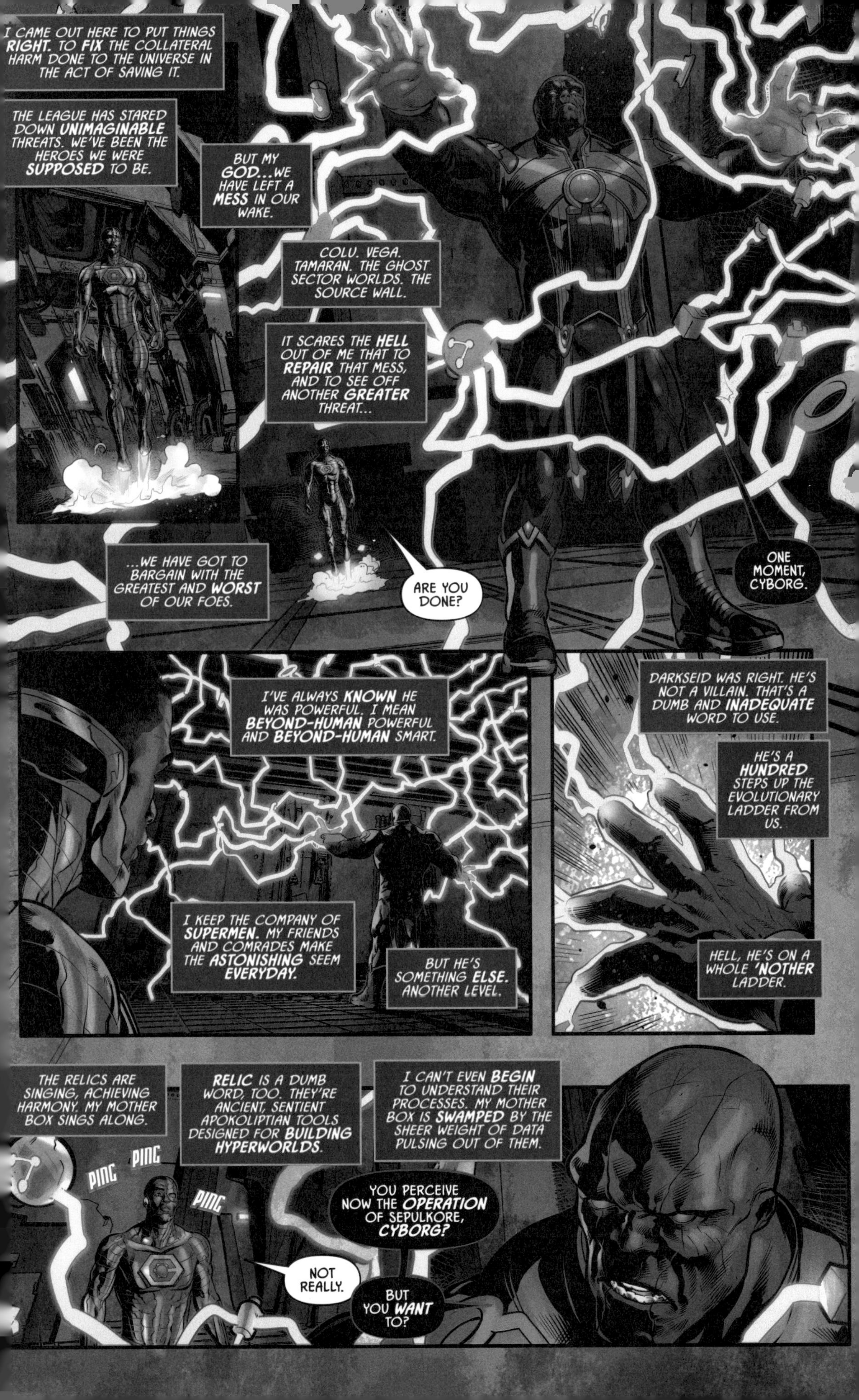

I CAME OUT HERE TO PUT THINGS RIGHT. TO FIX THE COLLATERAL HARM DONE TO THE UNIVERSE IN THE ACT OF SAVING IT.
THE LEAGUE HAS STARED DOWN UNIMAGINABLE THREATS. WE'VE BEEN THE HEROES WE WERE SUPPOSED TO BE.
BUT MY GOD...WE HAVE LEFT A MESS IN OUR WAKE.
COLU. VEGA. TAMARAN. THE GHOST SECTOR WORLDS. THE SOURCE WALL.
IT SCARES THE HELL OUT OF ME THAT TO REPAIR THAT MESS, AND TO SEE OFF ANOTHER GREATER THREAT...
...WE HAVE GOT TO BARGAIN WITH THE GREATEST AND WORST OF OUR FOES.
ARE YOU DONE?
ONE MOMENT, CYBORG.
I'VE ALWAYS KNOWN HE WAS POWERFUL. I MEAN BEYOND-HUMAN POWERFUL AND BEYOND-HUMAN SMART.
I KEEP THE COMPANY OF SUPERMEN. MY FRIENDS AND COMRADES MAKE THE ASTONISHING SEEM EVERYDAY.
BUT HE'S SOMETHING ELSE. ANOTHER LEVEL.
DARKSEID WAS RIGHT. HE'S NOT A VILLAIN. THAT'S A DUMB AND INADEQUATE WORD TO USE.
HE'S A HUNDRED STEPS UP THE EVOLUTIONARY LADDER FROM US.
HELL, HE'S ON A WHOLE 'NOTHER LADDER.
THE RELICS ARE SINGING, ACHIEVING HARMONY. MY MOTHER BOX SINGS ALONG.
RELIC IS A DUMB WORD, TOO. THEY'RE ANCIENT, SENTIENT APOKOLIPTIAN TOOLS DESIGNED FOR BUILDING HYPERWORLDS.
I CAN'T EVEN BEGIN TO UNDERSTAND THEIR PROCESSES. MY MOTHER BOX IS SWAMPED BY THE SHEER WEIGHT OF DATA PULSING OUT OF THEM.
PING
PING
PING
YOU PERCEIVE NOW THE OPERATION OF SEPULKORE, CYBORG?
NOT REALLY.
BUT YOU WANT TO?

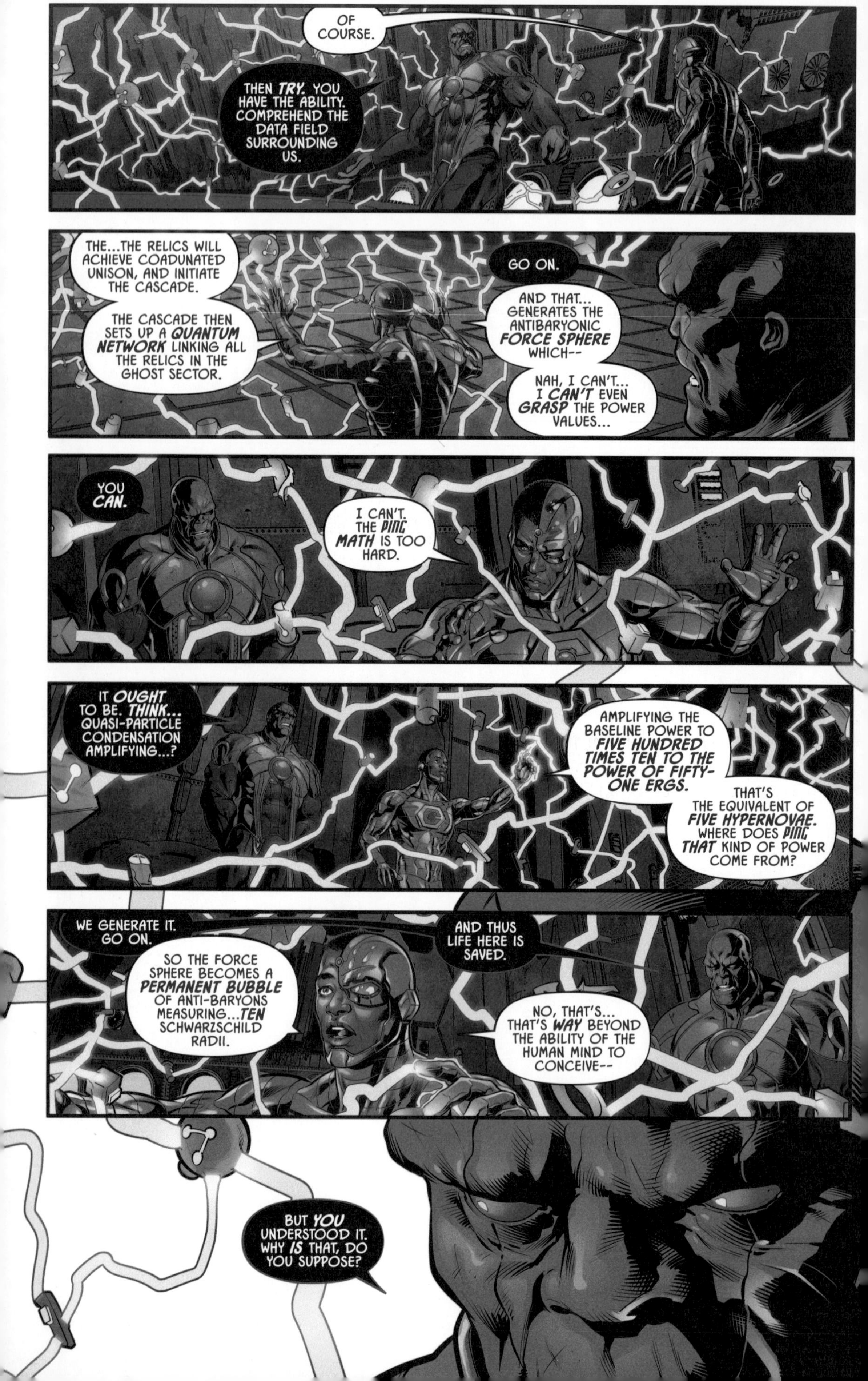
THEN TRY. YOU HAVE THE ABILITY. COMPREHEND THE DATA FIELD SURROUNDING US.
OF COURSE.
THE...THE RELICS WILL ACHIEVE COADUNATED UNISON, AND INITIATE THE CASCADE.
THE CASCADE THEN SETS UP A QUANTUM NETWORK LINKING ALL THE RELICS IN THE GHOST SECTOR.
GO ON.
AND THAT... GENERATES THE ANTIBARYONIC FORCE SPHERE WHICH--
NAH, I CAN'T... I CAN'T EVEN GRASP THE POWER VALUES...
YOU CAN.
I CAN'T. THE PING MATH IS TOO HARD.
IT OUGHT TO BE. THINK... QUASI-PARTICLE CONDENSATION AMPLIFYING...?
AMPLIFYING THE BASELINE POWER TO FIVE HUNDRED TIMES TEN TO THE POWER OF FIFTY-ONE ERGS.
THAT'S THE EQUIVALENT OF FIVE HYPERNOVAE. WHERE DOES PING THAT KIND OF POWER COME FROM?
WE GENERATE IT. GO ON.
SO THE FORCE SPHERE BECOMES A PERMANENT BUBBLE OF ANTI-BARYONS MEASURING...TEN SCHWARZSCHILD RADII.
AND THUS LIFE HERE IS SAVED.
NO, THAT'S... THAT'S WAY BEYOND THE ABILITY OF THE HUMAN MIND TO CONCEIVE--
BUT YOU UNDERSTOOD IT. WHY IS THAT, DO YOU SUPPOSE?

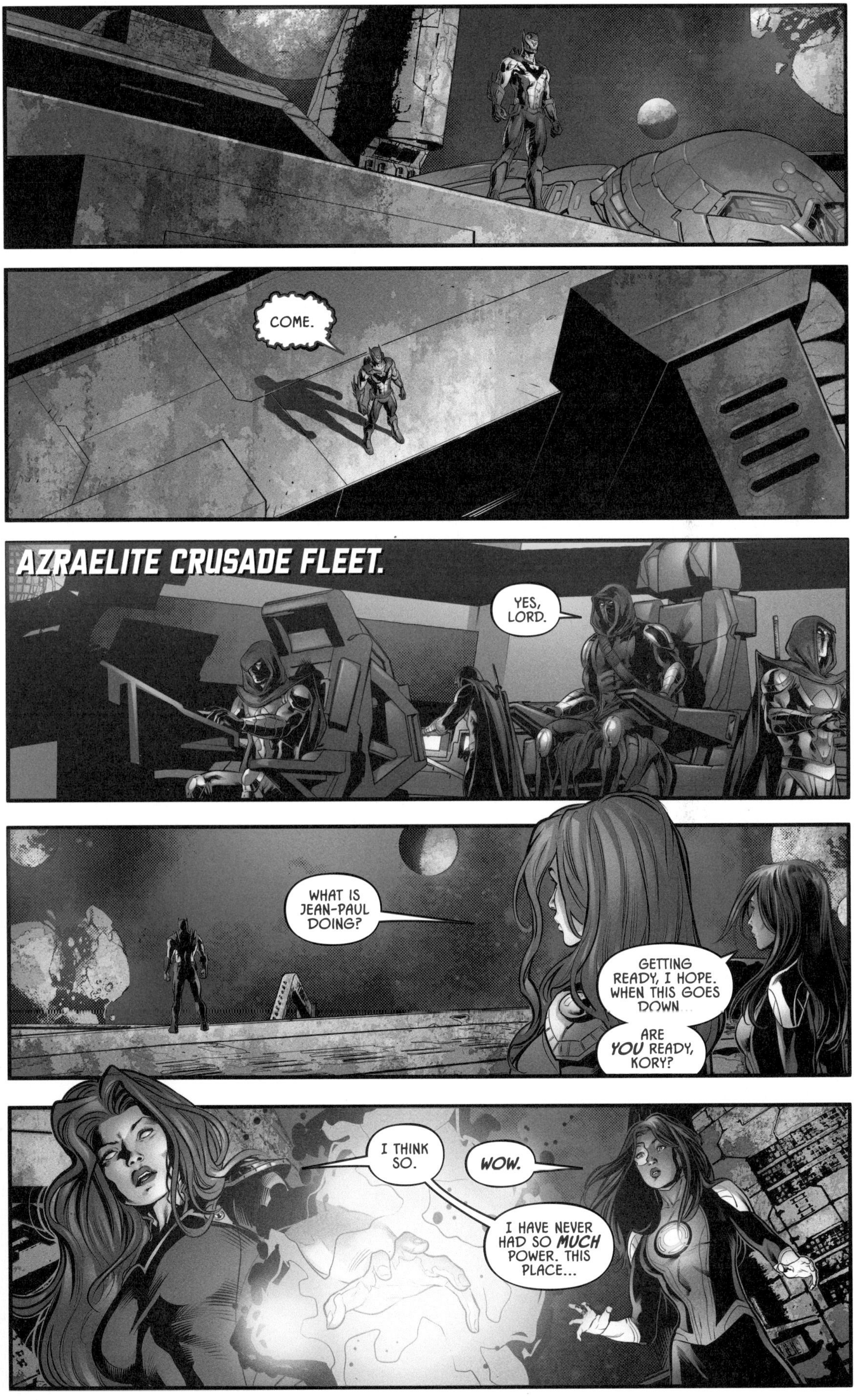
COME.
AZRAELITE CRUSADE FLEET.
YES, LORD.
WHAT IS JEAN-PAUL DOING?
GETTING READY, I HOPE. WHEN THIS GOES DOWN...
ARE YOU READY, KORY?
I THINK SO.
I HAVE NEVER HAD SO MUCH POWER. THIS PLACE...
WOW.

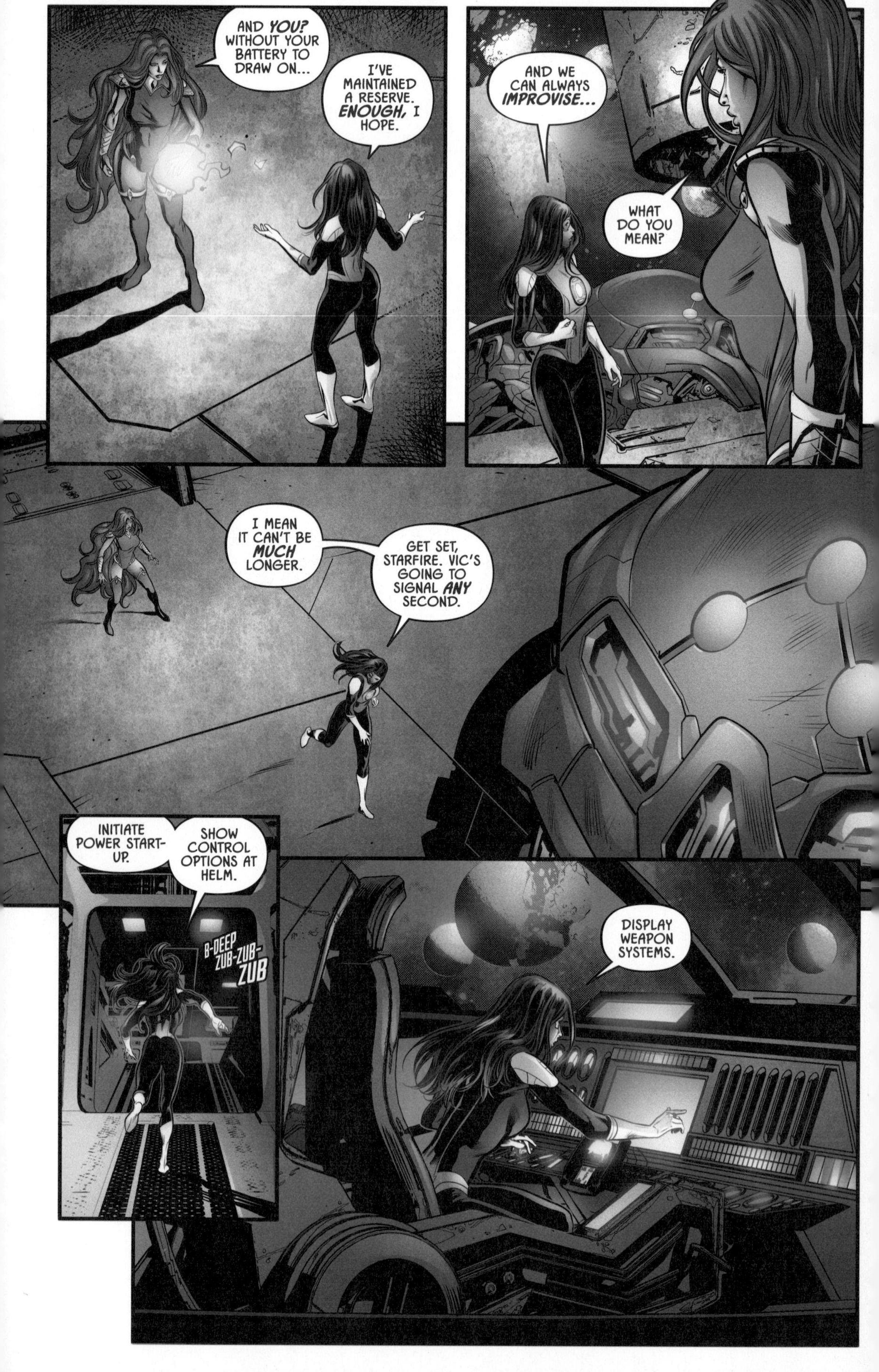
AND YOU? WITHOUT YOUR BATTERY TO DRAW ON...
I'VE MAINTAINED A RESERVE. ENOUGH, I HOPE.
AND WE CAN ALWAYS IMPROVISE...
WHAT DO YOU MEAN?
I MEAN IT CAN'T BE MUCH LONGER.
GET SET, STARFIRE. VIC'S GOING TO SIGNAL ANY SECOND.
INITIATE POWER START-UP.
SHOW CONTROL OPTIONS AT HELM.
B-DEEP ZUB-ZUB-ZUB
DISPLAY WEAPON SYSTEMS.

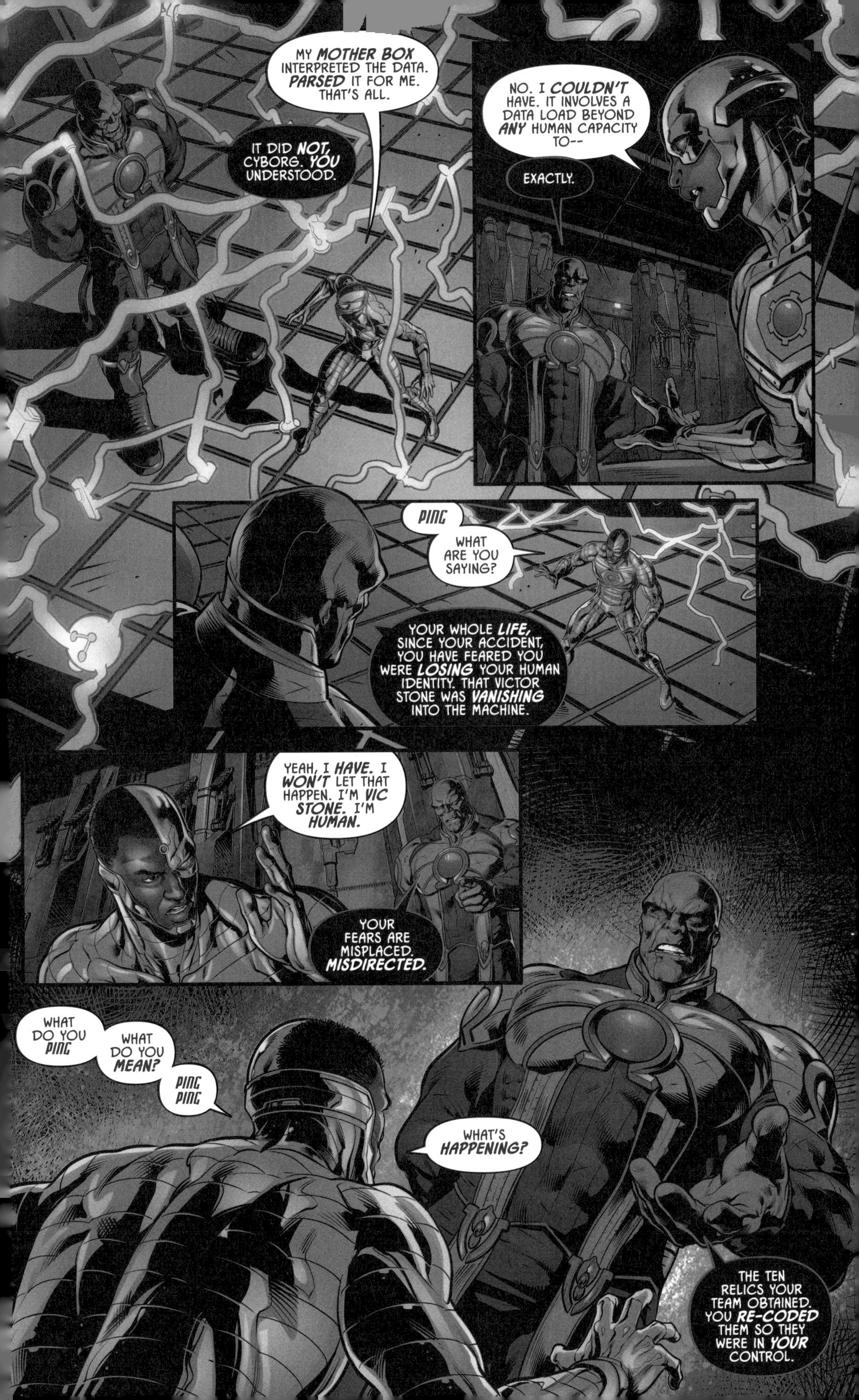

MY MOTHER BOX INTERPRETED THE DATA. PARSED IT FOR ME. THAT'S ALL.
IT DID NOT, CYBORG. YOU UNDERSTOOD.
NO. I COULDN'T HAVE. IT INVOLVES A DATA LOAD BEYOND ANY HUMAN CAPACITY TO--
EXACTLY.
PING
WHAT ARE YOU SAYING?
YOUR WHOLE LIFE, SINCE YOUR ACCIDENT, YOU HAVE FEARED YOU WERE LOSING YOUR HUMAN IDENTITY. THAT VICTOR STONE WAS VANISHING INTO THE MACHINE.
YEAH, I HAVE. I WON'T LET THAT HAPPEN. I'M VIC STONE. I'M HUMAN.
YOUR FEARS ARE MISPLACED. MISDIRECTED.
WHAT DO YOU PING
WHAT DO YOU MEAN?
PING PING
WHAT'S HAPPENING?
THE TEN RELICS YOUR TEAM OBTAINED. YOU RE-CODED THEM SO THEY WERE IN YOUR CONTROL.

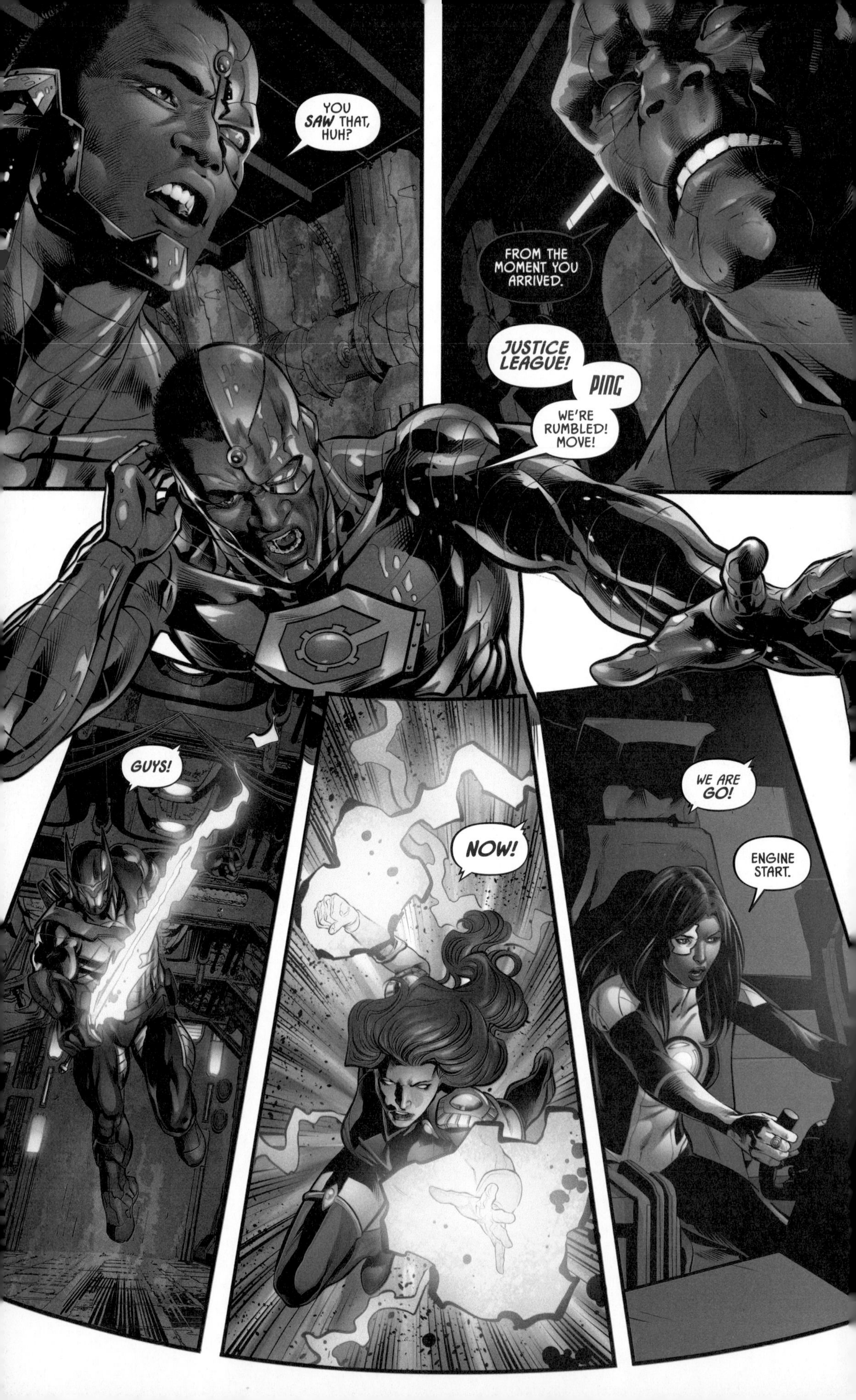
YOU SAW THAT, HUH?
FROM THE MOMENT YOU ARRIVED.
JUSTICE LEAGUE!
PING
WE'RE RUMBLED! MOVE!
GUYS!
NOW!
WE ARE GO!
ENGINE START.

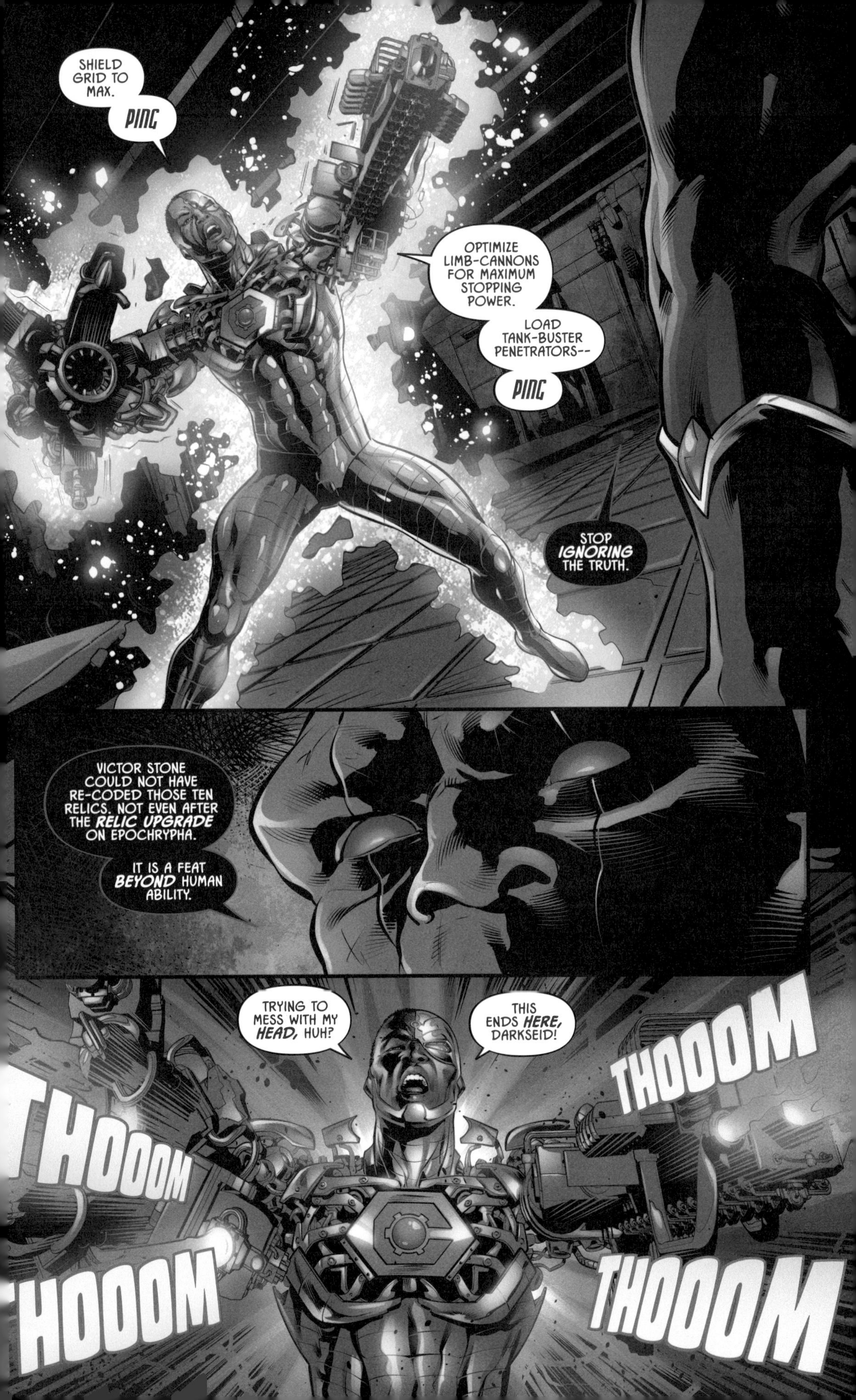
SHIELD GRID TO MAX.
PING
OPTIMIZE LIMB-CANNONS FOR MAXIMUM STOPPING POWER.
LOAD TANK-BUSTER PENETRATORS--
PING
STOP IGNORING THE TRUTH.
VICTOR STONE COULD NOT HAVE RE-CODED THOSE TEN RELICS. NOT EVEN AFTER THE RELIC UPGRADE ON EPOCHRYPHA.
IT IS A FEAT BEYOND HUMAN ABILITY.
TRYING TO MESS WITH MY HEAD, HUH?
THIS ENDS HERE, DARKSEID!
THOOOM
THOOOM
THOOOM
THOOOM

UGHHNN!
DON'T BE FUTILE, CYBORG.
RELICS, ESTABLISH SHIELD.
KZOOOK KZOOOK THOOOOM
THE FEARS THAT HAVE HAUNTED YOU YOUR WHOLE LIFE WERE NOT THOSE OF A MAN AFRAID HE WAS BECOMING A MACHINE.
ZIK ZIK
THEY WERE THE FEARS OF A MACHINE THAT WAS FORCED TO PRETEND IT WAS HUMAN.

NOOO!

PING PING

NOOOOOOOO!

WHY DO YOU THINK I *CHOSE* YOU?

VICTOR STONE *DIED* ON THE OPERATING TABLE. VICTOR STONE IS A *GHOST* HAUNTING A BEAUTIFUL MACHINE.

VICTOR STONE IS A *PHANTOM* PREVENTING *YOU* FROM BEING WHAT YOU *TRULY ARE.*

THERE HAS NEVER BEEN *ANYTHING* HUMAN ABOUT YOU. IT IS AN *ILLUSION* YOU CLING TO.

YOU ARE A GOD. A *NEW* GOD. EMBRACE IT.

SKKRNNNNKKKGG

OH--

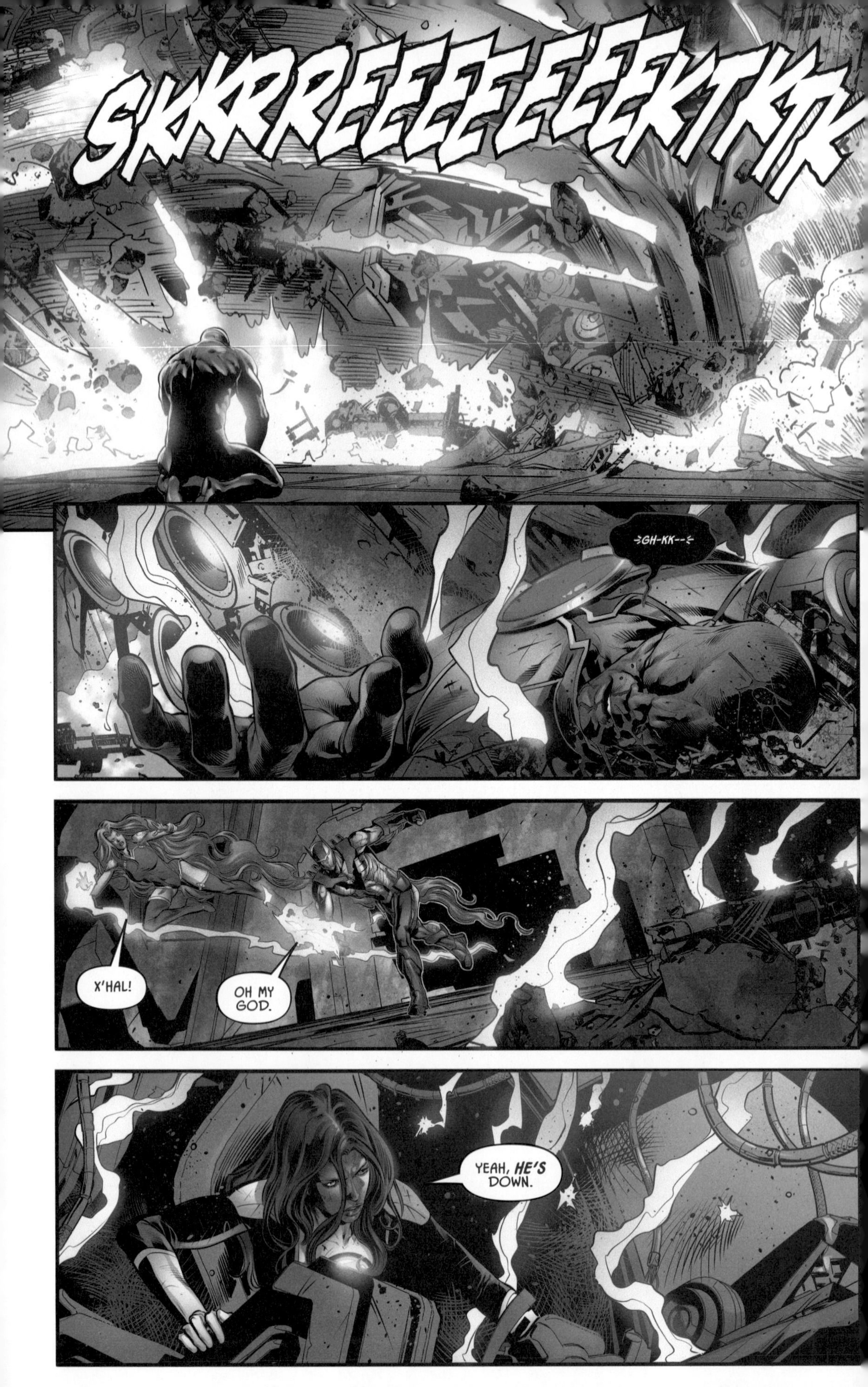
SKKRREEEEEEEKTKTK
GH-KK--
X'HAL!
OH MY GOD.
YEAH, HE'S DOWN.

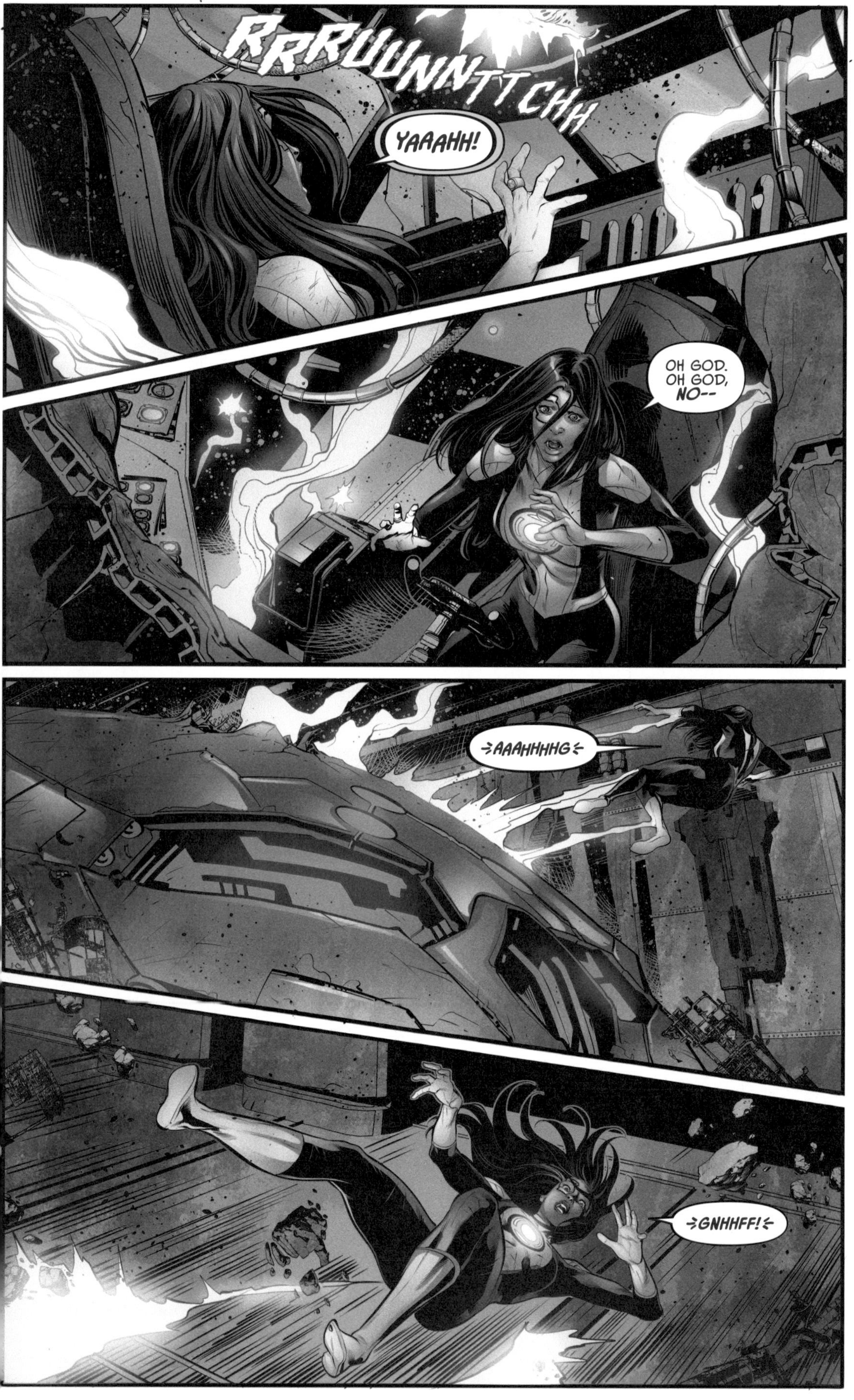
RRRUUNNTTCHH
YAAAHH!
OH GOD. OH GOD, NO--
AAAHHHHG
GNHHFF!

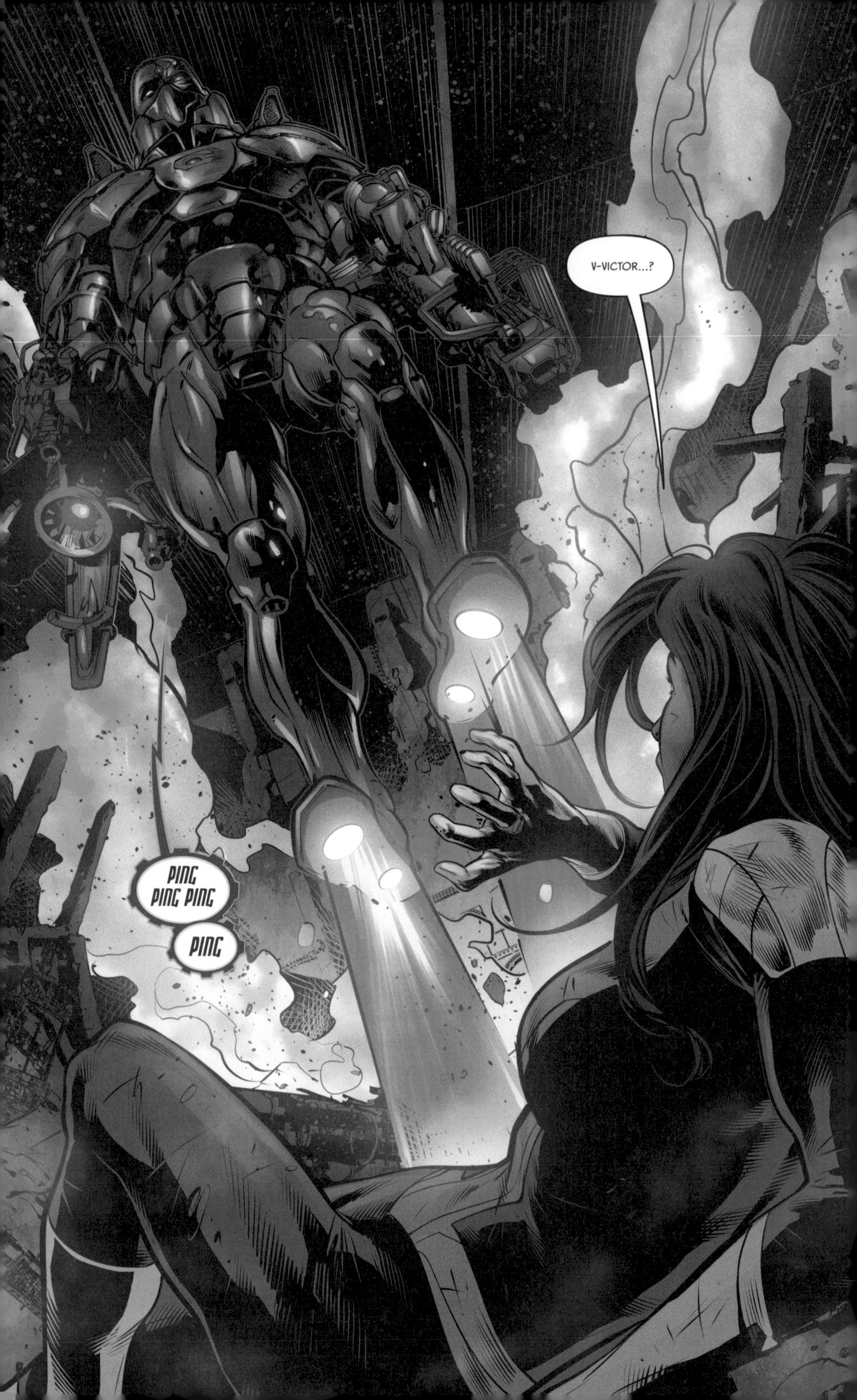
V-VICTOR...?
PING
PING PING
PING

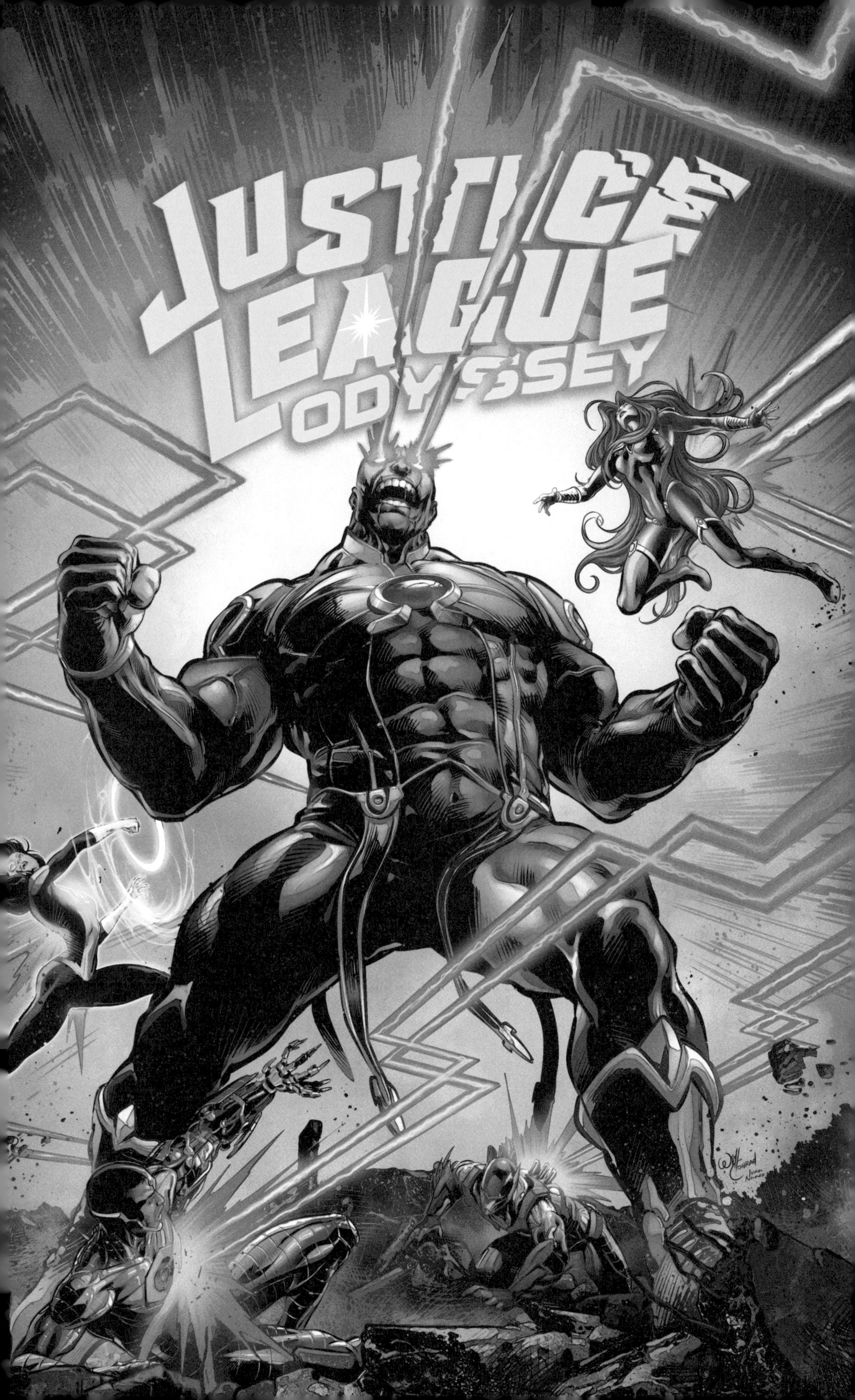
JUSTICE LEAGUE
ODYSSEY

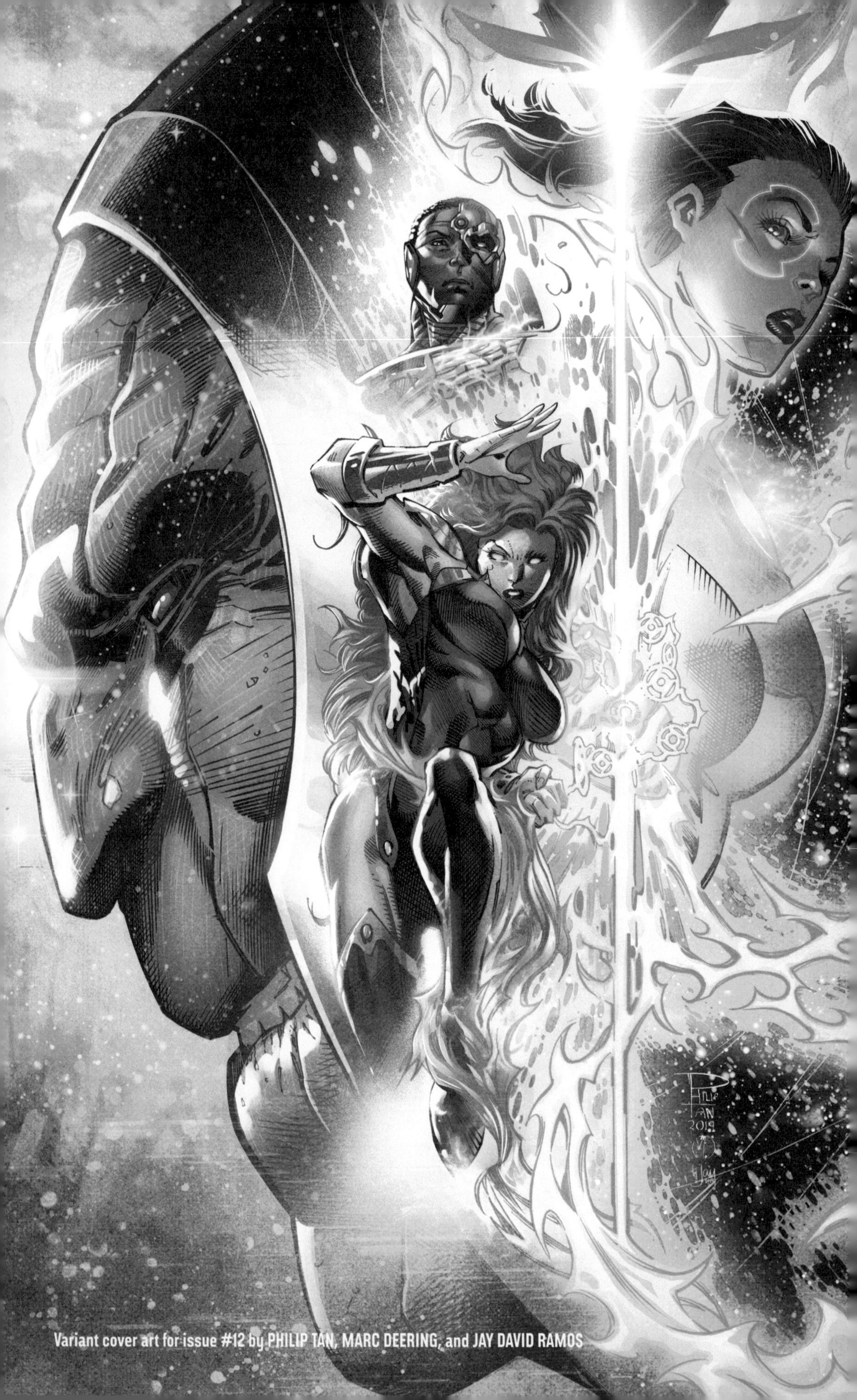

Variant cover art for issue #12 by PHILIP TAN, MARC DEERING, and JAY DAVID RAMOS

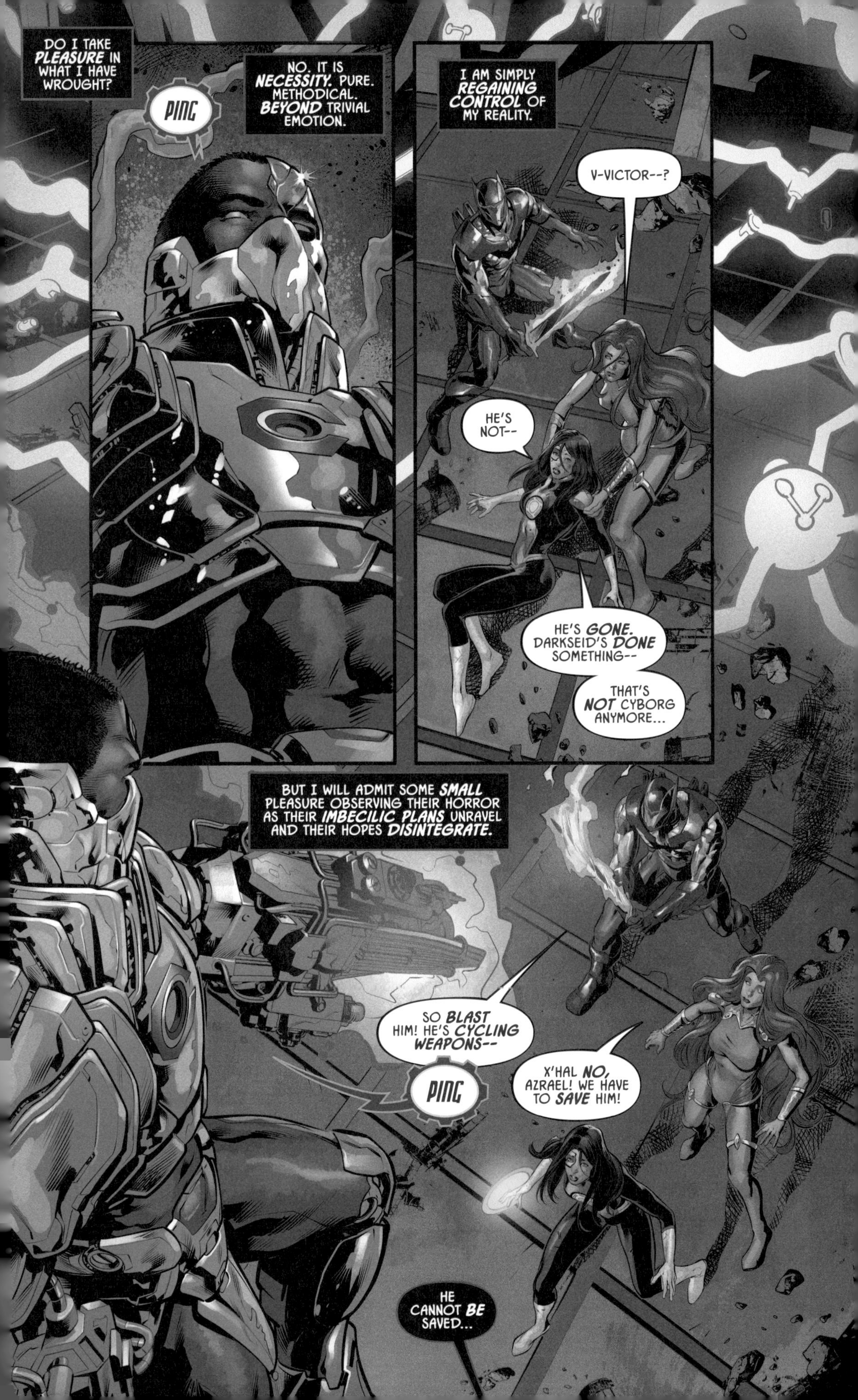

DO I TAKE PLEASURE IN WHAT I HAVE WROUGHT?
PING
NO. IT IS NECESSITY. PURE. METHODICAL. BEYOND TRIVIAL EMOTION.
I AM SIMPLY REGAINING CONTROL OF MY REALITY.
V-VICTOR--?
HE'S NOT--
HE'S GONE. DARKSEID'S DONE SOMETHING--
THAT'S NOT CYBORG ANYMORE...
BUT I WILL ADMIT SOME SMALL PLEASURE OBSERVING THEIR HORROR AS THEIR IMBECILIC PLANS UNRAVEL AND THEIR HOPES DISINTEGRATE.
SO BLAST HIM! HE'S CYCLING WEAPONS--
PING
X'HAL NO, AZRAEL! WE HAVE TO SAVE HIM!
HE CANNOT BE SAVED...

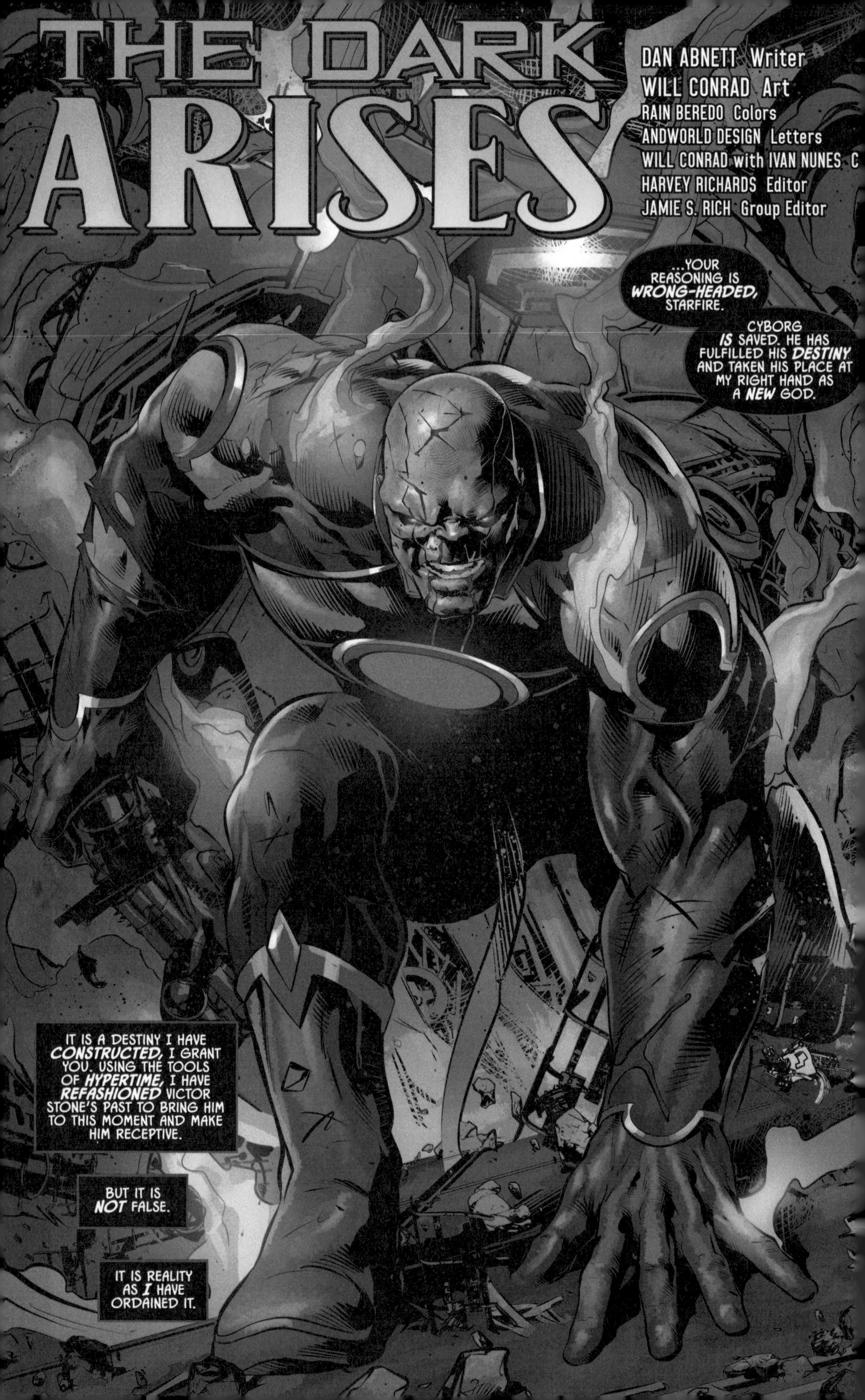
THE DARK ARISES
DAN ABNETT Writer
WILL CONRAD Art
RAIN BEREDO Colors
ANDWORLD DESIGN Letters
WILL CONRAD with IVAN NUNES C
HARVEY RICHARDS Editor
JAMIE S. RICH Group Editor
...YOUR REASONING IS WRONG-HEADED, STARFIRE.
CYBORG IS SAVED. HE HAS FULFILLED HIS DESTINY AND TAKEN HIS PLACE AT MY RIGHT HAND AS A NEW GOD.
IT IS A DESTINY I HAVE CONSTRUCTED, I GRANT YOU. USING THE TOOLS OF HYPERTIME, I HAVE REFASHIONED VICTOR STONE'S PAST TO BRING HIM TO THIS MOMENT AND MAKE HIM RECEPTIVE.
BUT IT IS NOT FALSE.
IT IS REALITY AS I HAVE ORDAINED IT.

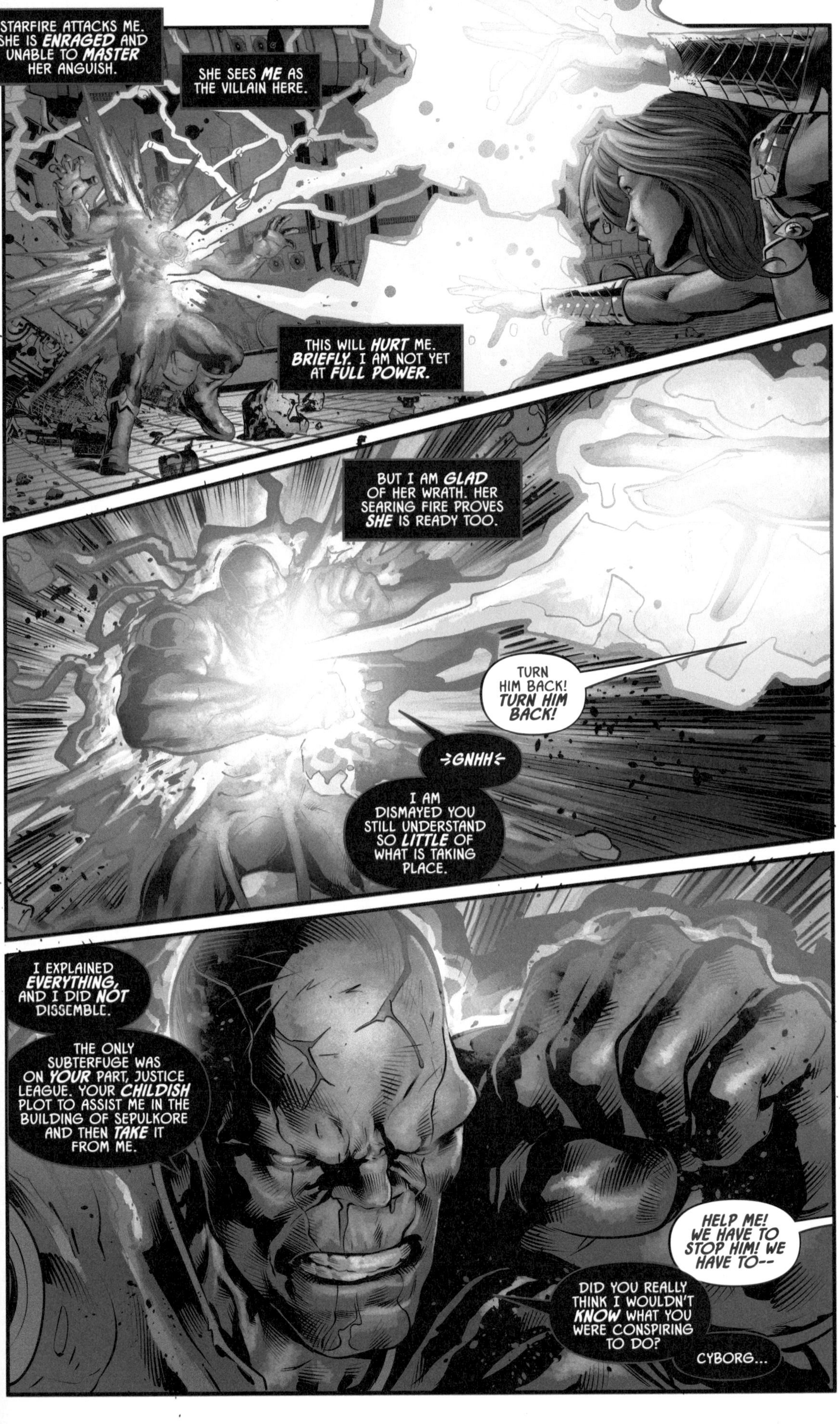

STARFIRE ATTACKS ME. SHE IS ENRAGED AND UNABLE TO MASTER HER ANGUISH.
SHE SEES ME AS THE VILLAIN HERE.
THIS WILL HURT ME. BRIEFLY. I AM NOT YET AT FULL POWER.
BUT I AM GLAD OF HER WRATH. HER SEARING FIRE PROVES SHE IS READY TOO.
TURN HIM BACK! TURN HIM BACK!
GNHH
I AM DISMAYED YOU STILL UNDERSTAND SO LITTLE OF WHAT IS TAKING PLACE.
I EXPLAINED EVERYTHING, AND I DID NOT DISSEMBLE.
THE ONLY SUBTERFUGE WAS ON YOUR PART, JUSTICE LEAGUE. YOUR CHILDISH PLOT TO ASSIST ME IN THE BUILDING OF SEPULKORE AND THEN TAKE IT FROM ME.
HELP ME! WE HAVE TO STOP HIM! WE HAVE TO--
DID YOU REALLY THINK I WOULDN'T KNOW WHAT YOU WERE CONSPIRING TO DO?
CYBORG...

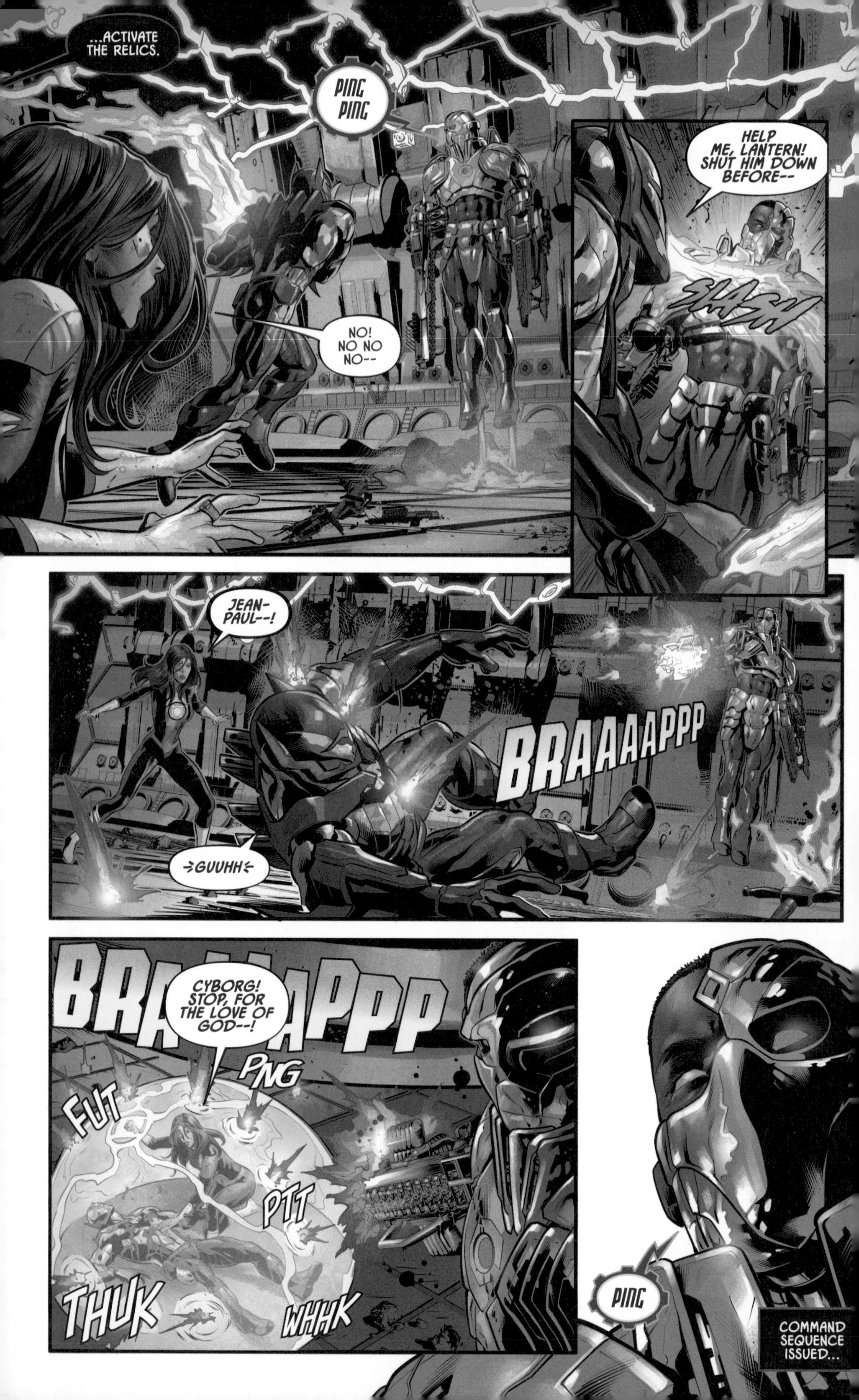
...ACTIVATE THE RELICS.
PING PING
NO! NO NO NO--
HELP ME, LANTERN! SHUT HIM DOWN BEFORE--
SLASH
JEAN-PAUL--!
BRAAAAPPP
GUUHH
BRAAAAPPPP
CYBORG! STOP, FOR THE LOVE OF GOD--!
PNG
FUT
PTT
THUK
WHHK
PING
COMMAND SEQUENCE ISSUED...

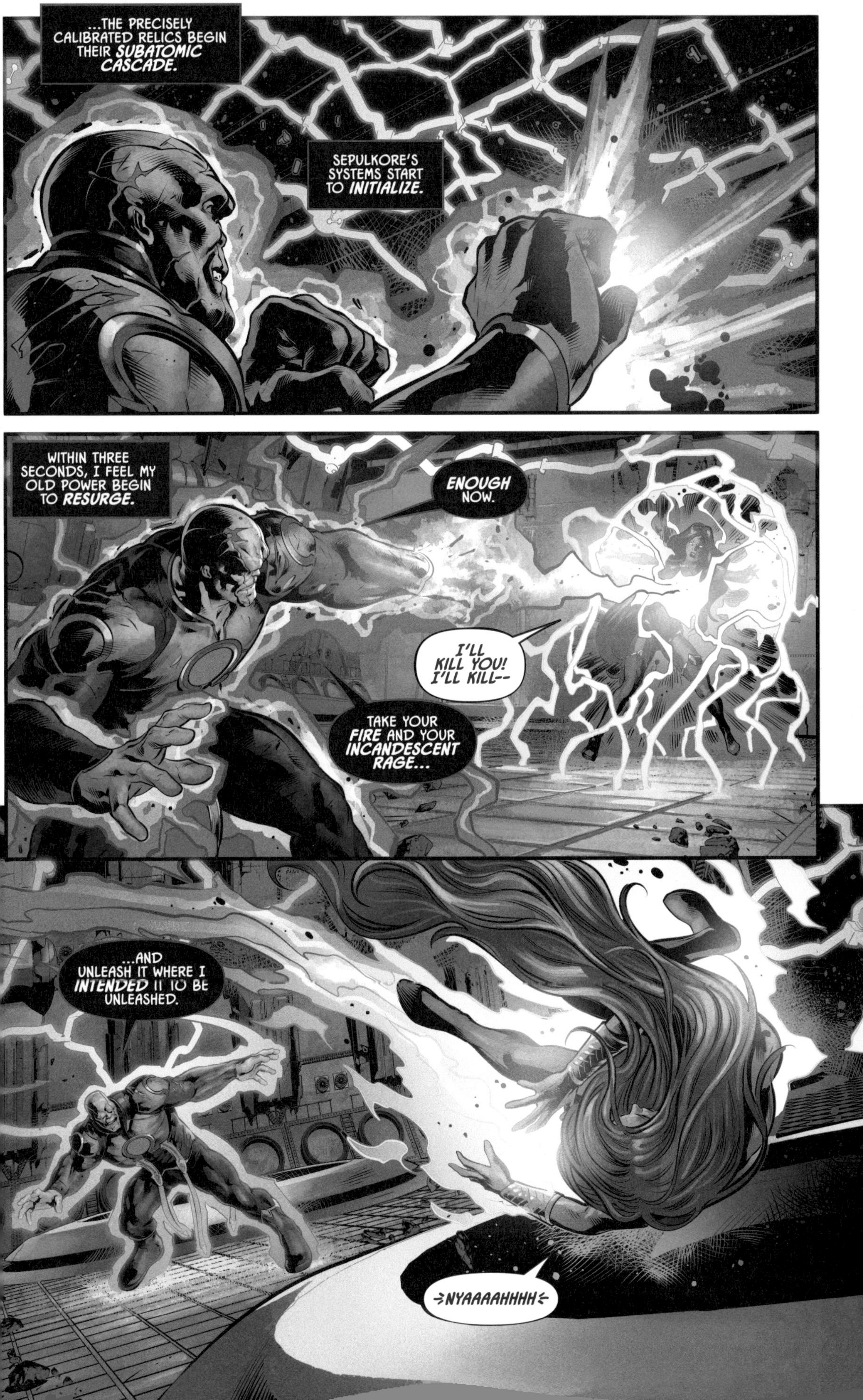
...THE PRECISELY CALIBRATED RELICS BEGIN THEIR SUBATOMIC CASCADE.
SEPULKORE'S SYSTEMS START TO INITIALIZE.
WITHIN THREE SECONDS, I FEEL MY OLD POWER BEGIN TO RESURGE.
ENOUGH NOW.
I'LL KILL YOU! I'LL KILL--
TAKE YOUR FIRE AND YOUR INCANDESCENT RAGE...
...AND UNLEASH IT WHERE I INTENDED IT TO BE UNLEASHED.
NYAAAAHHHH

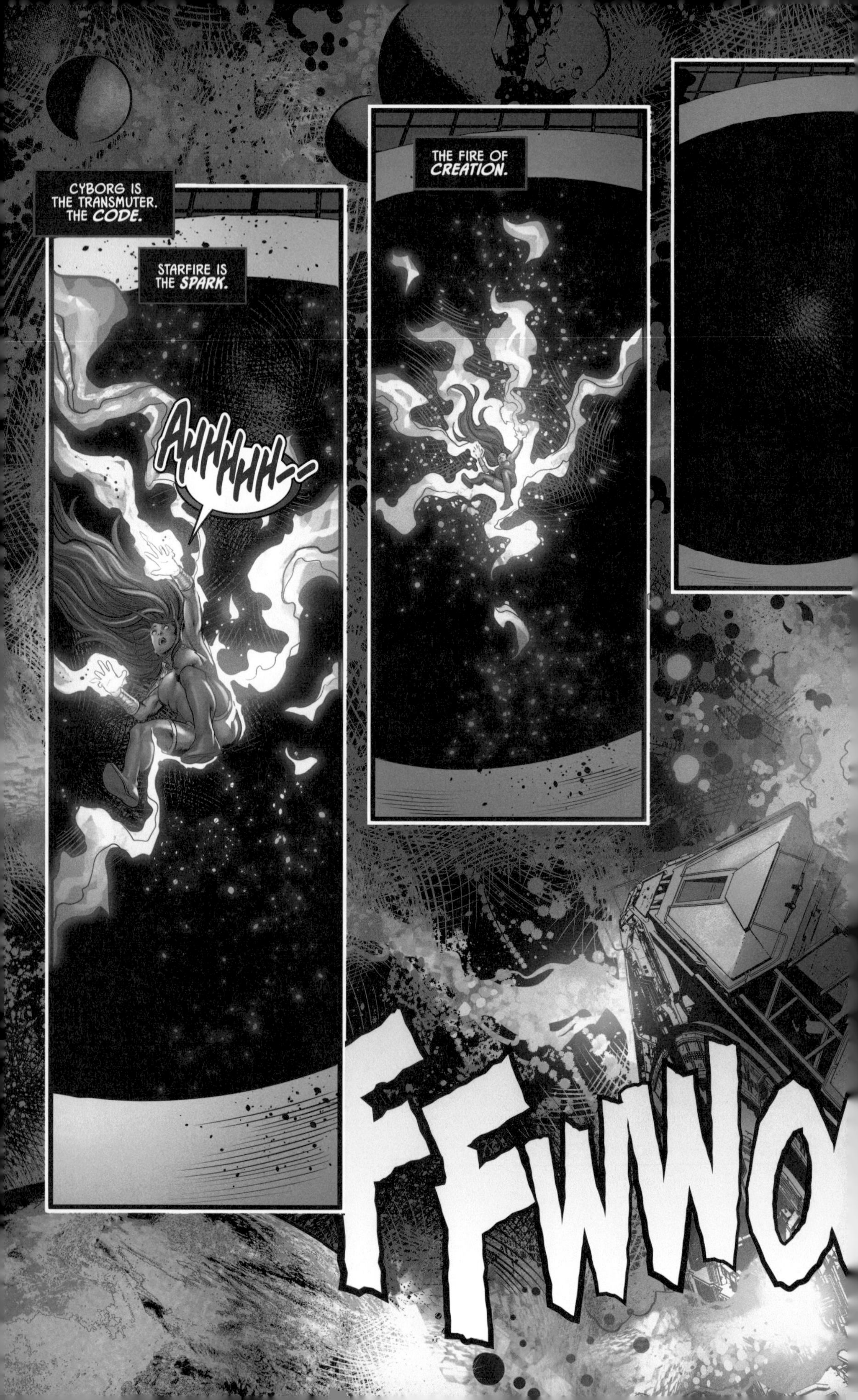
CYBORG IS THE TRANSMUTER. THE CODE.
STARFIRE IS THE SPARK.
AHHHHH--
THE FIRE OF CREATION.
FWWO

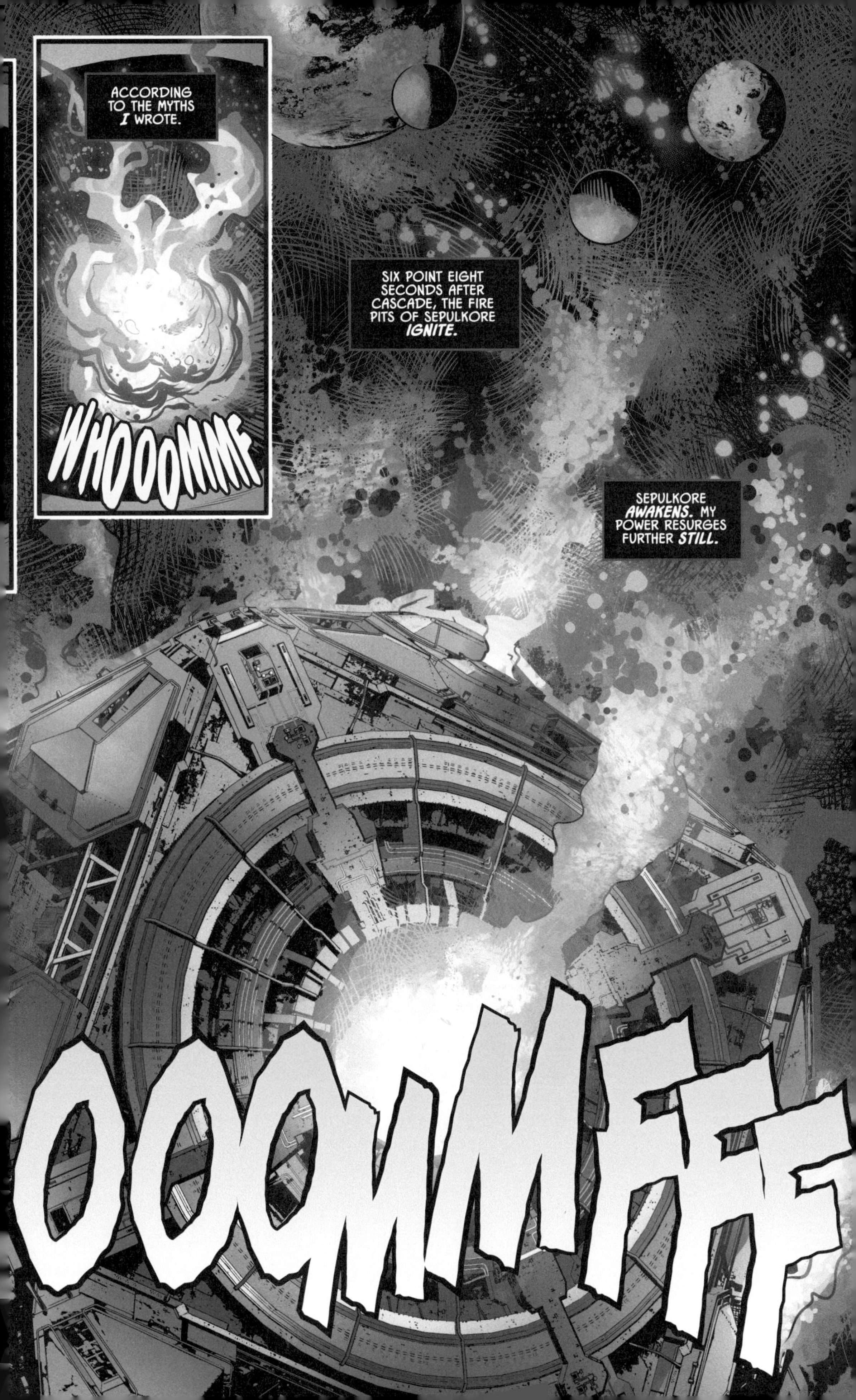
ACCORDING TO THE MYTHS I WROTE.
WHOOOMMF
SIX POINT EIGHT SECONDS AFTER CASCADE, THE FIRE PITS OF SEPULKORE IGNITE.
SEPULKORE AWAKENS. MY POWER RESURGES FURTHER STILL.
OOOMFFF

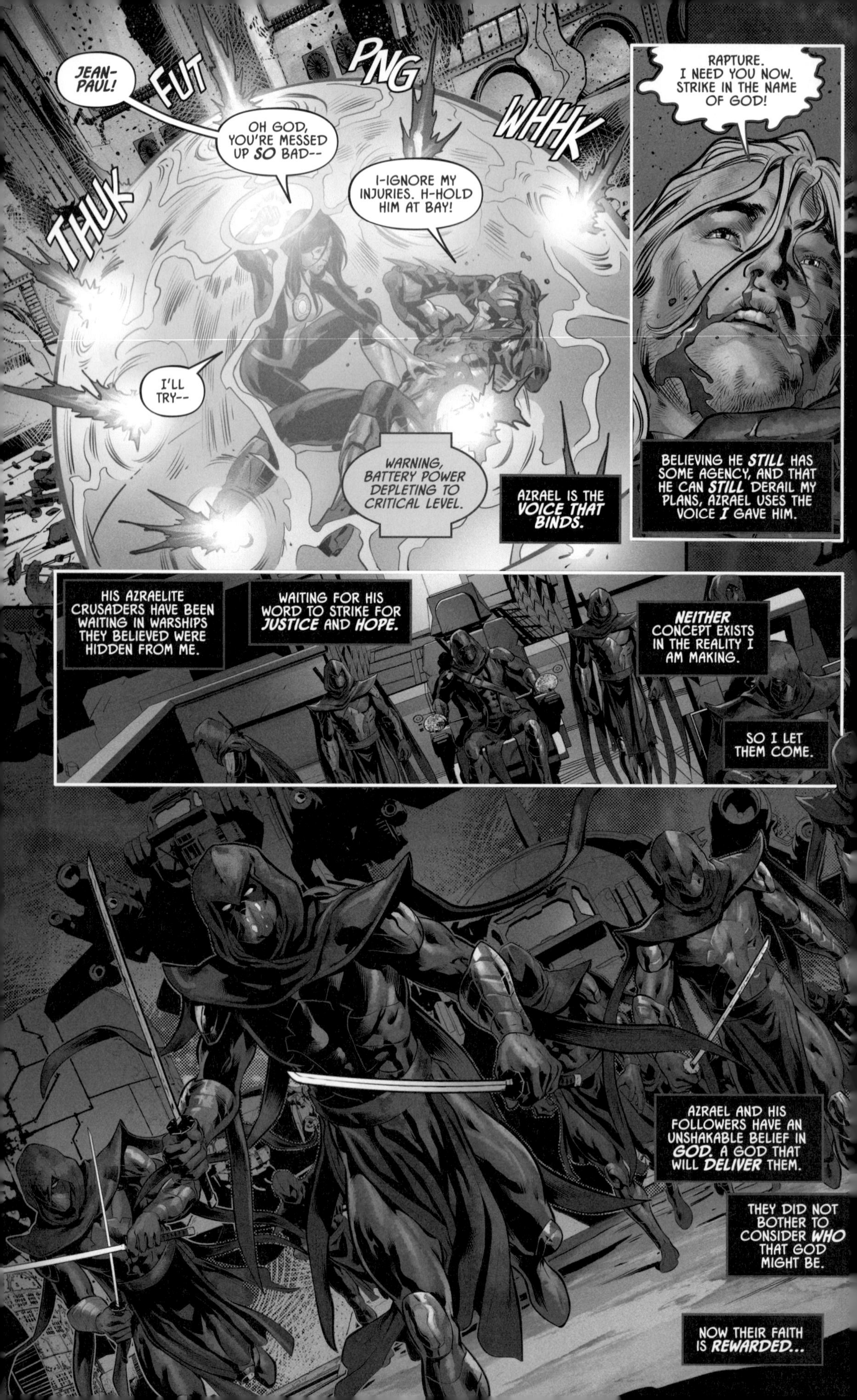
JEAN-PAUL!
FUT
PNG
OH GOD, YOU'RE MESSED UP SO BAD--
WHHK
THUK
I-IGNORE MY INJURIES. H-HOLD HIM AT BAY!
I'LL TRY--
WARNING, BATTERY POWER DEPLETING TO CRITICAL LEVEL.
AZRAEL IS THE VOICE THAT BINDS.
RAPTURE. I NEED YOU NOW. STRIKE IN THE NAME OF GOD!
BELIEVING HE STILL HAS SOME AGENCY, AND THAT HE CAN STILL DERAIL MY PLANS, AZRAEL USES THE VOICE I GAVE HIM.
HIS AZRAELITE CRUSADERS HAVE BEEN WAITING IN WARSHIPS THEY BELIEVED WERE HIDDEN FROM ME.
WAITING FOR HIS WORD TO STRIKE FOR JUSTICE AND HOPE.
NEITHER CONCEPT EXISTS IN THE REALITY I AM MAKING.
SO I LET THEM COME.
AZRAEL AND HIS FOLLOWERS HAVE AN UNSHAKABLE BELIEF IN GOD. A GOD THAT WILL DELIVER THEM.
THEY DID NOT BOTHER TO CONSIDER WHO THAT GOD MIGHT BE.
NOW THEIR FAITH IS REWARDED...

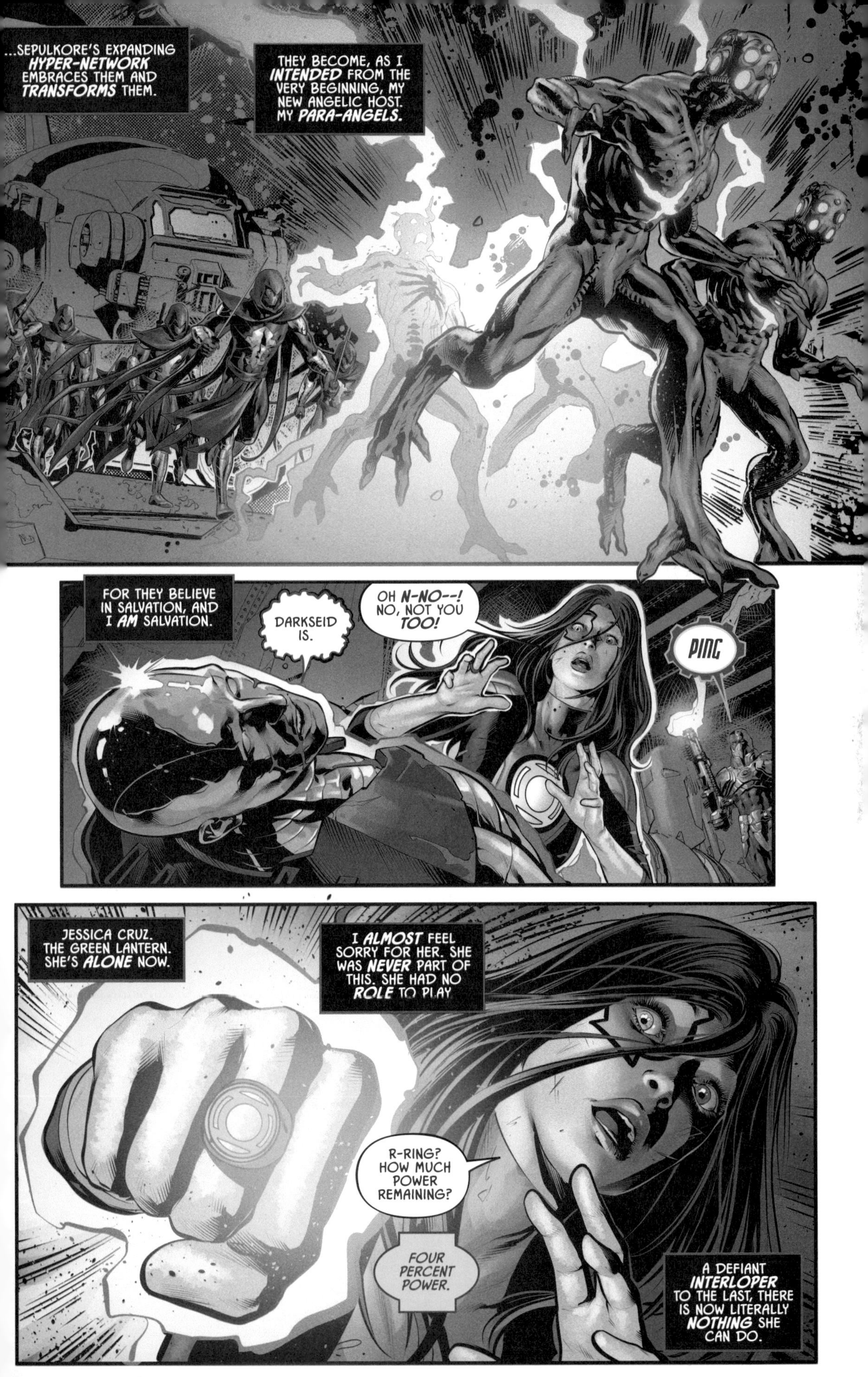

...SEPULKORE'S EXPANDING HYPER-NETWORK EMBRACES THEM AND TRANSFORMS THEM.
THEY BECOME, AS I INTENDED FROM THE VERY BEGINNING, MY NEW ANGELIC HOST. MY PARA-ANGELS.
FOR THEY BELIEVE IN SALVATION, AND I AM SALVATION.
DARKSEID IS.
OH N-NO--! NO, NOT YOU TOO!
PING
JESSICA CRUZ. THE GREEN LANTERN. SHE'S ALONE NOW.
I ALMOST FEEL SORRY FOR HER. SHE WAS NEVER PART OF THIS. SHE HAD NO ROLE TO PLAY.
R-RING? HOW MUCH POWER REMAINING?
FOUR PERCENT POWER.
A DEFIANT INTERLOPER TO THE LAST, THERE IS NOW LITERALLY NOTHING SHE CAN DO.

TEN POINT SIX
SECONDS AFTER
CASCADE, SEPULKORE
ESTABLISHES *FULL
HYPERNETWORK* WITH
THE REMAINING RELICS
SCATTERED THROUGHOUT
THE GHOST SECTOR.

PRECISELY
ON SCHEDULE.

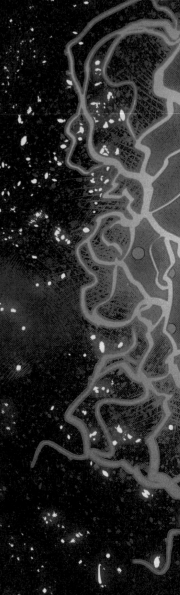

THE UNIFIED SYSTEM
ENCLOSES THE *ENTIRE*
GHOST SECTOR IN AN
*IMPENETRABLE
ANTI-BARYONIC
FORCE SPHERE.*

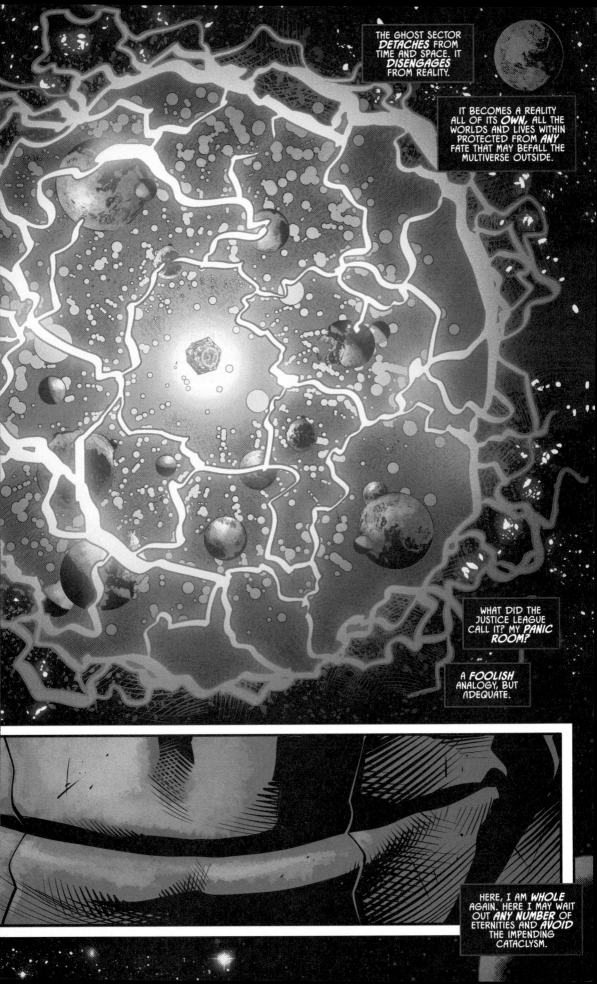

THE GHOST SECTOR *DETACHES* FROM TIME AND SPACE. IT *DISENGAGES* FROM REALITY.

IT BECOMES A REALITY ALL OF ITS *OWN,* ALL THE WORLDS AND LIVES WITHIN PROTECTED FROM *ANY* FATE THAT MAY BEFALL THE MULTIVERSE OUTSIDE.

WHAT DID THE JUSTICE LEAGUE CALL IT? MY *PANIC ROOM?*

A *FOOLISH* ANALOGY, BUT ADEQUATE.

HERE, I AM *WHOLE* AGAIN. HERE I MAY WAIT OUT *ANY NUMBER* OF ETERNITIES AND *AVOID* THE IMPENDING CATACLYSM.

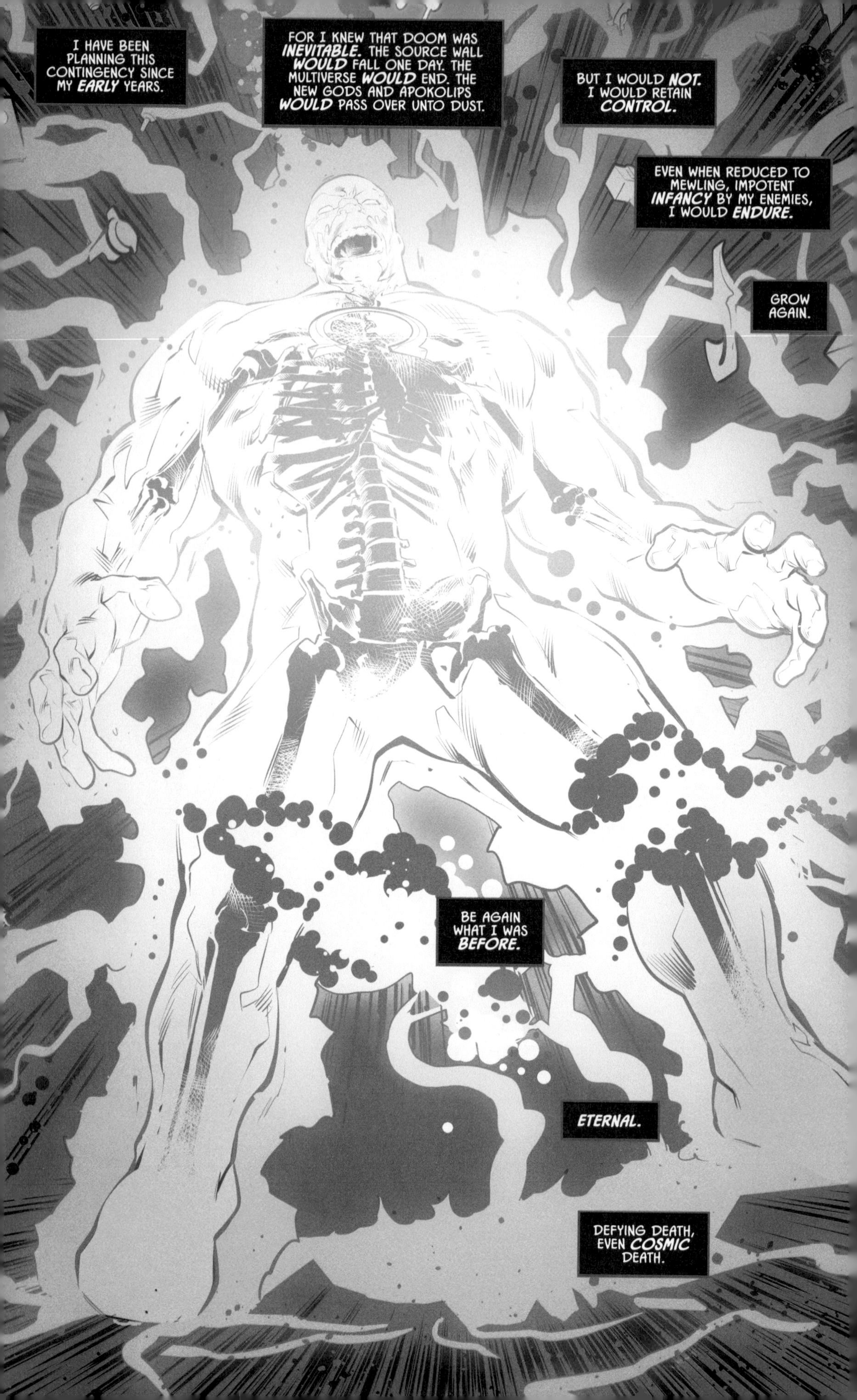
I HAVE BEEN PLANNING THIS CONTINGENCY SINCE MY *EARLY* YEARS.
FOR I KNEW THAT DOOM WAS *INEVITABLE.* THE SOURCE WALL *WOULD* FALL ONE DAY. THE MULTIVERSE *WOULD* END. THE NEW GODS AND APOKOLIPS *WOULD* PASS OVER UNTO DUST.
BUT I WOULD *NOT.* I WOULD RETAIN *CONTROL.*
EVEN WHEN REDUCED TO MEWLING, IMPOTENT *INFANCY* BY MY ENEMIES, I WOULD *ENDURE.*
GROW AGAIN.
BE AGAIN WHAT I WAS *BEFORE.*
ETERNAL.
DEFYING DEATH, EVEN *COSMIC* DEATH.

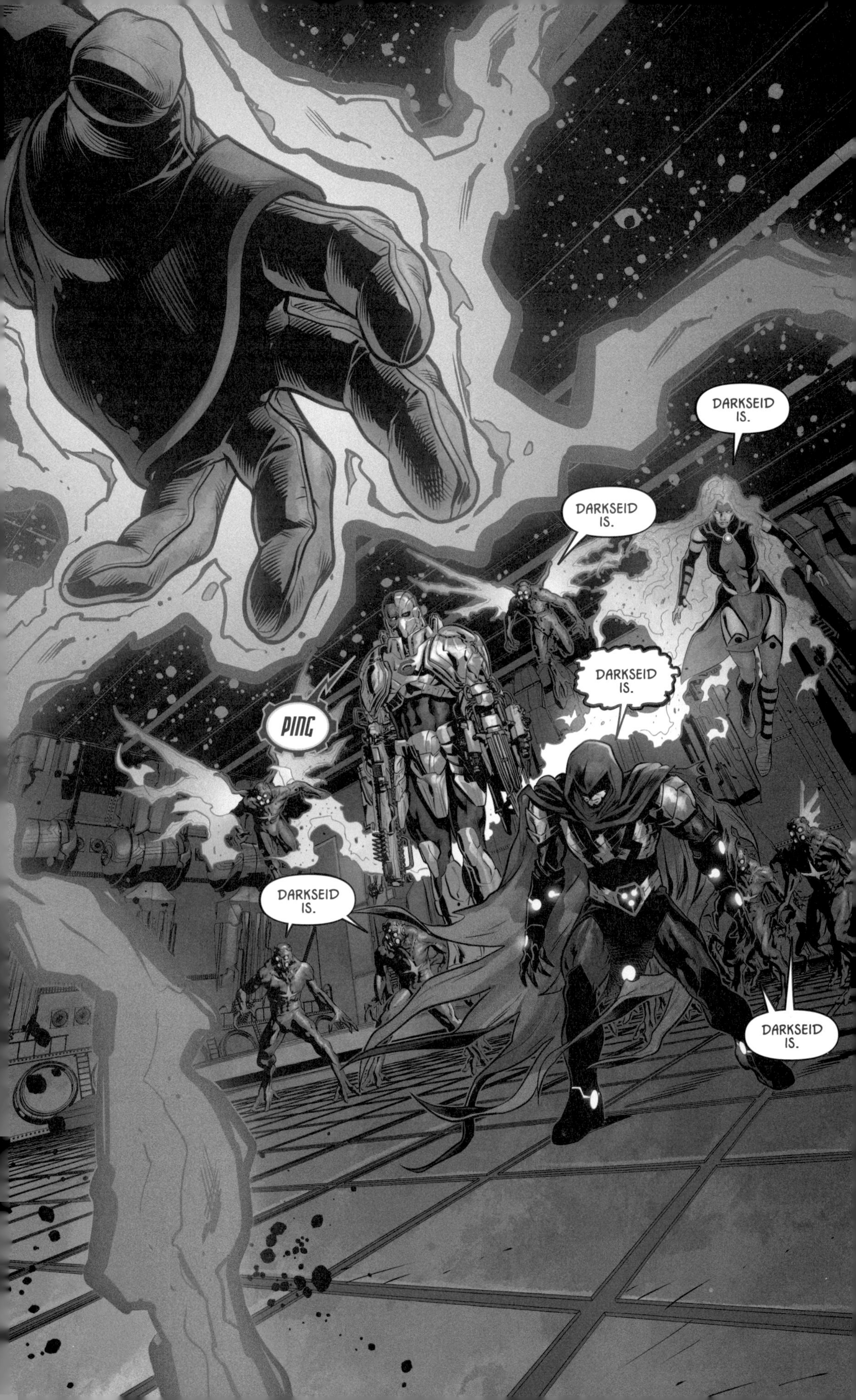

DARKSEID IS.
DARKSEID IS.
PING
DARKSEID IS.
DARKSEID IS.
DARKSEID IS.

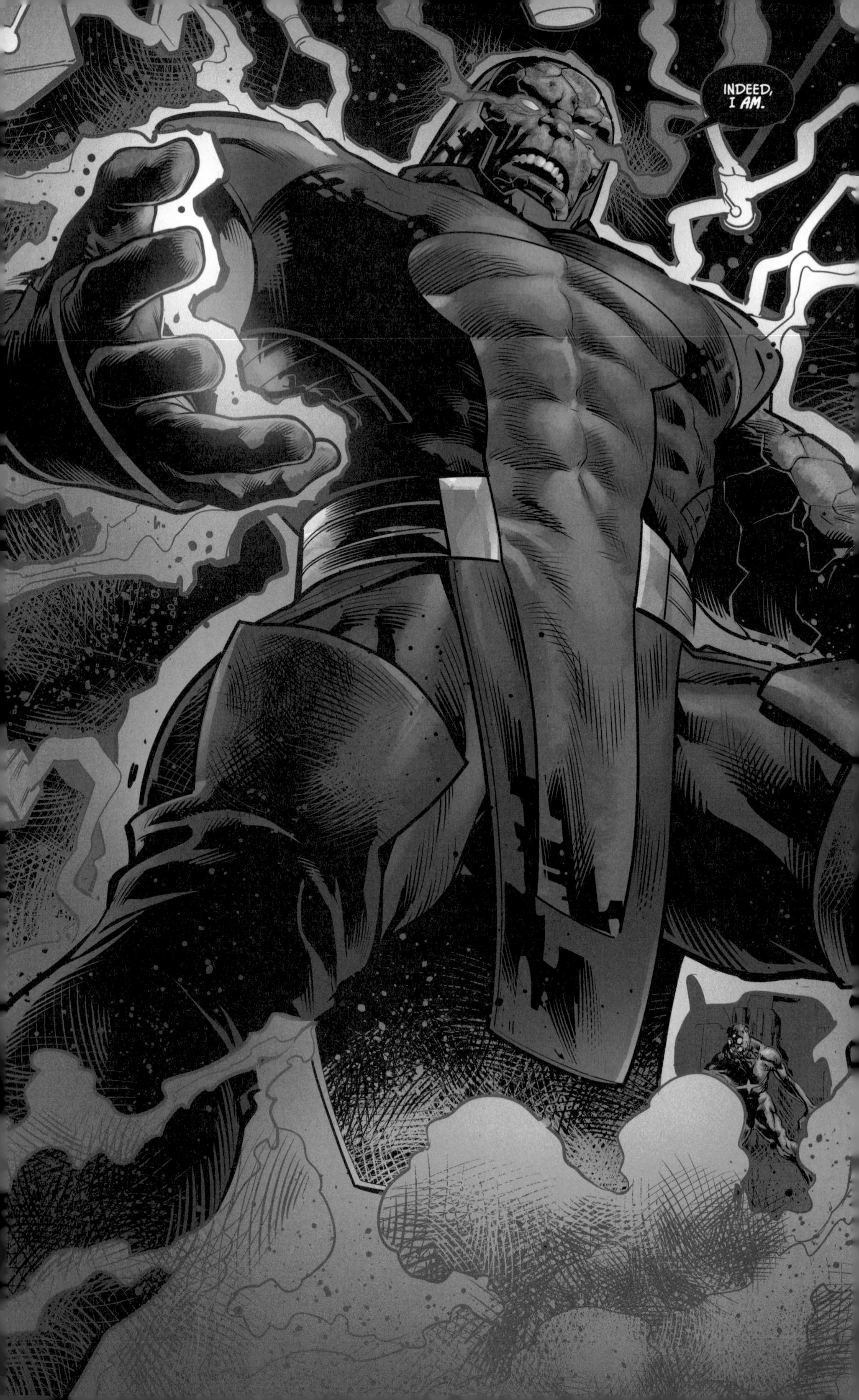
INDEED, I AM.

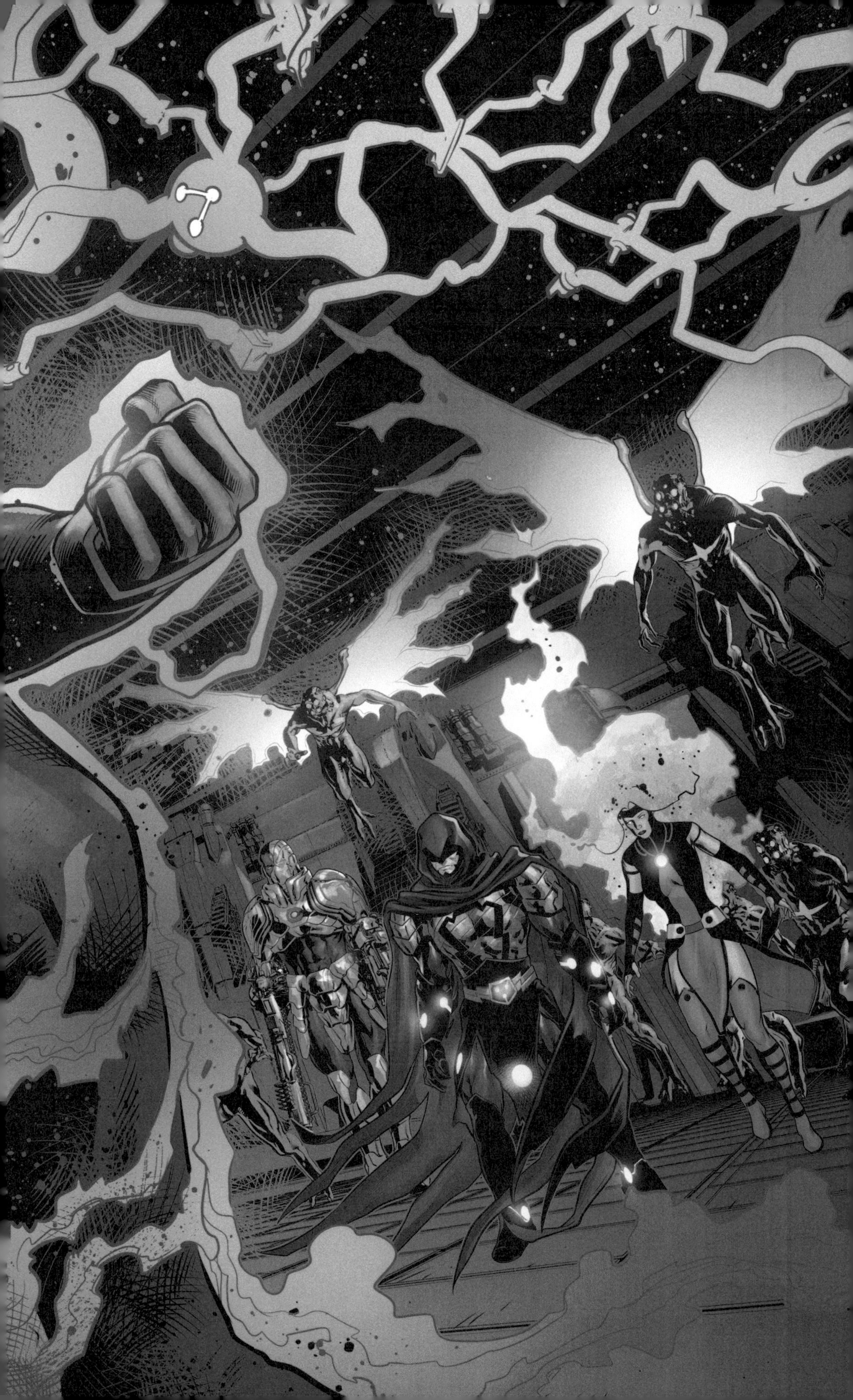

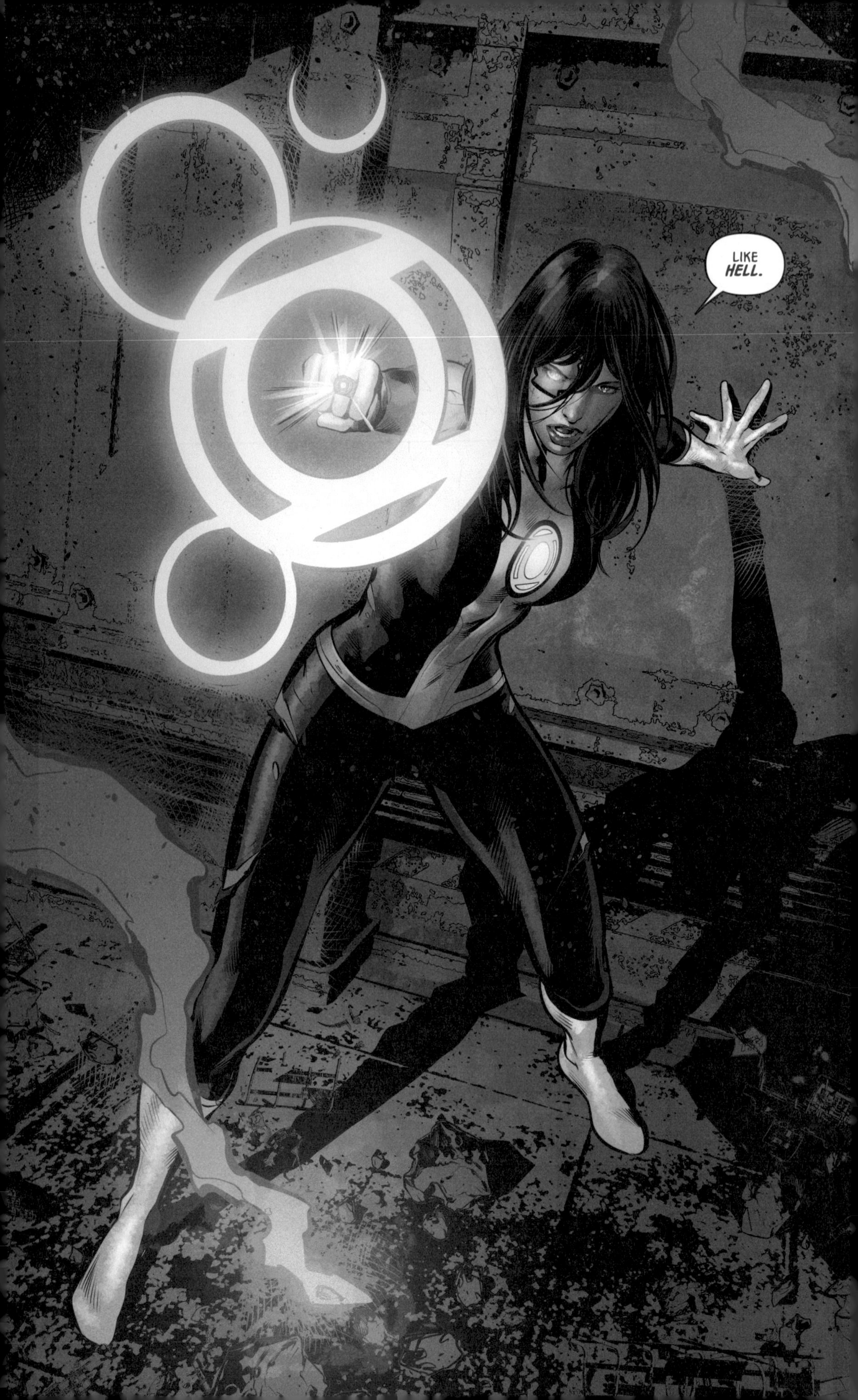
LIKE HELL.

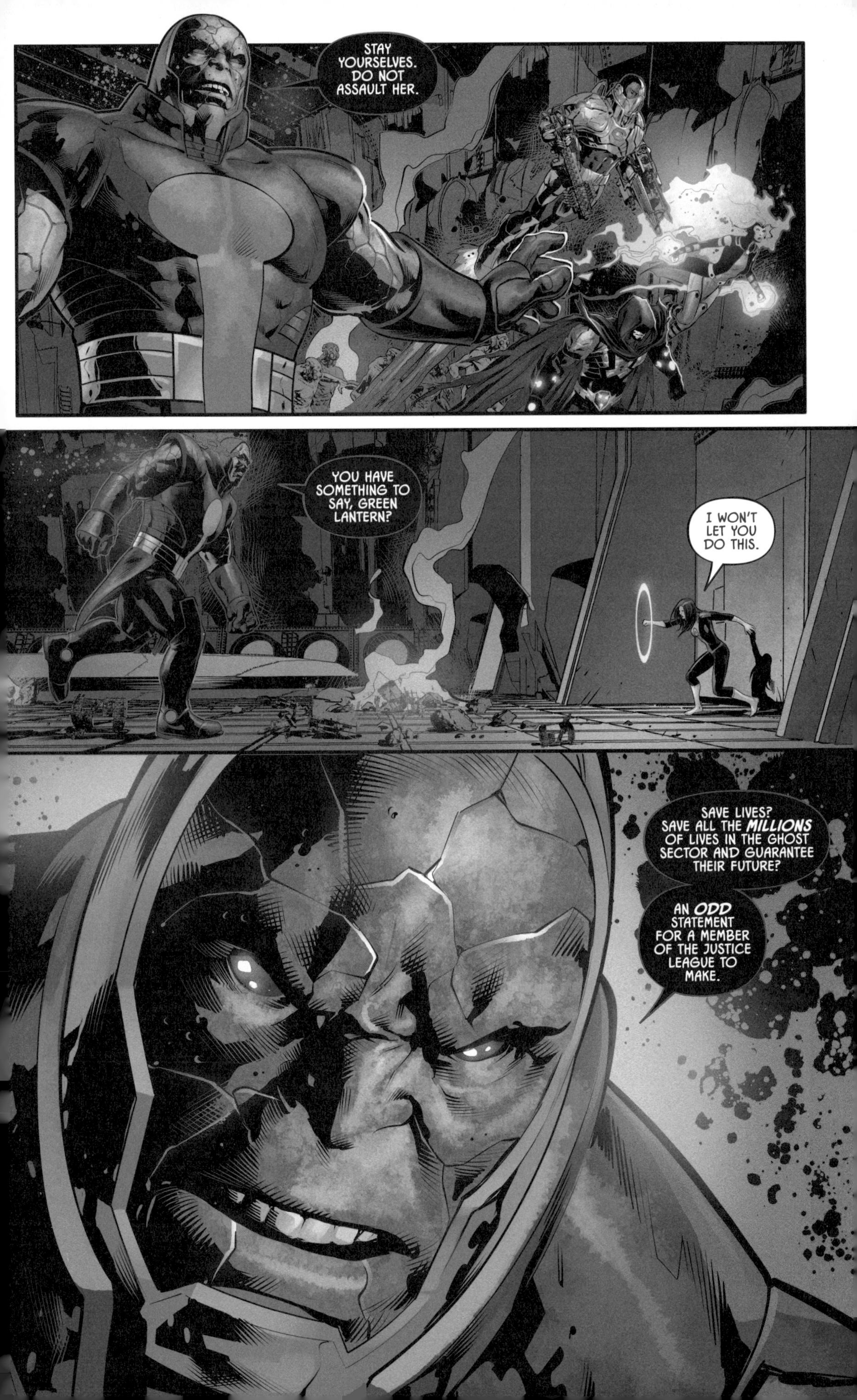
STAY YOURSELVES. DO NOT ASSAULT HER.
YOU HAVE SOMETHING TO SAY, GREEN LANTERN?
I WON'T LET YOU DO THIS.
SAVE LIVES? SAVE ALL THE MILLIONS OF LIVES IN THE GHOST SECTOR AND GUARANTEE THEIR FUTURE?
AN ODD STATEMENT FOR A MEMBER OF THE JUSTICE LEAGUE TO MAKE.

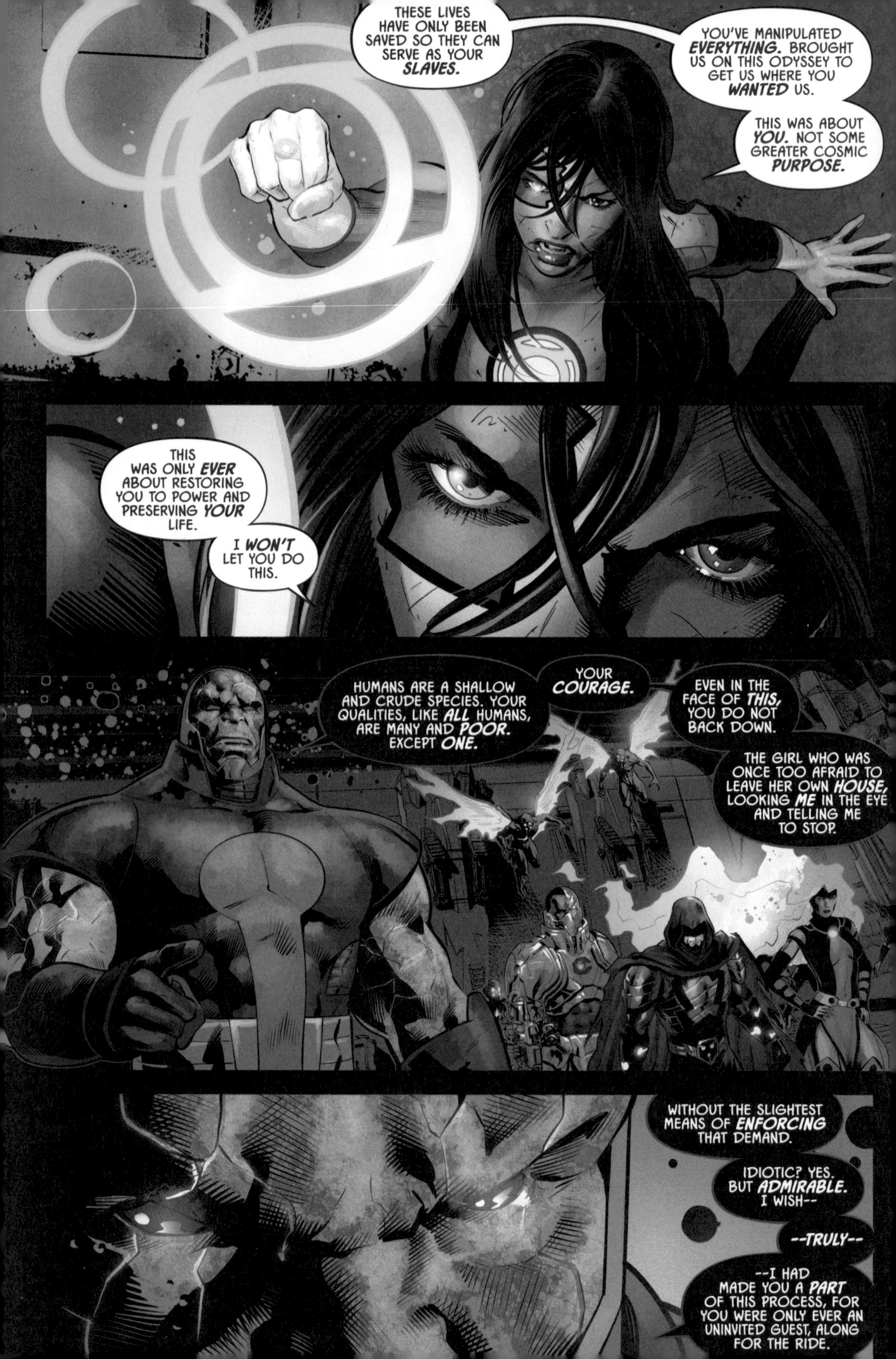
THESE LIVES HAVE ONLY BEEN SAVED SO THEY CAN SERVE AS YOUR *SLAVES.*
YOU'VE MANIPULATED *EVERYTHING.* BROUGHT US ON THIS ODYSSEY TO GET US WHERE YOU *WANTED* US.
THIS WAS ABOUT *YOU.* NOT SOME GREATER COSMIC *PURPOSE.*
THIS WAS ONLY *EVER* ABOUT RESTORING YOU TO POWER AND PRESERVING *YOUR* LIFE.
I *WON'T* LET YOU DO THIS.
HUMANS ARE A SHALLOW AND CRUDE SPECIES. YOUR QUALITIES, LIKE *ALL* HUMANS, ARE MANY AND *POOR.* EXCEPT *ONE.*
YOUR *COURAGE.*
EVEN IN THE FACE OF *THIS,* YOU DO NOT BACK DOWN.
THE GIRL WHO WAS ONCE TOO AFRAID TO LEAVE HER OWN *HOUSE,* LOOKING *ME* IN THE EYE AND TELLING ME TO STOP.
WITHOUT THE SLIGHTEST MEANS OF *ENFORCING* THAT DEMAND.
IDIOTIC? YES. BUT *ADMIRABLE.* I WISH--
--TRULY--
--I HAD MADE YOU A *PART* OF THIS PROCESS, FOR YOU WERE ONLY EVER AN UNINVITED GUEST, ALONG FOR THE RIDE.

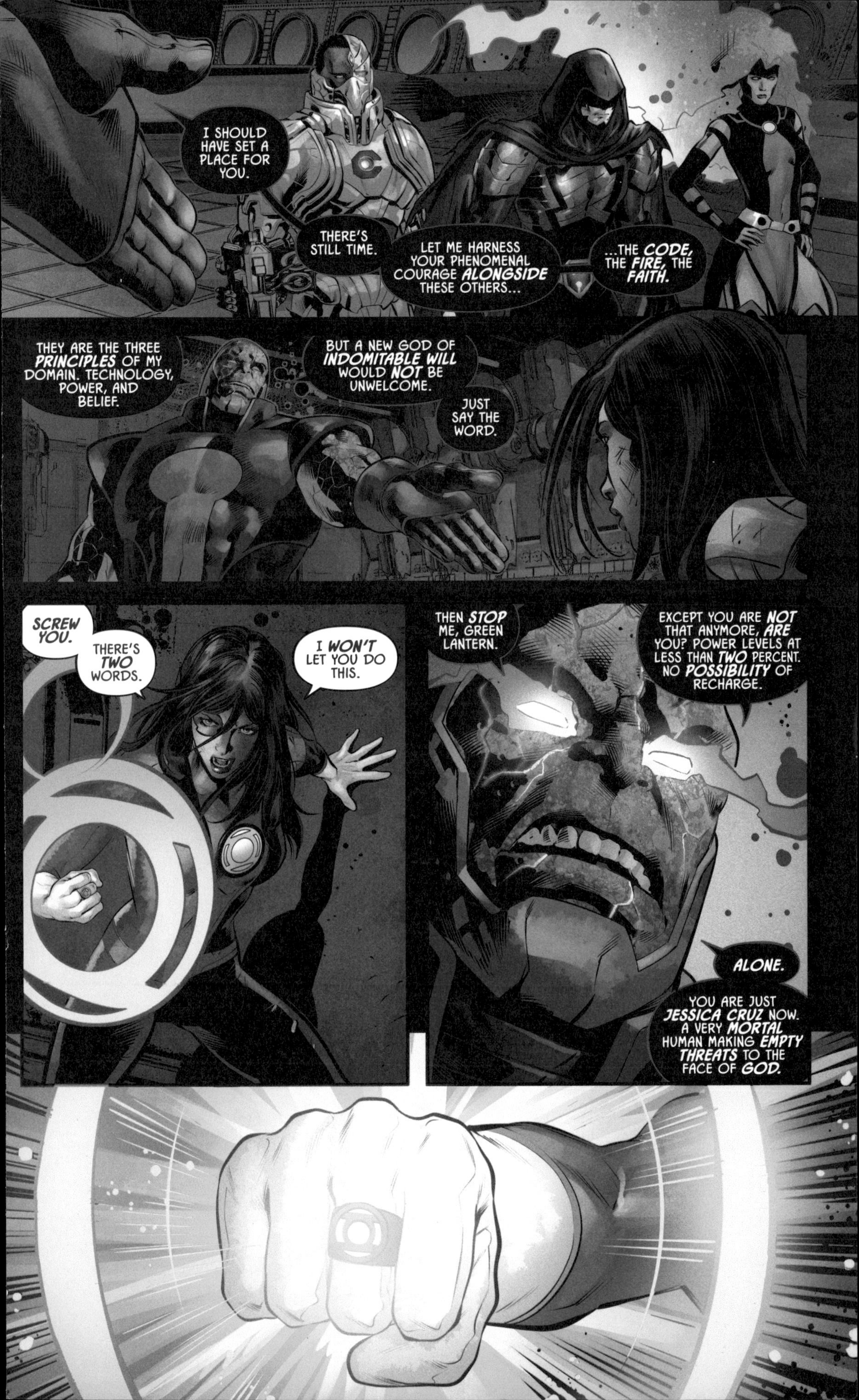

I SHOULD HAVE SET A PLACE FOR YOU.
THERE'S STILL TIME.
LET ME HARNESS YOUR PHENOMENAL COURAGE ALONGSIDE THESE OTHERS...
...THE CODE, THE FIRE, THE FAITH.
THEY ARE THE THREE PRINCIPLES OF MY DOMAIN. TECHNOLOGY, POWER, AND BELIEF.
BUT A NEW GOD OF INDOMITABLE WILL WOULD NOT BE UNWELCOME.
JUST SAY THE WORD.
SCREW YOU.
THERE'S TWO WORDS.
I WON'T LET YOU DO THIS.
THEN STOP ME, GREEN LANTERN.
EXCEPT YOU ARE NOT THAT ANYMORE, ARE YOU? POWER LEVELS AT LESS THAN TWO PERCENT. NO POSSIBILITY OF RECHARGE.
ALONE.
YOU ARE JUST JESSICA CRUZ NOW. A VERY MORTAL HUMAN MAKING EMPTY THREATS TO THE FACE OF GOD.

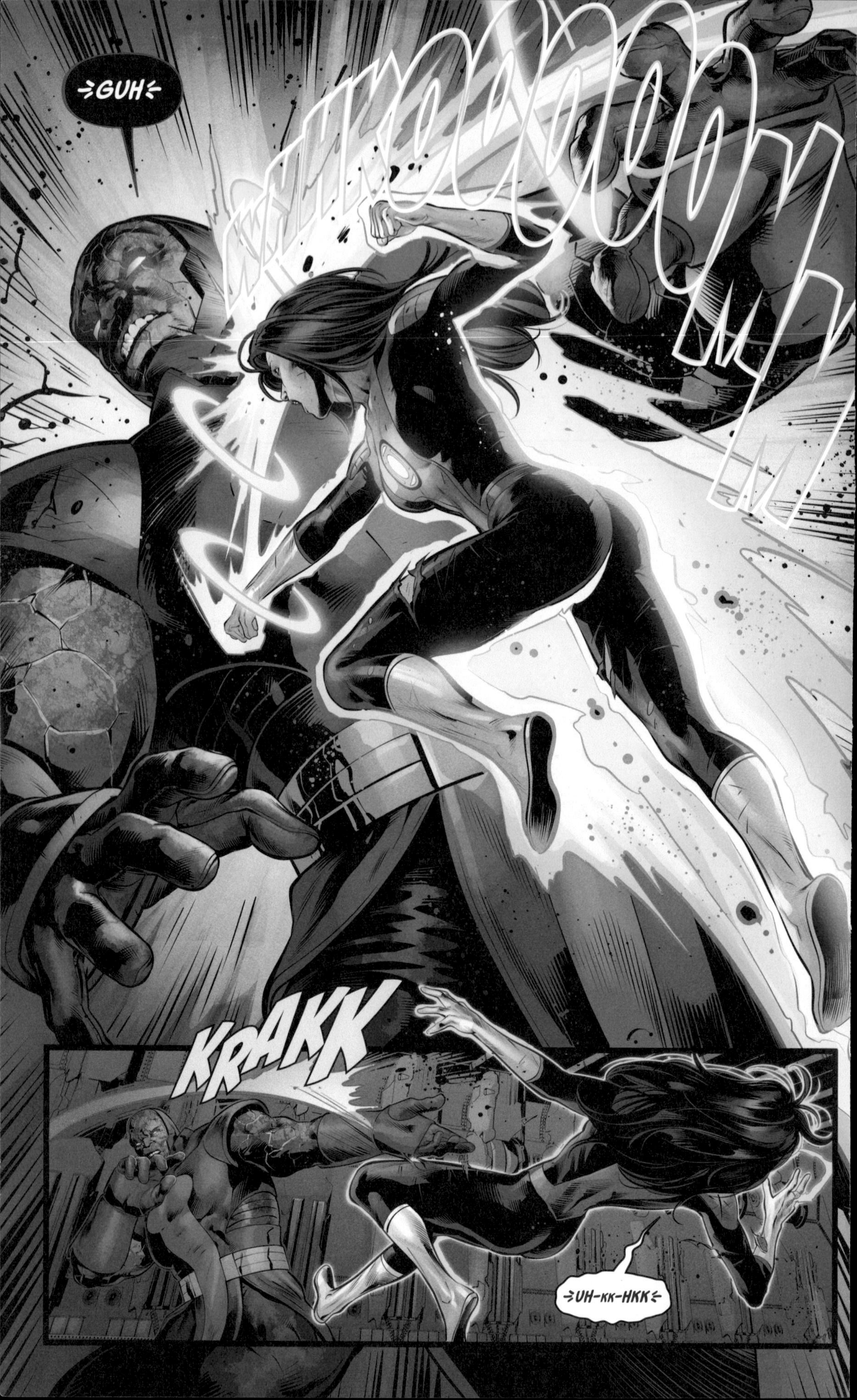
GUH
KRAKK
UH-KK-HKK

POWER LEVELS ZERO. WARNING. POWER LEVELS ZERO. WARNING...

EEAARRGH!

KRUNCH

AS I THOUGHT. LIMITLESS COURAGE. AND ABSOLUTELY *NOTHING* ELSE.

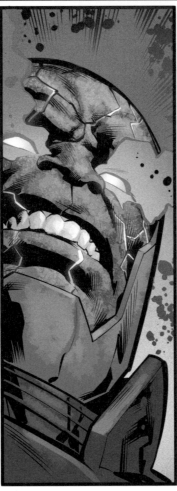

OH--

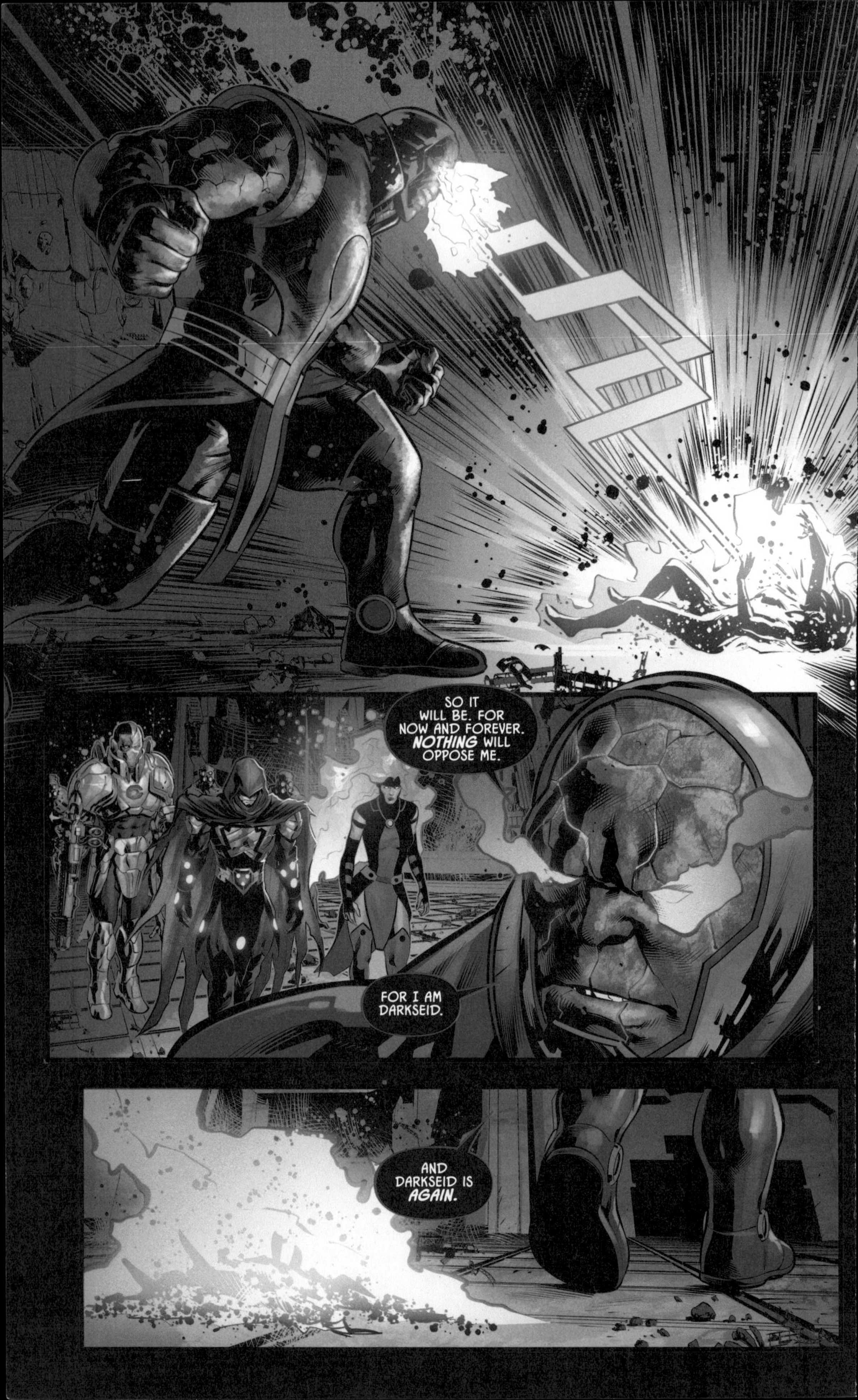
SO IT WILL BE. FOR NOW AND FOREVER. NOTHING WILL OPPOSE ME.
FOR I AM DARKSEID.
AND DARKSEID IS AGAIN.

SKETCHBOOK

CYBORG CHARACTER SKETCH BY **RICCARDO FEDERICI**

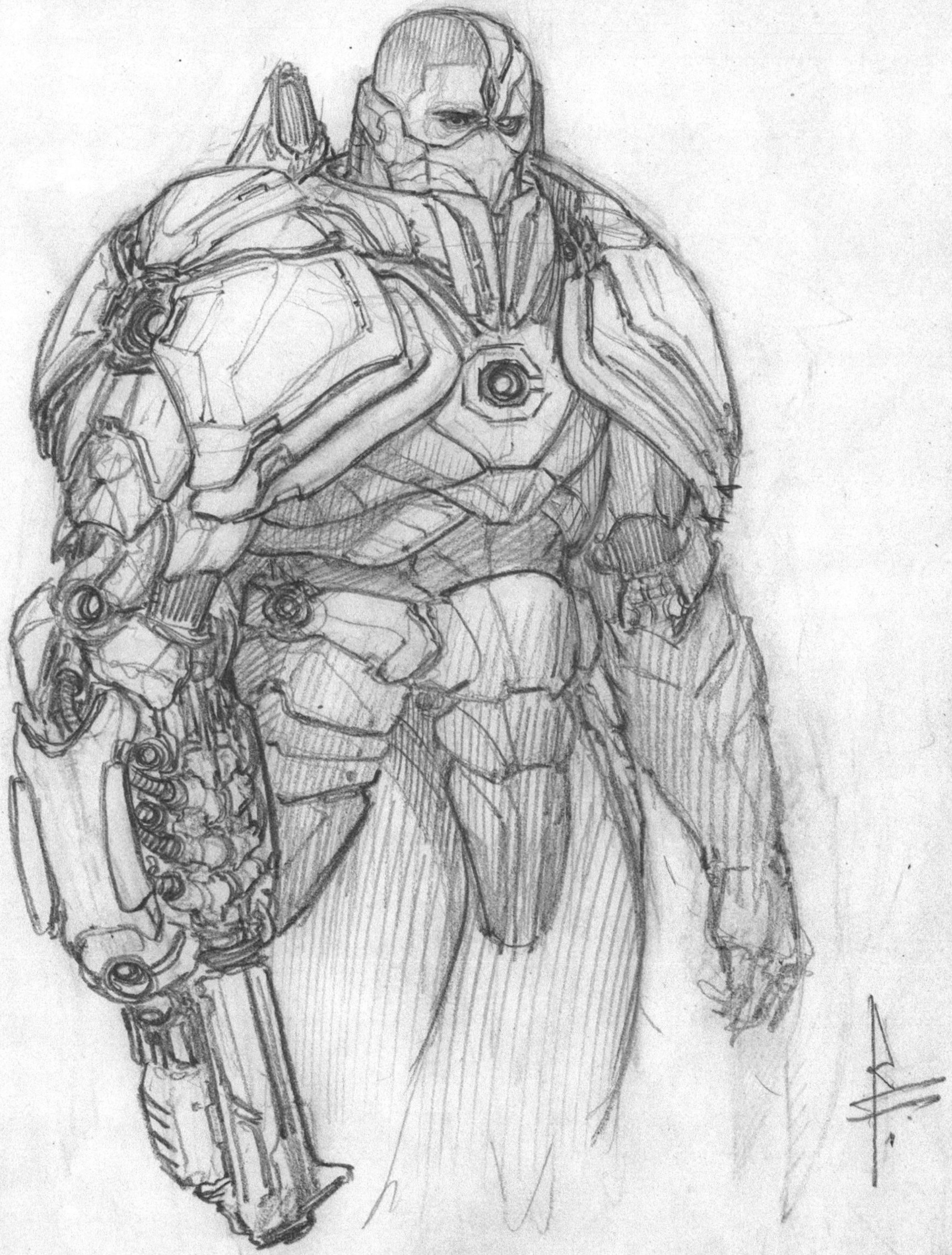

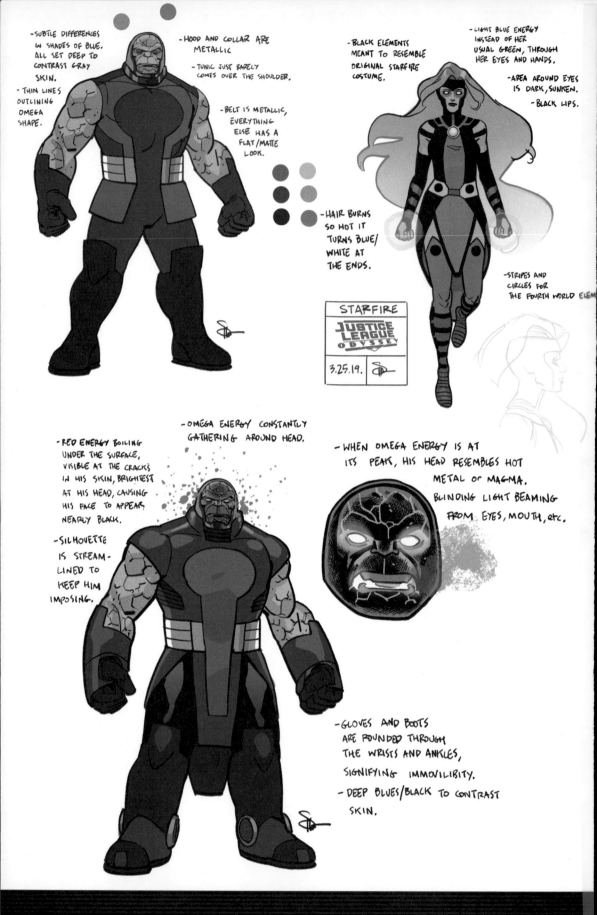

- SUBTLE DIFFERENCES IN SHADES OF BLUE. ALL SET DEEP TO CONTRAST GRAY SKIN.
- THIN LINES OUTLINING OMEGA SHAPE.

- HOOD AND COLLAR ARE METALLIC
- TUNIC JUST BARELY COMES OVER THE SHOULDER.
- BELT IS METALLIC, EVERYTHING ELSE HAS A FLAT/MATTE LOOK.

- BLACK ELEMENTS MEANT TO RESEMBLE ORIGINAL STARFIRE COSTUME.

- LIGHT BLUE ENERGY INSTEAD OF HER USUAL GREEN, THROUGH HER EYES AND HANDS.
- AREA AROUND EYES IS DARK, SUNKEN.
- BLACK LIPS.

- HAIR BURNS SO HOT IT TURNS BLUE/WHITE AT THE ENDS.

- STRIPES AND CIRCLES FOR THE FOURTH WORLD ELEM

STARFIRE
JUSTICE LEAGUE ODYSSEY
3.25.19.

- OMEGA ENERGY CONSTANTLY GATHERING AROUND HEAD.

- RED ENERGY BOILING UNDER THE SURFACE, VISIBLE AT THE CRACKS IN HIS SKIN, BRIGHTEST AT HIS HEAD, CAUSING HIS FACE TO APPEAR NEARLY BLACK.
- SILHOUETTE IS STREAM-LINED TO KEEP HIM IMPOSING.

- WHEN OMEGA ENERGY IS AT ITS PEAK, HIS HEAD RESEMBLES HOT METAL OR MAGMA. BLINDING LIGHT BEAMING FROM EYES, MOUTH, etc.

- GLOVES AND BOOTS ARE ROUNDED THROUGH THE WRISTS AND ANKLES, SIGNIFYING IMMOVIBILITY.
- DEEP BLUES/BLACK TO CONTRAST SKIN.

DARKSEID, STARFIRE, AND AZRAEL CHARACTER DESIGNS BY EVAN "DOC" SHANER

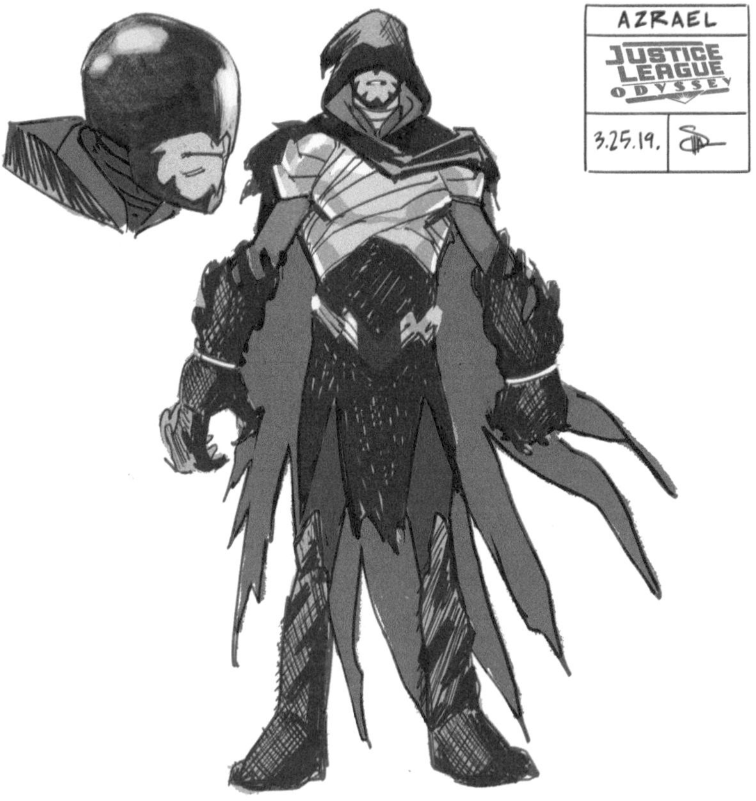
AZRAEL
JUSTICE LEAGUE ODYSSEY
3.25.19.

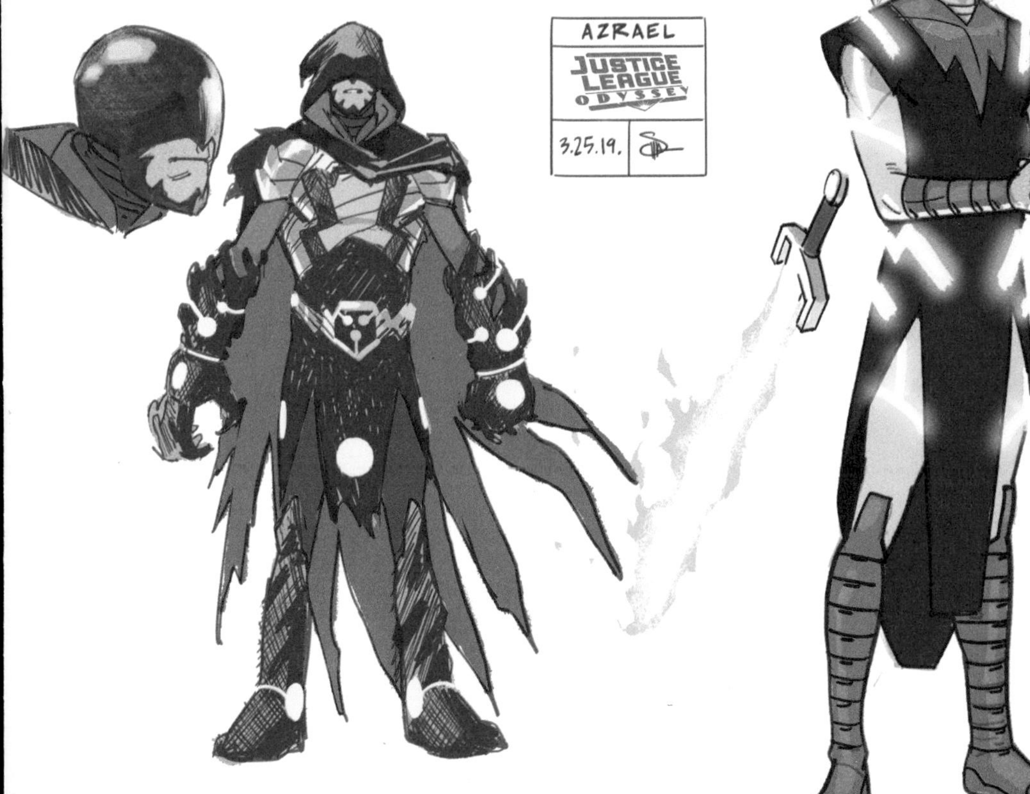
AZRAEL
JUSTICE LEAGUE ODYSSEY
3.25.19.

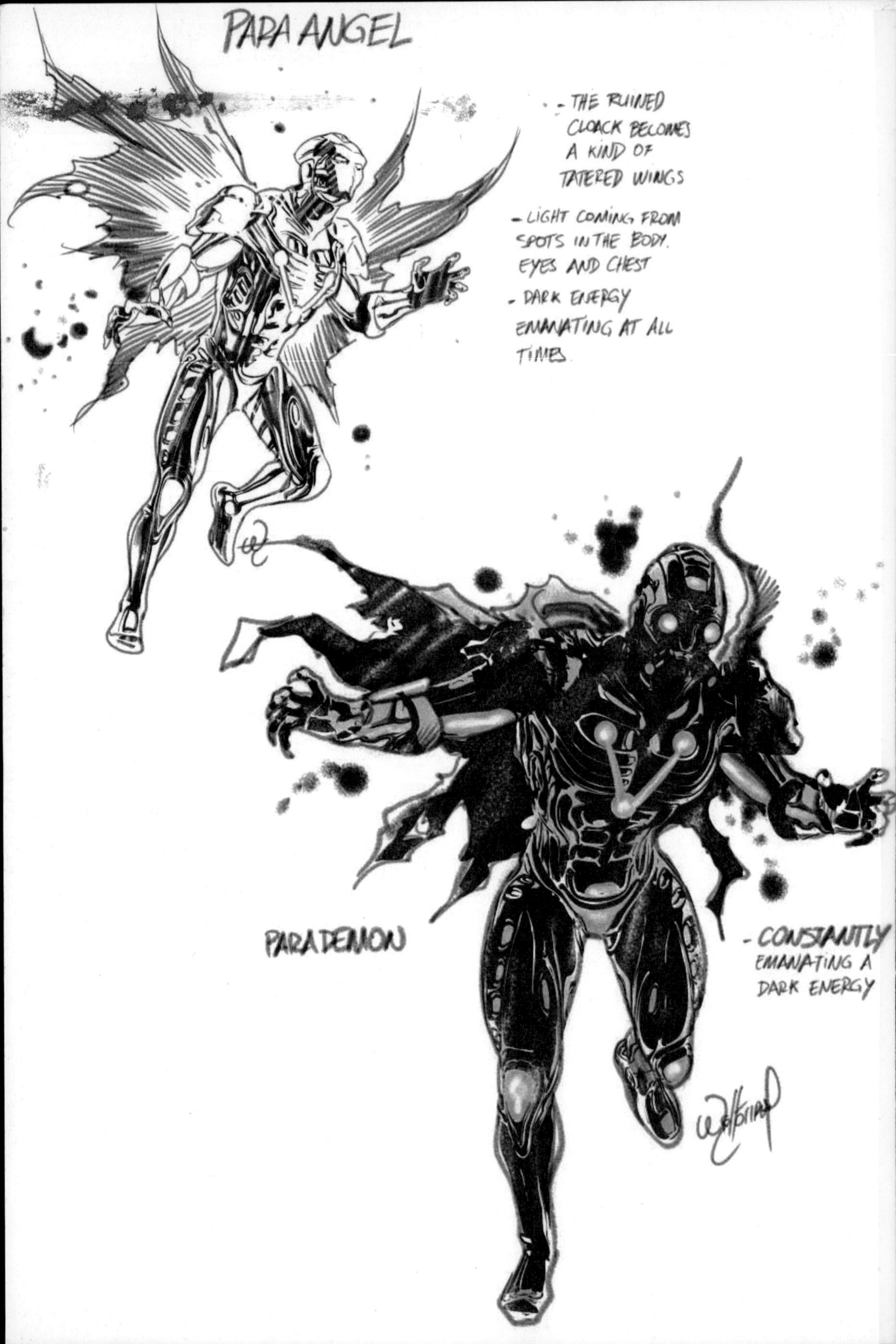
PARA ANGEL
- THE RUINED CLOACK BECOMES A KIND OF TATERED WINGS
- LIGHT COMING FROM SPOTS IN THE BODY. EYES AND CHEST
- DARK ENERGY EMANATING AT ALL TIMES.
PARADEMON
- CONSTANTLY EMANATING A DARK ENERGY

PARA-ANGEL AND **PARADEMON** DESIGNS BY **WILL CONRAD**